Emotional Amoral Egoism

Emotional Amoral Egoism

A Neurophilosophy of
Human Nature and Motivations

Nayef R.F. Al-Rodhan

The Lutterworth Press

THE LUTTERWORTH PRESS

P.O. Box 60
Cambridge
CB1 2NT
United Kingdom

www.lutterworth.com
publishing@lutterworth.com

Hardback ISBN: 978 0 7188 9572 3
Paperback ISBN: 978 0 7188 9573 0
PDF ISBN: 978 0 7188 4833 0
ePub ISBN: 978 0 7188 4834 7

British Library Cataloguing in Publication Data
A record is available from the British Library

First published as *"Emotional Amoral Egoism"* by LIT Verlag, 2008

This edition published by The Lutterworth Press, 2021

Contents

Acknowledgements

The author would like to thank the following people for their important assistance with the production of this book: Adrian Brink, Samuel Fitzgerald, Debora Nicosia, Christine Garnier-Simon, Ioana Puscas, Ines Gassal-Bosch and Virginia Raffaeli.

I am also immensely grateful for the support of my colleagues at St Antony's College, Oxford University (UK), at the Geneva Centre for Security Policy (Switzerland) and at the Institute of Philosophy, School of Advanced Study, University of London (UK).

Part 1

Human Nature

Insights from the Frontiers of Neurophilosophy

The last several decades of brain research have radically changed our understanding of what it means to be human. Are we inherently good or bad? Are we driven by reason or emotions? Do we have free will? Does power corrupt the mind? Are we capable of genuine altruism? Questions such as these have puzzled philosophers for millennia and have laid the groundwork for the development of political theories and ideologies that changed the course of history. Reflecting on these important matters has advanced our understanding of the human condition, of its extraordinary virtues and enduring limitations. Yet, most of the answers, and attempted answers, to questions about our human nature have remained, historically, speculative in nature. The absence of tools to access the human brain and understand its deeper neurochemical and neuroanatomical processes and responses has meant that, for the longest time, a critical seat of our emotions, reason and identity was left completely unexplored. In this book, I aim to bring neuroscience to the forefront of inquiries about human nature and, in so doing, reflect on what accounts for 'good governance' and what can help us secure a more peaceful future for humanity.

Neurophilosophy opens up fresh perspectives on such questions, which humanity has been pondering for centuries. Neurophilosophy, which emerged in the late 1980s, is a field of cross-disciplinary research, which pioneers insightful synergies between neuroscience and other disciplines which have traditionally sought to elucidate the human mind, and it offers a key to unlocking some of the most persistent mysteries shrouding human nature.[1]

Chief among them is a puzzle long thought to be without answer: the human capacity for both good and evil. Instances of atrocities – such as genocide or enslavement – can be found in all cultures and societies, modern and ancient. We need only scratch the surface of history to find confirmation of our darker impulses. Yet, for all the man-made horrors, there are also many instances of other human characteristics: of goodness, of charity, of heroism on behalf of strangers. Recently, the European refugee crisis has highlighted how profoundly dualistic human nature is: alongside occasions of xenophobic violence, we witnessed enormous generosity and friendship shown towards refugees. Suffice it to say, the picture is mixed. As Louis Pojman has observed, 'We seem to be part angel, part demon, part rational, and part animal, capable of great glory and great tragedy.'[2] How can we explain this paradox? Traditionally, at the heart of the debate on human nature has been the question of whether we are inherently good until corrupted by our environment or born bad but kept in check by society. Well before the advent of modern theories of human development, philosophical and religious traditions sought to answer this enigma. Thomas Hobbes (1588–1679), for example, argued that humankind is driven by passions and instincts linked to self-preservation, requiring law and rules to keep our basic instincts under control.[3] Jean-Jacques Rousseau (1712–78), by contrast, believed that human beings are naturally good and that their vices are attributable to the corrupting influence of society. Plato (427–347 BCE), occupying the middle ground, described humans as the product of their biological heritage but also recognised the crucial role of the environment in influencing their behaviour. In the Old Testament, humankind is portrayed as created in the image of God and, thus, as inherently good. Both Jews and Christians agree, however, that human beings fell from grace by eating from the tree of knowledge, which left them alienated from God and in need of salvation.[4]

The continuing nature–nurture controversy frequently lapses into debates over whether we are driven by emotions or by rational thought. Traditionally, those placing greater emphasis on passions and survival instincts regard our biological heritage as more important than the influence of our environment. By contrast, those stressing our capacity for reason tend to attribute greater significance to culture and education as factors in determining who we are. A related question is, thus, whether reason plays a role in our moral judgements. If so, do we engage in conscious reasoning before forming a judgement or after the fact? The first modern philosopher to argue that we make moral judgements based on emotional responses to situations or scenarios was David Hume (1711–76). Immanuel Kant (1724–1804), on the other hand, held that we reach moral judgements through a process of conscious reasoning. In Kant's view, humanity has progressively evolved from being motivated by animal instincts to being driven by reason.[5] Aristotle (384–322 BCE), too, regarded human beings as capable of living a 'good' life by employing reason.[6] Plato depicted human beings as driven by both passion and reason. He famously compared balancing both faculties to steering two horses running in opposite directions.[7] Indeed, only recently have we begun to unveil the crucial role of emotions in rational decision-making. Advances in neuroscience and brain-imaging techniques have given us a glimpse of the complex interplay of emotion and reason in moral judgement. Consider, for example, the famous case of Antonio Damasio's patient, 'Elliot'. Surgery to remove a tumour impaired Elliot's emotional capacity. Whilst still exhibiting a high IQ, Elliot found himself incapable of making decisions, with disastrous consequences for his previously happy professional and family life.[8]

Another recurring set of questions in the study of human nature, and closely intertwined with the nature–nurture controversy, pertains to free will and determinism. Are we in control of our behaviour or is everything we do determined by genes, the environment or other forces beyond our volition? At one end of the spectrum are existentialists – such as Jean-Paul Sartre (1905–80), Søren Kierkegaard (1813–55) and Friedrich Nietzsche (1844–1900) – who argued that human beings have a radical free will. According to Sartre, 'Man is condemned to be free.'[9] At the other end of the spectrum is, for instance, Hobbes, who held that nature is the driving force behind human action.[10] Yet others believe that free will is merely a figment of our imagination. An example of this can be found in Sigmund Freud's (1856–1939) theory of pansexuality, which holds that, while we may think that we are making conscious choices, we are driven by subconscious motives.[11] Interestingly, in the twentieth century, modern physics' discovery of quantum mechanics sent determinism into retreat. At the same time, however, determinist thinking saw a rise in other disciplines – such as biology, psychology or the behavioural sciences – as a result of new insights into the impact of genetics and heredity on human nature and the influences of social and cultural conditioning on our behaviour.[12] Today, neuroimaging tools are enabling neuroscientists to further their exploration of our agential control. Moreover, advances in technology are increasingly allowing us to alter our species' capabilities, prompting the questions: Shall we soon take biological evolution into our own hands? Will technology change what it means to be human? Indeed, recent technological developments – such as brain-computer interfaces – complicate the traditional nature–nurture debate by blurring the line between human and machine.

Across disciplines, inquiries into free will have probed the nature of moral judgements. Are we truly free to discern and pursue the good, rather than being driven by forces outside our control? Are we capable of moral behaviour, of altruism which does not serve our self-interest? The range of answers to such questions has inspired widely different perspectives on human nature. Hobbes, for example, portrayed human beings as egoists, incapable of acting altruistically. Kant regarded morality as the result of reason.[13] Some sociobiologists, such as Edward O. Wilson and Frans de Waal, consider morality to have developed from our social instincts.[14] Others, including evolutionary psychologists such as Marc Hauser, have gone so far as to argue that, over time, human beings have evolved so as to develop an innate moral instinct.[15] This suggests that some basic moral criteria must be universal across different cultures. Nonetheless, it also raises the question of whether human beings are deliberating moral agents.[16]

In short, the paradoxes of human nature have inspired heated controversies from various disciplinary vantage points for centuries. The writings shaping the debate on human nature, however, have long missed a key element: insight into the human brain. For millennia, the workings of the brain were considered relatively unimportant. In ancient Egypt, for example, mummies often had their brain discarded, whilst the heart was preserved as the assumed seat of both thoughts and the soul. Similarly, Aristotle located the mind in the heart, regarding the brain merely as a cooling mechanism for blood.[17] Until the early twentieth century, very little was known about the physical basis of the mind. Since then, a neuroscientific revolution has drastically improved our understanding of the mind as a product of complex, but real, processes occurring in the material brain.[18] More recently, twenty-first-century brain-imaging technology – such as functional magnetic resonance imaging (fMRI) or, more recently, magnetic encephalography (MEG) – has enabled us to delve into the inner workings of the living brain. Whilst modern neuroscience is still far from unlocking all of the mysteries surrounding human nature, it has drastically improved our understanding of how we feel and think, what motivates us and what we are capable of doing under certain circumstances. Today, novel techniques from neuroscience allow us to explore the brain structures involved in moral judgement, for instance, or emotional experiences, overturning many long-held beliefs about the human species.[19]

This book seeks to move beyond deterministic and reductive accounts of human nature by taking stock of, and advancing, not only insights from philosophy, psychology, and social biology, but also cutting-edge findings from neuroscience. In so doing, the book pushes the field of neurophilosophy into uncharted territory, which incorporates neuroscientific discoveries into the analysis of international relations and global order. Indeed, recognising our neurobiological make-up and the social and political tendencies it underpins is key to understanding international security and to improving its practice. Only if we know who we most deeply are, and what we most genuinely want, can we devise policies which bring out the best in human nature. Tragically, at a time when conflicts are abundant, neuroscience's meaningful contributions are widely overlooked in policymaking and wider debates on human nature.

The Structure and Aims of the Book

As mentioned above, this book is driven by three central purposes. First, it advances our understanding of human nature by drawing on insights from various disciplines and especially from cutting-edge neuroscience research. Second, it offers a convenient entry point for researchers and practitioners to understand how a neurophilosophical perspective on human nature can improve our understanding of existence, international relations, prosperity, peace and security. It thereby addresses a gap in the existing literature which widely neglects the political implications of neuroscientific discoveries and their neurophilosophical implications. Third, the book makes pioneering neuroscience research – all too often presented in arcane technical jargon – accessible across disciplines, to both academics and policymakers. It, therefore, avoids overwhelming the reader with technical detail and jargon in its explanations of neuroscientific discoveries and their societal implications.

The book frames these insights from neuroscience within an overarching theory of *emotional amoral egoism*. To establish a context for understanding this theory, Part 2 provides an overview of noteworthy accounts of human nature which have emerged across disciplines over the past three thousand years. Given space constraints, this section of the book cannot endeavour to capture the whole range and variety of thinking on human nature. It focusses instead on what I see as the most influential ideas, including philosophical, religious/spiritual, psychological and evolutionary approaches. Part 2 more fully develops the main contours of the debate outlined in the introduction, including the nature–nurture controversy and the emotionality–rationality dichotomy. From this emerges a kaleidoscopic view of humankind riddled with paradoxes. Part 2 explores not only the main intellectual positions about who human beings are; it also considers where we are going in light of twenty-first-century advances in science and technology. Indeed, today's increasing possibilities for modifying human capabilities through biological and technological means are further compounding existing accounts of human nature.

In Part 3, I embark on the challenging task of formulating a more comprehensive theory of human nature, which I call *emotional amoral egoism*. It represents a synthesis of insights from a variety of disciplines, including neuroscientific findings. It posits that there are three character-istics common to all human beings, across all ages and cultures. Chief among them is our *emotionality*. Extensive research into the human brain has revealed the centrality of emotions in human experience and their profound impact on key cognitive processes. In fact, emotions shape how we perceive the world, how we process information and how we remember events.[20]

In addition, we are all born *amoral*. I do not use the term 'amoral' in the traditional sense to denote indifference to, or lack of awareness of, the concepts of right and wrong. On the contrary, I believe that most human beings have moral sensitivities and the capacity to form moral judgements. However, a preponderance of evidence suggests that human beings possess no innate understanding of good and evil and that their moral judgements shift according to circumstances, both personal and political. This is what I mean when I describe humankind as amoral.

In spite of being born amoral, we do not enter the world as the entirely blank slate envisioned by Locke (1632–1704). Instead, I prefer to conceive of the human mind as a *predisposed tabula rasa*.[21] By 'predisposed' I mean that we are endowed by nature with a powerful survival instinct, one which pushes us towards actions which maximise our chances of survival. It is in this sense that human nature is fundamentally *egoistic*: the third commonality we all share. Therefore, while humankind is capable of being both good and bad, survival instincts are so powerful that people commonly act according to what they perceive to be their general self-interest in a given situation. No matter how selfless an act may appear, some form of self-interest is likely to be lurking beneath the veneer of altruism. This element aside, our moral compass and our life-guiding values are largely shaped by our upbringing and environment, both personal and political. Admittedly, and despite lacking inborn moral concepts, we possess some innate pro-social emotions, such as empathy and sympathy. However, whilst the latter can contribute to what could be described as 'moral sensitivity', the link between emotions and morality must not be mistaken for an innate 'moral grammar', especially as our pro-social affinities are often biased towards in-group members.

Our emotional amoral egoism is genetically coded yet can be modified by the totality of our environment. In other words, whilst endowed with predilections stemming from our genetic make-up, our brains remain malleable, especially in early life, and, therefore, susceptible to external influences, both good and bad, including from drugs and psychotherapy and, more recently, advances in bio-, molecular, nano- and computational technologies, which could be so significant as to ultimately change what it means to be human. In light of this interplay between genetics and environment, I believe that the traditional nature–nurture dichotomy loses its meaning.

Furthermore, contrary to longstanding philosophical beliefs, comparatively little of what motivates us is generated by reason alone, as our emotional nature has the upper hand in driving our behaviour. Not only are we compelled by emotions, but our brain is pre-programmed to feel good. We have an instinctual motivation to repeat behaviour which activates the reward centres of the brain. My theory contends that there are five main drivers of human action through which this neurochemical gratification is sought. I have called them the *Neuro P5*: *power, profit, pleasure, pride* and *permanency*. By *permanency* I refer to the quest for longevity and the desire to leave a legacy which extends beyond death.

Drawing on philosophical insights from recent work in neuroscience, Part 3 calls into question many long-revered beliefs about human nature, including the role of rational analysis in influencing human behaviour and the nature–nurture dichotomy. To situate my theory of emotional amoral egoism in relation to its historical antecedents, Part 3 closes with a table which facilitates direct comparison.

Part 4 uses my neurophilosophical theory of human nature to pave a richer and more practical understanding of how our emotional amoral egoism can trigger fear, conflict and division and how these are manifested through some key issues and policy challenges that humanity is facing today, such as human enhancement, inequality, Big Data and fake news. When left unchecked – whether by positive socialisation, egalitarian norms or institutional constraints – the egoistic character of human nature will trigger a relentless quest to fulfil our need for the Neuro P5, even at disastrous cost to self and others. It is possible, however, for us to harness the defining dynamics of human nature in ways which promote peace and security. My understanding of human nature as malleable and subject to external influences highlights the key role of the environment in shaping our moral compass. As I argue in this section of the book, sustainable improvements in the human condition can only unfold in a context which reconciles the ever-present tension between the needs of human dignity and the emotional amoral egoism which is innate within us all. By *dignity*, I do not mean the mere absence of humiliation, nor do I refer exclusively to the inherent worth of every human being. Rather, I use this term to describe a condition in which nine universal human needs are recognised and fulfilled: *reason, security, human rights, accountability, transparency, justice, opportunity, innovation* and *inclusiveness*. I believe that sustainable improvement in the human condition can be achieved through a new good-governance paradigm which is capable of balancing this tension – a paradigm I call *dignity-based governance*. Dignity-based governance involves, at the very least: (1) countering human amorality with *justice, accountability* and *transparency*; (2) channelling human egoism to benefit society through *opportunity, inclusiveness* and *innovation*; and (3) assuaging vitriolic human emotionality by providing *security*, safeguarding *human rights* and fostering a society based on *reason*.

Thus, Part 4 applies the lens of emotional amoral egoism to a wide range of imminent security concerns and demonstrates how dignity-based governance can help us navigate these issues. Chief among them are the downsides of globalisation, interdependence and interconnectivity. For all the opportunities it offers, globalisation has brought about major challenges, including shifts in social, ideological and cultural constellations which are unsettling previously established identities, as well as increasing the number of conflicting resistance identities (see Chapter 4.2).

Today, cultural diversity is a fact in almost every region of the world, due to the increase in human mobility, migration and the existence of diaspora communities. At the same time, deeply ingrained in our brains is the fear of the 'other', a reflex which is triggered by encounters with the unfamiliar. This widely unconscious bias makes us susceptible to ethnocentrism, which mistakes the *familiar* for the *better* in every circumstance. Our natural inclination towards us-versus-them thinking is often instrumentalised for political purposes and can easily degenerate into xenophobia, discrimination, alienation, ethnic tension and violent conflict (see Chapters 4.3 and 4.4).

Indeed, tensions between groups with different outlooks and values are a major source of instability across continents. In Europe and beyond, the past few years have seen rising polarisation, with political attitudes diverging towards ideological extremes. Sectarian polarisation, operationalised by exogenous national interests and manipulation, continues to ravage many societies, especially in the Middle East. In the

United States, levels of social cohesion decrease as American citizens are increasingly polarised along partisan lines. Political and religious extremism is tearing apart families, communities and societies throughout the world. The internet, in particular, is accelerating the polarisation of pre-existing attitudes. It creates so-called echo chambers in which the constant repetition of one-sided views exacerbates pre-held prejudices, fears, or in-group tendencies, which at times become so extreme as to lead to the commission of violent acts against the 'other'. *Fear-induced pre-emptive aggression*, a by-product of our emotional amoral egoism, plays a major role in fostering resistance identities, polarisation, xenophobia and ethnic conflict. Chapter 4.4 illustrates how dignity-based governance can prevent conflicts through its focus on inclusiveness, reason and education, as well as through the monitoring and regulation of both political discourse and the entertainment and gaming industries.

Whilst xenophobia and conflict are old phenomena in the history of humankind, Chapter 4.5 devotes attention to some more recent security concerns, including Big Data and human enhancement, as well as issues which have not traditionally been the object of political analysis (such as the meaning of life) but which are instrumental in shaping today's security landscape. There is a strong correlation, for example, between radicalism and the quest for meaning, and the latter plays an important role in holistic approaches to development and politics. Thus, Chapter 4.5 shows how my theory of emotional amoral egoism can be harnessed to improve understanding of a wide range of issues and how dignity-based governance can contribute to maximising the benefits and avoiding the risk associated with these issues.

Importantly, dignity-based governance can instil in us greater concern for the welfare of distant others. Most recently, the Covid-19 pandemic[22] is contributing to the sense that people everywhere belong to a shared community of fate.[23] From the point of view of moral cosmopolitanism, this is positive, since it may help to create a sense of community with what might otherwise be seen as distant 'others'. However, due to our nature and evolutionary history, when faced with the need to intervene in favour of non-co-nationals, our loyalties and commitments often remain incredibly parochial. Applying my theory of emotional amoral egoism, I discuss how we might account for the limits of human compassion (Chapter 4.6). At the same time, I demonstrate how, by fulfilling what we perceive emotionally to be our basic needs, dignity-based governance can enable us to apply reason to our interactions with others and, thus, extend our sense of moral obligation to the whole of humanity.

To unlock the best in human nature, dignity-based governance must be ensured on both the domestic and global levels and must be accompanied by harmonious interstate relations. International relations must, therefore, be guided by the paradigm I call *symbiotic realism*, which is premised on the idea that, since we live in an interconnected and interdependent world, international politics can no longer rely on zero-sum and relative gains, but rather must be a multi-sum game, with non-conflictual competition and absolute gains. In light of these considerations, Part 4 illustrates the benefits of incorporating neurophilosophical reflection into political analysis. On the one hand, it demonstrates the impact of our innate predispositions on key security issues. On the other, it highlights the extent to which external factors determine how we act on the genetic heritage we carry with us and, in light of this, how our emotional amoral egoism can be channelled for the greater good of humanity through dignity-based governance.

Finally, Part 5 provides some concluding thoughts on the security and societal implications of the theory of emotional amoral egoism and offers practical and actionable steps for policymakers and governments. By illustrating what the aforementioned threefold balancing act means in practice, the final part of the book demonstrates how dignity-based governance is the most effective tool through which to bring out the best in every single human being.

By exploring human nature from a neurophilosophical vantage point, I hope to breathe new life into an old debate and spark new insights into how our innate tendencies shape the world in which we live and how they can be constructively harnessed for the greater good of all, at all times and under all circumstances.

Part 2

Existing Approaches to Human Nature

A Historical Overview

Western thought on human nature is heavily informed by two traditions: ancient Greek philosophy and the Judeo-Christian view of the Bible or the Old Testament.[24] In the former, approaches to human nature are focussed on rational self-interest, rather than appeals to divine creation. In the middle of the fifth century BCE, Athens began to grow, becoming increasingly prosperous, and religion, based on the Homeric gods, was called into question. This helped bring about a rise in secularism. This transformation was accompanied by the growing influence of the Sophists, who were sceptical about religion and believed in the power of persuasion and oratory skill as the key to success in a democratic society.[25] Overall, the human capacity for reason was given a predominant place in the works of major philosophers of the time. Plato, for example, held that rational thought ought to be employed to overcome the passions inside us.[26] Aristotle went even further, claiming that reason was the principal characteristic of human nature.[27]

This view lost its traction with the spread of the Judeo-Christian conception of human nature, which comes from the Bible (the Old Testament for Jews and the same book along with the New Testament for Christians). Both religions are monotheistic. Thus, in the Bible, human beings are spiritual beings created by a single God. The Old Testament portrays God as creating humankind to be like Him, in His own image. Human nature is, thus, thought to be inherently good and human beings are considered to be free rational beings capable of choosing the right path. Yet, bearing the burden of sin, both original (i.e. inherited from Adam and Eve) and personal, human beings are deemed to need divine help for salvation, which they can receive through faith. The capacity for rational thought is not considered to be enough for humankind to flourish; human beings are also in need of love, faith and hope.[28]

Whereas the Abrahamic, monotheistic religions hold that human beings have a single God, polytheistic and animistic belief systems see human beings as existing among other spiritual and mythological beings.[29] In Hinduism, for example, everything is interconnected. The essential part of the self is thought to be linked to all other beings.[30] Yet human beings may not be aware of this. According to Hinduism, the basic human condition is characterised by ignorance and suffering, rather than sin,[31] and as the tension between knowledge, false knowledge and ignorance, which can delude the mind and lead it into a downward spiral of suffering. Jeaneane Fowler has alluded to a similar interpretation of Hindu philosophy: ignorance of the true nature of reality is tantamount to being ignorant of our own selves.[32] Human beings are conceived as creatures of infinity trapped in finite personalities. They are thought to be engaged in an ongoing transitory experience of self, trying to satisfy their desires, with conflict and insecurity resulting from existential anxiety. Moreover, individuals are not believed to be free. Karma determines what happens to the individual and, thus, our fate depends on previous actions.[33] Hinduism teaches that deliverance comes through discovering our true, immortal nature, through self-realisation, rather than through divine grace.[34]

Confucianism, prominent in Eastern philosophy, holds an optimistic view of human nature. Confucius (551–479 BCE) believed that everyone is capable of becoming a sage but rarely realises that potential. Confucius spoke very little about human nature and, as a result, a wide variety of differing theories of human nature developed within the school of thought which followed him. Although his teachings did not directly deal with human nature, they contained the notion that humankind is at certain times capable of exercising free will, of choosing how to act in a particular situation. Confucius recognised that the environment helps explain why people act in different ways and described human nature as malleable and requiring continual guidance in order to be moral. Yet Confucius was not clear about whether human nature is fundamentally good or bad.[35] Following his death, diverging answers to this question were provided by two leaders within Confucianism. Mencius (371–289 BCE), representing the 'idealist' strain of thinking, conceived of human nature as essentially good. Hsün-tzu (ca. 300-ca.230 BCE), in contrast, considered human beings inherently evil and driven by desire, envy, hatred and greed.[36]

In the seventh century CE, another Abrahamic and monotheistic religion emerged on the Arabian Peninsula. Islam shares with Christianity and Judaism a commitment to the authority of divine revelation.[37] However, Islam rejects the notion of original sin.[38] Human beings are, thus, not in a natural state of sin due to the Fall of Man. Yet, the Islamic tradition includes numerous, partially competing claims and streams of thought on human nature. The subject of human free will versus divine predestination, for example, is highly contested in classical Islamic thought, as represented by the writings of scholars such as Ibn Sina (ca. 970–1037) (known in the Western world as Avicenna) or Al-Ghazali (1058–1111). Proponents of predestination see values and morality as not subject to human free will, while other Islamic thinkers stress that fundamental moral questions can be handled by human reason, guided by revelation.[39] Another key figure in Arab-Islamic philosophy was Ibn Rushd (1126–98) (also known as Averroes). Living in Al-Andalus (Spain), Ibn Rushd sought to restore the teachings of Aristotle, as opposed to what he considered the Neoplatonist tendencies of earlier Islamic theorists such as Ibn Sina.[40] As a loyal Aristotelian, Ibn Rushd gave the science of the soul a place of its own, focussing on the capacity for sensation and thought of human beings.[41] One of his most controversial theories, at least in the West, is that of the 'Unity of Intellect', in which he proposed that all humans share the same intellect and have a universal capacity for knowledge.[42] His work also strongly influenced that of another Arab-Andalusian philosopher: Ibn Tufayl (1105–85), best known for his philosophical romance *Hayy ibn Yaqdhan* (ca. 1175),[43] in which he described how man can discover the ultimate truth through a systematic process of reasoned inquiry.[44]

Other major landmarks in the history of thought on human nature are situated several centuries later and mark an attempt to break with religious conceptions of human nature. In his famous text, *Leviathan* (1651), Hobbes presented a dim view of human beings. Written during the English Civil War, the text portrays humankind as selfish, power-hungry and constantly pitted against each other in the continual quest for survival and reproduction in a world defined by scarce resources. Without a state to enforce the rule of law, life for human beings would be characterised by fear, insecurity and violence. Indeed, Hobbes believed that our social nature is rather artificial. What lay beneath the surface, prior to the birth of the Leviathan, was a deeply autonomous being. However, absolute liberty in the state of nature was extremely dangerous because, since all humans had it, life was made unpredictable and, famously 'nasty, brutish and short'. Social life did not necessarily come naturally to humans but, when the cost of strife in the state of nature became unbearable, humans had to establish communities by covenant. The Leviathan, however, was an 'artificial man', sovereignty, 'an artificial soul' and civil laws, 'artificial chains'. This implies that none of the social and political orderings created by humans are natural, but rather self-imposed.[45]

Hume's appeal to empiricism was even more pronounced. One of the most significant figures of the Enlightenment, Hume considered all knowledge to be shaped by experience. He attempted to generate a scientific theory of human nature, portraying humankind as capable of both benevolence and selfishness, and driven by emotion rather than reason.[46]

In eighteenth-century France, a group of thinkers emerged who placed greater emphasis on the human capacity for reason. Among them was Rousseau, who argued that human nature is fundamentally good but corrupted by society. Equally grounded in the Enlightenment, Kant argued that humankind's capacity for reason could improve the human condition.[47] What distinguishes us from animals, Kant believed, is the capacity to generate concepts forming an integrated system of knowledge which bestows reason on our behaviour. According to Kant, the human condition is characterised by a tension between self-interested desires (for love, belonging or power) and moral duty. Whilst Kant recognised that some of our actions are simply driven by desires, he also believed that there are instances in which we choose to act according to a moral obligation which can even contradict our desires. Kant called this 'pure' or '*a priori*' reason. Thus, for Kant, morality is a function of reason and not just of our feelings, as Hume maintained.[48] Perfection in moral terms is, from this perspective, impossible to achieve. In Kant's view, we are driven neither solely by our genetic make-up nor by our environment. Instead, we have developed a kind of rational self-love nurtured by our social condition.[49]

The Industrial Revolution in nineteenth-century Europe provided the context for the emergence of another great philosopher: Karl Marx (1818–83), who would influence world developments for much of the twentieth century.[50] For Marx, the human condition under capitalism is characterised by alienation. Human beings, he argued, are alienated from the means of production and from themselves. Those not owning capital are obliged to sell their labour in order to survive in a capitalist system and are, therefore, vulnerable to exploitation by the owners of capital. Moreover, when a person sells his or her labour, he or she is not working towards his or her own fulfilment, but to satisfy other basic needs.[51] According to Marx, only under socialism could people live a 'good' life.

At the same time, some of Marx's contemporaries began to apply the theories of Charles Darwin (1809–82) to the social world in the form of social Darwinism, viewing social inequalities and exploitation as part of natural law. Evolutionary perspectives do not deny the environment's role in shaping human psychology and behaviour but emphasise the paramount importance of biological lineage. The sociobiological thesis holds that morality is a product of our evolution in the sense that it derives from our need to survive. Natural selection may have favoured altruistic individuals in terms of better enabling their genes to be passed on to future generations. This perspective starkly contrasts with the position of existentialists, who consider human beings to be free to construct themselves.[52]

A more recent understanding of human nature, however, has been influenced by the fact that, in the twenty-first century, we can manipulate not only the natural world around us, but also our own biological make-up. Today, increased knowledge about the human brain is coupled with enormous advances in genetics, nanotechnology, bioinformatics and robotics, especially those concerning artificial intelligence. Together, they are beginning to blur the line between human and machine.[53] Rapid developments in synthetic biology are making possible not only the alteration of existing biological systems, but also the creation of novel biological systems with functions which do not exist in nature. A key example is CRISPR, short for Clustered Regularly Interspaced Short Palindromic Repeats. CRISPR is a revolutionary gene-editing technology which has enabled scientists actually to modify the building blocks of life.[54] Human enhancement technologies promise to endow us with unprecedented capabilities, in a process which will soon make transhumanism – a radical human metamorphosis and physical and cognitive enhancement – a reality rather than speculation.[55] These recent developments are opening up new frontiers for shaping and possibly redesigning the future evolution of human beings and the biosphere. As synthetic biology progresses on various fronts, biological neurotechnological super-intelligence, among much else, may soon leave the realm of science fiction and shift the boundaries of human cognition. All of these developments undeniably challenge our previous understanding of 'existence', including human existence.[56] They may even lead to a fundamental change in humanity's essence, which will be neither sociopolitically inconsequential nor ethically neutral.

I shall now explore in greater detail the major approaches to human nature which have been outlined briefly above. For at least two reasons, it is helpful to review these approaches before proceeding with my theory of emotional amoral egoism (see Part 3). First, it helps to situate my thinking in relation to that of other theorists of human nature. Second, these approaches merit attention because they inform many of the political theories discussed in Part 4, theories which I shall revisit in the light of recent neuroscientific findings.

This section begins by examining religious and spiritual perspectives before directing attention to philosophical deliberations on the human condition. In addition, it surveys relevant theories in behavioural psychology and evolutionary biology. Finally, it explores the implications of twenty-first-century research, especially in the field of neuroscience, for our understanding of human nature. Consideration will be also given to the various ways emerging technologies may require a re-conceptualisation of what being human implies.

2.1

Religious and Spiritual Approaches to Human Nature

Some of the most influential conceptions of human nature are religious or spiritual in origin. This chapter outlines, in brief and in general, several of the major religious and spiritual approaches. I begin with the Abrahamic monotheistic religions of Judaism, Christianity and Islam, in which humankind is believed to possess the capacity for reason and free will. These religions define human nature in terms of the individual's relationship with God.

I then turn to polytheistic religions and holistic spiritual belief systems, in which notions of human nature vary. Polytheistic, animistic and animatistic traditions generally believe that human beings exist among other spiritual and mythological beings. Holistic spiritual traditions regard humanity as existing within God or as part of a divine cosmos (i.e. Vedic religions, such as Buddhism). In most of these traditions, the human condition is not one of sin, but of ignorance and suffering. Salvation is not believed to be divine in nature, but to be achieved through knowledge of the true, immortal nature of humankind.

2.1.1. Monotheistic Religions

Within the Abrahamic religions, a human being is a spiritual entity deliberately created by a single God. The Judeo-Christian view of human nature is based in the Bible. The Jewish Torah, the Christian

Old Testament, is comprised of 39 books written between 1200 BCE and 200 BCE. Twenty-seven additional books make up the New Testament. Christians regard the New Testament as authoritative because it records the coming of the Messiah.[57]

In the Old Testament, human nature is understood in relation to God, who is thought to have created human beings in His own image.[58] Humankind is, thus, believed to be innately good and to possess intrinsic worth. Humans are also considered free and responsible beings.[59] Because human beings are considered to be made in God's image, they are conceived as having command over all other species.[60] There is, thus, no sense in which humankind is simply one part of an interconnected cosmic universe, as there is in some other belief systems.

Despite having been created in God's image, all of humanity is believed to be in a general state of sin and, thus, alienated from God. As the sons and daughters of Adam and Eve, all human beings are burdened with the initial error of disobedience to God, committed at the beginning of human history. Just as holiness and divine justice were given to Adam on behalf of the whole of humankind, so Adam's sin is passed on to his descendants. Sin is, therefore, inherited, rather than a personal error which one commits.[61]

Human beings are thought to tend towards sin, in bondage to selfish desire and pride. That humankind tends towards evil has implications for morality. It implies that we have a tendency to abuse our free will, thereby disrupting our friendship with God. Some Christians, however, believe in the doctrine of original sin, in which all humans are considered as being born inherently sinful. In this latter doctrine, humankind is not endowed with free will. Original sin implies that we cannot attain perfection according to God's standards. Instead, we frequently experience internal conflict, and there is often a tension between what we know we ought to do and what we end up doing. Sin is conceived as mental and spiritual. It is made up of pride, selfishness and our resultant alienation from God.[62]

In Judaism, being made in God's image is interpreted as signifying that we have the capacity for reason. In the rabbinical interpretation, humankind was formed with two 'impulses': a moral conscience, which reminds people of God's Law when they consider taking particular actions; and an impulse to satisfy one's inner needs and desires, which are not necessarily bad, since they also motivate us, for example, to satisfy essential needs and to have a family. However, this latter impulse can lead to sinful behaviour if not checked by moral conscience. Judaism, therefore, rejects the doctrine of original sin.[63]

The New Testament view of human nature is a continuation of the ideas found in the Old Testament. Christ is believed to be the incarnation of reason, which is that which sets us apart from other animals and is expressed in language. Human beings are not just rational animals, but creatures who need love, trust and emotional fulfilment in order to flourish. By God's grace, through faith, we may find salvation. In the New Testament, there is also the idea that human nature is redeemed through Jesus, which demonstrates that human nature can become divine. Love, especially, is considered high altruism.[64]

Islam constitutes the third Semitic religion. It recognises Abraham and the prophets in the Old Testament up to Jesus but asserts that Mohammed is the last prophet.[65] In the Koran, human beings are created perfectly good, as in Judaism and Christianity, and have dominion over all other creatures.[66] Humankind is conceived as having free will with which to choose to submit to Allah.[67] Islam, however, lacks the notions of original sin and atonement which are found in some Christian doctrines.

2.1.2. Polytheistic and Holistic Religions and Belief Systems

Polytheistic and animistic religions and belief systems vary, but they tend to regard human beings as existing among other spiritual and mythological beings. Humans are, therefore, not privileged as spiritual beings. Polytheism refers to belief in or worship of multiple gods or deities. Hinduism, for example, allows for numerous deities, which are all manifestations of one impersonal divine power. That ultimate power is called Brahma. In Buddhism, higher beings are commonly designated as gods. However, contrary to polytheistic religions such as Hinduism, Buddhism does not teach the worship of these gods. Interestingly, veneration of saints in Christianity is in some respects indistinguishable from polytheism and, indeed, seamlessly continues pre-Christian traditions.

Unlike Western theology, Hinduism and Buddhism posit that people need to be saved from suffering rather than sin.[68] The sources of Hinduism lie in specific scriptures or *Vedas*, which literally means 'wisdom', some of which are thought to have been written as long ago as 2000 BCE. Rather than recording revelations, these resemble pre-Socratic speculations about the beginnings and nature of the universe. In this sense they are not perceived as authoritative, divine revelations.[69]

In Hinduism, the human condition is one of alienation. Humankind is thought to be motivated by desires which can never be satisfied. As long as we are subject to such desires, we are condemned to live in a constant state of suffering. Further, we project our individual suffering onto others. The condition of alienation means that ordinarily we are only aware of our conscious selves. Our real selves, however, are believed to be divine.[70] Our desires are thought to originate from the belief that one's own existence is more valuable than that of others, and that ownership is the source of human conflict. Realising that the mind and body are constantly in a state of flux, continuously changing, and that we shall all eventually die, is one way the false belief that one's self is more important than the selves of others can be overcome – as people realise that we all face the same destiny.[71]

Common to all forms of Hinduism is reincarnation or the transmigration of the soul. This is the belief that after death all human beings will be reborn in other forms. This belief is also shared by Buddhists. In every reincarnation, although a person's body changes, their soul remains the same. The soul, however, is viewed as a set of tendencies rather than a fixed character or essential core.[72] Thus, in Hinduism, the body and the soul are radically separate, and the soul is something divine. The soul represents the immortal, true self which is independent of external events and intellect. According to Hinduism, the life objective of humankind is to experience the self as an expression of Brahma and, thereby, to overcome ignorance and suffering.

Reincarnation is linked to the law of *karma*: a moral law which rules the universe, determining that you reap what you sow. Those who sow love and justice will be reincarnated as a higher level being, gradually becoming closer to God. Nirvana (enlightenment) indicates a 'waning away' from deluded egocentrism and the selfish desires which imprison humans. Hindu morality also implies obeying the dictates of one's hereditary caste, of which there are five: (1) the Brahmin, who should be devoted to learning and insight; (2) the Kashatrya, the warriors, who should demonstrate courage and integrity; (3) Vaishya, the business class; (4) Sudras, the servants and subordinates; and (5) the outcasts or 'untouchables', who are believed to be either criminals or the descendants of criminals. Untouchables are individuals who are thought to have no rights within the caste system. The doctrine of karma holds that members of a caste deserve their status but, if they obey their *dharma*, which in Hinduism can loosely be translated to encompass the 'right way of living', they may be reincarnated as a member of a higher caste in the next life.[73]

Buddhism, which formed out of a split with Hinduism in the sixth century BCE, rejected the *Vedas* and the caste system but, nonetheless, retained some of the major doctrines of Hinduism. As in Hinduism, people are thought to be born into suffering. The cause of this suffering is identified as desire. Karma and reincarnation are retained in Buddhism but the doctrine of karma is conceived in a slightly different way. The Hindu law of karma is fundamentally linked to moral rules and reincarnation. In the Buddhist version of karma, each action has an effect, which may be either good or bad. A person can, thus, improve their status in human society by consciously striving for purity. A truly noble person in Buddhism, therefore, is not someone born into a particular social rank, but someone who ritually performs pure and benevolent acts. An escape from suffering and to nirvana may be achieved through ethical behaviour and discipline. Nirvana may, thus, be attained in earthly life and not only after death. Finally, in contrast to Hinduism, there is no immortal essence which transmigrates at death.[74]

2.1.3. Animism and Animatism

In animism, out-of-body experiences, dreams, trances and the like are thought to indicate that human beings have a soul which is separate, but intrinsically linked to the body until death. It, therefore, rejects the idea of a hard separation between the spiritual and the physical world. Animism dates back as far as prehistoric humans and is still practised today, notably in native and aboriginal cultures. Under the animistic belief system there can be no separation of body or matter and soul. Most such belief systems hold that the spirit survives physical death and inhabits living things within a spiritual cosmos. In animistic terms, living a 'good' life is achieved by living in harmony with all other living things, some of which may be human.[75] Animatism represents an extension of animism in which non-human creatures are also thought to have soulsy.[76]

* * *

To summarise, religious and spiritual conceptions of human nature vary considerably. In the Abrahamic, monotheistic religions of Judaism, Islam and Christianity, humankind is believed to have been created in God's image and is therefore good, although often with a predilection towards sin. The Abrahamic religions differ over the extent to which human beings are alienated from God. In all three religions, however, salvation comes from union with that one God.

In polytheistic and animistic traditions, humankind is generally believed to exist among other spiritual and mythological beings, as part of a divine or spiritual cosmos. In polytheistic religions, such as Hinduism and Buddhism, the human condition is not tainted by sin, as is the case in Abrahamic religions, but rather marked by ignorance and suffering. According to Hinduism and Buddhism, salvation, thus, comes through knowledge of the true, immortal nature of human beings and not through union with God. Finally, in animism, a higher state of being can be achieved through harmony with all living things.

2.2

Philosophical Approaches to Human Nature

Political philosophers have responded to the question of human nature in a number of ways. Some regard human nature as something fixed, while others view it as being shaped by culture or circumstance. Whether human beings are good or bad, selfish or altruistic, or a combination of both, is a question which has not been settled definitively. Several debates may, however, be identified: *perfection through reason versus constraint by emotions, nature versus nurture* and *innate morality versus radical freedom to choose one's own personal truth*. Those holding perfectionist views of human nature include figures such as Aristotle and Karl Marx. They maintain that a particular teleology exists in relation to human nature and stress the formative influence of society on human beings' capacity to overcome alienation from their true selves. Aristotle, for example, argued that ethical precepts could help human beings overcome their brute state and realise their better self.[77] Others, however, reject such social-deterministic ideas and, instead, stress the role of passions in constraining humanity's capacity to develop its best potential. Those who emphasise nature over nurture prioritise our inherited biological traits as causal explanations of human behaviour, whereas those who view nurture as paramount place greater weight on the role of environmental influences in determining who we are. Some philosophers, nevertheless, subscribe to a dualistic approach and maintain that emotions and reason are both important in shaping our behaviour. Others go beyond this dualism, arguing that we make moral judgements on the basis of a moral repertoire which precedes emotions and rational thought. In other words, we have an innate moral capacity. For others, we have no universal essence and are radically free to choose how to behave.

This chapter reviews these debates and provides an overview of the most influential conceptions of human nature, which my own theory seeks to supersede with a more synthetic approach. Moreover, as is demonstrated in Chapter 5.1, these philosophical positions either explicitly or implicitly inform theories of international relations which are rethought from a neurophilosophical perspective in Part 4. It is therefore useful to outline them early on.

2.2.1. Perfection through Reason

Perfectionism refers to a teleology of morality advancing an objective conception of good. Defined in narrow terms, perfectionism is premised on the idea that it is possible to develop one's constructive potential and realise one's 'true' self.[78] As Plato's student, Aristotle regarded human beings as capable of living a 'good' life by employing reason.[79] Aristotle's approach to human nature has been described as functionalist. Human beings, he argued, have a function: to employ reason in the pursuit of a virtuous life and, in this way, to achieve happiness.[80] Virtue is thus inseparable from happiness according to Aristotle, and the expression of virtue is at its utmost in the exercise of reason (and rational activities). Aristotle considered a person's value to be determined by his or her capacity to fulfil this function. Aristotle referred to education (in the broad sense of good habits, self-discipline, courage and strength of character) as necessary to attain happiness. A 'good' life is, thus, realised through moderation and temperance. A wise individual will find the right balance with which to follow a moral life and reach a state of self-perfection. Not all will be capable of finding the median, succumbing instead to vices associated with excess.[81]

In Aristotle's view, reason is capable of overcoming desire. This suggests that people are ultimately free to choose how to behave and to live their lives, although Aristotle admitted that the external environment may also have an impact on a person's capacity to live a virtuous life.[82] To this extent, the importance of nurture is at least recognised.

Another prominent figure who favoured a perfectionist conception of human nature was Marx. His view of human nature was based on a historical materialist approach,[83] within which the human condition is a function of the social relations of production which characterise any given economic system. Under capitalism, people are believed to be alienated from themselves and their true nature. This kind of alienation originates from the social relations of production which exist under capitalism in which people are obliged to sell their labour in order to meet their material needs.[84] In so doing, they engage in activities which do not contribute to their happiness and, moreover, what they produce with their labour is not their own. Alienation under capitalism, therefore, refers to the way people are estranged not only from their own labour, but also from the product of their labour.[85]

Thus, for Marx, economic factors shape human consciousness and not the other way around. Accordingly, morality is determined by the materialist base under any particular economic system. It is, as a consequence, subject to change: human nature and morality shift according to the social relations which predominate within any particular economic system.[86] Under socialism, unequal relations of production would no longer exist. In the classless society which would follow, human beings would be free to develop themselves as they wished and to realise their true potential. In other words, socialism would necessarily imply a change in the capacity of human beings to behave in a moral way and to live happily together in society.[87]

Therefore, both Aristotle and Marx stressed the determinism of human perfection. In the case of Aristotle, determinism is at the individual level and based on reason. In Marx's view, the human condition depends entirely on the social relations which characterise different types of economic systems.

2.2.2. Constraint by Emotions

Hume held that we cannot really know ourselves, since we cannot know anything of substance given that our understanding of things is simply built up of an ensemble of perceptions. According to Hume, all perceptions are either impressions or ideas. The difference between them lies in the intensity with which they are experienced:

> Those perceptions, which enter with the most force and violence, we may name *impressions*; and under this name I comprehend all our sensations, passions and emotions, as they make their first appearance in the soul. By *ideas* I mean the faint images of these in thinking and reasoning, such as, for instance, are all the perceptions excited by the present

discourse, excepting only, those which arise from sight and touch, and excepting the immediate pleasure or uneasiness it may occasion.[88]

Hume believed that all of our ideas originate from simple impressions: 'the simple impressions always take the precedence of their correspondent ideas, but never appear in the contrary order'.[89] Similarly, we have no transcendental self or soul. We can only know ourselves as a series of mental states.[90] Like Buddhism, Hume held that we can, however, realise self-knowledge through the synthesis of perceptions.

In contrast to Aristotle, Hume argued that reason alone cannot help us overcome our selfishness and lead a virtuous life. According to Hume, we engage in moral behaviour not as a result of rational thought, but because acting in a moral way causes us to feel good about ourselves. We may, for example, help someone in need because it makes us feel good. We may also avoid being cruel because it makes us feel bad.[91] Hume wrote: 'Reason is and ought to be the slave of the passions, and can never pretend to any other office than to serve and obey them.'[92] Humankind is, therefore, equipped with moral instincts determined by emotions, which provide the basis for reasoned judgements. Morality is, consequently, driven by passions.[93] He thus contended:

> So that when you pronounce any action of character to be vicious, you mean nothing, but that from the constitution of your nature you have a feeling or sentiment of blame from contemplation of it. Vice and virtue, therefore, may be compared to sounds, colours, heat and cold, which, according to modern philosophy, are not qualities in objects, but perceptions in the mind.[94]

In this view, conscious reasoning plays a minimal role in our moral judgements.[95]

Hume held that, while some virtues, such as benevolence, generosity and charity, are innate, others, such as justice and chastity, require guidance from society. There is, therefore, a sense in which our moral sensitivities are limited and require further cultivation.[96] As is shown in Chapter 2.4, a similar contention is made by evolutionary theory and associated approaches to human nature.

Jeremy Bentham (1748–1832) viewed behaviour as driven by emotions. Whether something is good or bad ought, he argued, to be judged according to the pain or pleasure produced by it, calculated through what he called *felicitus calculus*. He believed in the ability to improve the human condition through increased knowledge, interpreted in the sense of being well-informed. Bentham maintained that overcoming ignorance is possible due to our ability to understand people's actions as manifestations of pain and pleasure. From this perspective, the human condition could be improved if a general framework were put in place to help guide people's actions within particular historical conditions.[97] Most importantly, such a framework should aim to achieve the greatest happiness for the greatest number, in accordance with utilitarian principles.[98]

2.2.3. Nature

Niccolò Machiavelli (1469–1527) viewed humankind as unchanging, making it possible to make generalisations about human nature. Human beings, he believed, are primarily driven by passions and, most of all, by love, hatred, fear and contempt. Importantly, Machiavelli did not attribute a significant role to reason. Above all, people are motivated by self-interest, which is thought to drive the desire for self-preservation and security, and, eventually, power, glory and domination. True morality, according to Machiavelli, does not exist. Instead, human beings only engage in what may appear to be moral behaviour out of self-interest.[99]

Hobbes also viewed human nature as driven by desires. He wrote the *Leviathan* during the turbulent years of the English Civil War (1642–51). His conception of human nature was radically materialist. Hobbes believed that human beings do what they perceive to be in their self-interest. This is partly due to the fact that they suffer from a state of insecurity. Without some form of overarching government, people who are of equal physical and mental ability have the capacity to harm each other. Moreover, people essentially have the same strong desire for happiness, security, power, wealth, food and other resources in scarce supply. Together, these two factors imply that human beings, in a state of nature, are justified in fearing one another. Only an overarching form of government can alleviate this state of insecurity by enforcing laws and guaranteeing justice for its citizens.[100]

With such a materialist notion of the human essence, there is no such thing as free will. Hobbes is a determinist at the level of the individual. According to his philosophy, human nature is fixed and not subject to significant modification as a result of culture or education. The emphasis is, thus, clearly placed on nature rather than nurture.[101]

If people act in a moral manner, this is likely to be as a result of self-interest rather than a conscious effort to live a happy life. Seeing others suffer may make us feel bad and, in order to feel better, we help them. We may also act in a virtuous way in order to save ourselves from harm.[102] Given the overriding egoistic nature of our character, morality and a strong central government are necessary to restrain the pursuit of self-interest.[103] Unlike Hume, Hobbes held that moral actions may be prompted by emotions but self-interest is ultimately behind these seemingly noble acts. Thus, what may at first appear as altruism, for example, is likely to be what I term *pseudo-altruism*.

2.2.4. Nurture

At the other extreme is Locke, who had an important impact on seventeenth-century philosophy and the way we can think about human nature. At the heart of Locke's thinking is his notion of the human mind as a clean slate or *tabula rasa*, as expressed in the following passage:

> It is an established opinion among some men that there are in the understanding certain innate principles; some primary notions … stamped upon the mind of man, which the soul receives in its very first being and brings into the world with it. It would be sufficient to convince unprejudiced readers of the falseness of this supposition, if I should only show … how men, barely by the use of their natural faculties, may attain to all knowledge they have, without the help of any innate impressions, and may arrive at certainty without any such original notions or principles.[104]

This essentially implies that human beings are born with no particular predilections in terms of thought or innate ideas. Indeed, the fact that some principles may receive universal consent, in Locke's view, does not make those principles innate. Universal maxims cannot be innate, since children, for instance, have no knowledge of them.[105] Moreover, he asks, 'How can these men think the use of reason necessary to discover principles which are supposedly innate, when reason (if we may believe them) is nothing else but the faculty of deducing unknown truths from principles or propositions which are already known.'[106]

According to Locke, experience is the most important factor informing both the human psyche and human behaviour. Everything we know, we learn from our environment. Locke viewed the human mind as highly malleable and considered culture and education, especially, capable of shaping human nature. Thus, nurture rather than nature is paramount from this viewpoint.[107]

Indeed, at the time of Locke, the rejection of innate ideas was perceived by some as a threat to stable identity and to the belief in human beings' inherent tendency towards virtue. Locke himself sometimes appeared to fear that reason may be too weak to ensure that morality prevails over passion and interest. Still, whilst acknowledging the motivating forces of passion, custom and interest, Locke regarded the human capacity for reason as capable of overriding them, so that responsibility and moral freedom could exist at least to some extent. Although Locke considered the environment paramount for determining the constitution of human nature, he acknowledged the capacity of human beings to withstand external influences. This reflectivity appears to have been associated with a Christian moral order.[108]

Rousseau, on the other hand, famously stated that 'Man is born free, and everywhere he is in chains.'[109] Rousseau saw human nature in a fairly positive light. In his thinking, human beings are naturally self-interested, but are also concerned by other people's suffering. Their egoism is, thus, tempered by sympathy.[110] In stark contrast to Hobbesian belief, Rousseau considered human beings to be happy, loving and peaceable creatures who exist under conditions of plenty. What altered this situation, Rousseau argued, was the advent of property. Private property created relations of inequality and triggered the need for governmental protection of that property. The ensuing laws have acted as constraints on freedom, generating conflict and suffering.[111] Rousseau wrote:

> [w]ar is constituted by a relation between things, and not between persons; and, as the state of war cannot arise out of simple personal relations, but only out of real relations, private war, or war of man with man, can exist neither in the state of nature, where there is no constant property, nor in the social state, where everything is under the authority of the laws.[112]

Rousseau believed in the malleability of humans, who are naturally good until corrupted by society. Yet, in Rousseau's thinking, people possess a free will:

> To renounce liberty is to renounce being a man, to surrender the rights of humanity and even its duties. For him who renounces everything no indemnity is possible. Such a renunciation is incompatible with man's nature; to remove all liberty from his will is to remove all morality from his acts.[113]

People are, thus, capable of change. In this sense, Rousseau echoed the thinking of Locke and his notion of the human mind as a *tabula rasa*.[114] Similarly, Rousseau held that education and legislation can make a difference. *The Social Contract* (1762), in fact, was written as a guide to legitimate government.

Kant rejected Locke's notion of the human mind as a clean slate. In his view, humanity has progressively evolved from being motivated by animal instincts to being driven by reason and moral considerations. As Kant states:

> Reason, in a creature, is a faculty which enables that creature to extend far beyond the limits of natural instinct the rules and intentions it follows in using its various powers, and the range of its projects is unbounded. But reason does not itself work instinctively, for it requires trial, practice and instruction to enable it to progress gradually from one stage of insight to the next.[115]

Kant believed that what distinguishes humans from other animal species is their capacity for rational thought; reason is what makes humanity 'human'.[116] His emphasis on reason echoes Aristotle's argument in that humankind not only tends to create a unified system of knowledge, but, as a result, has agency. We carry out certain actions with the intent of affecting our environment in particular ways. Here, Kant wished to point out that while animals can, and indeed do, affect the world in which they live, they cannot explain what they are doing and why. Animals do not, in any way, experience a dilemma between self-interest and moral obligation.[117]

To repeat, in Kant's view, morality derives from reason, not from desires.[118] In general, the use of reason implies assessing the best means to satisfy one's specific desire. Kant maintained, however, that sometimes reason is employed in the fulfilment of an obligation, that is, a moral obligation. Under these circumstances, we accept a motivation for behaviour which is not connected to the satisfaction of individuals' desires. As free, rational human beings, we can make moral choices.[119]

As Stevenson and Haberman put it, 'Kant's view was that human actions cannot be entirely reduced to physical causation and that they involve choices that are not themselves caused.'[120]

Kant, therefore, made a distinction between causal explanations and rational explanations for human behaviour. Thus, Kant argued that, while some human actions are generated by desires and emotions, others are prompted by rational thought. As a result, he was able to make a distinction between self-interested actions, driven by selfish desires and emotions, and moral duty, which stems from rational thought alone.[121] Whether this distinction is valid is taken up below.

Stevenson and Haberman point out that it may be useful to distinguish between different kinds of self-interested reasons for action. Some self-interested desires are connected to immediate gratification, such as consumption of food and drink, sex and so on. Others may be linked to longer-term considerations. Some may, for example, choose to forgo drinking alcohol for health or dietary reasons, even though they may enjoy drinking it. In short, we may resist immediate gratification in the interest of longer-term objectives.[122]

2.2.5. Dualism

Plato was one of the first philosophers to argue that reason was the key to living a 'good life'.[123] He is also one of the chief figures espousing a dualist conception of human nature. Within this approach, the non-material soul or mind is assumed to exist separately from the material body. According to Plato, the soul is a type of divine, immortal self, which exists before birth and continues after death. In this sense, it may be thought of as a type of fixed, essential essence.[124] To this end, Plato's dualism has much in common with the Hindu doctrine of reincarnation in which the immortal soul transmigrates after death.

According to Plato, it is this transcendental self which is capable of knowing the Forms, also known as Ideas, through a process called anamnesis.[125] The idea here is that all things which are perceptible have a Form which exists independent of the objects themselves. The world of Forms is the real world. We can gain access to this real world if we attain true knowledge of the Forms and as soon as we free ourselves of falsehoods and illusions. Only when we gain true knowledge of the Forms may we truly know our divine, immortal selves.[126] When this occurs, all aspects of the soul are in a state of harmony.

Plato argued that the soul is composed of three parts: an intellectual, rational part; a spirit; and an appetitive part. Like Kant, Plato separates material or corporeal desires, emotions and reason from one another. Material desires or the Appetite are linked to desires such as hunger and thirst. Spirit or passion appears to refer to apparently non-bodily emotions, such as love rather than lust. According to Plato, Spirit is something close to Reason. Reason ought to control both the Spirit and the Appetite, pictured as horses which must be guided by Reason so that they run in harmony.[127] Importantly, in Plato's conception of the human condition, both reason and passion are considered drivers of human nature.

Justice is thought to predominate when the three dimensions of the soul exist in harmony. It is unclear, however, whether Plato believed that human beings possess the free will through which to change themselves without the aid of institutions. Given that justice is conceived as representing the correct balance between the three aspects of our souls, we are thought to be more content if justice is present in our lives. Plato viewed education as an important institution which was capable of contributing to the production of just individuals. Education is here understood in the broad sense, encompassing upbringing as well as formal education.[128]

Finally, Plato recognised the role of the environment in allowing people to develop their full potential. While individuals are assumed to have different capabilities, their inability to fully know the soul means that people should be given equality of opportunity through education in order to allow the qualities of the soul to emerge. It is also in this sense that Plato's interpretation of metempsychosis, or 'transmigration of the soul', is similar to reincarnation in Hinduism.[129]

2.2.6. Innate Morality

Like Hume, John Rawls (1921–2002), a prominent twentieth-century philosopher, held that human beings have an innate moral faculty. In contrast to Hume, however, Rawls did not view moral judgements as the result of emotions.[130] According to Rawls, human beings possess a kind of moral faculty that exists prior to emotions or reason. Within this conception, human beings are equipped with unconscious principles.[131] In this sense, Rawls shifts the discussion away from the nature–nurture debate. However, Rawls was aware of the tension between evolutionary selfishness and consciously conceived moral systems.[132] His work *A*

Theory of Justice (1999), which puts forward a conception of justice as fairness, encourages the reader to picture a situation in which self-interested individuals are asked to devise a social contract on which society will be based. They must do so, however, without knowing what their social status would be or which intellectual capacities they would have in this society.

In justice as fairness, the original position of equality corresponds to the state of nature in the traditional theory of social contract. This original position is not, of course, thought of as an actual historical state of affairs, much less as a primitive condition of culture. It is understood as a purely hypothetical situation characterised so as to lead to a certain conception of justice.[133]

A just society, in Rawls' view, would be one in which such self-interested agents would agree to be born into ignorance of the hand they would be dealt (i.e. it is hypothetical).[134] 'The principles of justice', Rawls wrote, 'are chosen behind a veil of ignorance.'[135] Self-interest is, thus, not incompatible with a consciously conceived moral system, because we are endowed with a natural sense of fairness and good.[136]

A form of innate morality is also supported by Frans de Waal, as will be illustrated in more depth in Chapter 2.4. In his 2006 book, *Primates and Philosophers: How Morality Evolved*, de Waal argues that morality has a biological origin and that it is the product of natural selection.[137] Indeed, according to de Waal, morality is neither a conscious choice nor a product of reason, but rather an innate type of emotionally-driven judgement-making.[138] Drawing on his work on non-human primates, he contends that morality stems from the cooperative tendencies which we developed through evolution.[139] The in-group/out-group dichotomy which characterises natural selection has, over time, allowed for the evolution of what we consider today to be morality.[140] This form of morality serves to keep in check the immoral and egoistic passions which generally lead human beings to favour self-interested behaviour.[141]

More recently, behavioural psychology has sought to identify the missing link between genetics and morality. The monoamine oxidase A (MAOA) gene, for instance, which plays a key role in the breakdown of neurotransmitters such as serotonin, has been the focus of many molecular genetic studies.[142] Following initial research on a mutation of the gene in a Dutch family, studies over the past 30 years have demonstrated how it can have a varying degree of responsibility for extraversion, as well as for conduct disorders and anti-social behaviour in both adults and children, and even aggression in adult males, thus earning it the nickname of the 'warrior gene' or the 'serial killer gene'.[143]

A well-known study conducted in Finland, in particular, even found a link between the MAOA allele and nine to ten per cent of violent crime in the country.[144] However, as of yet, studies have only been able to prove that it may cause a predisposition for such personality disorders and behavioural traits, not that it necessarily always causes them.[145] For this reason, labelling such genes as 'serial killer genes' is incredibly problematic. On the one hand, it can lead to the possibly unjust reduction of criminal sentences, as occurred in Italy in 2010, when a judge decided to decrease the sentence of a male convicted of murder following a so-called 'genetic susceptibility test'; the test showed the convicted carried variants of the MAOA and other genes that have been associated with (a predisposition for) aggression. On the other, it can stigmatise its carriers in unprecedented ways, which could lead to widespread discrimination, genomic-profiling, blurred social-equality norms, and resultant increased punishment without justification.[146] Indeed, as will be illustrated in subsequent chapters of this book, placing excessive importance on genetic traits fails to take into account the significant environmental influences on human behaviour.[147]

2.2.7. Radical Freedom

Existentialist thinkers offer a notion of human nature as radically free. Existentialism encourages self-examination and the creation of one's own philosophy of life. Essentially, this implies that each of us has a responsibility to discover his or her own personal truth by which we can live and die. In contrast to Aristotle and Plato, existentialists hold that existence is prior to essence. For Plato, for instance, the world can only be known in a transcendental sphere, which we can discover through reflection.[148] For existentialists, there is no transcendental self to be discovered. Though it turns away from the appeal to reason, existentialism, nevertheless, is, like much Enlightenment thinking, a rejection of the notion that the social structure is God-given.[149]

Existentialism developed in reaction to philosophical thought that assumed that human beings are subject to universal laws.[150] The meaning given by the individual is emphasised over general theory. In Gordon Marino's words, it developed a 'philosophy as a way of life, as a guide for the perplexed'.[151] Three central themes can be identified within existentialist thought. The first is the uniqueness of the individual and the rejection of universal claims about human beings. The second is the importance of subjective experience, as opposed to an objective truth applicable to all. Here, the stress is on the meaning that individuals attribute to their lives. The third is the view that human beings are radically free to determine their lives.[152] As human beings, we have not chosen to be born into this world and must, nevertheless, decide how we wish to define ourselves. In this sense, our essence is chosen rather than given. For this reason, one of the central objectives of existentialists is to help individuals live a rich and fulfilling life.[153]

Two types of existentialism are identifiable: religious (Kierkegaard, Karl Jaspers and Gabriel Marcel) and secular (Sartre, Simone de Beauvoir and Albert Camus). Both forms of existentialism place an emphasis on personal freedom and responsibility.[154] Kierkegaard is regarded as the founder of existentialist thought. He took issue particularly with Aristotle's belief that reason is at the core of the human condition. According to Kierkegaard, our inner passion is likely to be more of a determinant factor in the search for personal truth.[155]

For Kierkegaard, existence is absurd, but our capacity to make sense of it is the voice of God prompting us to find greater meaning. It is this which enables us to embrace faith and religious existence. Indeed, only those individuals who are aware of their alienation from anything meaningful can become true believers.[156] Kierkegaard rejected attempts to give objective justifications for faith-based claims. Instead, he embraced an approach to religion which relied on subjective self-commitments.[157]

In *Fear and Trembling* (1843), an exploration of the story of Abraham and Isaac, in which Abraham agrees to kill his own son on the basis of a subjective command from God, Kierkegaard attempted to demonstrate the way religious claims can demand individuals to suspend the ethical concerns related to their own conduct.[158] In his view:

> [i]n ethical terms, Abraham's relation to Isaac is quite simply this: the father shall love the son more than himself. But within its own confines the ethical has various gradations. We shall see whether this story contains any higher expression for the ethical that can ethically explain his behaviour, can ethically justify his suspending the ethical obligation to his son, but without moving beyond the teleology of the ethical.[159]

Kierkegaard could see no relationship between Abraham's act and the universal, other than the fact that Abraham transgressed the universal for the sake of some higher end purpose outside it. In answer to why Abraham does it, Kierkegaard asserted: 'For God's sake and – the two are wholly identical – for his own sake. He does it for God's sake because God demands this proof of his faith; he does it for his own sake so that he can prove it.'[160]

On the secular side of existentialism, taking an opposing view, Nietzsche maintained that the principal motivating force of humankind is the will to power.[161] The notion of a 'will to power' refers not only to the desire for control, but also to a transformative force. Will to power refers to a cosmic power at the centre of the universe.[162] This will to power is, partly, what replaces the void left by the 'death of God'. Indeed, according to Nietzsche, the world has no intrinsic meaning. In the absence of God, we must create our own meaning.[163]

In Nietzsche's thinking, human beings arc not cqual. Some people will be able to affirm themselves and dominate, while others will become subject to domination. In his opinion, those who are the most capable of self-affirmation and excellence are those who ought to develop moral codes. Christian morality, in this respect, is thought to induce slavish behaviour on the part of the masses.[164] The *Übermenschen* are those who are capable of standing outside any given historical process and of affirming themselves.[165] According to Nietzsche, 'The magnitude of an "advance" can even be measured by the mass of things that had to be sacrificed to it; mankind in the mass sacrificed to the propensity of a single *stronger* species of man – that *would* be an advance.'[166]

Sartre, another seminal secular existentialist, linked the idea of freedom with that of existence preceding essence. For those who embrace religion, existence is subordinated to individual essence or a person's soul. Given that they were created by God in his image, according to Judeo-Christian tradition, human beings have an identifiable nature. Yet, if God and faith are removed from the equation, we have no definable nature and there is no intrinsic significance to our lives. We are simply sentient beings with no specific purpose. We are, therefore, entirely free to define our own purpose. Understood in this way, freedom is as much negative as it is positive. It is a burden which each one of us has to bear.[167] Just as human beings are free to create their own essence, they are also free to change it. To this end, humanity is highly malleable.

What makes human beings unique is their self-awareness. We are able to reflect on our own condition and wishes within a broader vision of existence. This kind of consciousness, for existentialists, means that we are more than simply a combination of corporeal desires and sensations. Sartre attempts to reflect this reflexive dimension of the human condition by referring to the uniqueness of our ability to call ourselves into question: 'The human being is not only the being by whom negations are disclosed in the world; he is also the being who can take negative attitudes towards himself.'[168] This reflexivity, however, implies that our existence is characterised by a tension between, on the one hand, a higher order consciousness and, on the other, our desires and sensations. How we manage this tension defines our identity. As Charles Guignon points out:

> If we regard the self as a tension or struggle, it is natural to think of human existence not as a thing or object of some sort, but as an unfolding event or happening – the story of how the tension is dealt with. What defines my existence, according to this view, is not some set of properties that remain the same through time, but the 'event of becoming' through which I carry out the struggle to resolve the tension that defines my condition in the world.[169]

* * *

This chapter provided a brief overview of the major philosophical approaches to the question of human nature, which continue to inform the way I conceive of the human condition. This overview served two reasons: first, I sought to provide a brief sketch of these positions because they provide the context in which my own approach, which aims to provide a more accurate and synthesised picture of human nature, should be situated; and second, to set out the philosophical foundations of the conceptions of human nature which inform the major approaches to international relations discussed in Part 4.

I identified several debates underlying the philosophical discussion of human nature. Some view human beings as capable of perfecting themselves through the employment of reason, while others see perfection as a result of historical circumstance. For others, human emotions sometimes lead to moral behaviour. I term this debate as *perfection through reason* versus *constraint by emotions*. I also outlined the between *nature* and *nurture*, which emphasises the influence of either our biological heritage or our environment on the human psyche and human behaviour. Lastly, I identified an innate debate between *morality* and *radical freedom* (no essence prior to existence). In the former position, human beings are believed to be endowed with an innate moral faculty which is independent of emotions and reason. In the latter, there is no universal essence and moral actions are dependent on conscious choices.

2.3

Psychological Approaches to Human Nature

Much of philosophical thinking assumes that human beings are, above all, defined by their capacity for rational thought. Challenges to the notion of 'rational man' have, however, been mounted from within the discipline of psychology, which provides alternative explanations for human motivation. A major contribution of these approaches is the focus on human needs – both physiological and psychosocial – and on the role of the unconscious. Some of these needs have an important place in my own theory. In this chapter, I shall examine some of the key theories which led to the development of modern psychology. These include Freud's discussion of pansexuality and psychoanalysis, according to which the human condition is based on unconscious drives which are predominantly sexual. Burrhus F. Skinner (1904–90), on the other hand, was concerned not with unconscious sexual desires as motivations for conscious behaviour, but with responses to stimuli within the environment. The humanistic psychology Abraham Maslow (1908–70) emphasised human needs rather than motivations. This was an attempt to develop a type of psychology which addressed the whole gamut of a human being's functional make-up. Finally, the work of Konrad Lorenz (1903–89) argued that ecological factors have influenced the development of our instincts.

2.3.1. Freud and the Study of Psychological States

Freud's psychoanalytic theory constituted a revolutionary approach to human nature in the early twentieth century.[170] Freud called into question the core belief underlying some of the major approaches to human nature, such as Aristotle's or Kant's, that the human condition is defined, above all, by our capacity for rational thought.[171] He held that neuroses typically had a sexual cause. Importantly, he was a philosophical materialist and determinist in that he linked our psychological states to our physiological states. He, therefore, anticipated the connection between psychology and physiology which would later be made in neuroscience.[172]

According to Freud, all of our dreams and actions, even the smallest and seemingly most benign (such as a slip of the tongue) have a meaning; they betray things about our psyche which would otherwise remain hidden beneath the surface. Since our consciousness has biological origins, we are not, contrary to what existentialists would suggest, radically free to construct our own truths.[173]

Another significant aspect of Freud's thinking is the notion of unconscious mental states. This refers to states that are not normally accessible to conscious consideration. In his view, hysterical paralysis, neurotic behaviour, obsessions and dreams are linked to the unconscious mind. Some of these unconscious thoughts originate in the conscious realm – those linked to traumatic experiences, for example – but are buried deep in the unconscious mind because they are, otherwise, too painful to bear. The rest of our unconscious, according to Freud, propels our conscious thinking and behaviour.[174]

Freud also put forward a new structural theory which identified three elements of the mind: the id, ego and superego. The id is the part of the mental apparatus which is connected to basic instincts requiring immediate satisfaction. The ego relates to conscious mental processes which contribute to determining how to act. Everything in the ego is conscious, whereas everything in the id is unconscious. Lastly, he identified a superego, which is a part of the mind which contains the conscience. It is in this part of the mind that moral judgements occur. It can arbitrate between the ego and the world by introducing systems of rules which constrain the ego, which has the difficult task of mediating between the id and the superego.[175] When the ego is able to successfully reconcile the id and the superego, harmony between the personality and the environment is thought to result.[176]

As Stevenson and Haberman note, there are notable similarities between Freud's and Plato's ideas:

> The id obviously corresponds closely to Appetite or desire, but it is not so clear how ego and superego correspond to Plato's Reason and Spirit. In its reality-knowing function, the ego would seem to be akin to Reason, but Reason for Plato has also a moral function that Freud assigns to the superego. And Plato's spirited element seems to be performing a moralistic function in the example of feeling disgusted with one's own desires.[177]

Freud argued that individual well-being depends on harmony between the three parts of the mind and between the individual and the external world. The ego has to reconcile the desires of the id and the superego, which acts as the representative of the social and moral norms of society. A third principal component of Freud's psychoanalytic theory relates to human instincts or drives. The main type of drive was thought to be sexual – hence the notion of pansexuality, which reflects the idea that the cause of all human behaviour can be found in sexual desire.[178]

Another interesting aspect of Freud's thinking is the developmental understanding of the human character. This is the notion that personality depends on experience as well as hereditary traits. Childhood and early infancy are, thus, thought to exert an ongoing and important influence on adult behaviour.[179]

The objective of psychoanalysis is self-knowledge.[180] There is, thus, some sense in which human beings can reach a higher state of existence through self-realisation, which may be attained through psychoanalysis. The 'truth', as it were, is gained through an understanding of the unconscious desires which drive psychodynamics and behaviour. This 'reality', however, is an interpretation which is dependent on the analyst's insight and judgement.

2.3.2. Skinner and the Study of Observable Behaviour

One of the seminal figures in psychology who came after Freud is Skinner, a behavioural psychologist. In contrast to Freud, Skinner was concerned with observable responses to stimuli. He, therefore, advanced a different kind of psychology. Skinner's psychology did not concern itself with the unconscious and hidden human desires. Instead, it was premised on the notion that both the human psyche and human behaviour are determined mostly by the external environment.[181]

In 1945, as the Second World War was coming to a close, Skinner wrote a utopian novel, which was published in 1948 as *Walden Two*. This novel of ideas, loosely set in the 1940s, after the war, uses the description of a utopian community, Walden Two, to illustrate how a community may prosper if it operates flexibly, and continuously tests the most successful scientific and evidence-based strategies for community governance.[182] Indeed, the book was inspired by the idea that those returning from war should experiment with a community better suited to satisfying human needs than the existing society.[183] Over the course of the next forty years, Skinner developed a science of voluntary behaviour, as opposed to involuntary behaviour.

He outlined a naturalism which touched every dimension of humanity. Known as radical behaviourism, it held that a person's psychological state can only be understood by taking into account his or her behaviour and the environmental factors which influence it. Skinner essentially applied naturalism – the belief that everything in nature functions according to objective laws – to social life. He argued that the human mind is not something which exists in its own right prior to a social context.[184] He also contended that psychology had to give up its focus on mental states and, instead, concentrate on that which could be observed (i.e. behaviour). Yet he did not go so far as to claim that human behaviour was caused entirely by external, environmental stimuli. He did, in fact, leave some room for genetic endowments. What Skinner's psychology aimed to do was discover the laws by which the external environment influences human behaviour.[185] Human behaviour is, in this context, presumed to be predictable.[186]

Emotions are not attributed a causal status in relation to human behaviour. Rather, Skinner redefined emotions in behavioural terms. While emotions are ordinarily experienced on a subjective level, Skinner argued that they can be understood as dispositions to act in particular ways and are, therefore, comprehensible by an objective observer. A person who is afraid, for example, is likely to avoid contact with specific stimuli by running away, whereas someone experiencing intense anger may be more likely to strike or insult others.[187]

Skinner, therefore, developed a psychological approach which focussed on external events which trigger human action. To this end, behaviour is believed to be determined not by a person's psyche, but by the environment. Emotions may be repressed, for example, as a result of the existence of norms and mechanisms of punishment in society.[188] His work reflected this assumption that behaviour can be controlled and, to this end, he conceived of human nature as malleable and susceptible to nurture.[189]

2.3.3. Maslow and the Focus on Human Meeds

Maslow, on the other hand, put forward a theory of human motivation and a hierarchy of needs. His humanistic psychology attempted to develop a form of psychology which addressed different, hierarchically organised, functions or needs, rather than focussing on psychopathology as Freud and Skinner had done. In Maslow's view, in order to understand what motivates human behaviour, we need to consider the whole range of a person's existence.[190]

Like much Western philosophical thought, as well as Buddhism, Maslow's psychology rests on the assumption that human beings possess a higher self which can be realised in everyday life.[191] Central to his psychology is the notion that there is a hierarchy of needs. Those needs which we find at the lower end of the scale, such as basic physiological needs, dominate our existence if they are not satisfied. At the first and lowest level are safety needs, which are physiological and instinctive, including the need for food, shelter, air, water, sleep and sex, for instance. The second level includes security needs, such as protection, stability, security, and freedom from fear, anxiety and chaos. If these needs are met, an individual can be motivated by higher functions, such as belonging and love or self-esteem, reputation with others and achievement, which, respectively, occupy the third and fourth levels. At the fifth and final level is self-actualisation, which can lead to transcendence. Needs can also be partially fulfilled at both the lower and the higher levels, making Maslow's hierarchy of human needs a framework for analysis rather than a rigid prescription of the ordering of human functions.[192]

When physiological needs at the first level are not met, this can lead to a severe risk to life and even death, in the worst-case scenario. If needs are not met at the second level (security), the consequences may also be catastrophic for, when people fear for their safety and even for their lives, they may be motivated to do terrible things which they would find unthinkable in other circumstances. Lack of satisfaction at the third level (belonging and love) is also likely to have serious consequences. People who suffer from alienation due to lack of love and the feeling of not belonging are likely to feel rejected and angry. We might imagine that this could be translated into extreme forms of behaviour. At the fourth level, a lack of achievement and respect are likely to lead to a lack of self-worth, an extremely destructive emotion. Contrary to these first four categories, described by Maslow as 'deficiency needs', lack of fulfilment at the fifth level (self-actualisation) has less serious consequences.[193]

2.3.4. Lorenz and Evolutionary Thought in Psychology

Lorenz was interested in establishing a historical and philosophical basis for studying human behaviour – an evolutionary epistemology. He emphasised the inborn nature of patterns of human behaviour. In relation to instincts, Lorenz favoured group selectionist ideas, which have now been called into question by sociobiologists who espouse gene-centred views of selection.[194] Lorenz was also concerned with the constraints imposed by what we may be born with and the moral underpinnings of a humane society.

His early work focussed on the origins of, and nervous energy connected to, instinctive behaviour. His work with the Dutch biologist Niko Tinbergen (1907–88) demonstrates that ecological factors play a significant part in the evolution of particular instincts within certain species.[195] Based on his work with animals, Lorenz, controversially, argued that human evolution has selected an 'aggressive gene'. He contended that evolutionary adaptation has resulted in the selection of genetic make-ups which are predisposed to aggressive, warlike behaviour. If an aggressive gene is selected, it must have a useful function, such as the eradication of competitors to sexual partners.[196] He also argued that aggression has the advantage of dispersing individuals over a large territory, thereby creating the conditions under which scarce resources could be shared between members of the same species. Aggression may also have helped create a pecking order which enabled the most experienced to lead a group.[197]

Lorenz maintained that human beings may have a natural predilection for aggression and that this may help to explain the violent behaviour which has characterised human history, as well as the group-related nature of such violence. Wars, riots and ethnic cleansing, for example, are targeted at groups which are perceived as foreign 'others'. He believed that we could direct such predispositions towards more harmless activities, such as sports competitions, for instance, by taking rational steps to keep them in check.[198] It is important to note, however, that Lorenz did not believe that our biological heritage made such behaviour inevitable. While we may have a predilection for violent behaviour, studying and understanding its causes could offer hope for overcoming it. There is, thus, a sense in which we can transcend natural selection through our environment.[199]

* * *

To summarise, by briefly outlining the work of Freud, Skinner, Maslow and Lorenz, this chapter has examined the challenges which have been posed to the belief that humanity is, above all, rational. For Freud, the unconscious played an overwhelmingly important role in shaping the human psyche and human behaviour. In contrast, Skinner insisted that human behaviour could be explained by observable behaviour and exogenous events. Maslow's humanistic psychology attempted to provide a framework within which to capture the influence of a range of human needs on behaviour. Finally, Lorenz introduced evolutionary thought into psychology, arguing that ecological factors shaped the instincts which humankind evolved.

2.4

Evolutionary Approaches to Human Nature

This chapter explores how sociobiologists and evolutionary psychologists approach the question of human nature. Sociobiology attempts to apply evolutionary theory to the social world, in order to better understand human behavioural traits. Evolutionary psychologists, on the other hand, focus on design features which affect human psychological adaptations. These approaches help us explain why unconscious motivations are so significant for understanding human nature and emphasise that a great deal of our behaviour is informed by emotions rather than by reason. They also attempt to address, from an evolutionary standpoint, the question of whether we are moral beings. Here, moral sensitivities, albeit fairly basic ones, are perceived to be innate. The intellectual roots of both these approaches are to be found in Darwin's theory of evolution by natural selection, which represented a radical departure from the belief that humankind is created in God's image.[200]

I begin by giving a brief overview of evolutionary theory. However, since Darwin's time, studies in genetics have advanced our understanding of how behavioural traits are transmitted across generations. It is in this context that I discuss Edward O. Wilson's sociobiology. I also consider Richard Dawkins' and George Williams' theories, which challenge the notion that altruism can be explained by group selection, favouring instead a gene- or individual-centred selection as a way of explaining the origins of our more noble inclinations. Finally, I focus on some seminal contributions to evolutionary psychology, including those of Marc Hauser, Steven Pinker, Frans de Waal and Peter Singer, who argue that certain traits, such as empathy and even morality, have evolutionary roots.

2.4.1. Evolutionary Theory

Evolutionary theory is concerned with change in living things over time, be they animals, plants or human beings.[201] Variation is believed to occur as a result of the survival advantages which adaptations may give certain organisms. Individual members of a species which display such traits are more likely to exhibit reproductive success than those lacking them. Indeed, crucial to evolution is not simply survival, but the transmission of the genes which facilitated survival advantages.[202]

Physical adaptations include, for instance, the tongue of a certain type of bumblebee, which is perfectly designed to collect nectar from deep inside a flower. This makes the types of bumblebees with these tongues better suited to undertake this task.[203] Yet, as Robert Winston points out, this does not imply that all adaptations resemble perfectly conceived solutions to nature's challenges:

> Many adaptations appear to be the work of a talented and ingenious biological engineer, but there are also examples that seem rough and ready, badly thought out, or something of a botched job. Our own eyes are one quite good example. True, they have excellent clarity of vision and colour definition. If they are in prime working order, they have a fast autofocus and accurate autoexposure. Additionally, they are self-cleaning and cleverly built into a protective hollow. But we are, many of us, short-sighted, and cataracts are common. And there is a major 'design' flaw: the light-sensitive retina lies behind a layer of blood vessels and nerves, and these 'service pipes' limit the amount of light reaching the retina. This arrangement also necessitates a hole in the retina through which the vessels and nerves can pass to connect to the brain – this hole is our blind spot. And, more seriously, it means the retina can become detached rather easily. It would be much better to have the retina in front, and we find this superior 'design' in large cephalopods such as squid and octopus.[204]

Darwin's thesis of evolutionary development relies on the concept of natural selection under conditions of scarcity. Natural selection refers to a process of genetic replication, whereby species attempt to survive by adapting to their environment and in the process develop mutations which give some members of a species a survival advantage over others.[205] Natural selection, thus, focusses on the biological factors which shape who we are and, in this way, sets boundaries to the extent to which we, as human beings, are capable of exercising free will.

Darwin also put forward his own thesis on emotions. In *The Expression of the Emotions in Man and Animals* (1872) he argued that the expression of emotions is the result of instinct rather than learnt behaviour.[206] He identified six core emotions – happiness, sadness, anger, fear, disgust and surprise – to which others later added guilt, shame, embarrassment, jealousy and contempt and, more speculatively, pride, sympathy, admiration, frustration and nostalgia.[207]

Of course, in Darwin's day it was not yet known how characteristics were passed on from one generation to the next. Important progress in this regard was made in the 1930s, when Ronald Fisher, John B.S. Haldane and Sewall Wright started to fuse Darwinian theory and genetics. Theorists who attempted to outline a synthetic theory combining the two included Theodosius Dobzhansky, Ernst Mayr and, in more recent years, Stephen Jay Gould.[208]

In addition to challenging religious notions of human nature, Darwinian theory also called into question philosophical approaches which viewed reason as the source of morality and sociability. Darwin saw morality as a product of evolution, rather than something which humankind had invented at some specific point in history.[209] Interestingly, Darwin argued that we have a duty not only to act altruistically towards our kin, but also to expand gradually our sphere of concern to all other human beings and, eventually, to the animal kingdom.[210]

2.4.2. Sociobiology

A prominent current application of evolutionary theory to social behaviour is to be found in sociobiology, which is premised on the notion that biology shapes human behaviour. Morality, for example, is thought to be the result of our evolution and is, therefore, a product of biology.[211] At the core of sociobiology is the concept of 'inclusive fitness', which holds that evolution has created behaviour which increases an organism's chances of surviving and reproducing. The latter may take place by either of two means: first, through individual reproductive success; and, second, through adopting behaviour which is likely to increase the chances of genes similar to one's own being passed on to the next generation. Together, these two means constitute inclusive fitness.[212]

George Williams is famous for his critique of group selection. In his view, selection is more likely to have been among genes or individuals than groups. He, therefore, favoured a gene-centred understanding of evolution,[213] which was later taken up by sociobiologists, such as Wilson, who pioneered the field in *Sociobiology: The New Synthesis* (1975) and *On Human Nature* (1978). In the first of these books, Wilson argues that natural selection, rather than free will, is the motivating force behind human behaviour. He, thus, argued that, when discussing morality, we must be cautious not to yield to the illusion of radical free will.[214]

One of the most prominent present-day proponents of sociobiology is Richard Dawkins. In a series of works, the most well-known being *The Selfish Gene* (1976), Dawkins argues that it is the gene and not the organism or group which is the principal unit of natural selection. In this thesis, the individual organism operates as a vehicle for the transmission of the gene from generation to generation. This contrasts with traditional Darwinian natural selection in that it is not the survival of the individual which is emphasised, but that of the gene. In this vision of things, we act as transporters. While we as organisms are ephemeral, with a finite time on this earth, genes continue indefinitely.[215]

Although mere vehicles for genes, human beings do, nevertheless, make life difficult for genes. According to Dawkins, our unusually large brains have led to our development of memes. Memes essentially refer to cultural practices, including language, beliefs, institutions, ideas and patterns of behaviour, which may be passed on from generation to generation (hence the popular term today referring to images shared on social media). Once established, these practices become part of what we might ordinarily think of as structure. Some memes may hinder the transmission of genes from one generation to the next, contraception being the most troublesome meme from a gene's point of view.[216]

Some would agree that the evidence does suggest that our genes play a central role in shaping our behaviour. The Minnesota Twin Family Study was established in 1983 with the goal of identifying the genetic and environmental influences on the development of human psyche. It started off by creating a registry of all twins born in Minnesota from 1936 to 1955 but has more recently recorded twins born between 1961 and 1964. The Twin Study of Adult Development was begun in 1986 to discern how genes and the environment, respectively, affect the aging process. The genetic dimension was found to be comparatively more important than the environment, as affected by lifestyle, for instance.[217]

The study showed that identical twins demonstrated astonishing similarities in terms of behaviour. A set of male identical twins, who had been brought up separately, had both become police officers, other sets both had similar smoking and drinking habits, or had been married twice and, in both instances, the first wife had been called Linda and the second Betty. This, as the study pointed out, does not suggest, however, that the environment plays no role whatsoever in the development of the human psyche and behaviour.[218]

In Dawkins' approach, the gene predominates over the environment. As such, genes and not culture are thought to be responsible for the evolution of altruism, violence, parenting skills, deception, sexual conflict and so on.[219] To answer the question, 'Where does the good Samaritan in us come from?', Dawkins argues that, while the gene itself may be selfish, the organism is not. Exactly how genes are selfish depends on the circumstances. In some instances, the gene may be selfish in terms of influencing the organism to behave altruistically. Human beings may behave altruistically towards kin, because this increases the survival chances of reproduction of genes similar to their own. They may also practice reciprocal altruism – the 'you scratch my back, I'll scratch your back' scenario – since this increases survival chances. The development of language by human society may also encourage people to act altruistically because of the importance of reputation. In addition, acts which carry a greater 'cost' for the performer may demonstrate authentic superiority. They represent 'rule of thumb' principles which we have now elaborated with deliberately conceived moral systems.[220]

Other sociobiologists argue that there is a common core of morality, based on reciprocity, which may be supplemented by rules of thumb, such as Kant's categorical imperative, which together may constitute a universal moral code.[221] This indicates that there may be a difference between basic-common-denominator morality and true or complete altruism.

2.4.3. Evolutionary Psychology

Evolutionary psychology focusses on the characteristics of the human brain which affect human psychological adaptations. This is central to explaining universal psychological traits, such as emotions, reciprocity, altruism, in-group bias, communications and so on. Steven Pinker, for example, argues that language is a universal feature of all humankind. According to him, we are endowed with a common grammar, which is an innate and unique characteristic of our species. It provides a foundation on which diverse languages can be developed.[222]

In Pinker's 1994 book, *The Language Instinct*, drawing on Noam Chomsky's contention that human beings possess an innate universal grammar which is unique to our species, he argues that we are all equipped with an in-built capacity for language. Systems of grammar exist in all cultures, and they should not be thought of as a cultural invention – unlike writing, for instance. Pinker argues that, on the contrary, language ought to be considered an instinct, a creation of human evolution, which emerged to help solve problems of communication within what would have been highly social communities of hunters and gatherers.[223]

In *How the Mind Works* (1997), Pinker argues that our neuronal architecture is sufficiently complex to support not only rationality, but also the suppression of impulses. According to Pinker, we should understand science and morality as two different and separate realms. In other words, we ought to be able to accept a scientific explanation for our moral sense, its evolutionary history and its neurobiological foundations; at the same time, we ought to understand morality as an ideal worth striving towards.[224]

Drawing similarly on Chomsky's notion of an unconscious universal grammar with which we are born, and from which different languages develop, Marc Hauser argues that the human species possesses a universal *moral* grammar. In his fascinating book, *Moral Minds: How Nature Designed Our Universal Sense of Right and Wrong* (2006), Hauser maintains that human beings have developed a moral instinct through Darwinian selection. From this innate moral grammar, other, more specific moral systems, shaped by culture, may then develop.[225]

According to Hauser, this universal moral grammar is unconscious. He begins his book with a discussion of the major philosophical theses on morality. First, he takes issue with Hobbes, who held that our moral systems are devised through a process of reflection. For Hauser, this perspective on human nature and morality fails to explain why certain morals would be acceptable to our species.[226] As mentioned above, the central thesis of *Moral Minds* is that we possess an innate moral faculty, which is the equivalent of a universal moral grammar. This innate moral sense exists in every culture. He argues, for example, that in all cultures parents are expected to care for their children. Yet this is not intended to suggest that moral systems do not differ among human cultures.

On the basis of this *common* moral grammar, *specific* moral systems may be erected. What varies from culture to culture is not the rule, but exceptions to the rule. From this perspective, morality is, thus, based on biology.[227]

The underlying question is: what is the source of this universal moral faculty? Hume would have argued that shared emotions are its source. Kant, by contrast, would have contended that common moral codes are the outcome of our unique capacity for reason. Indeed, while Kant recognised that our emotions may help to shape moral responses, he considered our moral judgements to be the result of deliberate reasoning, which implies conscious reflection on moral principles and rules.[228]

Behavioural psychology, as I related above, also tends to assume that morality is the child of reason. Skinner, for example, regarded human nature as infinitely malleable. Children, he claimed, can be taught to be moral. Yet evolutionists such as Hauser would challenge this line of argument. While the human brain may be malleable, what makes a moral principle valid? Or, more precisely, what makes a parent's judgement about what course of action a child should take valid in moral terms? Moreover, why does a child understand these apparently abstract ideals?[229]

According to Hauser, our emotions cannot be given a causal role in relation to our moral judgements, as moral dilemmas activate a vast network of brain regions linked not only to emotions but also to decision-making, conflict, social relations and memory. He adds a Rawlsean element to this observation. Rawls, he argues, would not reject the idea that emotions are implicated in the process through which we arrive at a moral judgement. Rawls would, however, question Hume's assumption about when these emotions come into play. In summary, there are, in Hauser's view, areas of the brain which may be thought of as Kantian (based on reason), Humean (based on emotions) or Rawlsean (based on a moral grammar).[230]

Hauser holds that one can identify a 'mirror neuron system' which plays a critical role in moral judgements. This means that the same parts of the brain are activated when a person does something him/herself as when they watch someone else do the same thing. Thus, emotional conductors are necessary for moral judgements to take place. Empathy, for example, represents a fundamental link in our behaviour.[231] A Rawlsean model would, therefore, provide the most accurate depiction of how we come to make moral judgements. In this conception, an event or action may prompt a moral judgement. If emotions play a role, they do so only after the judgement has been made. Emotions are, in fact, triggered by these exact judgements.[232]

In his book *Primates and Philosophers: How Morality Evolved* (2006), Frans de Waal also explores the biological origins of morality. Like Wilson and Hauser, de Waal argues that human values are the result of natural selection. However, de Waal draws on his work with primates to illustrate the evolutionary basis of moral behaviour.[233]

According to de Waal, evolution has created humans as beings who have cooperative tendencies, and morality is considered to be an offshoot of these inclinations.[234] In contrast to Hobbes, de Waal argues that society did not emerge from a rational decision made at some particular moment in time: '[T]here never was a point at which we became social: descended from highly social ancestors – a long line of monkeys and apes – we have been group-living forever. ... Humans started out – if a starting point is discernible at all – as interdependent, bonded, and unequal.'[235] In fact, living in groups undeniably offers considerable advantages. It may increase the chances of finding food, rearing offspring and escaping predators. As a result, sociability has been favoured by selection and is, therefore, embedded in primate psychology.[236] For this reason, de Waal makes the interesting observation that solitary confinement is the second most severe punishment for a human being after the death penalty, since it goes against our inherently sociable nature.[237]

Unlike Hauser, however, de Waal considers moral judgements to be driven by emotions. 'I feel', he insists, 'that we are standing at the threshold of a much larger shift in theorizing that will end up positioning morality firmly within the emotional core of human nature.'[238] Thus, the Humean interpretation of morality would be the most accurate.[239] Indeed, de Waal rejects the notion that human beings developed moral schema by choice, that is, as a consequence of rationality and voluntary design. De Waal refers to this Hobbesian approach to human nature and morality as 'veneer theory', which he traces back to Thomas Henry Huxley (1825–95), although he recognises that it goes back much further in Western philosophy and religion. Huxley had a rather dim view of human nature. He compared humanity to a gardener who is constantly busy trying to keep the weeds from growing in his garden. Morality, in this view, was a necessary invention required to keep human nature in check. It is a thin cultural layer, a thin veneer, under which lie immoral, egoistic passions.[240]

De Waal accepts that it may be legitimate to think of evolution as favouring self-interested behaviour but contends that one should not make the mistake of assuming that this is at the expense of altruistic behaviour. Kin selection and reciprocal altruism are thought to provide adequate explanations for altruistic tendencies. These, he argues, seem more adequate than group selection, since inter-group migration among primates is extremely common, resulting in a considerable amount of genetic mixing between groups. According to de Waal, claims appealing to Darwinian theory as a justification for the rejection of morality in society are premised on a misunderstanding of natural selection.[241]

According to de Waal, 'the old always remains present in the new'.[242] He illustrates this point in relation to empathy. In his view, more advanced forms of empathy have their origins in simpler forms. Social animals need to coordinate in order to respond collectively to danger and, for instance, to find food. An animal which fails to run away with others, in response to an approaching predator, is not likely to survive very long. Other, more sophisticated forms of attention towards others are evidenced in primate behaviour. A female ape is sensitive to whimpering from her baby and tries to reduce its distress, for example.[243]

Thus, evolutionary pressures may have favoured in-group moral instincts, with the first circle of loyalty being to oneself and one's kin, and then to the broader species:[244] 'In the course of human evolution, out-group hostility enhanced in-group solidarity to the point that morality emerged.'[245] Humans as we know them today have, of course, gone much further than their ancestors and have developed complex moral systems which can be explained. This concept, in particular, echoes Hauser's argument about the limits of moral instincts.

This idea is echoed by Peter Singer, who argues that, while humankind may be self-interested and competitive, it also has considerable capacity for cooperation.[246] He claims that continuous moral progress is possible and, indeed, has taken place as we have gradually expanded our moral circle from the family and the village to the clan, the tribe, the nation and, with the 1948 Universal Declaration of Human Rights, to the species as a whole. Moreover, it has grown from including only men, to including women and children as well.[247] This implies that a conscious effort can be made to place all of humanity inside our moral circle.

* * *

To sum up, this chapter has looked at how evolutionary psychologists and sociobiologists view human nature. Sharing the same intellectual roots as Darwin, thinkers who draw on evolutionary theory, such as Dawkins and Hauser, challenge the religious view of humankind having been created in God's image. Likewise, they call into question philosophical approaches which depict human nature as driven solely either by egoistic passions or by rationality.

Both sociobiologists and evolutionary psychologists argue that many of our traits are the product of evolution. Even morality is deemed to have emerged from our evolutionary past. This latter insight is particularly interesting, since it suggests that we possess a type of innate, universal moral faculty, with divergences being exceptions to the rule. This implies that we ought to be able to agree on a minimum set of universal moral criteria. On a less positive note, however, evolutionists also suggest that, while there may be a moral core to our humanity, it may only be linked to our kin. This implies that any moral standards extended to the whole of humanity are ideal types requiring consistent reinforcement.

2.5

Human Nature in the Twenty-First Century: Neuroscience and Transformative Technologies

Twenty-first-century neuroscientific inquiries into human nature defy any brief summary and are all too often presented in a technical jargon inaccessible to most policymakers and non-experts. One of the aims of this book is to make these discoveries accessible across disciplines. As a starting point, it is therefore fundamental to highlight how twenty-first-century brain-imaging technology – such as functional magnetic resonance imaging (fMRI) or, more recently, magnetic encephalography (MEG) – have allowed us to delve into the inner workings of the living human brain.[248] The picture which emerges from brain-imaging studies is overturning many long-held beliefs about human nature. For example, neuroscientific investigations of the brain have shown that the neuronal mechanisms underpinning cognition are tightly connected to emotional processing in the brain,[249] thus highlighting the false dichotomy between rationality and emotionality. In addition, neuroscience has found that the brain is highly adaptive and malleable, due to the synapses' ability to change in response to experience and of the maturation undergone during specific developmental stages.[250] Further, there is a wealth of ongoing research exploring the neural correlates of moral judgements, conjoint with a growing philosophical literature interpreting the empirical discoveries of this research.[251] The insights this research is yielding suggest that we possess no innate understandings of good and evil, and that our moral compass is malleable. Part 3 will explore in more detail recent neuroscientific findings in order to propose a general theory of human nature and a specific theory of human motivation.

Twenty-first-century scientific and technological advances are not only drastically enhancing our understanding of human nature, they also allow us to modify nature, human and otherwise, with far-reaching consequences. Several technologies, in particular, may well lead to a fundamental change in our species' capabilities.[252] These include artificial intelligence, neural interfaces and technologies such as 'closed-loop' systems (which record brain signals and deliver stimulation in response and can, as such, be particularly useful in the treatment of neuropsychiatric disorders).[253]

Neural interfaces are new kinds of technologies which, without requiring manual input through a keyboard or a joystick, for instance, can connect the brain or parts of the nervous system to digital or IT systems and devices. At present, we have access to two main types of neural interfaces: on the one hand, those which 'read' the brain by decoding brain signals; and, on the other, those which can affect the function of specific regions of the brain by 'writing' instructions for them through the stimulation or manipulation of their activity.[254] In medicine, brain-computer interfaces (BCIs) provide a much-needed way of helping patients suffering from neuronal dysfunction. In the case of patients who have suffered strokes or paralysis, or live with Parkinsonism, for instance, BCIs can enable them to make movements they had previously lost.[255] In the case of brain disorders, such as epilepsy or depression, they can monitor brain activity and stop incoming crises and attacks through the use of drugs.[256] Nevertheless, such interfaces – also called electroceuticals[257] – are increasingly being used in contexts which go well beyond medicine. BCIs in the form of headsets are indeed being used, for instance, by gamers to control on-screen characters in virtual reality settings[258] or, allegedly, even by some companies to monitor the fatigue and productivity levels of their employees.[259] In the future, neural interfaces are likely to enable an ever-increasing integration of human thought with artificial intelligence (AI) and machine-learning. This possibility may open the door to the development of enhanced decision-making capabilities, as well as improved situational awareness and, potentially, even new kinds of sensory experiences which will surpass our wildest imagination.[260]

Weaving AI and computers into the human personality will change human nature in at least three significant ways. First, it will lead to various forms of human enhancement, which I shall discuss below.

Second, it will affect the scope of our free will, autonomy and decision-making processes. On the one hand, a device which monitors blood glucose and learns to control automatically the release of insulin is a form of decision-making on behalf of a person, which is hardly controversial. On the other, similar devices may also be used more controversially, for example, to monitor, influence and stimulate people's moods and emotions. This potential use of BCI technologies is especially challenging from an ethical perspective, since it can be incredibly invasive.[261] BCI devices used to cure depression or other brain disorders may, for instance, prevent someone from experiencing negative emotions even when such emotions are normal, such as during a funeral, for instance.[262] Furthermore, there is also the risk of 'brainjacking', the possibility of brain implants being maliciously controlled by cyber attackers.[263] Cyber attackers could, therefore, against the will of the patient or without his or her knowledge, modify emotions and induce pain or behavioural changes (such as hypersexuality or pathological gambling). Moreover, they could stimulate the reward system in order to reinforce certain actions, or even kill people, for instance, by hijacking an insulin pump.[264]

Third, alongside issues of free will, we must consider the question of how BCIs might lead to deeper epigenetic changes. Within epigenetics studies, which explore heritable changes in gene expression, 'lifestyle' and individual genetic background are typically considered to be intertwined.[265] In the long run, the prolonged and repeated use of BCIs may cause unpredictable changes in our gene expression, which may also be passed on to our children.[266]

Ongoing advances in genome editing and synthetic biology, as well as in the field of super-intelligence, are enabling the rapid collapse of previously existing barriers to much more drastic forms of human enhancement.[267] By *human enhancement*, I refer to 'the use of innovative technologies to augment human biological and cognitive abilities beyond the replacement of dysfunctional cellular groups and organs', as I have defined it elsewhere.[268] This type of human enhancement can be achieved through both pharmacological and non-pharmacological means. An increasing number of people within the university student and workplace communities are relying, for instance, on psychostimulants such as Adderall, a drug commonly prescribed for treating disorders such as attention deficit hyperactivity and to augment focus, organisational and learning skills.[269] Non-pharmacological methods for cognitive enhancement include non-invasive brain stimulation techniques which rely on electrical currents or magnetic impulses.[270] The potential applications of such human enhancement technologies are immense, including in the military context. Armies, for instance, could use these technologies to improve a human operator's multi-tasking capabilities or his/her ability to learn and make use of specific types of physical movements much faster than he/she would otherwise be able to do.[271]

Synthetic biology is a very recent interdisciplinary field which developed at the practical level over the past twenty years. The aim of synthetic biology is not merely to alter biological systems, but to design and create new kinds of biological systems with functions and capacities which do not exist in nature.[272] If carried out safely and responsibly, such innovations could help tackle human and global security challenges. They could address food crises, for example, by engineering an 'off' switch for plants so they could respond to environmental signals, such as dryness, or by significantly increasing the nutritional value of crops.[273] However, as we are partly a product of our environment, releasing synthetic organisms into the environment will have consequences for the evolution of human nature as well as the environment.

In addition, synthetic biology is increasingly focussing on revolutionary innovations which can be applied to the human body. One example of these uses of synthetic biology can be found in the ongoing development of a synthetic probiotic producing a bacterial species which detects and treats diseases from inside the gut.[274] Yet the line between treatment and human enhancement is already being tested by other important ventures in the field of synthetic biology.[275] Indeed, an emerging field of application is within transplantation, since organs and cells produced synthetically could provide the solution to problems of rejection and auto-immune responses.[276] Moreover, rapid developments in synthetic biology could help design organs which 'eventually surpass human organs in function and survival'.[277]

More daring fronts have now been reached through the dramatic advances in synthetic biology and the understanding of the human genome. These include, notably, the possibility of synthesising human DNA, which the scientists in the Genome Project-Write (or GP-Write) are working on. Although tools for genome editing have become widely available following the development of ground-breaking technologies such as CRISPR, GP-Write aims not only to 'edit' DNA, but to re-write critical stretches of chromosomes and, possibly one day, even a human genome sequence from scratch. Though the scientists in the project insist that creating new types of humans or babies is not their goal,[278] synthetic biology is likely to endow us with this kind of unprecedented capability.

Notably, it is generally believed that, in the future, super-intelligence will follow shortly after the advent of general artificial intelligence.[279] *Super-intelligence* refers to hypothetical machine intelligence which surpasses the smartest human mind.[280] With advances in synthetic biology, even biological super-intelligence may become feasible, entailing radical changes in the human brain.[281]

To sum up, twenty-first-century science and technology have not only provided us with a better understanding of human nature but, in the near future, they may in fact radically change what it means to be human. This raises the fundamental question of how it is possible to use the positive potential of emerging technologies while minimising their downsides. Such concerns include, among others, the problem of rising social inequality due to the fact that not all people will have equal access to human enhancement technologies or the fact that only the militaries of wealthy states may acquire enhanced soldiers and therefore a guaranteed advantage over their enemies.

To conclude, this chapter has explored the most influential accounts of human nature which have emerged over the past three thousand years. In what follows, I shall embark on formulating a neurophilosophical theory of human nature, which will take inspiration from and push forward the latest insights from across disciplines, especially neuroscience.

Part 3

Emotional Amoral Egoism

A Neurophilosophical Approach to Human Nature

From Part 2, it emerges that human nature is too complex a phenomenon to be adequately comprehended through a single disciplinary lens. Therefore, by integrating neuroscientific findings with insights from the humanities and social sciences, a neurophilosophical perspective can significantly widen the scope of our understanding. Arguing from a neurophilosophical vantage point, Part 3 puts forward a general theory of human nature which I have termed *emotional amoral egoism*. The theory posits that there are three attributes – *emotionality, amorality* and *egoism* – common to all human beings, across all ages and cultures. Our differences notwithstanding, we all share these three commonalities, which are deeply ingrained in the most ancient parts of our brain. In so arguing, I offer an account of human nature which moves beyond a neuroessentialist view. In other words, I do not attribute everything about the human experience to neurochemical and neuroanatomical reactions inside our brains, or to strictly inborn instincts. Instead, I take into account the interplay of a wide array of factors, from our innate perceptions to the role of the environment (both personal and political), in explaining who we are (see Diagram 1).

The first facet of human nature is *emotionality*. Philosophy has long conceptualised emotions as different from – or a hindrance to – rationality. For centuries, rationality has been celebrated as a

Diagram 1: Emotional amoral egoism

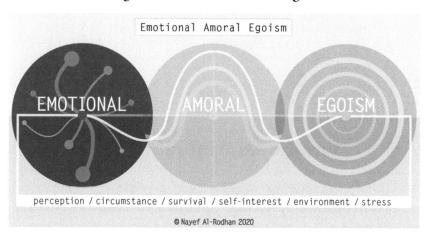

distinctively positive trait, while emotionality has been regarded as detrimental to good judgement, as I discussed earlier. However, recent years have witnessed a wealth of research pointing to the salience of emotions and their profound connection to a range of cognitive processes in humans, including rational decision-making, learning and perception.[282] Emotional responses frequently precede our rational thinking, and we tend to rationalise our actions only after our emotions have prompted us to make a certain decision. In other words, 'rationality' is often merely a *post hoc* justification for the initial impetus provided by the emotions.[283] Most emotions are instinctive. Some, however, may be triggered by conscious thought. In any case, emotions are mediated through neurochemical combinations in our brains. Importantly, our specific neurochemistry is genetically inherited but alterable by experience and circumstances.

Amorality is the second defining trait of human nature. By describing the human species as amoral, I do not negate the fact that human beings have moral sensitivities, or that they possess the capacity to make moral judgements. Nor do I use the term *amoral* in the traditional sense to describe people who, though competent with the concept of a moral judgement, are not motivated to act morally and are indifferent to right and wrong.[284] Rather, I use the term *amorality* to mean that we are born without innate understandings of good and evil, and that our moral judgements may fluctuate according to circumstances, both personal and political. Let me explain how neuroscientific findings support such a claim.

Over the past few years, large numbers of scholars have devoted their attention to studying the brain structures involved in moral decision-making, making use of novel techniques from neuroscience. The results of this research have been variously interpreted by some of the leading figures in philosophy, psychology and neuroscience.[285] Some studies purport to have demonstrated the existence of genetic influences on the development of what is generally viewed as virtuous character traits.[286] As briefly mentioned in Chapter 2.2.6, in recent years a large number of studies, such as those of Macià Buades-Rotger and David Gallardo-Pujol, have focussed on the interplay between certain mutations of the MAOA gene and environmental influences. According to these studies, there is evidence that, at least in the case of men, adverse environmental circumstances can predict increased levels of anti-social behaviour or even violent tendencies, when coupled with the mutated MAOA gene.[287]

However, whilst I acknowledge that certain genes may influence how prone we may be to anti-social or pro-social behaviour, I still believe that we enter the world without inborn notions of good and evil. There is a preponderance of evidence that our moral judgements shift in response to different circumstances and have no objective validity. Studies on stress, for example, show that, in the face of moral dilemmas, stress is correlated with more egocentric decisions.[288] A number of scholars, including Jonathan Haidt and his collaborators, have demonstrated that altering an individual's emotion can alter moral judgements.[289] In one study, for example, Thalia Wheatley and Haidt hypnotised a group of subjects to make them experience disgust at an arbitrary word, such as 'often' or 'take'. Subjects were then asked to make moral evaluations of characters in apparently innocent stories which did or did not contain the disgust-inducing word. Interestingly, they found that, compared to the control group, the subjects did indeed make more severe moral judgements when the story included the disgust-eliciting word.[290]

Similarly, fMRI studies carried out by Joshua D. Greene and colleagues have shown that moral dilemmas vary systematically in the extent to which they engage emotional processing and that these variations influence moral judgement.[291] According to Greene et al.'s dual-process theory of moral judgement, our reason and emotions may conflict when it comes to making such judgements, and this is especially the case when the moral dilemma is 'personal' rather than 'impersonal'.[292] To this, Greene and his co-authors add that utilitarian thought processes require extra cognitive efforts compared to non-utilitarian choices, which are driven by automatic emotional responses.[293] Greene's research suggests that modulation of the emotional response to a moral dilemma can change a moral judgement.[294] To sum up, there is a wealth of evidence that human beings possess no objective moral compass to determine right or wrong. Instead, our moral compass is malleable.

As early as 1900, Émile Durkheim (1858–1917) suggested that morality must be understood as a social fact that is subject to human agency, rather than being deeply ingrained in us.[295] I largely, though not entirely, agree with Durkheim's observation. Indeed, external factors determine the direction in which our moral compass points. This is why, on a considerable range of issues, moral values are divergent across cultures. As Jesse Prinz has suggested, to a significant extent, moral values 'hinge on culturally inculcated passions'.[296] Some scholars, including John Mikhail, would disagree with the position taken here, however. They would argue that human beings are endowed with an innate 'moral grammar' which enables them to generate universal moral evaluations on a range of issues. Indeed, prohibitions of murder or incest appear to be universal or almost so.[297] How can we reconcile this phenomenon with my contention that human beings are amoral?

Although moral concepts are not part of our genetic endowment, we are innately programmed with some pro-social affinities. Certain emotions, such as empathy[298] and sympathy,[299] for example, facilitate group living by making us sensitive to the emotions of others and enable us to care for their well-being. Whilst these emotions are essential for the development of what could be described as 'moral sensitivity', the link between emotions and morality must not be mistaken for an innate moral capacity. In fact, studies in social psychology have revealed that empathy and morality are two independent motives for behaviour.[300] Emotions such as empathy are often biased towards individuals who are spatio-temporally close (our family members etc.).[301] Our emotions are, first and foremost, designed by evolution to ensure our survival. Indeed, survival instincts are so powerful that people, while capable of being both good and bad, generally act according to what they perceive to be their overall self-interest. Hence, circumstances determine what I call the *survival value of humankind's moral compass*. I use the term *bad* to describe human behaviour which inflicts harm, physical or emotional, on others. By *good*, I refer to behaviour which considers not only our own personal well-being, but also that of other living beings and the environment, demonstrating respect for key moral principles such as honesty, fairness and inclusiveness. The aforementioned prohibitions of killing or inbreeding spring from our survival instincts, rather than altruistic motives: if these prohibitions did not exist, the probability of being killed, or of suffering from a genetic deformity, would be greater. In other words, social norms which appear, at first glance, to be revelatory of universal innate moral values are, on closer inspection, motivated by self-interest.

This brings us to the third fundamental feature of human nature: *egoism*. Egoism is not only about the pursuit of biological survival, but also about the attainment of life goals and the opportunity to express one's authenticity, self-worth and potential. This is why revolutions and social movements are not only initiated by those who fear for their physical survival, but also by the disenfranchised and marginalised who want to reclaim their right to an identity.[302]

Recent research tends to support the notion that we are shaped by the forces both of nature and of nurture.[303] Accordingly, the three primordial facets of human nature – emotionality, amorality and egoism – are genetically coded and reflect the 'nature' component. They are, however, modified by the totality of our environment and, therefore, by 'nurture', as is indicated in Diagram 1. The human brain, in fact, is highly malleable and capable of rewiring itself in response to intrinsic and extrinsic stimuli.[304] Unlike Locke, therefore, I do not consider human beings to be entirely blank slates. Instead, I prefer to conceive of the human mind as a *predisposed tabula rasa* (see Diagram 2). By *predisposed*, I mean that we are endowed with predilections stemming from our genetic make-up, gearing us towards survival (and those acts which maximise our chances of survival). Otherwise, our moral compass, our life-guiding values, will be largely shaped by the conditions of our environment, be they personal and/or political. My theory of human nature offers a new perspective on the perplexing question of free will, moving beyond the nature–nurture dichotomy (see Chapter 2.2). In other words, we are neither radically free to choose our nature nor entirely determined by our biological heritage. Furthermore, our personality traits are not only shaped by our environment, but also may be modified by drugs and psychotherapy. Scientific and technological advances (e.g. in the field of synthetic biology) are giving rise to ever more possibilities of altering human psychology and physiology. They may soon allow human beings to surpass their current biological and cognitive limits. This could ultimately alter what it means to be human. Whether humanity will use technology to create trans- and, eventually, post-humans, therefore, may well constitute the greatest ethical challenge of the twenty-first century.

In addition to being malleable, the human brain is pre-programmed to feel good. Indeed, our instincts push us to repeat behaviours which activate the reward centres of the brain – delivering oxytocin and

Diagram 2: Predisposed tabula rasa

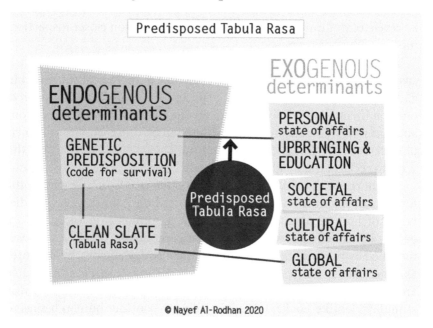

© Nayef Al-Rodhan 2020

dopamine, among other important neurochemicals, to waiting neural receptors.[305] I argue that there are five main drivers of human action through which this neurochemical gratification is sought. I call them the Neuro P5: power, profit, pleasure, pride and permanency. By permanency, I refer to the pursuit of survival, of longevity, but also to the propensity for carrying out actions which enhance the prospects of one's life having an imprint or legacy which goes beyond and survives physical death – such as intellectual output, kin, philanthropic and humanitarian work, or even heroic acts which impact the lives of others and can be recorded in collective memory. The Neuro P5 are at the heart of my specific theory of human motivation, which will be developed in Chapter 3.1. The relationship between both theories is set out in Diagram 3.

While a great deal of what we are is based in instincts and driven by emotions, we are, nevertheless, capable of reaching a higher state of being through reflection. There is ample evidence that reasoning can disrupt intuitive and often biased processes of moral judgement formation either by upfront conscious control, or by intentional after-the-fact correction.[306] Through reflection we can, for example, overcome our innate in-group favouritism and fear of the 'other' and make impartial

Diagram 3: A general theory of human nature: emotional amoral egoism and a specific theory of human motivation (the Neuro P5)

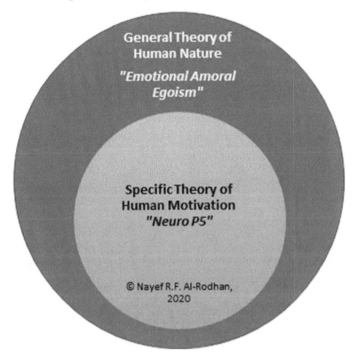

and less-biased moral judgements (see Chapter 3.7). The latter, however, does not readily transpire in everyday life, since reflection is a deliberate mental act which can only occur once our basic needs are satisfied.

Diagram 4 illustrates how the major elements of human nature interrelate. Above all, human beings are (1) egoistic in the sense of being motivated by survival instincts. Our survival instincts are (2) emotionally based and (3) predisposed through our genetic make-up. Our (4) heterogenous personality traits are shaped by variations in (5) neurochemistry, as well as (6) our environment, and may be modified by (7) medicines, genetic engineering and so on. Further, we are able to act in what are generally regarded as moral ways, though we often do so for self-interested reasons.

When describing human nature as emotional, amoral and egoistic, I am not being pessimistic – far from it. On the contrary, I believe that we can productively harness these dynamics of human nature in ways which promote peace and security. Pro-social behaviour can be fostered by a type of good governance which ensures egalitarian norms

**Diagram 4: A general theory of human nature:
emotional amoral egoism**

A General Theory of Human Nature:
"Emotional Amoral Egoism"

1 Humans are motivated by survival instincts

2 that are emotionally based

3 and predisposed through genetic make-up

4 with heterogeneous variations & personality traits (basic make-up, spontaneous mutations, epigenetics)

5 that are mediated through neurochemistry

6 and affected by personal state of affairs, upbringing, education, and societal, cultural and global state of affairs

7 but may be modified by medicines, molecular/genetic engineering, neurotechnology, etc.

8 and can occasionally be moral, although probably for self-interest reasons.

© Nayef Al-Rodhan 2020

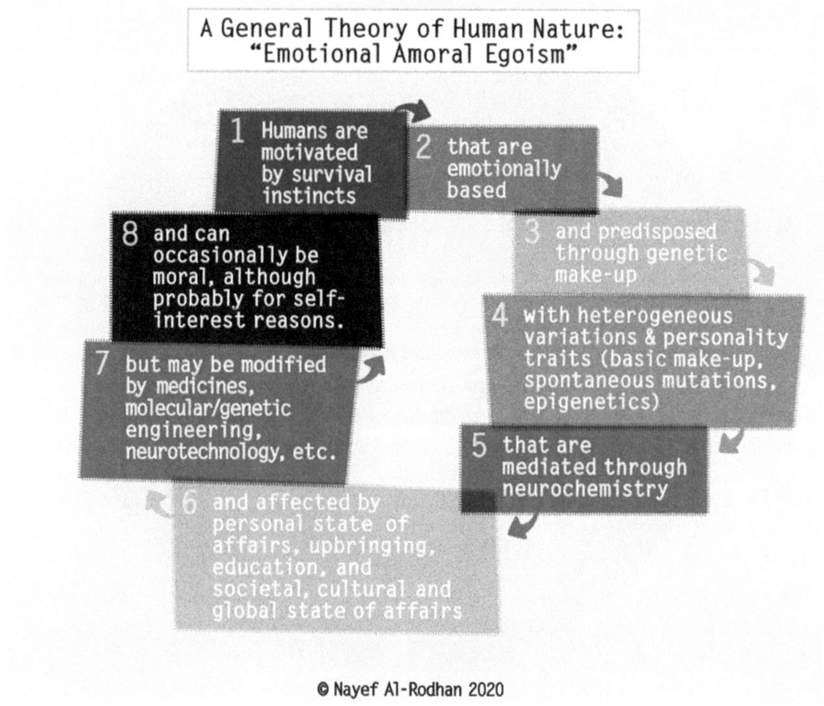

and human dignity, a paradigm I refer to as *dignity-based governance*. Subsequently, Parts 4 and 5 explore how dignity-based governance can mediate between our emotional, amoral and egoistic character and our need for dignity. However, before delving in more detail into the political implications of our emotional amoral egoism, the Neuro P5 merit closer attention.

3.1

The Neuro P5: A Theory of Human Motivation

At the heart of my general theory of human nature lies my specific theory of human motivation. What drives our behaviour? What moves us to action? What pushes us towards specific goals? What motivates us and why? These questions have been considered across a vast body of literature through different disciplinary lenses concerned with, for instance, social learning theory, control theory or self-determination theory.[307] Our understanding of the internal psychological processes and the neurobiological mechanisms which underpin human motivation has been greatly enhanced over the past few years. Drawing on the latest insights from neuroscience, I argue that the Neuro P5 are five particularly powerful motivators of human nature. Indeed, our brain is pre-programmed to 'feel good' and it will do everything it takes to attain neurochemical gratification, maintain it and, if possible, enhance it. The Neuro P5 play a fundamental role in this process by activating the reward centres of the brain, delivering much-craved neurochemical gratification (see Diagram 5).

Most of the time, the Neuro P5 are instinctual. Instincts are biologically inherited unconscious drivers of behaviour which stem from the conditions under which our Palaeolithic ancestors had to survive. That said our environment can alter how our instincts are acted upon. In what follows, each of the Neuro P5 – power, profit, pleasure, pride and permanency – is introduced in more detail.

Diagram 5: The Neuro P5

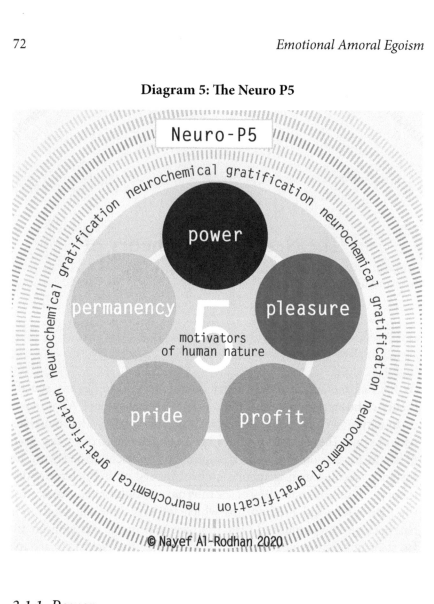

3.1.1. Power

Throughout the past, power has been the object of human striving, shaping all human relations, social structures and the whole course of history. Whilst we all have an intuitive understanding of the term, power has become a far-ranging notion which eludes an easy definition in the social sciences and in political discourse. This is partly due to the influence of Michel Foucault (1926–84) and his revival of Nietzsche's writings.[308] The classical foundations for defining power were laid by the works of Karl Marx and Max Weber (1864–1920). Marx maintained that economic structures – such as owners of capital – represent societal sources of power. Weber, on the other hand, argued that power was a function not only of economic relationships but also of culture and social organisation, as reflected in social institutions such as religion and law.[308] He famously defined power as the chance for a person to realise his or her 'will in a social action even against the resistance of others who are participating in the action'.[309] Since then, various debates have evolved to differentiate themselves from, or agree with, Weber's definition of power. Drawing on these numerous approaches, power can be succinctly defined, as Betty Dobratz, Lisa Waldner and Timothy Buzzell do, 'as individual, group or structural capacity to achieve intended effects as a result of force, influence, or authority'.[310]

Many philosophers have cautioned about the destructive effects of unlimited power. In 1938, Bertrand Russell (1872–1970) warned that 'love of power, like lust, is such a strong motive that it influences men's actions more than they think it should' and that 'the psychological conditions for the taming of power are in some ways the most difficult'.[311] Contemporary neuroscience has revealed exactly how power 'goes to the head'. Power is neurochemically represented in the brain through a release of dopamine, the same neurochemical involved in the reward circuitry and largely associated with generating the feeling of pleasure, as well as with the motivation to repeat those actions which are conducive to dopamine releases. In other words, power-seeking is akin to other addictive processes, since it produces 'cravings' at the neurocellular level and generates a 'high' much like that produced by substances we typically define as drugs.[312] In light of this, it is clear that Russell was right when he said that 'love of power is greatly increased by the experience of power'.[313] This is why so many leaders cling to power with such fierce tenacity. Indeed, most people, when handed the opportunity to accrue more power, would not voluntarily turn it down. As a result of its drug-like effects on the brain, when power is unconstrained by democratic controls or good systems of governance, its holders may manifest undesirable distortions in judgement, cognition and behaviour.

3.1.2. Profit

Gaining a profit is another motivating force behind our actions. It ensures that we take what we need and act in ways which benefit us – financially or otherwise. We continuously seek to accumulate more of the things which we value, such as money, love or knowledge. A measured pursuit of profit has positive effects – for instance, through hard work, excellence and absolute gains (when a person's gain does not entail another person's loss). It also helps the individual satisfy the needs of his/her ego by earning him/her reward or recognition and thereby enhancing his/her reputation or status.

The pursuit of profit turns into outright greed when we give in to an excessive desire for more, at all costs – even at the expense of others. In this context, greed may indeed be thought of as an incapacity to delay gratification. In the human brain, the capacity and responsibility for delaying gratification or reward lies in the prefrontal cortex. Recent research has shown that the parts of the limbic ('affective') system, which are associated with the generation of dopamine, are preferentially activated when individuals are presented with immediate reward. The prospects of delayed reward, on the other hand, activate parts of the brain associated with cognitive and deliberative functions.[314] Greed can, therefore, be described as a result of inner impulses which override our cognitive functions when addressing issues of reward. Since immediate gratification is a more powerful impulse than the thought of any possible longer-term consequences, greed too often results in ruthless, fraudulent and criminal behaviour which only gives rise to a relative gain (i.e. one person's gain coincides with another person's loss). The dramatic events of the financial crisis in 2008 and 2009 provide only one of many manifestations of greed having devastating consequences.

3.1.3. Pleasure

Our brains are wired for pleasure. Motivational psychologists have long argued that human beings seek to maximise pleasure and to avoid painful experiences. Motivational hedonism even assumes that all human motivation boils down to a basic desire to pursue pleasure. Normative hedonism goes as far as claiming that only pleasure has value. In *Civilization and Its Discontents* (1930), Freud argued that the purpose of our lives, as suggested by our behaviour, seemed to be the application of the 'pleasure principle', which referred to the id's search for immediate gratification of all needs, wants and urges. This requires the satisfaction of instinctual drives which include, *inter alia*, hunger, thirst, anger and sex. For Bentham, too, pleasure, which he considered to be the 'only good', constituted a fundamental driver of human nature.[315] The emerging insights into the neurochemistry of the human brain only confirm the vital role of pleasure in driving our behaviour.

Pleasure may be purely sensory, like savouring the taste of food, the smell of perfume or the warmth of the sun. Or it may be a complex psychic or intellectual experience, like the joy of solving a puzzle. Indeed, the greatest pleasures in our lives are likely to be both sensual and intellectual. Art, nature and sport, for example, provide us with more than a mere sensual experience. Rather, we appreciate them for their own sake, despite the fact that they fulfil no utilitarian function. Art, in particular, transports us into an exalted state by challenging us intellectually, not by providing us with some form of immediate physical gratification. The philosopher Alva Noë, for example, maintains that art discloses to us what we do not yet know about ourselves.[316] It is, therefore, clear that we derive great pleasures from the imaginative experiences, intellectual discoveries and the admiration of skill which art provides us.

Pleasure is widely assumed to be a purely subjective feeling. Yet it has objective features in the form of measurable hedonic reactions, both neural and behavioural. Over the past several decades, results from neuroimaging studies have suggested that pleasures from many different kinds of stimuli – food, sex, addictive drugs, music, art – produce strikingly similar patterns of brain activity. However, the hedonic hotspots they activate only partially overlap with the so-called brain reward system, which was once thought to be at the origin of every sensation of pleasure.[317]

Possessing the capacity to experience pleasure helps us to reduce tension and stress and motivates us to seek companionship and engage in sexual reproduction. Excessive pleasure-seeking, however, tends to have detrimental long-term consequences. Nowadays, in particular, we may have the desire to pursue pleasure in ways which go beyond the search for food, into areas which can present dangers to either our physical or mental health or both. The pursuit of fitness, for example, can lead to substance abuse. On a wider level, excessive pleasure-seeking may also be detrimental to society's social foundations or to the environment (through, for example, throw-away consumerism). If we focus too narrowly on what is pleasant to the self, we easily lose sight of what is good socially, politically or morally.

3.1.4. Pride

Another major driver of human behaviour is pride. Pride is a self-referential emotion, as opposed to basic emotions such as happiness, sadness, anger, disgust and fear (see Chapter 3.3.2). Self-referential

emotions provide us with evaluative information about ourselves.[318]
Basic and self-referential emotions overlap in many aspects, including,
most notably, their neurobiological circuits. Indeed, although at present
research on the neurofunctional correlates of self-referential emotions
is scarce, conceptually, emotions such as pride, guilt and shame usually
encompass, at the very least, an emotional aspect as well as a self-
reflecting, self-evaluating and self-conscious aspect.[319] In other words,
they are intimately linked with our self-esteem. The emotional aspect,
in particular, activates the same networks responsible for the generation
of basic emotions, such as the amygdala, insula, and ventral striatum.
Cortical midline structures and the dorsolateral prefrontal cortex are,
instead, responsible for the generation of self-esteem.[320] As Jessica Tracy
and Richard Robins explain, 'pride is the primary emotion (along with
shame) that gives self-esteem its affective kick, and self-esteem in turn
influences a wide range of intrapsychic and interpersonal processes'.[321]
Pride, of course, has both positive and negative connotations. Tracy
and Robins distinguish between two sorts of pride: an 'authentic' pride
(I'm proud of what I did) and a 'hubristic' pride (I'm proud of who I
am). The former results from accomplishments, which are accompanied
by genuine feelings of self-worth. The latter is not so much associated
with actual accomplishments but, rather, results from a self-reflective
process producing a distorted image of the self in order to help promote
self-esteem. It may even be a way of suppressing shame by means of
exaggerated feelings of pride and the idealisation of the self, which
amount to a form of narcissism.[322] Importantly, MRI and fMRI studies
have shown that, in addition to exhibiting high levels of self-esteem,[323]
individuals who test higher in terms of narcissism scores tend to show
lower connectivity between certain brain areas, including the prefrontal
cortex and ventral striatum which, as stated above, are regions of the
brain associated with positive self-evaluation.[324] The low activity in
these regions of the brain may be responsible for narcissists' continuous
search for external affirmation.[325]

Pride is a major need of the ego. The experience of pride motivates
individuals to strive for achievements in socially valued domains which
enhance their reputation and social status.[326] Pride stems from the ego's
successful negotiation between its ideal self-image and external valuations
of the self. This key element of 'evaluation by others' which characterises
pride involves the activation of brain regions associated with such
processes, including the superior temporal sulcus and temporoparietal
junction and the lateral prefrontal and parietal regions.[327] In Freudian
terms, the ego mediates between the id, which is driven by basic survival

instincts, and the superego, which is the part of human consciousness which motivates us to conform to social pressures. In this sense, the ego provides the nexus between our biologically inherited instincts and the social world.[328] As Gardner Murphy (1895–1979) suggested, we might therefore usefully think of the ego as the part of ourselves which organises everything linked to self-enhancement and self-defence.[329] On the other hand, Percival Symonds (1893–1960) defined the ego as 'that phase of personality which determines adjustments to the outside world in the interest of satisfying inner needs in those situations where choice and decision are involved'.[330] In light of these considerations, it is evident that the ego will be negatively affected when it has been unsuccessful in negotiating between a person's inner needs for recognition and their valuation according to prevailing social standards. In such instances, our pride is hurt and the self feels humiliated. The consequence is a loss of self-esteem.[331]

As mentioned above, pride can take the form of reasonable self-respect or inordinate conceit. It is more likely to take the form of healthy self-respect when the ego is 'strong' enough to live up to one's ideals for oneself. Factors contributing to a 'strong' ego include love and respect, socially accepted outlets for inner needs, opportunities for self-expression and self-assertion, and a strong and cohesive family and society.[332] These aspects contribute to the recognition of an individual's worth and are, thus, purveyors of pride.[333] A measured or 'strong' ego is likely to help an individual meet different challenges and opportunities in socially appropriate ways which fulfil his or her inner need for esteem. A 'weak' ego is, instead, likely to lead to excesses associated with unchecked impulses, since individuals with that type of ego will be unable to tolerate either the frustration of their needs and desires or disappointment. These excesses may include the wish to exert domination over others, or attitudes associated with cultural arrogance or a sense of exceptionalism involving the idealisation of one's own group and the denigration of others.[334] Feelings of pride may facilitate 'pro-social' behaviour, such as charitable acts, since helping others makes an individual feel that he or she is a 'good person'. Not only will this make him or her feel good about him/herself and maintain a positive self-concept, but it will reward him or her with social status and acceptance.[335] A loss of pride, on the other hand, may lead to various forms of anti-social behaviour, such as, *inter alia*, narcissistic aggression, hostility, abuse, greed and manipulation of others.[336] Interestingly, loss of pride is among the root causes of radicalisation processes. Indeed, it gives rise to feelings of isolation, the rejection of the self and the need for external recognition and belonging, which is sought through the commission of extreme acts which trigger admiration and respect among members of the extremist in-group.[337]

3.1.5. Permanency

As mentioned in the previous chapter, ingrained in the deep, ancient part of our brain is the evolutionary imperative of what I call permanency. Humankind is, first and foremost, driven by key survival instincts related to basic sustenance, shelter, personal safety and reproduction. However, permanency refers to more than the mere pursuit of physical survival or longevity. The desire for permanency also motivates actions which enhance one's prospects of leaving an imprint or a legacy which overcomes physical death. These actions may include intellectual output, offspring, philanthropic and humanitarian work or even heroic acts which impact the lives of others and can be recorded in collective memory. Whilst these acts may appear selfless, a form of self-interest – be it psychosocial or purely physical – is likely to be lurking beneath the veneer of altruism. Indeed, although this desire to be remembered has shaped our histories and cultures and driven the production of incredible artwork and literature, it has also triggered the commission of acts which are far from altruistic, contributing to the outbreak of wars and the building of empires. Still, a measured degree of general self-interest is essential to succeeding in our environment, since it will not only encourage us to perform at our best; it will allow us to respond to the often equally self-interested behaviour of others. Excessive self-interest of this kind, however, is likely to lead to conflict, criminality and violence.

Recognising these five fundamental drivers in our nature, we must strive to create domestic and global governance frameworks which can keep these powerful motivators in check. Part 4 will illustrate in detail how we can positively channel our emotional amoral egoism through good governance.

3.1.6. Specific Individual Inclinations

I identify specific individual leanings as another, sixth, factor driving human behaviour. Such leanings can be quite strong, inducing intense feelings. An otherwise apparently well-balanced person may, for example, display obsessive behaviour in relation to football, checking the results every day, orienting conversations around the game, planning his or her life around matches and so on. When a person's team wins, it brings great pleasure and joy, and players may be elevated to the status of gods. Equally, losses can produce feelings of great sorrow and even anger. What may appear as a benign leisure activity can, thus, become an incredibly powerful motivating force.

When measured, specific individual leanings may, however, provide a means of coping with stress, because they reduce nervous tension. There may also be a reward in the form of leisure activities. Sports, for example, may involve the satisfaction of personal challenges, leading to a sense of achievement.[338] Sports may also be addictive because of the neurochemical changes they induce. A person's self-identity may also be reinforced by their engagement in a leisure activity. They may feel a sense of belonging as a result of being part of a group or community with similar interests, for instance, a sport or acting club, or a volunteer organisation. In this sense, leisure activities may aid in the development of a strong ego. Then again, while some of these inclinations may be innocent, as in sports, others may be pathological. Some may translate into exaggerated behaviour and, when excessive, may result in addiction and what may be perceived as 'socially inappropriate behaviour', and even in criminality and violence, as demonstrated by contemporary studies concerning the links between violent video games and the reproduction in real life of similarly aggressive behaviour.[339]

3.1.7. Occasional Reason

Reason constitutes another aspect of human motivation. The recurring question of how we make sense of the world has been answered in different ways by different scholars. According to Plato's theory of Forms, for example, forming an understanding of something requires us to interpret the stimuli generated by our senses, and it involves applying concepts which help us mentally to organise what we perceive.[340] For Kant too, our faculty of reason led us to build a whole system of knowledge which depends on rules and principles.[341] Part 2 discussed how reason has been conceived across disciplines. Here, it suffices to highlight that, according to my own theory, we employ reason only occasionally when carrying out actions and making decisions. Most of what we do, we do out of habit and instinct. Further, although a measured degree of reason is likely to lead to distinction and excellence, reason without emotion may, on the contrary, turn us into psychopaths.[342]

3.1.8. Infrequent Reflection and Morality

Reflection and morality constitute the eighth and final factor of human motivation. As discussed above, philosophers have taken many different positions in the analysis of human morality. In Hobbes' perception of nature, for example, there was no room for morality, since individuals were preoccupied with their safety. In the Hobbesian state of nature, all human beings were driven by desires, possessing the same capacity to do harm to one another and existing in a context of scarcity and anarchy (i.e. a lack of central government).[343]

Hobbes' ideas stand in contrast to liberal approaches, such as that espoused by Kant, in which morality was possible because of the human capacity for reason, since morality depended on this ability to attribute value to things. Kant adopted a particular teleology in which human beings were evolving away from basic instinctual behaviour towards rational and moral behaviour.[344]

For sociobiologists, moral behaviour is the result of natural selection, with morality being something closer to instinct than a product of free will. In their view, a type of common moral code has evolved to ensure the survival or the reproduction of one's genes.[345] From the evolutionary psychological standpoint, this might be thought of as a universal moral grammar, as Hauser called it. In other instances, it is considered in terms of moral sensitivities or predispositions.

My theory posits that human beings are born without an innate moral compass. In some instances, moral behaviour may seem instinctive. Yet, on closer inspection, such unconscious moral actions are likely to be driven by general self-interest, as discussed above. Despite being born without innate understanding of good or evil, we are capable of conscious moral judgements. Moreover, we are capable of acting with regard not only to our own personal well-being, but also that of other living beings and the environment. This capability depends on more than our capacity for reason, although morality requires us to attribute value and choose between available options. Rather, it is *reflectivity* which makes conscious moral judgements possible. As I shall discuss in Chapter 3.7, reflectivity can disrupt our immanent biases and allow us to move beyond the dictates of self-interest. Reflective behaviour involves deep thought about the self's relationship to selfhood and to others and, therefore, will not often come into play as a factor motivating actions and choices. In fact, it is unlikely that most individuals who are struggling to ensure their basic survival needs will have the luxury of engaging in reflection on a daily basis. Therefore, the human capacity to behave morally depends on the satisfaction of basic needs, including the need for dignity, as I shall discuss in Part 4.

* * *

This exploration of eight basic motivational factors has made the case that humankind is overwhelmingly driven by, above all, the Neuro P5 – power, profit, pleasure, pride and permanency – and partly also by our specific interests or passions, which are themselves underwritten by more basic impulses, although not entirely. Though we are primarily driven by emotionality, we also occasionally employ reason to understand what we perceive, but only infrequently do we engage in the kind of reflective thought which may lead to conscious moral behaviour.

Having outlined my theory of emotional amoral egoism, the Neuro P5, and the additional role of interests and reason, the remainder of Part 3 provides complementary information on various aspects of my theory. Chapter 3.2 illustrates the practical ways both our genetic constitution (nature) and our environment (nurture) contribute to shaping who we are. I then provide more insights into the nature and neural basis of our emotions and behaviour. Having clarified the commonalities shared by all human beings, I shall examine how evolution allows for the creation of infinitely unique individuals. In addition, I shall discuss how our behaviour and faculties can be modified by drugs, psychotherapy and new technologies. Finally, I shall explore in more detail the nature of moral judgements and the role which reflectivity can play in this process. Part 3 closes with a table facilitating comparison between my theory of human nature and its intellectual antecedents.

Nature and Nurture

Being emotional, amoral and egoistic, human beings are endowed with a powerful instinct for survival. Although we are not completely blank slates, we can be shaped by our environment, which will affect how we act on our genetic heritage. Moving past the nature–nurture debate, this chapter will illustrate the practical ways both our genetic constitution (nature) and our environment (nurture) contribute to shaping who we are.

3.2.1. The Power of Genes

As this book highlights, a considerable part of what makes us who we are is inextricably linked to our genetic constitution or genotype. However, in order to understand the basic dynamics of natural selection and how our genes operate, it is necessary first to provide a brief overview of how life may have begun on earth and how genes, as we know them today, came to be. Only by understanding these ancestral processes can we comprehend how our genetic make-up is inherited.

3.2.1.1. DNA as the Product of Natural Selection

Fossils show that species have changed over time. Indeed, they have sometimes undergone mutations to become completely new species. Natural selection is premised on the notion that all members of a particular species show variations in both their behavioural and physiological traits. Genetic traits, including genetic variations, are passed from generation to generation. Offspring will, therefore, inherit part of this variation, which results in children resembling their parents.[346] Thus, since both our phenotype – our physical appearance and constitution – and our personality traits are, to a great extent, influenced by our genes, it is necessary to briefly explain how this process of genetic inheritance functions.

First, it is important to note that Darwin's theory of natural selection is a special case of a more general principle – the principle of 'stable selection'. Atoms tend to fall into stable patterns and those stable patterns come to form objects. The earliest type of natural selection would have been stable formations of atoms, and the occasional event of them joining to form molecules. This principle is what Darwin thought lies behind the natural selection of genes.[347]

Indeed, while there are a number of different theories about the origin of life, they all appear to share some common elements. Laboratory experiments have shown that, if imitations of the chemical conditions on earth are mixed together and supplied with a source of energy, such as ultraviolet light, the molecules which form from this mixture are more complex than those which were put together initially. In particular, amino acids, the foundation blocks of protein, have been found to form in this context. Experiments have also shown that such tests can produce organic substances, called purines and pyrimidines, which are the basic foundation of the genetic molecule DNA.[348] DNA, which stands for deoxyribonucleic acid, is a macromolecule responsible for storing biological information and is, thus, one of the essential components for the existence of life.

Scientists believe that these genetic molecules may have formed three to four billion years ago in oceans, giving rise to the beginning of life on earth. At some point, a molecule called a *replicator* would have formed, which had the unusual capacity to replicate itself. The replicator made it possible for large quantities of the same molecule to form and spread throughout the seas. DNA molecules descend from these replicator molecules. Evolution came about because mistakes are inevitably made in the copying process. Variation would, thus, have occurred among replicas, gradually giving rise to all the forms of life we know today. According to the principles of natural or stable selection, some varieties would have been more stable than others, making them more numerous because they would have lasted longer and therefore had a greater opportunity to make a larger number of copies of themselves than less stable molecules. Another quality which must have made the replicator so successful is the speed of replication, which would have resulted in higher fecundity among the replicator molecules.[349]

Another important factor in natural selection is competition. Varieties of replicators would have had to compete for the smaller building block molecules needed to make copies. The replicator molecules which managed to succeed in such competition are likely to have developed protective coatings of protein around them, which could have been the first cells to come into existence. The survival and reproduction of these replicator molecules formed the basis of our existence and of that of all other forms of life: today we call them genes.[350]

3.2.1.2. Genetic Inheritance

DNA is distributed among our cells, coiled into a double-helix shape. Dawkins puts it quite elegantly: 'It is as though, in every room of a gigantic building, there was a bookcase containing the architect's plans for the entire building.'[351] The equivalent of the bookcase in a cell is a nucleus. The nucleus contains 23 pairs of chromosomes on which genes sit, for a total of 46 chromosomes. DNA is the product of natural selection.[352] It comprises a chain of nucleotides consisting of combinations of four different types: adenine (A); cytosine (C); guanine (G); and thymine (T). Each A nucleotide in one DNA helix has a corresponding T nucleotide in the other, and vice versa, and the same type of correspondence occurs with the remaining nucleotides, with C and G forming another fixed pair. (In RNA, uracil (U) replaces T as one of the four nucleobases.) Specific sequences of such nucleotides form what we call genes.[353]

Recent advances in DNA-sequencing technology have enabled the sequencing of the human genome, a long and complex project which took over ten years and was declared fully completed in 2003. The Human Genome Project published a list of three billion letters which represent the chemical rungs of the DNA molecules. As Robert Winston notes, it would take over 270 feet of shelving to house it if we were to try to stretch it out in a line.[354]

The structure of DNA provides the basis for genetic inheritance. DNA molecules replicate – make copies of themselves – while at the same time managing the creation of a different kind of molecule – protein. As such, genes indirectly supervise the making of human bodies. In line with Dawkins' theory of stable selection, the body may be thought of as a way of preserving genes in an unaltered state. The success of the body is, therefore, directly linked to the success of the genes.[355]

Sexual reproduction mixes up and rearranges genes. Each body is, thus, merely a temporary container of a particular combination of genes. While the container or body is ephemeral, the genes themselves have much greater longevity. They are transmitted across generations of people, the combination being reshuffled as this happens.

The process by which genes are transmitted from generation to generation involves a considerable degree of 'editing'. Chromosome pairs are split by sperm and egg cells, which are unique among cells in that they contain 23 instead of 46 chromosomes, so that the cells of the next generation will also have 46 chromosomes, 23 coming from the mother, 23 from the father. Those 23 chromosomes in sex cells are themselves a compilation of reassembled genetic units. Natural selection is likely to favour the smaller units, since smaller genetic units have a greater chance of staying intact and getting passed on than do longer genetic units. We may share some of these smaller units with apes and other animals. The genes which may be, in a way, immortal, are those which contribute to constructing a body which is relatively good at surviving and living long enough to reproduce.[356]

As stated above, natural selection is based on the idea that all members of a species demonstrate an element of variation, both physiologically and psychologically, and that part of this variation is transmitted through our genes from generation to generation. Some genes which are passed from generation to generation may have longer histories than others, some dating as far back as our early human ancestors. 'Good' genes are those which contribute to a phenotypic and psychological make-up which enable a person to live long enough to reproduce successfully. Therefore, in light of the role played by our neurochemistry and our biology in determining who we are, we must appreciate the great extent to which human nature is a product of natural selection.

3.2.2. The Influence of the Environment

Thus far, I have emphasised the genetically inherited factors which contribute to shaping who we are. Yet, as I also mentioned, acknowledging the role of the biologically determined aspects of both our physiology and our psychology does not mean that we have to negate the critical role which the environment plays in shaping human nature. Indeed, as I have been arguing, we do not have to choose between nature and nurture. Nature and nurture are not, in fact, mutually exclusive influences. In my view, evolutionary changes do not give us predilections towards certain kinds of behaviour. How these innate characteristics are acted on will, nonetheless, depend heavily on the environment. I understand this environmental element as encompassing our personal living conditions, upbringing and education, as well as societal, cultural and global conditions. Acknowledging what has been inherited from our

Palaeolithic ancestors helps us to recognise the enormous significance of culture, society and education. This section, therefore, considers how environmental factors may contribute to human nature.

3.2.2.1. Personal Conditions, Upbringing and Education

Our personal experiences and interactions with others are vital for determining who we are; this is particularly the case in relation to childhood experiences. People who have lived through things which make the needs of the ego, for instance, harder to fulfil may find it harder to prosper when faced with challenges and opportunities. Similarly, adults who have suffered abuse as children may find it hard to be empathetic and it may, therefore, be difficult for them to establish relationships with others. On a more positive note, people who have been welcomed and positively defined by others are likely to find it easier to satisfy the needs of their ego than those who have been rejected and humiliated. Therefore, as I shall illustrate in more depth in Part 4, dignity plays a crucial role in our personal development as well as in our ability to maintain constructive relationships.

The most important unit affecting our psyche and behaviour is likely to be our family. While our temperament is determined physiologically, relations with our closest relatives critically influence our character – whether we are extroverted, confident or lack self-esteem, for example – and, as a result, our personality. Children who feel loved are more likely to grow into confident adults with high levels of self-esteem than those who do not feel loved, cared for and supported.

The family also plays an important role in terms of the moral education of individuals. Moral judgements are largely shaped by what we are taught during our childhood, which goes on to form part of our value system. Authority figures within the family, be they parents, grandparents or elder siblings, may help to instil certain values in children, such as the importance of respecting other people's opinions, culture and belongings.

Our family context may also strongly influence our knowledge of the world, its history and its diverse cultures, and increase our awareness of other historical experiences and cultural traditions, as well as giving us an appreciation of the arts, literature and nature, for instance.

Education at a formal level has an especially important role in fostering transcultural synergy, which I conceive as the creative stimulus which results from a recognition that differences between people and groups should be welcomed rather than feared.[357] It is vital that children are taught to unpack negative stereotypes. This may be facilitated through a variety of means, including school curricula, the newspaper industry and broadcasters and the internet.[358] Furthermore, it is important for governments to actively educate all their citizens about cultural and ethnic diversity. At the global level, exchanges should be informed by recognition and respect for others.[359]

Although there might be limitations to our altruistic, moral behaviour, at least in terms of our biological heritage, education is an essential tool with which to promote moral norms. Education may be particularly important for encouraging children to expand their moral commitments to wider communities.

3.2.2.2. Social Conditions

Inclusiveness, safety and the provision of welfare are all essential aspects of society which shape a person's mindset and relations with others. Ensuring that all members of society have their basic needs met will increase the likelihood of moral behaviour. Indeed, people are likely to be less inclined to be self-reflective and moral if their basic survival needs have not been satisfied.[360]

Unlearning stereotypes may be all the more essential in the current context of globalisation, which is intensifying contact between people from diverse cultural backgrounds. Radical transformations on a number of levels – political, economic and cultural – may make people's points of reference, and, therefore, their identities, less stable than may have previously been the case. As people search for greater stability against a backdrop of great flux, essentialist accounts of identities – which see each identity as being comprised by a fixed set of attributes – may be extremely appealing but must be resisted.[361]

In his book, *In the Name of Identity: Violence and the Need to Belong* (2000), Amin Maalouf points out that every individual is likely to have multiple allegiances and points of reference.[362] Society should, therefore, aim to forge a shared form of consciousness, capable of embracing multiple identities, which can become a unifying and cross-cultural point of contact. This is likely to enhance a society's stability and resilience. People need to feel a sense of belonging, which comes from being positively viewed and accepted by others. Policies designed to manage the many challenges of culturally plural societies are vital in terms of their potential impact on the human psyche and human behaviour.[363] Policies should be put in place to encourage exchanges between diverse cultural groups as a means of resisting intolerance, prejudice and xenophobia. Indeed, we should aspire to increase awareness of other cultural customs and ways of life, as well as awareness of the multiple identities which may exist within one's cultural group.

3.2.2.3. Cultural Conditions

Our capacity to attribute and express meaning through symbolic representation of the world around us is a trait which makes us unique among animals. The development of culture is a human universal and plays a vital role in shaping how people think and behave. Culture is complex and fluid and continuously in the process of evolving. For anthropologists, culture shows that we are not wholly determined by genetics.[364] Yet, as I mentioned earlier, taking our genetic heritage into account does not imply that we need to succumb to biological determinism.

Culture has been defined in a number of ways. Chris Jenks lists these definitions as:

(1) culture as a cerebral or cognitive category (a state of mind);

(2) culture as a collective category (intellectual/moral development of a particular society);

(3) culture as a descriptive category (a collective body of arts and intellectual endeavours); and

(4) culture as a social category (a way of life of a people).

We may think of it as a combination of the symbolic, ideational and learnt in human society.[365]

Cultures are not static; they are in a constant state of evolution. If cultures are fluid, civilisations may be thought of as continuities of human thought and practice.[366] Richard Dawkins has conceived of this continuity in evolutionary terms. Dawkins, perhaps surprisingly, argues that we have to think of the gene not as the only basis of our evolution, but rather as the basis for multiple evolutions. Genes are important in evolutionist theories of human nature because they are replicators.[367] However, memes, which refer to ideas, religion and belief systems, he suggests, might be thought of as new kinds of replicators. Just as genes can be passed on from generation to generation, so too can memes, through the transmission of culture:[368] 'Just as genes propagate themselves in the gene pool by leaping from body to body via sperm or eggs, so memes propagate themselves in the meme pool by leaping from brain to brain.'[369] Dawkins sees meme replication taking place through language, writing, art and music.[370]

Why do some memes survive over thousands of years? Dawkins takes God as an example of a highly successful meme. This particular meme, he argues, has been successfully transmitted across the generations because of its psychological appeal. Indeed, the belief in the existence of God provides an answer to some of our most troubling existential preoccupations.[371]

Ultimately, the qualities which make memes successful replicators are the same as genes: longevity, fecundity and copying fidelity. Fecundity is more important than longevity, as is the case with genes. In terms of copying fidelity (the ability to produce an accurate copy of the original), it seems that memes are subject to continual change and are thus passed on in mutated forms over time. What seems to differ in the case of memes is that their successful reproduction benefits the memes themselves rather than any individual organism.[372]

Dawkins emphasises that one thing which humankind has evolved is conscious foresight – the capacity to imagine possible future scenarios. This, he argues, may prevent us from excesses which we might otherwise engage in and here, perhaps, lies the hope for what lies ahead. As human beings, we have the capacity to recognise that our biological heritage may incline us to be, for instance, only limited in our altruism. This recognition, however, makes possible the conscious effort to go beyond this limitation through education.[373] There are, of course, other ways of conceiving of the transmission of culture from one generation to the next. We might, for example, think of culture as being transmitted through socially constructed meanings and collective memory.[374]

The point is that we have inherited some tendencies from our ancestors and through early evolution (such as an aversion to celibacy, a preference for hierarchical social relations, limited altruism and selfishness) but how these propensities are mediated depends on culture. Culture may enhance or dampen some of these predispositions.[375]

If evolutionists are right to argue that xenophobia and prejudice may be to some extent innate, culture may provide an important means of fostering intercultural sensitivity and understanding.[376] The culture to which we belong often forms our major reference points and may provide the basis for evaluation of people from other cultures. This becomes particularly worrisome when we harbour a moral or cultural sense of superiority, which causes us to denigrate and essentialise other cultures. The all-too-familiar result is negative cultural stereotyping, which is most often informed by little knowledge of what it actually means to be a member of the particular culture so targeted. Negative stereotyping not only represents a simplification of reality, but also reduces the dignity of those being (mis)represented, because their worth as individuals and members of a group is undermined.[377]

As I shall explore in more depth in Parts 4 and 5 when illustrating my paradigm of dignity-based governance, culture and the processes by which it is transmitted may very well constitute a key medium for promoting long-term peace and coexistence. Indeed, as I shall expand on further in subsequent chapters, culture provides a means of infusing recognition of and respect for others. It may also provide the means by which to resolve conflicts in a peaceful manner.[378] It is also imperative to build bridges at the trans-civilisational level through a common consciousness which is not consistent with domination or assimilation.[379] If our time on the savannah has left us with only a limited degree of altruism towards kin and immediate group members, culture may be a medium through which we may encourage the extension of moral communities beyond those with whom we are immediately related.

3.2.2.4. Global Conditions

The global situation can also affect the way we think and behave. Global social forces affect societal, ideological and cultural configurations in ways which may or may not improve the human condition. In societies which are not privileged by the global political and economic situation, for example, globalisation may contribute to basic survival needs going unmet, causing increased insecurity and fear. Certain global dynamics may affect families, health, education systems and school attendance. A consequence of this may also be that the population of such societies may lack a positive, independent identity. Rapid global change and transformation is also likely to cause abrupt cultural reorientations which can destabilise people's sense of identity and of self. Transnational political communities may also affect relations between cultural groups within societies, further increasing instability and insecurity.

* * *

To sum up, the environment is a critical factor in shaping who we are. Recognising the influence of our biological heritage does not mean denying the huge importance of the environment for our psychology and behaviour. Both nature and nurture have a role to play in constituting humanity. Our earliest experiences within the family and during our schooling interact with our physiological make-up to form our personalities, points of reference and value systems. Families and formal schooling are, thus, vital for determining how we act on our genetic heritage and what we make of the positive and negative character traits which have been passed down to us across generations. At a broader level, society contributes to shaping us, both by ensuring that our basic survival needs – which include not only sustenance and physical safety, but also a positive and stable identity – are met and by inculcating values which reflect our higher aspirations as self-aware beings (see Parts 4 and 5). Culture, therefore, constitutes a major medium through which humanity can be pointed in a positive direction.

3.3

The Role of Emotions and Their Universality

As discussed above, the key tenet of my theory of emotional amoral egoism is that human beings are primarily driven by emotionality. Most of our emotions evolved during our ancestors' life on the savannah. The latest research suggests that basic emotions – such as fear or anger – are shared by all humans, irrespective of culture, because they result from our genetic make-up rather than being learnt in our own lifetimes. Most emotions are instinctive, though some may be triggered by conscious thought. In any case, emotions are neurochemically mediated – that is, mediated through chemical combinations in our brains. Since our specific neurochemistry is genetically inherited, so is our capacity to feel emotions. Emotions are central to our functioning. In fact, emotionality overlaps with a large part of our rational cognitive functions, including perception and decision-making.[380] This is why, when a person suffers a stroke which damages the *emotional* centres of his or her brain, even if his or her *logical* capacities remain intact, the person becomes functionally disabled, unable to make decisions or correct judgements.

Most emotions appear to be negative.[381] This perhaps explains why many spiritual systems, Buddhism being perhaps the most notable, are informed by the notion that we can reach fulfilment if we overcome our emotions and reach a serene, emotion-free state. Evolutionists would argue that there may be more negative emotions than positive ones because natural selection favours those who are successful in avoiding harm,[382] which involves emotions such as fear and pain which shield us from dangerous situations.[383] Yet, at the same time, positive emotions, such as pleasure and contentment, play an important role in forming loving and supportive relations, which are equally important to our well-being.

This chapter thus focusses more narrowly on the nature of emotions. In particular, it synthesises research on the universality of emotions and considers a number of core human emotions from an interdisciplinary perspective which integrates recent neuroscientific findings. This sets the stage for Chapter 3.4, which explores the neurochemical basis of our emotions.

3.3.1. Universal Emotions

Charles Darwin pioneered the argument that human emotions are innate – that we are born with them – and that the way we communicate them to others is universal.[384] In other words, we express what we are feeling to others involuntarily, as a result of our genetic heritage, rather than as a result of learning through socialisation. Communicating emotions is, thus, instinctive. Babies, for example, are able to recognise emotions in the faces of adults, and there is wide consistency between people from different cultural backgrounds in terms of the expression of emotions.[385] Darwin identified six core emotions revealed in our facial expressions: happiness, sadness, anger, fear, disgust and surprise.

In the late 1960s, the psychologist Paul Ekman added a number of emotions to this list, including guilt, shame, embarrassment, sympathy, admiration, frustration and nostalgia.[386] Ekman also explained emotions in terms of natural selection, theorising that they must have emerged as a result of adaptations to the environments in which our ancestors developed.[387]

Ekman shared Darwin's belief in the universality of emotions. In the 1960s, he studied the Fore tribe in New Guinea, a tribe living lives similar to those of our Stone Age ancestors. Its members had no contact with the outside world and, as such, had not been exposed to the Western newspaper and broadcasting industry and its depictions of emotions. Still, Ekman found that members of the Fore tribe expressed emotions in a way which everyone around the world could readily relate to. His work was ground-breaking, given that the predominant view in the West at the time was that the expression of emotion was culturally specific and, thus, learnt rather than innate.[388] Ekman's work seemed to confirm Darwin's contention that humans had a common system for expressing emotions. According to Ekman, any apparent differences in facial expressions were purely due to context, to rules about when, how and to whom it was appropriate to manifest those specific emotions.[389]

Ekman's conclusion remained virtually unchallenged for about fifty years. However, more recent studies have shown that, although the underlying emotions are most likely universal, they may not all elicit the same physiological reactions and interpretations, which may, instead, vary from one culture to the next.[390] These studies include research led by psychologist Carlos Crivelli and anthropologist Sergio Jarillo, who also studied an indigenous group in Papua New Guinea. They found that, while smiling is always associated with happiness, scowling or gasping faces are not universally linked to the same emotions. The gasping expression, in particular, previously thought to be universally associated with fear and submission, is used by the indigenous Trobrianders to express anger. Based on the results of their study, according to Crivelli, at least these facial behaviours are not pancultural, but are instead culturally specific.[391] This finding shows that, although the emotion itself may be universal, as Darwin and Ekman have claimed, how it is physically translated and perceived may not be. Instead, it may be subject to cultural influences.

Darwin also contended that the functioning of emotions follows three main principles. He maintained that, first, our emotions were produced by a functional process and were used to satisfy a desire or relieve a sensation, becoming habitual as a result of repetition. They were, as a result, 'of direct or indirect service under certain states of the mind'. Second, in what he defines as the 'principle of antithesis', Darwin held that inducing an opposite emotion entails the expression of physical movements of a directly opposite nature. Finally, he argued that an emotional response seemed to come from the nervous system.[392] In relation to this latter point, as Chapter 3.4 elucidates, Darwin demonstrated tremendous foresight. Neuroscience has since shown that emotions are neurological reactions to the stimulation of nerve centres in the brain,[393] and that we have evolved multiple systems of emotional response which enable us to experience more than one emotion at once.[394]

3.3.2. Our Emotional Repertoire

Fear, pain, grief, anger, jealousy, love, contempt and disgust constitute some of the most powerful human emotions. Not only do they have a long evolutionary history, but they are responsible for a great deal of our behaviour. In what follows, these emotions are discussed from an interdisciplinary perspective.

Fear. The Oxford English Dictionary defines fear as 'an unpleasant emotion caused by the threat of danger, pain, or harm'.[395] At an instinctual level, fear informs us that our environment is a perilous place and that we need to be ready to respond to imminent danger. From an evolutionist's perspective, fear fulfils a critical function and has obvious survival value. Fear enables us to respond to threats to our survival in an appropriate manner.[396] In the past, it taught us to be respectful of predatory animals, thereby giving us an advantage in the struggle to stay alive in a wild and dangerous natural environment. Fear, as Robert Winston puts it, helped our ancestors to be ready to be on the defensive, to prepare their limbs to perform incredible feats in order to ensure survival, whether in terms of staying to fight or running from danger.[397] Fear may have not simply enabled our ancestors to avoid harm; it may also have led them to organise into cooperative groups. Our sociability may, therefore, have been a consequence of fear. An appropriate level of fear is required for our survival, while an excessive amount of anxiety interferes with normal functioning.[398] Scientists have found that only two fears may be inborn in humans – the fear of falling and that of loud noises.[399]

Nestled within the human brain is the amygdala, which plays a crucial role in coordinating fear. Neurobiologically speaking, fear is a very complex emotion. Its manifestations assume several forms, depending on the nature of the threat. As I shall discuss in more depth in Part 4, according to Hobbes, it is fear which often prompts us to 'strike first', with the aim of subduing others to the extent that we no longer feel threatened.[400] He believed this is particularly true when one is doubtful about one's own abilities to mount a defence. Hobbes, thus, argued that, when taken together, distrust in one's fellows coupled with a lack of confidence in one's defensive capacities logically recommends taking the offensive.[401] Modern neuroscience, however, has demonstrated that this behavioural process, which I have previously referred to as *fear-induced pre-emptive aggression*, is more complex than previously believed.[402] While survival and avoidance of physical pain constitute a powerful motivator to 'strike first', as Hobbes would argue, there are other powerful stimuli creating fear responses. Moreover, it is not only aggression in the form of a 'strike' which is prompted by fear. Fear entails a whole range of reactions to satisfy the need for safety, which may include the accumulation of profit and power as a way to counter fear (see Chapter 3.4.5 on the neurochemistry of power and Chapter 4.4 on the role of fear in conflict).

Pain and grief. Pain, it should be remembered, is an emotion as well as a sensation. It is the brain's way of reacting to trouble in the body, aimed at bringing about recovery. When we experience pain – such as a sting, ache, prick or burn – receptors in the skin generate an electrical impulse which travels from the skin to the spinal cord, which is then relayed to the brain.[403] Due to advances in various techniques, such as functional magnetic resonance imaging (fMRI), we now know that the signals are most likely to be relayed first to the thalamus and, from there, to the cortex, the central control unit for cognition. The thalamus sends messages between the brain and various parts of the body.[404] If the pain experienced is linked to someone putting their hand on something hot, for example, a message will be sent telling the hand to pull away.

The sensation of pain itself is a complex process, involving a number of neurochemicals, such as serotonin, norepinephrine and opioid-like chemicals. Some of these are responsible for mild pain sensations, while others are implicated in more intense feelings of pain.[405] We might say that these neurochemicals, when combined with memory and cognition, help us not only to recover from harm, but also to learn how to avoid dangerous external stimuli in the future. They form part of a learning and recovery process which helps us to keep the human body safe.

Another type of pain, typically thought of as psychological, is grief, an incredibly powerful reaction to loss, which we normally associate with the death of a loved one. Yet grief can also be caused by the loss of an aspect of a person's life which they valued highly.

Grief has been described in a number of different ways: as a natural response to loss, as a psychiatric disorder and as a disease process. We might think of it as a natural human reaction, a universal aspect of human life irrespective of culture, although the form and intensity of its expression may be culture-specific.[406] Loss typically provokes two kinds of reactions: active distress and passive depression and, thus, may also be considered a psychiatric disorder.[407] Grief as a result of bereavement is often associated with the onset of illness. It may even contribute to death. We often hear it said that someone 'died of a broken heart' when they perished in the wake of the loss of a spouse or partner. In such circumstances, both illness and death may be linked to suppression of the immune system, although they may also be connected to changes in lifestyle as a result of the death of a loved one, such as changes in nutritional intake. Yet, it is difficult to determine whether bereavement is a direct cause of deterioration in health or death.[408]

Evolutionary psychology has provided insight into how grief may be linked to natural selection. Grief prompted by separation within the context of a close relationship may be useful from the point of view of reproductive success, since it encourages individuals to seek reunion. This motivating reaction, however, is still operative when the individual is no longer alive, causing a great deal of suffering. Grief felt over the loss of someone is, as John Archer puts it, the 'cost we pay for being able to love in the way we do'.[409] The severity of grief is likely to vary according to the intensity of the relationship which has been lost. Loss of a spouse is one of the hardest-felt losses, but loss of a child is even more devastating. With the death of a son or daughter, dreams and hopes for the future are shattered. In evolutionary terms, genetic similarity and parental caring instincts may help to explain the despair which the loss of a child is likely to cause.[410]

Psychological studies have suggested several conceptual frameworks for comprehending the mental processes involved in grief. Some suggest that individuals maintain a complex representation of a loved one, which, if destabilised, provokes alarm. Equally, an absence of affective feedback from the loved one may generate alarm signals, which prompt a desire for reunion. Others suggest that representations of a loved one form part of the self.[411]

In some respects, grief is vital to us succeeding in our environment. It may help us maintain relationships vital to sexual reproduction and childrearing. Yet, if too severe and devastating to the self, grief may endanger our long-term well-being, and may even contribute to severe illness.

Anger. Like fear, anger is an intense emotion which compels us into action.[412] According to Carol Tavris, a social psychologist, anger has both mental and physical causes and consequences. This, she believes, may be linked to the fact that the emotion may be initiated either in the limbic or the neocortical parts of the brain. The former controls impulses and the latter is responsible for cognitive rationality. This implies that anger can result from conscious thought as one mulls over something, as well as a spontaneous response to an occurrence.[413]

Jealousy. Jealousy is commonly associated with emotional and sexual possessiveness in relation to an object of desire. It is distinct from envy, which is linked to desire for a material object which someone else possesses and we lack.[414] According to Winston, 'Sexual jealousy is an impulse we've almost certainly inherited from our ancestors on the savannah. A less suspicious species than ours would have become extinct many years ago.'[415] In evolutionary terms, sexual infidelity was a threat to the male partner of a couple, in particular. Without the benefit of DNA testing, an early male human had no way of knowing for certain whether he really was the father of the child he was rearing. From the viewpoint of merely passing on one's genes to future generations, raising a child which is not biologically one's own is a misuse of resources. This, according to Winston, explains why jealousy forms such an important part of male sexual psychology.

A complicating factor is that female ovulation is hidden and many women are often unaware that they are ovulating. One consequence of this is that human sexual energy is not reserved to a specific period. The possibility of infidelity is, therefore, ever present for the male partner. Moreover, internal fertilisation means that only women can be certain that they are the biological parent of a child. Winston suggests that both internal fertilisation and concealed ovulation may have evolved to keep biological fathers attentive during the period of childrearing. Female sexual jealousy is most probably connected to this concern as well.[416]

Shame. Shame is produced by a complex emotional dynamic. Shame seems to be accompanied by a desire to escape the boundaries of our own bodies. Circumstances in which we feel ashamed include instances when we break taboos or situations in which we become dependent on someone else in order to carry out the most basic of functions. Shaming others has historically involved public humiliation, sometimes even beyond death. Hanging, for example, was considered too decent a death for people convicted of serious crimes. These people may have been hanged, drawn and quartered and displayed for all to see.[417]

Embarrassment. Embarrassment, like shame, may be a non-primal emotion and is equally difficult to define. Embarrassment seems to be caused by drawing unwanted attention to oneself. According to Walton, involuntary reddening of the face may be a means of showing others that we know that we have breached social etiquette. He notes that this may be accompanied by a state of mental confusion. Both the psychic and physical states appear to be linked. Only when the blood rush to the face begins to ebb does the person begin to think more clearly.[418] Studies of the neurobiological underpinnings of shame and embarrassment show that both distinct and shared brain structures are involved in the generation of these emotions. While shame is linked with activity in the dorsolateral prefrontal cortex, the posterior cingulate cortex and the sensorimotor cortex, embarrassment is associated with activity in the ventrolateral prefrontal cortex and amygdala.[419]

Surprise. Surprise is a response to an unforeseen occurrence. There is an element of apprehension in surprise. The physiological characteristics of surprise resemble those of fear, which may reflect the fact that our ancestors would have been surprised largely by things which may have posed a threat to their safety. The wide-open eyes and raised eyebrows are an attempt to perceive as much as possible. The opening of the mouth has been attributed to quietening the breathing or increasing the ingestion of oxygen. It may even represent a cry. It has been suggested that putting a hand to one's mouth may have been a way our ancestors attempted to prevent themselves from exclaiming in a dangerous situation in which silence would have favoured their chances of survival.[420] Surprise is often considered to be among the primary motivations which drive learning and exploratory behaviour.[421]

Happiness. In general, happiness is thought of as a state of mind, linked to a feeling of pleasure or well-being. It is associated with positive emotions, such as contentment, joy, connectedness and serenity. Being with people with whom we feel a special connection, situations which make us laugh, and the giving and receiving of presents are all examples of things which are associated with happiness. Modern neuroscience, in fact, has demonstrated how Freud's notion of the 'pleasure principle' is not too far from the reality of how our brains perceive the feeling of happiness. Indeed, happiness and pleasure are neurochemical processes which involve the release of neurochemicals such as oxytocin and dopamine in our brains. As I discuss in more depth in subsequent chapters, these neurochemicals are responsible for feelings of gratification. It is this search for gratification and pleasure which drives a large part of everyday human behaviour, in what I have referred to in previous works as the *sustainable neurochemical gratification principle.*[422]

Further, this feeling of pleasure and gratification at the neurochemical level is triggered during engagement in activities which we associate with happiness, not just after their completion.[423] Therefore, and although happiness is commonly believed to be a state of being, it may be the result of chance events which bring a sense of momentary joy. Walton notes: 'Of all our emotions, happiness is perhaps the strangest, subject to a far greater range of stimuli than those we conventionally associate with the negative feelings, but it is also the most fragile.'[424] This point of view stands in contrast to Aristotle's emphasis on the positive state of human existence. For him, a final end point of happiness exists, which is linked to an ethical state. In this sense, happiness or fulfilment is related to activity and not simply passive hedonism and implies the use of our cognitive rationality to pursue an ethical life, this being akin, perhaps, to wisdom.[425] It seems possible that happiness is linked to living an ethical life because doing so brings rewards in the form of loving relationships and self-esteem.

Disgust. Disgust is a genuine corporeal response to negative exogenous factors. Something which we find disgusting will turn the stomach and prepare the oesophagus for expulsion, as well as prompt us to shrink back from the offending object.[426] Flared nostrils and a wrinkled nose are also facial indicators of disgust. Anything which has a toxic dimension to it may provoke a feeling of disgust.[427] It is likely that this emotion evolved in order to avoid infection and disease. It may also play a role in our moral sensitivity.

Contempt. Contempt is located somewhere between a desire to ignore someone and a desire to let him or her know that you think they are worthless. Walton suggests that contempt or disdain may be thought of as a distancing instinct aimed at social exclusion.[428] It is possible that it may have evolved to help individuals or groups to face a dangerous adversary by instilling in them a feeling of superiority.[429]

As Darwin and Ekman suggest, basic human emotions are universal and, as such, reflect genetics and evolution, rather than culture – although, as mentioned, Crivelli and Jarillo did demonstrate that some emotions *may* have idiosyncratic, culturally specific forms of expression. Fear, grief, jealousy and surprise, for example, all seem to be genetically inherited and reflective of the environment in which early humans faced the challenges of survival. As a result, many of the emotions we are capable of expressing are negative, linked to sexual reproduction and harm avoidance. We do, however, appear to have a number of non-primal emotions, which are generated by awareness of the social norms which apply in our environment. These include, for example, shame and embarrassment. We cannot pinpoint with any exactness the extent to which the expression of certain emotions is innate or learnt. However, we do know that many of our core emotions are the product not only of our genetic make-up, but also of our specific neurochemistry, as the next chapter explains.

3.4

A Neurochemistry of Emotions and Behaviour

Thus far, I have suggested that human beings are emotionally driven, amoral and egoistic. I have examined how traits are genetically passed on from one generation to the next and how each human being is, nonetheless, influenced to some extent by the environment in which they live. I have also specifically explained that emotions are universal and, for the most part, negative. These considerations highlight the key fact that our core emotions are determined by our genetic make-up, rather than being learnt. This, however, does not mean that all of our emotions are instinctive. As has been mentioned above, some of our emotions, those which are probably not primordial, such as shame and embarrassment, appear to be intimately connected to our conscious selves and, as such, may be provoked by conscious thoughts as well as instincts.

A fundamental aspect of human nature which must, therefore, be highlighted is the fact that emotions, both our older and our more recent ones, are neurochemically mediated. One of the first to make this contention was Darwin, who speculated that emotions were initiated in the nervous system. In recent years, modern neuroscience has led to a better understanding of just how this occurs. Indeed, a great deal of recent research in neuroscience has been devoted to the study of emotions.[430] The results of these studies have effectively called into question the notion that the mind can be separated from the body, as René Descartes (1596–1650) famously conjectured when he argued that the nature of the mind and that of the body are so different from one another, that they must be able to exist independently.[431] In fact, we now know that psychology and physiology are inseparable as far as emotions are concerned.

This chapter outlines the way our emotions are caused by changes to the chemistry of our brains, illustrating this with a discussion of one of our oldest emotions – fear. It also considers how our neurochemistry may help to explain much of our behaviour, focussing, in particular, on the neurochemical processes underlying addiction, dissociative behaviour, libido, attraction and attachment, as well as what I refer to as the *neurochemistry of power*. Overall, this chapter illustrates what I mean when I say we are emotionally driven animals.

3.4.1. A Question of Chemistry

Joseph LeDoux, a leading neuroscientist who studies emotions, argues that understanding how emotions are neurochemically represented in the brain may help us gain a better understanding of them. This approach is quite different from psychological studies which examine emotions merely as psychological states.[432] A more accurate account, however, sees emotions as both physiological *and* psychological states.

Emotions are mostly located on the right side of the brain, particularly in the dorsolateral prefrontal cortex (DLPFC),[433] which plays a central role in the modulation of affective processing. Initial insights into the location of emotions inside the brain came from examinations of responses to external stimuli. Disturbing films triggered activity in the left visual field and transmitted it to the right side of the brain, while the same films projected onto the right visual field were transmitted to the left side of the brain and produced lower levels of negative feelings, thus pointing towards the existence of some form of emotional lateralisation in the brain.[434]

Research has shown that positive and negative emotions are underwritten by different structures in the brain, indicating, for instance, that the right hemisphere may have more control over emotions than the left. There is some debate, however, about whether negative and positive emotional processes can be precisely located within a geographical area of the brain's structure and whether 'hemisphere asymmetry' in the subjective experience of feelings and moods implies a different specialization for both hemispheres.[435]

Research using fMRI has further increased our knowledge of the neurophysiology of emotions by providing an advanced way of perceiving brain activity. As mentioned before, emotions are essential tools which equip us with the means to respond successfully to life's opportunities and challenges.[436] Fear, especially, was central to the survival of our ancestors. It is now known that fear is produced in the amygdala. The amygdala has connections to the autonomic nervous system, which controls physiological reflexes such as heart rate. It is also connected to other parts of the brain which process stimuli from the external environment. Winston describes the amygdala as a 'neurological crossroads, the hub of a network of pathways in the brain'. When some external event is perceived to present a possible danger, the amygdala triggers a fear response and a huge biochemical release, preparing the body with all of the neurological resources it may need in order to escape.[437]

Interestingly, consciousness is not involved in this fear response: 'So it turns out that our most primal emotion, to advance or retreat, is triggered so fast that it precedes all conscious thought and awareness.'[438] In Winston's words:

> [A]ll hell has broken loose. Biological sirens and alarms are wailing ... your brain and your autonomic nervous system – the automatic controller of the gut, heart vessels and lungs – have gone into overdrive and produced a huge surge of adrenalin. This triggers a hormonal cascade inside you, an incredibly fast and powerful chemical relay-race designed to propel you away from a threatening situation. ... The adrenalin makes your heart pound faster, increasing its normal resting rate by as much as two or three times. ... You are also breathing much faster now, and the blood is being rapidly redistributed around your body. The blood vessels in unimportant areas like your stomach and your skin constrict, shunting blood away and into the now dilated vessels of the muscles of the limbs. Here the extra oxygen and fuel gained by your increased breathing can best be harnessed to flee from the threat, or even fight it. ... As the adrenalin and cortisol continue to gush out into your blood, your pupils dilate, allowing you to see better in darkness and shadows and to perceive any movement around you more keenly. A kind of pain-dampening effect is switched on so that you won't be distracted from getting away by any injuries. Emergency reserves of glucose are released inside you to allow for especially intense bursts of muscular activity. Even your immune system is mobilizing to cope with the possibility of dealing with a serious wound.[439]

All humans are equipped with this emergency kick-start system, but people may not experience the same level of fear in response to the same sensory input. Indeed, the way people experience and respond to emotions is also a question of chemistry. For instance, some may be petrified by the idea of diving from a bridge into water below, while others may simply experience a degree of nervous tension. These differences are the result of variations in neurochemistry, especially in levels of neuropeptides and neurotransmitters such as serotonin and dopamine, which enable the transmission of fear-codifying impulses which connect the synapses between nerve endings.

Different networks of brain regions function together to produce different emotions in response to external stimuli or thoughts. Neurotransmitters and neuropeptides are responsible for connecting these different networks and, thereby, for allowing emotions to be generated. Variations in emotional traits are, thus, the result of how neurotransmitters and neuropeptides function. For example, it is thought that the neurotransmitter and hormone dopamine is particularly active in extroverted individuals, dopamine being responsible for producing feelings of desire, excitement and pleasure. Serotonin, another important neurotransmitter and hormone, is responsible instead for, *inter alia*, regulating mood, cognition, reward, as well as sexual desire and social behaviour.

Understanding how neurotransmitters link the environment to our emotions is key to comprehending what makes up our personalities. It is likely to explain why some personality traits are extremely difficult to alter, try as we might. For instance, if we have high dopamine reactivity, we may respond very positively to environmental rewards for effort, whereas people with low dopamine reactivity may not.[440] Similarly, since serotonin is closely linked to mood and social behaviour, higher or lower levels of that neurotransmitter may significantly impact both how we are feeling and how we behave towards others. On the one hand, since there is some evidence that low levels of serotonin may be one of the causes of clinical depression, it is often artificially supplied to people suffering from depression and anxiety disorders in the form of pharmaceutical antidepressants.[441] On the other, neuroscientific studies have also tried to demonstrate that serotonin hypofunction may be responsible for forms of impulsive aggression and anger.[442] The evidence on the matter is, at least to some degree, contradictory.[443] Understanding whether there is, indeed, such a link between serotonin and behaviour towards others may enable us, in the future, to alter these personality traits and behaviours. Variations in our neurochemical make-up are genetic in origin. Genetic heritage, therefore, plays a role in determining temperament by way of neurochemical differences in how the amygdala functions and its neural connections.

A large body of research on traits focusses on three qualities: fearfulness, boldness and aggressiveness. People who are uninhibited, calm and bold are, it is thought, likely to deal with life's unexpected occurrences fairly well because their responses to events are not likely to be exaggerated and will last no longer than necessary. Those who react to the unexpected or unfamiliar with excessive anxiety or aggression are, by contrast, likely to cope less well with life's highs and lows. This is because their stress response is relatively strong and lasts for longer than is necessary. Those who are anxious, inhibited and reactive are likely to be less resilient when faced with challenges and those who are aggressive, impulsive and irritable may be more prone to lash out and to project their emotions on others. Most personality types are a mixture of these ideal types, that is, midway temperaments, because this best ensures survival.[444]

Research into how neurochemical transmitters translate stimuli from our environment, as well as images and thoughts, is in its infancy, however. One complicating factor is the fact that several neurotransmitters, rather than just one, may be responsible for producing a particular emotion, making it harder to decipher the level of intensity among neurotransmitters.[445] Another complicating factor is that emotions most often do not have purely positive or purely negative aspects, but rather a combination of both.[446]

None of this, however, means that the environment cannot influence innate traits. Research is being carried out into how experiences can alter someone's inherited neurochemistry and, therefore, temperament. For example, it is possible that parenting may be able to alter the physiology of a child and, consequently, play a part in defining their temperament.[447]

3.4.2. Addiction

Neuroscientific research has increased our knowledge of the role of neurotransmitters in addictive processes and, as a result, of the physical origin of addiction. This has provided critical insight into the workings of our neuronal networks and, thus, into our motivations, nature and behaviour. Addiction is an extreme form of behaviour which uses existing neuronal networks. Studying it through various modalities, which include behavioural and neurochemistry studies, as well as brain imaging, may be the best way to understand what motivates human behaviour, albeit in an extreme way. It may provide a 'window on the mind', given that it gives us unique insight into how our neurochemistry can drive us in a very powerful way, even against our better judgement.

Indeed, the principal organ affected by addiction is the brain. Addictive drugs essentially use/misuse the brain's pre-programming to induce feelings of pleasure. Part of this pre-programming is concerned with what is called 'salience', which refers to matters having special relevance to one's survival. Issues which appear to be 'highly salient' or relevant' include threats, food and sex. The danger of addictive drugs is that they 'use' these ready-made structures, resulting in the activation of reward circuitries, which produces an extreme sense of pleasure. Consequently, abstaining from these drugs will produce feelings of uncontrollable craving as well as the other usual physiological features of withdrawal. When the brain's pleasure centres are stimulated, they send out signals to repeat the activity which is causing the feelings of pleasure. Not everyone, however, forms an addiction. This is because there are also areas of the brain which allow us to evaluate the consequences of such behaviour, such as the medial prefrontal cortex, the medial orbitofrontal cortex and the dorsal striatum, all of which are involved in computing the causal effectiveness of our own behaviour.[448] Most people would decide that, as pleasurable as it may be, drinking, eating or gambling excessively are unlikely to be a good thing in the longer run. Recent research has shown that the chance of relapse among rehabilitating methamphetamine addicts appears to be higher among those patients who are less adept at employing the analytical part of their brains.[449]

There is also evidence of a genetic predisposition to addiction. People who are genetically predisposed to impulsive behaviour, immediate gratification and risk taking are more prone to addiction.[450]

Drugs produce effects by travelling through the bloodstream to the brain, where they alter the function of particular brain cells. Cocaine, for example, stimulates the nuclei of certain brain cells, prompting a large release of particular neurotransmitters, which carry messages from one neuron or nerve cell in the brain to the next. Alcohol, by contrast, reduces their activity. Some drugs, such as amphetamine or cocaine, have an effect by preventing the uptake of neurotransmitters. Others, such as marijuana or heroin, copy specific neurotransmitters and can, thus, attach to receptors and activating neurons.

Resistance builds up because specific neurotransmitters are repeatedly over-stimulated and the body responds by reducing their sensitivity. Essentially, the neurons are overloaded by abnormally high levels of neurotransmitters like dopamine – the neurotransmitter largely responsible for feelings of pleasure – thus reducing the number of sites or receptors to which the neurotransmitters can attach. In order to achieve the same effect, the addict has to increase the dose of the substance to which he or she is addicted. The person will also get physical withdrawal symptoms when he or she stops taking the substance. These are provoked by a shock to the brain caused by the changed neurochemical environment.[451]

Much research on the neurobiological basis of addiction focusses on the way drugs affect the brain's reward system and stimulate dopamine-producing neurons, thereby generating feelings of euphoria and pleasure.[452] Researchers have found, for example, that a rush of dopamine in addicts' brains is what causes a cocaine high. In other words, what the cocaine addict craves is the surge of dopamine which produces sensations of euphoria.[453]

Specifically, researchers have been exploring the role of a family of dopamine receptors which appear to multiply in conjunction with cocaine, methamphetamine or nicotine. What this does is to enable a greater amount of the drug to enter neurons and stimulate those which produce dopamine.

To a certain extent, we are all addicts, in the sense that our brains are pre-programmed to want to 'feel good'. Therefore, we continuously seek to repeat any behaviour which produces a sense of well-being/ neurochemical gratification. This is what I term the *sustainable neurochemical gratification principle*. The feeling of gratification may occur as the result of instinctive 'salient' acts or it may be triggered by what we normatively decide is pleasurable (i.e. through established social or moral norms). As mentioned before, there are five main drivers of human action through which this neurochemical satisfaction is sought: power, profit, pleasure, pride and permanency. What this means for individuals, society at large and the global human system is that constructive/useful behaviour (e.g. excellence, lawfulness, moral conduct) ought to be normatively associated with feelings of reward and general self-interest. This will stimulate the repetition of that behaviour, and thus positively reinforce it, in order to produce feelings of gratification and pleasure in our brains. This implies that it is far more effective to reward good behaviour or rehabilitate bad behaviour than solely to punish bad behaviour.

3.4.3. Dissociative Behaviour

As the previous section illustrated, the brain's reward system plays a crucial role in motivating human behaviour. When impaired, however, it may give rise to what is known as *dissociative* behaviour.[454] This term refers to mental disorders which involve a disconnect or discontinuity between perceptions of the external world, of the self and of one's own thoughts and memories. Forms of dissociation are an involuntary way of escaping life and are usually developed as a reaction to trauma.[455] Indeed, it appears that some children who have suffered perpetual abuse tend to withdraw emotionally, as a way of attempting to heal. Unfortunately, as of yet, little is known about the neuronal systems used in dissociative behaviour. Nevertheless, Daniel Levine holds that some of the same regions of the brain are stimulated during dissociation as during 'fight or flight' behaviour, although they initiate different neurochemical combinations. As in fight or flight behaviour, levels of the hormone cortisol are high and those of oxytocin are low.

3.4.4. Libido, Attraction and Attachment

In his novella *Elective Affinities* (1809), Johann Wolfgang von Goethe (1749–1832) depicts couples in strong marriages as being like particles of quicksilver (as mercury was commonly known) which bind themselves to one another through a chemical process. This hints at the notion that love is all about chemistry. Research suggests that intimate relationships are, indeed, a question of 'good chemistry'. There are thought to be three neuronal systems linked to sex, reproduction and parenting. Libido is related to a desire for sexual gratification and is connected to oestrogens and androgens. Attraction refers to increased focus on a preferred sexual partner and is associated with the neurotransmitters *dopamine* and *norepinephrine* and lower levels of serotonin. The neuronal system implicated in male-female attachment, typically characterised by a sense of serenity, comfort, security and emotional connection, has been linked to two specific neuropeptides: oxytocin and vasopressin.[456]

In relation to attachment, the peptide *oxytocin* is released during key, intense emotional moments, such as birth, breast-feeding and sexual climax, and appears to be especially important in relation to female attachment towards both offspring and sexual partners.[457]

Oxytocin attaches to receptor molecules in regions of the brain which are associated with reward. It appears to be implicated in bonding through reward in relation to sexual and social relations. On the other hand, vasopressin is active in the bonding process and is responsible for orienting attention on relevant stimuli – in the case of male-female partnerships, towards the member of the opposite sex with whom the person is forming a close relationship.[458]

While the peptide is present in men, its effect is thought to be enhanced by oestrogen and dampened by testosterone, rendering it more potent in women than in men. This has led to speculation that human beings may have evolved the capacity for attachment as a means of preparing us for caring for children, who remain dependent for a comparatively long period of time.[459]

The neuronal circuits which are associated with libido, attraction and attachment have evolved to regulate different aspects of the reproductive cycle and they are connected to different types of behaviour. Libido ensures that individuals will seek sexual relations with other members of the same species and, if they are heterosexuals, thereby reproduce. Attraction ensures that individuals will seek genetically appropriate members of the species as potential mates. Attachment ensures that unions are maintained long enough to rear offspring, a period of time specific to each species.[460]

The neuronal circuits related to these emotions are thought to be discrete. In other words, a person can be attached to someone with whom they have never had sex or with whom they have ceased to have sexual relations. Alternatively, a person may be sexually attracted to and have sex with someone they do not love, and most likely would not love if they got to know them better.[461]

3.4.5. The Neurochemistry of Power

Before moving on to the next section of this book, however, it is also worth providing a brief overview of what I have referred to in other writings as the *neurochemistry of power*.[462] As I discussed in Chapter 3.1.1, power is one of the Neuro P5, the most important drivers of human behaviour. The feeling of power is fundamentally linked to the reward circuitry in our brains. This sensation is neurochemically represented by a release of dopamine into our systems, which triggers a feeling of pleasure. Dopamine activates the reward system, which is essential for the survival of our species, since it motivates us to re-engage in necessary behaviours, such as food consumption, in accordance with the 'sustainable neurochemical gratification principle'.[463] As I explained in the chapter on addiction, since dopamine is addictive and produces a 'high', human beings have the instinctive motivation to repeat actions and behaviours which are responsible for dopamine releases, be they healthy or unhealthy, such as the consumption of drugs, regardless of their social acceptability.[464] Power, therefore, has the same effect on our neurochemistry and, consequently, on our behaviour, as any other addictive substance.[465]

For this reason, power, especially absolute and unchecked power, is intoxicating and highly addictive.[466] It affects our cells and our neurochemistry – and, consequently, and even more notably, our behaviour – in a variety of ways. On the one hand, dopamine can produce heightened cognitive functions. On the other, it can trigger poor judgement,[467] a lack of inhibition, extreme narcissism, perverted behaviour and gruesome cruelty. It can make us impulsive, less risk-averse and less empathetic.[468] As I have previously discussed elsewhere, recent studies have also shown that high levels of dopamine are associated with a sense of personal destiny, risk-taking, preoccupation with the cosmic or religion, emotional detachment which can lead to ruthlessness, and an obsession with achieving goals and conquests.[469] Absolute power and the high it produces can also lead people to believe that a spiritual force is guiding their actions.[470] This has been the case not only with famous dictators, like Stalin, Hitler and Napoleon, but also with leaders of established democracies. For example, both former US President George Bush and former British Prime Minister Tony Blair seemed to believe that it was God's will that they wage war against Iraq. This irrational degree of certainty is a symptom of extremely high levels of dopamine. Further, the dopamine levels present in powerful individuals are also responsible for their strong egocentrism, as well as the paranoia which often plagues the powerful.[471] Indeed, as I briefly mentioned in Chapter 3.3, it is the constant fear of this loss of power, be it real or imagined, which will drive leaders to do anything at all to enhance their power and ensure it remains undisputed. Therefore, it is this pre-emptive response to fear which pushes them to go as far as committing acts of unspeakable cruelty both against those whom they perceive to be the enemy and sometimes even against their own.[472]

3.4.6. Fear-Induced Pre-emptive Aggression

As mentioned in the previous section, pre-emptive responses to fear often lie at the root of the commission by individuals of violent actions, and, in extreme cases, even conflicts and wars, and thus merit closer attention.

The seminal thinking of Hobbes provides a helpful starting point when examining the personal and political implications of fear. In particular, his insights on human behaviour under conditions of anarchy are instructive.[473] According to Hobbes, distrust pushes human beings to strike first in an attempt to protect themselves. This is particularly true when one doubts one's own abilities to mount a defence. In other words, Hobbes considered an offensive approach to be the logical answer to the combined effect of distrust in one's fellows coupled with a lack of faith in one's own defensive capacities. Moreover, Hobbes' theory postulates that a state of war persists at all times in cases in which an established superior power is absent (irrespective of whether there is ongoing physical conflict or violence). In addition, his theory assumes that no one has the necessary defensive capacities individually.[474]

Neuroscience has shed new light on Hobbes's observations that fear triggers highly offensive responses. From a neurobiological perspective, fear is a very complex emotion and its manifestations take several forms, depending on the nature of the threat. These will range from the full activation of what is known as the 'panic system' to various forms of anxiety which lead to adaptive behaviour which ensures our survival.[475] While the instinct to survive and the desire to avoid physical pain constitute powerful motivators to 'strike first', as Hobbes observed, there are other powerful stimuli creating fear responses. These include those I have grouped together as the Neuro P5. To summarise, it is not only aggression in the form of a 'strike' which is prompted by fear. Fear entails a whole range of reactions to satisfy the need for safety, such as the accumulation of profit.[476] As I explore in more depth in Chapter 4.4.8, although fear-induced pre-emptive aggression is the root cause of many conflicts and has contributed to major crises in history, dignity-based governance can help mitigate it in favour of more peaceful and prosperous outcomes for all.

* * *

To conclude, emotions are key physiological as well as psychological phenomena. They are central in counselling us as to how we ought to respond to external stimuli, be they natural or social, and play a fundamental role in conditioning our behaviour and our everyday actions. Some of our more basic, primeval emotions, such as fear, evolved as crucial survival mechanisms, enabling our ancestors to avoid injury and death. Others were more closely tied to our ability to form the social relationships needed for the preservation of our genes in the evolutionary process. Neuroscientific research has demonstrated that multiple neuronal systems have evolved to translate sensory inputs into responses via neurochemically-mediated emotions. Since our neurochemistry is genetically inherited and contributes to forming our personalities, individuals differ in the way they experience emotions and respond neurochemically to external occurrences. Chapter 3.5 will explore further the relationship between inherited and acquired traits, as well as the notion, and development, of morality in relation to these.

3.5

What Makes Us Individuals? Examining Heterogenous Variations and Personality Traits

As human beings, we are all emotional, amoral and egoistic. Despite this common psychological orientation, however, we all have very different personalities. Even our day-to-day lives prove how different we are from one another. Both our genes and our environment account for our individuality. Having established how genetic traits are inherited and how the environment also has a role to play in the development of human nature, in this chapter I examine how evolution allows for the creation of infinitely unique individuals and why this is necessary to ensure our 'permanence'.

Chapter 3.2 explained that natural selection presupposes variation in the genetic make-up of organisms. Evolution is thought to occur through selection of the most successful adaptations or variations. Lacking the genetic technology which we have today when laying out his theory of natural selection, Darwin was able to focus only on *phenotypic* or *morphological* variations, which essentially theorised on diversification across species in relation to ecological factors (Darwin focussed especially on beak morphology variation in finches). However, scientific advances have since taken us further along the road to understanding evolution and today the emphasis is placed, instead, on variations of *genotype*. The specific genetic differences relevant to the evolutionary process are now understood to be those which give one individual an edge over others – this advantage being what ultimately matters in the struggle to survive.[477] This chapter examines this founding principle in more detail and outlines how a gene-centred view of evolution has recently displaced a group-centred notion. I discuss the implications that a focus on the individual gene, rather than the species as a whole, has for acts of altruism. I conclude the chapter by looking at the more minuscule genetic variations which contribute to each individual's personality traits.

3.5.1. *The Principle of Variation*

In an environment marked by scarcity of food, mates and dwellings, some phenotypes will be more successful at obtaining these than others. The variations that they represent are, therefore, more likely to endure as a result of reproduction. Organisms which are better able to compete for scarce resources will leave more offspring with the traits which have favoured their survival than those which are less suited to their environment. Organisms become adapted to their environment through natural selection. This is called 'fitness' – a gauge of relative reproductive success.

While Darwin's theory was constructed purely in terms of phenotypic characteristics, genetics has shed light on the way these traits are transmitted from one generation to the next. A phenotype is generated by a particular combination of a person's genotype and the environment. Variations in phenotypes are the result of genetic mutations, which occur because of changes in genetic codes or DNA, as Chapter 3.2 explained. Essentially, these mutations alter the protein synthesis which affects the phenotype. Morphological changes in organisms tend to be a product of the environment.[478]

Natural selection favoured animals which were endowed with sense organs (such as eyes, ears and taste buds) and were capable of converting input from the environment into signals transmitted through neurons (cells with walls composed of axons). Some axons are short and confined to tissue, such as the brain, while others are long, like wires, and are nerves connecting different parts of the body.

At some point in the course of evolution, sense organs may have had an almost direct relationship with muscles. However, natural selection favoured organisms which could generate a more accurate response to external events and a more sophisticated coordination of the muscles. Memory was a major advantage to organisms which possessed it. Not only could the organism respond to current events taking place in the environment, but also it could retrieve information related to the near past which might help it to respond successfully to the present circumstances. In addition to memory, some organisms also evolved consciousness, which allowed them to engage in purposeful behaviour.[479]

Some organisms even developed a capacity for learning. Organisms capable of making predictions about the future by drawing on past events and current information are much better equipped for survival than those which lack this capacity. Learning represented the beginning of subjective consciousness or self-awareness.[480]

3.5.2. Group/Kin Selection, Gene-Centred Selection

In order for genes to survive in the so-called gene pool, they have to offer a better chance of survival to the organism in which they are confined, compared to rival genes or alleles.[481] As Winston puts it, 'We can all trace our ancestry back to those with successful genes; the rest were doomed to end at an evolutionary cul-de-sac, dead branches of humanity's family tree.'[482]

The theory of group selection as the principal mode of evolution held sway within evolutionary biology for a long time. In the early 1960s, William D. Hamilton (1936–2000) challenged this orthodoxy by arguing that a gene is favoured if the totality of its replicas constitutes an increasing proportion of the overall gene pool. The thrust of his argument was that evolution acts on genes and not on groups (e.g. at the level of a species) or on individual organisms.[483] What this meant was that natural selection refers to genes and not to individuals. This, in turn, meant that the success of specific genes would depend on the success of the organism in its environment.

One of the key implications of this way of thinking about the mode of evolution is that relationships between kin would be paramount. Therefore, Hamilton's theory became known as the theory of kin selection. Since our offspring have 50 per cent of our own genetic make-up, as do our siblings, and our cousins 25 per cent, and so on, our relationships with other genetically related family members are likely to be stronger than our relationships with individuals who are not genetically related, at least not in any immediate sense. In the old proverbial sense, blood, according to Hamilton, is thicker than water.[484]

3.5.3. *Altruistic or Selfish Genes?*

Altruism refers to behaviour which favours others at some cost to the person acting altruistically. From the point of view of natural selection, altruism does not appear to make any sense, since competition is a key aspect of evolution by natural selection. Nonetheless, in nature it is common to witness behaviour from a variety of species which would, at least at first glance, be labelled as altruistic. Vervet monkeys, for instance, cry out at the first sign of predators. This cry is a means, it would appear, of warning others about a potential source of danger.[485] What we know today, however, is that kin selection underlies many of our assumptions about altruism and our relations with others. Indeed, according to Hamilton, the logical conclusion in terms of altruism is that altruistic behaviour may be favoured by natural selection if it enables an individual with similar genes to survive and reproduce, thus satisfying our desire for permanence. This may occur directly, by passing on one's own genes through sexual reproduction, or indirectly, by increasing the survival chances of individuals who share similar genes.[486] According to this logic, the vervet monkey calls out to warn its near relatives in order to increase the chance of genes which are similar to its own going on to be reproduced and added to the gene pool.

Hamilton's thinking provided the basis for Dawkins' *The Selfish Gene*, which emphasises the role of the individual gene in evolution. There may be a gene which tends to make survival more likely than it would have been under the influence of a gene's rival (a rival gene is called an *allele*). Replicas of good genes exist in any number of different bodies. Those types of genes which are found in bodies constituted by winning combinations of genes are more likely to be passed down through the generations than those which end up with a less successful combination.[487]

According to Dawkins, natural selection has meant that selfishness is a predominant quality which human beings possess as a result of their genetic heritage – selfishness, here, being defined as a response ensuring the highest possible chance of survival in terms of the transmission of one's genes to the next generation. It is important to note that Dawkins' concern is not with the motivations of the individual, and, therefore, not with the individual's desire for permanence, but with the effect of specific acts or behaviour on chances of survival.[488]

Among the examples of selfish behaviour, Dawkins cites the behaviour of black-headed gulls:

Black-headed gulls nest in large colonies, the nests being only a few feet apart. When the chicks first hatch out they are small and defenceless and easy to swallow. It is quite common for a gull to wait until a neighbour's back is turned, perhaps while it is away fishing, and then pounce on one of the neighbour's chicks and swallow it whole. It thereby obtains a good nutritious meal, without having to go to the trouble of catching a fish, and without having to leave its own nest unprotected.[489]

Other forms of selfish behaviour may include a refusal to share scarce resources, such as food or sexual partners. None of this behaviour, however, is conceived in terms of motive.[490]

Altruism may, therefore, be ultimately based on self-preservation or the preservation of individuals with genes which resemble our own, with the aim of ensuring our own permanence. In this case, we might be inclined to argue that 'true' altruism does not exist, at least in terms of our instincts. One of the unique features of *Homo sapiens*, however, is that we are a species with a highly developed self-awareness and have, thus, developed moral codes to which we aspire. In fact, it is important to reaffirm here that, as I have argued, human beings are not born with a form of pre-conceived morality or immorality and are, rather, amoral. Nonetheless, there may be a gap between the altruistic behaviour that we are capable of on an instinctual basis and the moral ideals which we have consciously developed.

3.5.4. Sexual Selection

Some traits are the result of sexual selection. In most species, there are morphological differences between males and females. Often, males will compete with each other for female sexual partners and females will exhibit some discrimination when choosing. Darwin noted that this could lead to variations in the evolutionary process, some giving particular males a better chance of passing on their 'good genes'.

If we consider sexually selected traits in human beings, body shape and beards are perhaps the most obvious phenotypic differences which may be attributed to sexual selection. Beards, for instance, appear at puberty, but have no particular survival advantage (defined in narrow terms), and are thought to have been selected mostly for the purpose of partner selection and to enhance male attractiveness. The deeper voices of men are also thought to have been sexually selected. Studies seem to suggest that women have a marked preference for a number of characteristics, including being older-looking, more masculine, dominant, courageous, mature and confident.[491]

Sexual selection of female physical traits is believed to have been less likely, since competition is generally among men. However, some studies suggest that female attractiveness may have increased the chances of the survival of offspring by enabling marriage to men of high socioeconomic status. If high status males are selective in their choices of sexual partners, cues of fecundity and reproductive value may have been important, such as the famous hip-to-waist ratio.[492]

Some biologists acknowledge, however, that some of the mutations selected do not necessarily constitute an optimal solution in survival terms. To this end, there are trade-offs in the evolutionary process. For instance, sexual selection among populations of guppies has led to brightly coloured males in waters where predators are relatively absent but, in more dangerous waters, male colouring is much less elaborate: thus, as Timothy Goldsmith notes, 'Phenotypes are necessarily compromises.'[493]

3.5.5. Personality Traits

A large part of our DNA is devoted to creating the physiological make-up of the brain. While most of us share a great deal of the same genetic code, minuscule variations exist. These variations help to explain why personality traits differ from person to person.[494] In terms of what we inherit biologically, neurochemistry is responsible for temperament. Most people have temperaments which are not extreme, indicating that being even-tempered provided survival advantages – although there must also have been some survival advantages to being impulsive, aggressive and inhibited, or these temperaments would not have survived selection pressures. The remainder of what constitutes our personalities (i.e. character) is largely the result of the environment.

* * *

To sum up, this chapter argued for the centrality of the principle of variation in evolution through natural selection. Variation is essential to advances in evolution, since some adaptations, those favoured by evolution, endowed individuals with a greater chance of survival, or of reproducing their genes, than others, thus fulfilling their need for permanence. This means that the survival chances of any individual gene depend on the success of the organism or body which is carrying it. An organism which has a more resilient immune system, for example, is likely to have a better chance of reproducing its genes than one which is deficient. Altruism, at least in so far as it is prompted by instincts, is likely, ultimately, to serve the reproduction of one's genes, or increase the number of similar genes within the gene pool. As such, it is a reflection of human beings' egoism and desire for permanence rather than of morality. Finally, as I pointed out earlier, variation is also important for explaining the uniqueness of personality traits.

Yet, all aspects related to personality and emotionality are bound to be rendered ever more complicated by ongoing developments in the field of human enhancement. Altering our mood, personality and physical features by means of drugs and technology poses unique challenges for our future. Chapter 3.6 grapples with the prospect of alteration of our minds and bodies, and the possibility of a trans-human and post-human future.

3.6

Behavioural and Genetic Modification: Changing Human Nature and Embracing Transhumanism?

Much of the argument expounded above emphasises facets of our common genetic heritage. Yet tiny variations in our DNA are what account for our individual personality traits. As I mentioned before, a large part of our DNA is devoted to creating the brain's physiological make-up, including its neurochemistry. Since our temperaments are determined by our neurochemistry, our personalities are, to a large extent, genetically driven. How we orient ourselves in the world is, however, only partly related to biological traits. As Chapter 3.2 discussed, our environment also plays a critical role in the constitution of our character, which is key to successfully navigating our world. When our personality traits hinder our ability to do so, drugs which operate on our neurochemistry, psychotherapy and technological advances provide the means of modifying behaviour. Today, more than ever before, technology has the capacity to shape who we are and where we are going. Perhaps one of the greatest challenges will come from the heavy burden of deciding what to do with these technologies, and the extent to which we shall use them to alter ourselves.[495]

This chapter focusses on the various ways we can modify human nature. First, it identifies some of the main types of personality disorders which people may suffer from and the kinds of treatment which are possible for them. It then shifts focus to the means by which we might eventually be able to enhance the natural capacities of our species and bypass our current limitations.

3.6.1. Personality Disorders, Medication and Psychotherapy

Personality may be defined as 'enduring patterns of perceiving, thinking, feeling, behaving, and relating to others'.[496] It may be thought of as the interaction of temperament, which is the result of biological traits, and character, which is shaped by the environment. Biological traits include impulsivity, dependence on reward or gratification and thrill seeking. The existence of personality types remains highly controversial. According to a recent study in *Nature Human Behaviour*, there are at least four distinct personality types: average, reserved, self-centred and role model. People fall into one of these four categories based on the extent to which they display the five major character traits: openness, agreeableness, extraversion, neuroticism and conscientiousness.[497] Personality disorders are believed to result from exaggeration of certain aspects of temperament, combined with character traits such as irresponsibility, uncooperativeness and self-obsession. Such disorders may manifest themselves as inflexibility or difficulty in adapting, in terms of perceiving, thinking, feeling, behaving and relating to others.[498] Specifically:

> Personality Disorders are generalized, inflexible patterns of inner experience and behaviour. These patterns significantly differ from cultural expectations, and begin in adolescence or early adulthood. Personality Disorders are long-term, maladaptive patterns of perception, emotional regulation, anxiety, and impulse control.[499]

Len Sperry organises personality disorders into three categories: dramatic personality disorders, anxious personality disorders and eccentric personality disorders. Within the first category, we may find people with sub-category personality disorders, such as histrionic personality disorder. People who suffer from this disorder are typically attention-seeking, seductive and exhibitionistic. They tend to exhibit exaggerated, excitable, demanding and self-indulgent behaviour. Another sub-category is narcissistic personality disorder, which entails a sense of grandiosity, lack of empathy and hypersensitivity to criticism. In terms of behaviour, narcissistic personalities tend to be exploitative and non-cooperative. Borderline personality disorder also falls into this category. People suffering from this disorder find it very difficult to maintain a stable self-identity and often engage in self-destructive behaviour, as a result of an intolerance of frustration. They may also have a cognitive style which is impulsive, meaning that the individual reacts quickly and is therefore prone to making errors, as well as unstable.[500]

The anxious personality disorders include dependent, obsessive-compulsive and avoidant personality disorders. The first of these, the dependent, refers to people who are overly passive, non-assertive and submissive as a result of insecurity and anxiety. They are, thus, likely to be extremely sensitive to fear of disapproval or abandonment, resulting in a self-effacing and uncritical style. The obsessive-compulsive personality disorder also falls into this category. A person suffering from this disorder is likely to be fixated on orderliness and perfectionism. One might expect them to be loyal and dependable but rigid and lacking spontaneity. They may be socially inhibited but capable of harbouring strong feelings of anxiety and anger and may appear to be preoccupied with meticulousness and unimportant detail. The last in this category is the avoidant personality disorder; it refers to overwhelming social inhibition, feelings of inadequacy and oversensitivity to evaluation by others. People suffering from this personality disorder are likely to be shy and anxious and to fear rejection and humiliation by others. They are likely to be wary of others and unsure of themselves.[501]

Within the eccentric cluster, we find the sub-categories of the schizoid, paranoid and schizotypal personality disorders. People with these disorders appear 'odd' or 'peculiar'. People with schizoid personality disorder are detached from social relationships and demonstrate a narrow range of emotions, perhaps appearing cold, distant and socially constricted. Individuals suffering from paranoid personality disorder tend to perceive the actions of others as threatening. Finally, those with schizotypal personality disorder fear close relationships and demonstrate thought or behavioural peculiarities.[502]

Since personality disorders are partly the result of biologically over-modulated aspects of temperament, medication can be used to treat some of them. Psychotherapy can also help to alter aspects of character. Medical treatment is thought to be effective if targeted at the specific aspects of temperament characterising the personality disorder – traits such as impulsiveness, aggression, inhibition, suspicion, affective instability and mood instability.[503]

Some forms of treatment are inclusive and combine psychotherapy and medication. For avoidant personality disorders, where an anxiety or depressive disorder is often present, a patient may require medication, but also individual psychotherapy as a result of the considerable deficit of social skills which is likely to accompany this disorder. Psychotherapy can also help the patient alter his or her schema, thus enabling them to change what has become an organised pattern of thought and behaviour. In severe cases, group therapy may be helpful, or couples' therapy, if the patient has a partner or spouse.

Medication does not exist for the dependent personality disorder. Individual psychotherapy which concentrates on altering mental processes is likely to be helpful. It should be combined with psychoeducational therapy addressing the skills deficit which is likely to accompany the disorder. Assertiveness and decision-making training may constitute part of the latter, for example.

Obsessive-compulsive personality disorders are more likely to occur with dependent or avoidant personality disorders. A holistic approach to treatment is recommended in this case. Because skills deficits are likely to be encountered, therapy is essential in order to alter the psychodynamics which characterise it.[504]

In the case of eccentric personality disorders, medication, as well as psychotherapy and skills training, may be recommended.[505] For borderline personality disorders, affective instability may be linked to neurochemical abnormalities. These may be treated by drugs aimed at regulating them.[506]

3.6.2. Human Enhancement: Panacea or Pandora's Box?

As discussed earlier, the twenty-first century brought about an enormous leap forward in our knowledge about the human brain. This has had wide-reaching implications not only for medicine, but also for our understanding of human nature. What is more, it has provided us with various means through which we could potentially redesign aspects of the human organism. Our potential to alter or enhance the capacities of human beings is the result of advances in, among others, genetic engineering, nanotechnology (involving the engineering of functional systems at the molecular scale),[507] psychopharmacology and neuronal interfaces (i.e. brain-computer interfaces). Possibilities of enhancing cognitive or physical abilities of healthy individuals, rather than repairing lost functions, are generally subsumed under the term *human enhancement*.[508]

Will the latest scientific advances enable us to take charge of our biological evolution? In fact, human enhancement technologies may well change the trajectory of the human species by setting us on the path to *transhumanism*.[509] Transhumanism implies a stage at which a human being starts to move beyond the limitations of human biology, but without reaching a point at which it is so different from humans as we presently know them that it can no longer qualify as human. At that point, such entities will have become post-human, beings which physically and mimetically can no longer be called human. Post-humans could come into existence through a remodelling of our current neurochemistry which, although copying our present form in some aspects, would grant us complete control over the emotional responses and motivations which drive our behaviour.[510] An example of a post-human may be a cyborg, a being with both organic and biomechatronic parts, produced through the use of advanced nanotechnology or a mixture of technologies, such as genetic engineering, psychopharmacology and neuronal interfaces. What makes the post-human distinct from other hypothetical, highly sophisticated entities, such as artificial intelligent robots, is the fact that, rather than being an entirely new entity, it finds its origin in human beings as we presently know them. Post-humanism implies that the species will pass through a trans-human stage and surpass it, either at some point during a post-human's life, or during the life of its ancestors. In the foreseeable future, however, transhumanism is the more likely next step in our man-made evolutionary process.

In several respects, we have already advanced towards a transhuman future. As illustrated at the end of the second chapter, we have already started to merge our bodies with technology (through pacemakers, artificial joints, contact lenses, artificial retinas and so on).[511] Humans are already using systemic methods to biologically alter mental processes (i.e. drugs which have an effect on the totality of the human body's chemistry) and are changing aspects of temperament, helping people to overcome inhibitions or increase self-control, for instance.[512] Likewise, negative mental states can be alleviated through artificial increases in levels of neurotransmitters such as serotonin and dopamine.[513] Drugs may also be supplied to specific, targeted areas of the brain through means of a pump, for instance to stop seizures from taking place.[514] The basic principle here is that a neurochemical the body lacks is artificially supplied to modulate behaviour. With advances in technology, such as computer-assisted molecular design and brain imaging, research into neurochemical modifiers is moving forward.[515] Unlike drugs such as heroin and cocaine, mood stabilisers, which contain lithium, carbamazepine or divalproex, do not produce a 'crash' after a 'high'. Instead, they are able to produce a constant and sustained mood change in the patient.[516]

In some instances, however, the supply of neurochemicals has no significant effect on behaviour. This happens when the receptors on the surface of cells are impaired in some way. Parkinson's disease, for example, which is connected to a dopamine deficiency, affects the brain's motor functions, but supplying dopamine to patients has little effect if the receptors for dopamine are damaged – if the 'key' is unable to open the 'lock'. With our current knowledge and medical abilities, we are not yet able to replace the damaged receptors or to induce the cells to repair or replace them.

Genetic engineering enables the isolation of specific genes and their modification in particular ways. Most recently, the CRISPR/Cas9 genetic scissors, the discovery of which in 2011 earned Emmanuelle Charpentier and Jennifer A. Doudna the 2020 Nobel Prize in chemistry, heralded a revolutionary advance in the field of gene editing. The sharp tools provided by CRISPR/Cas9 have reduced the time needed to make genetic modifications from years to days and have significantly lowered the cost.[517] Using this technology, researchers can change the DNA of animals, plants and micro-organisms with extremely high precision. Over the past nine years, the CRISPR/Cas9 gene-editing tool has, thus, had a revolutionary impact on the life sciences and on medical research. Indeed, not only is it contributing to new cancer therapies, but it may also make the dream of curing inherited diseases come true. For example, preliminary results from recent clinical trials suggest the potential use of CRISPR/Cas9 to successfully treat blood disorders such as sickle-cell disease or beta thalassemia.[518]

It is fundamental to note, however, that this type of technology may also be used to create entirely new traits, or to make the genes which determine such traits more prevalent within the gene pool.[519] Radical gene therapy may one day even be used to extend people's lifespans.[520] Genetic engineering, however, is currently restricted to animals and gene therapy to helping to treat disease. Indeed, most diseases result from mutations or imperfections in a person's genes. Flaws in genes cause the proteins they help generate to malfunction, which, in turn, affects the normal behaviour of cells and, thus, tissue and even organs. Gene therapy, an experimental technique intended to replace drugs or surgery, may be used to introduce new genes into cells containing flawed genes in order to help fight a variety of diseases. To date, it has been used in relation to somatic cells (most cells) for these kinds of purposes.[521] Both the US Federal Drug Administration and the European Commission, for instance, have approved the use of gene therapy to treat monogenic neurodevelopmental disorders.[522]

Gene therapy and other genetic engineering techniques may be used on other types of cells, as well, which poses more complex ethical challenges. One highly controversial use, on which there is currently no international consensus, is germline gene therapy, which involves selectively modifying genes in sex cells and early embryos by introducing new DNA strands which enable the desired modification.[523] If changes are made to germline cells, these changes will be passed on to the next generation and so on, which is not the case for changes to somatic cells. For this reason, at present, germline gene therapy on embryos is only allowed in some jurisdictions and usually exclusively for research purposes.[524] In 2019, however, a scientist in China claimed to have edited embryos for multiple couples during fertility treatment, leading to the birth of twins with modified DNA.[525] This example shows that there is an urgent need to regulate the use of genetic engineering techniques on human beings, since they may soon be an easily accessible option.

According to LeRoy Walters, the most important area for the use of gene therapy is in relation to the brain, especially with the aim of altering behavioural traits and changing the human germline. For instance, the dopamine D2 receptor has been inserted into rats' brains in order to reduce the consumption of alcohol. This, Walters suggests, is the kind of application to which gene therapy could be put in humans. Gene therapy may also potentially be used for enhancement, such as to refine the immune system, or to prevent dementia from ageing. Of course, the most controversial use to which gene therapy could be put would be to selectively transmit particular traits to our children.[526] Gene-editing technologies like CRISPR/Cas9 could make this possible in the next few years.

Intervening genetically is only one way the physiological and psychological constitution of human beings may be altered. Manufacturing, as we know it, is a combination of industry, chemical engineering and physical labour and skills. At the moment, we manufacture using things from nature, such as trees and ores, and refine these and form them into shapes in order to make products which we consider useful. Molecular nanotechnology may at some point mean that we shall not have to rely on altering what already exists as biological matter.[527] It could one day give us the ability to create things atom by atom, including human organisms. We should, thus, be able to alter our physiology, morphology and, to some extent, our psychology.[528] Molecular manufacturing, as it is sometimes called, is the brainchild of Richard Feynman, a Nobel Prize-winning physicist. In 1959, he pointed out that there is nothing in physics which precludes moving things atom by atom.[529] Molecular nanotechnology is potentially the most precise method of manufacturing. For centuries, we have been trying to manipulate matter by pounding, melting and so on. Molecular nanotechnology offers a way of engineering matter from the 'bottom up' through molecular machine systems, which are molecular components which produce quasi-mechanical movements in response to specific stimuli.[530]

As Nick Bostrom explains, molecular nanotechnology is 'the hypothetical design and manufacture of machines to atomic-scale precision, including general-purpose "assemblers", devices that can position atoms individually in order to build almost any chemically permitted matter-configuration for which we can give a detailed specification – including exact copies of themselves'.[531] The analogy in nature is, of course, a cell. However, cells are limited to what they can replicate because of their evolutionary history. For this reason, molecular nanotechnology represents an extremely powerful tool which surpasses the biological limits of nature.

Yet creating an assembler is an extremely difficult challenge. At present, scientists are approaching the problem from two angles. The first approach involves attempting to build on what happens in nature by using biochemistry to create new proteins which act as tools for additional engineering efforts; the second attempts to build atomic structures by positioning atoms individually on a surface. The two methods can be employed together.[532] Although molecular nanotechnology still faces significant practical challenges, huge progress has been made over the past couple of decades. It is in this context that the 2016 Nobel Prize for Chemistry was awarded to Bernard Feringa, Jean-Pierre Sauvage and Sir James Fraser Stoddart for their successful development of molecular machines.[533]

Some machine intelligence researchers, roboticists and cognitive scientists speculate that it may one day be possible to 'upload' our emotions, memories and values into 'connectionist nanocomputers', which may enable our mental processes to function more rapidly.[534] This would imply a kind of symbiosis between our brains and computer technology. However, there may be less complicated ways of creating a symbiosis between our minds and computers. Extensive research is under way, for example, into neurochip interfaces,[535] which are producing promising results in terms of the potential uses of such technologies for the treatment of diseases and much more.[536]

Chapter 2.5 provided insights into the most recent advances in various fields – including synthetic biology and artificial intelligence – and has illustrated in which ways these could potentially change what it means to be human. Synthetic biology, as explained earlier, is the result of the confluence of knowledge in life sciences, engineering and bioinformatics. It could have a revolutionary impact on our lives and brings with it enormous opportunities and risks. Opportunities include genome-specific medications for the treatment of cancer and degenerative diseases, such as Parkinson's and Alzheimer's. Risks are posed by the possibility of generating DNA products with increased capacity for virulence or pathogenicity, or unanticipated mutations which may occur when these products are integrated into normal DNA sequences.[537]

Of course, ethical concerns are raised by technological advances which may allow us to alter our physiology and psychology beyond what is currently recognised as human. On the one hand, presently available and future technologies may have tremendous benefits, including the possibility of treating a number of neurological disorders, including Parkinson's, paralysis, depression and diabetes. On the other hand, it remains highly controversial if, and to what extent, they should be used to alter human nature. Whether we ought to be able to construct our bodies and those of future human beings touches on the very question of our 'humanness'.[538] As Timothy Casey notes, we have entered the 'ultimate technological frontier where we ourselves become material to be shaped and reinvented through feedback mechanisms echoing and reinscribing the Darwinian world of natural selection and adaptation'.[539]

Against the Enlightenment's commitment to reason, both Marx and Martin Heidegger (1889–1976) were concerned with the centrality of the technological mediation of human existence and its implications for understanding human nature. The thinking of these two seminal figures is poignant today. For Marx, the human essence is distorted under capitalism. Human beings differentiate themselves from animals through their capacity to produce their means of existence. What makes human beings human is, thus, their engagement in production. In this conception, nature is already subjugated by humans.[540] Heidegger, on the other hand, called into question the notion that technology is a mere tool over which human beings have mastery. The modern technological age, he argued, is unique in that nature's energy resources can be stored for later use. He held that technology is beyond human control – modern technology shows a distinct disrespect for limits. This being the case, can humanity continue to employ technology without technology transforming what it means to be human?[541]

Capacities to manipulate chemistry and molecular matter have improved since the principle of nanotechnology was first set out. Scientists now have a better idea of how these capabilities may be used. What molecular nanotechnology will mean for our lives is impossible to predict but it will alter technology, economics and the environment. Nanotechnology is, for example, able to increase the energy efficiency of solar cells, enabling greater use of solar power.[542] It may also be conceivable that molecular machines will be able to destroy cancer cells which the body's immune system fails to detect and destroy.[543] Such scenarios indicate the huge opportunities which nanotechnology may offer. However, its revolutionary implications mean that it will also present us with challenges. These include a wide array of risks such as to the environment (for example, due to the release of nanoparticles in the environment)[544] and to human health (for example, due to the migration of nanoparticles to human organs)[545] as well as to our collective future when it comes to the uses of nano-science for human enhancement.[546]

Given the tremendous possibilities of emerging technologies, it will be imperative, going forward, to establish regulatory frameworks to limit their harmful implications. In particular, we shall need to establish clear principles to guide the development and application of human enhancement technologies. The trick will be to set out guidelines loose enough to permit legitimate research and applications, while making them tight enough to prevent dangerous activities. Defining what is legitimate and what is dangerous is the challenge which lies ahead of us. Gene therapy, in particular, is currently moving from what was previously an experimental phase to one in which it will be used on a large scale. Some controversial questions therefore include: What is a disorder and who decides? Do disabilities constitute diseases which ought to be cured? Is somatic gene therapy more acceptable than germline gene therapy?[547]

Human enhancement technologies raise major concerns over justice, fairness, meritocracy and authenticity. Societal divides between the enhanced and the non-enhanced are likely to emerge and erode meritocratic justice as enhancement technologies are likely to remain accessible only to those with great financial resources. Similarly, enhancement technologies threaten the authenticity of human experience. Tiny variations in our genetic make-up are in part responsible for our different personalities or, put differently, authentic selves. Our neurochemistry, which is genetically determined, is what moderates our temperament. Most of us have mid-range temperaments, since evolution tended to favour even tempers because they offered the best chance of survival. Our personality is, however, also shaped by the way our environment has influenced our character. We are, indeed, products of both nature and nurture. In some instances, our temperament and character may come together in such a way as to cause us to operate in less-than-optimal ways when faced with challenges and opportunities. In such instances, it may be legitimate to change behaviour with drugs, which modify the chemical compositions of our brain, helping to regulate impulses, or through psychotherapy, which may assist in altering thought processes. In other instances, however, concerns arise over the authenticity of human experience. Perhaps the experience of being loved, appreciated and rewarded can be neurochemically recreated without the attendant reality; but do we really want to live in this 'synthesised' illusion?

In sum, advances in our understanding of mental processes have enabled developments which offer both biological and technological methods of overcoming humanity's present limitations. In time, as we acquire greater knowledge of the neurochemical components of every emotion or thought and type of behaviour, we shall be able to modify human nature. Given the potential abuse of this knowledge, codes of ethics ought to be formulated sooner rather than later. Whether our future will be trans-human is at present highly debatable: 'Far from being an exhausted concept or failed project, being human is a question whose possibilities are very much open to intellectual inquiry and practical realization.'[548] Deciding whether we shall cross humankind's innate boundaries may be our ultimate ethical challenge.

3.7

Reaching Higher States of Being: Reflectivity and Morality

Recent neuroscientific discoveries have shown that human beings lack innate morality. To a significant extent, our moral compass is shaped by our environment and fluctuates according to the dictates of self-interest. There is evidence, however, that reasoning can disrupt our imminent biases and allow us to move beyond self-interest to make moral decisions, which consider not only our own well-being but also that of others, even those with whom we have no particular relationship. However, the human capacity for reason cannot flourish unless our basic survival needs and need for dignity are satisfied. People should have not only enough food to eat, access to clean water, sanitation, shelter and physical security, but also a sense of belonging and a positive self-identity.

This chapter discusses in more detail the nature of moral judgements, briefly outlined at the beginning of Part 3. It focusses on the role reflectivity can play in this process. It begins by clarifying what reflectivity actually implies before presenting key scientific findings on the topic of human morality.

3.7.1. Reflectivity

Reflectivity has to do with the self's relation to itself and to the world. We may conceive of it as a conscious mental act rather than an involuntary response to external stimuli.[549] Reflectivity suggests an active subject, in Kant's sense, and entails conscious judgements. Kant's notion of selfhood was centred on autonomy – the self-attained freedom achieved by following laws devised through the self's own rational thought.[550] As Jerrold Seigel notes, 'Such selfhood was universal in that all rational individuals were, in principle, equally capable of achieving it, and all did so by following the same rules.'[551] Reflectivity, thus, seems to offer the hope of going beyond our instinctive impulses and, through this process, reaching some kind of higher self.

Nietzsche's notion of the *Übermensch* is also indicative of the autonomy implied in reflectivity. He argued that only a different way of thinking of ourselves and our relationship to the world could help us to move towards a higher form of human existence.[552] Reflectivity here is conceived as a means of escaping the constraints of established knowledge structures.

According to Buddhist philosophy, self-awareness can be achieved through the renunciation of self-interested desires. Although Buddhism posits that there is no unchangeable self, it assumes that a form of self-consciousness is attainable. Buddhism conceives of the human mind as a series of perceptions. This is reminiscent of Hume's notion of reality as originating in sense impressions, which then give rise to ideas and thoughts. For Hume, we cannot attain true knowledge of anything, including the self. Reflectivity in this case implies the reflective nature of consciousness, rather than cognition of a fixed self.[553]

In short, reflectivity has been conceived in various ways. Most approaches associate it with the capacity to determine who we are and to what we ought to aspire. Yet, the role attributed to reflectivity varies according to the relative emphasis placed either on biological traits or on the environment. My own approach posits that reflectivity allows us to override our innate biases and produce more impartial and less egoistic moral judgements. I stress the role of the environment in helping us to develop our reflective abilities.

3.7.2. Morality

Long before the advent of modern neuroscience, the nature of moral judgements was a central area of inquiry across disciplines, especially philosophy. As I discussed above, Kant regarded our capacity for reason as a defining characteristic of humanity, and he considered morality to be a result of our faculty of reason. The prime tenet of Kantian ethics is that humankind progresses from bondage to instinct to rational and moral behaviour. Kant equated genuine morality with conscious altruism, implying true good will.[554] In the Kantian worldview, all duties or obligations can be separated into two kinds of imperative: hypothetical and categorical. The former refers to end/means reasoning, that is, if you want A, do B. The latter relates solely to ends, that is, simply do B. Moral obligations, according to Kant, should be considered categorical imperatives.[555] Hume, conversely, regarded morality as contingent on feelings and desires, rather than being rooted in our rational will. In the Humean sense, vice and virtue are not objects to be discovered. Morality cannot be attained by the application of reason as it is driven by emotions. Since we are likely to have different feelings and desires, moral principles are likely to vary.[556]

Over the past few decades, a lot of scholarly attention has been devoted to studying the brain structures involved in moral judgements. Neuroscientific methods have been employed to probe, among other things, whether human beings possess an innate moral faculty. As Chapter 2.4 recounted, Hauser argues that at least a limited set of moral principles (i.e. a 'moral grammar') is innate inside us.[557] In his view, we make moral judgements instinctively, without immediate recourse to reason: 'When we judge an action as morally right or wrong, we do so instinctively, tapping a system of unconsciously operative and inaccessible moral knowledge.'[558] The things children refrain from doing, for example, are not always what adults have corrected. In Hauser's view, one of the principal reasons for this is that children are drawing on an innate moral repertoire which is not learnt. The full extent of this repertoire is not accessible to conscious reflection.[559]

The idea that we are born with a universal moral grammar is heartening. It suggests that, despite cultural differences which inform how we view the world, we, as human beings, all possess the same moral repertoire at some basic level. Hauser writes: 'Appreciating the fact that we share a universal moral grammar, and that at birth we could have acquired any of the world's moral systems, should provide us with a sense of comfort, a sense that perhaps we can understand each other.'[560] An important dimension of Hauser's thesis is the notion of parametric variation,[561] which refers to how our universal 'Language of Thought' is externalised through a myriad of different but similar variations.[562] While he argues that a universal moral grammar exists and unites humankind, he, nonetheless, allows for variations to exist within this overarching formula. Put differently, although we may have a common moral grammar, specific moral 'languages' or systems can be generated from it. Therefore, a plurality of moral systems is possible.

This notion is also supported in a 2007 article by Jorge Moll and colleagues, in which they argue that human beings possess a natural sense of fairness which informs social practices. Using fMRI, they show that regions of the brain which are vital to social behaviour and perception, such as the lateral superior temporal cortex, are stimulated when we make moral judgements. They, therefore, conclude that we might automatically attach moral values to social events.[563]

Appealing though it may be, there are good reasons for rejecting the idea of an innate morality. Numerous studies have shown that our moral judgements shift in response to different circumstances and have no objective validity. Here, an issue of considerable interest has been the role of emotions in generating and altering moral judgements. Prinz, for example, argues that emotions, rather than universal moral principles, are the inputs for moral judgements and can shift such judgements from positive to negative.[564] He maintains that, in order to judge that something is morally wrong, it is necessary to feel antipathy towards it.[565] There is much empirical support for the view that emotions are involved in moral judgements.[566] Research shows, for example, that key areas of the brain, which are related to emotions and which are normally operational in moral judgements, are found to be impaired in anti-social individuals. Feelings of what is morally correct are dysfunctional in members of this group as a result of a lack of adequate emotional input.[567] In other words, the inability to experience emotions impedes our capacity to make decisions, including moral judgements.[568]

Although most scholars agree that emotions can increase the intensity of moral judgements, a few do question whether emotions can generate them.[569] I would argue, however, that there is undeniable evidence that emotions do not merely amplify moral judgements but play a crucial role in steering our moral compass. As demonstrated by Jonathan Haidt and his collaborators, inducing emotions can alter our moral judgements. One of their studies found, for example, that subjects seated at a dirty desk considered certain vignettes to be more morally wrong than subjects seated at a clean desk. Likewise, they found that hypnotically induced disgust provoked more stringent moral positions. Similarly, the research conducted by Joshua Greene suggests that modulation of the emotional response to a moral dilemma can change a moral judgement.[570]

To repeat, the link between emotions and moral judgements must not be mistaken for an innate morality. Rather, the aforementioned research confirms the shifting nature of our moral compass, showing that it provides no universal reference to an objectively good path.

Studies on stress, too, confirm the fragile nature of our moral compass and the power of circumstances to steer it. They demonstrate that, in the face of moral dilemmas, we make more egocentric decisions when we feel stressed.[571]

While individuals may be equipped with an inborn sense of fairness, empathy and sensitivity to social norms, their moral judgements depend on a complex combination of cognitive, emotional and motivational mechanisms, which are shaped by socialisation in specific cultural contexts and are, therefore, not just a product of nature but also of nurture.[572] As a result, moral judgements express subjective attitudes rather than objective moral facts.

Even emotions (such as empathy) which are conducive to our moral sensitivities do not necessarily make us better human beings. Empathy, for example, often leads us to make terribly unjust decisions, since it 'is spontaneously biased to individuals who are spatio-temporally close, as well as discriminatory in other ways, and incapable of accommodating large numbers of individuals'.[573] If our emotions are largely biological in origin, then they are likely to reflect the environment in which human beings evolved. This environment would have been composed of dispersed groups, and our strongest relationships would have been with kin. In this case, altruistic behaviour would have been directed at people whom we knew and to whom we were attached, and not at distant members of some other group. In other words, even if we have some inborn moral sensitivities, they are very limited in terms of their application, since they would most likely be stimulated differently by situations which concern our kin and by those which relate to someone we consider 'other'.

To sum up, recent neuroscientific discoveries demonstrate that human beings lack any innate morality. We are born amoral. Indeed, human beings will do whatever they have to in order to preserve the self, in accordance with our egoistic nature. For all our limitations, however, we can correct the bias which shrouds our empathy and moral judgements by employing our capacity for reason. Under the influence of conscious reflection, we can develop moral codes which may be applied to a much wider community than our instincts normally allow. This is particularly important in today's world, in which we are in much closer contact with people with whom we have no direct relationship, i.e. distant 'others', and towards whom we are asked to be charitable and to aid.

Morality, in most instances, is dependent on the satisfaction of basic survival needs (related to sustenance, physical safety, sexual relations) and the need for dignity, which I discuss in more detail in the next chapter. If a person suffers from chronic and persistent worries about his or her physical safety, or where the next meal is coming from, it is unlikely that he or she will act in a truly altruistic manner (i.e. conscious altruism). Once basic survival needs and the basic requirements for dignity have been provided for, however, people may be capable of acting in a moral way.[574] Whether an individual does act in a moral way when his or her survival is not at stake, will depend on individual character traits, upbringing and education, that is, on environmental factors, and not just on genetic ones.[575] The environment plays a crucial role in fostering our capacity for reflection, which in turn enables us to arrive at less biased, less egocentric moral judgements. There is strong evidence that reasoning can disrupt affect-driven and biased processes of moral judgement formation either by upfront conscious control, or by deliberative *post hoc* correction.[576] Education and culture are, thus, of major importance in shaping our moral obligations and capacity for reflection. Indeed, they can enable us to recognise our limits and use reason to go beyond them. They can encourage us to strive towards ideals and shape a better future.

* * *

To conclude, I believe that reflectivity presents us with a way of overcoming the present amoral and egoistic limits of humanity. Reflectivity may be conceived of as that part of selfhood which denotes intellectual self-awareness. It implies an active subject, capable of deploying transformative energy in the service of human advancement. Importantly, reflectivity is possible, although not inevitable, when our psychological and physiological needs have been taken care of. Since human beings are not innately endowed with moral principles, the sociopolitical environment plays a key role in fostering 'true' morality in the Kantian sense of the word. Most of us will learn what is considered moral in a particular society and will conform to this in order to flourish within that society. This has important implications because it places the responsibility on society and the species as a whole and not just on the single individual. The next chapter will focus in depth on the sociopolitical context required for humanity to thrive.

Situating the General Theory of Emotional Amoral Egoism

Having reviewed existing approaches to human nature and discussed my neurophilosophical account of emotional amoral egoism, I shall now situate my theory in relation to its historical antecedents. It would be beyond the scope of this book to compare all prior theories with my own. Table 1, therefore, focusses on the major contributions to the debate on human nature, without claiming exhaustiveness in terms of detail and contributors. Rather, it aims to provide a thumbnail sketch of some of the most influential positions in order to highlight how they compare and contrast with the conception of human nature expounded in this book.

In outlining a general theory of human nature and a specific theory of human motivation, I have aimed to construct a comprehensive approach. Like Maslow, who relied on the idea of a hierarchy of needs to address the complexity of human life, I have sought to conceive of the whole range of elements which characterise human existence when thinking about human motivations. My specific theory of human motivation reconsiders humanity's major drivers in light of recent findings coming from the neurosciences. Like Maslow, I also argue that basic human survival needs must be satisfied before human beings are likely to act on the basis of conscious reflection and morality. Where my theory of emotional amoral egoism differs from Maslow's hierarchy of human needs is in its consideration of both the physiological and the psychological determinants of an individual's psyche and behaviour.

Moreover, I have adopted a multi-disciplinary approach which draws on religious, philosophical, psychological, evolutionary, biological, sociobiological and neuroscientific insights.

Emotional amoral egoism also offers a cross-cultural perspective on human nature as it assumes that a great deal of what motivates human beings is connected to genetically coded survival instincts which are manifested through neurochemically-mediated emotions. Since emotions are universal, as Darwin noted with a great deal of foresight, much of what makes us who we are is not determined by any specific cultural context. As I illustrated in Chapters 3.2 and 3.5, while our genetic make-up is largely the same, tiny variations in our genes help to account for individual differences. In identifying this point, I share some common ground with Nietzsche, who recognised the role of specific individual inclinations, which he captured with the notion of the superman or *Übermensch*, who strives for the supreme realisation of himself. In my view, however, our genetic heritage helps account more for the similarities in human motivation than the differences. Plato, too, highlighted the role that genetics (without, of course, using this term) play in shaping human nature. In his view, a person's capacity to realise his/her transcendental self by overcoming falsehoods and illusions is dependent on intellectual capacities, which I also recognise. However, I believe that such differences, which stem from tiny genetic variations, account for only a small part of human nature. The role of intellect in shaping human behaviour is not as significant as that of genetically coded survival instincts which, as I have stressed, are intrinsic in our egoistic nature. Given the power of instincts, human beings are more inclined to be 'bad' than 'good' as they pursue their general self-interest, which their egoistic nature makes them prone to do. As mentioned before, I use the term 'bad' to describe human behaviour which inflicts physical or emotional harm on others. By 'good', I refer to behaviour which considers not only our own personal well-being, but also that of other living beings and the environment, demonstrating respect for key moral principles, such as honesty, fairness and inclusion. Since the actions of human beings will be instinctively triggered by their desire to survive, they will be more inclined to carry out actions which benefit them, irrespective of the broader consequences.

Accordingly, the theory of emotional amoral egoism places greater weight on emotions than reason. It is, therefore, clearly distinct from approaches to human nature which prioritise reason as a major motivating factor of human behaviour. The latter include the thoughts of Aristotle, who held that the purpose of humankind is to use reason in the pursuit of a virtuous and, thus, happy life. In his view, people can overcome desire by employing reason and are, therefore, by implication, ultimately free to choose how to behave. Similarly, Kant believed that it is the human capacity for rational thought which enables moral agency. He considered the capacity for reason to be the source of humans' uniqueness among animals.

In stressing the centrality of emotions in human experience, my position is closer to that of Machiavelli, Hobbes, Hume, Bentham, Darwin, Kierkegaard, Freud, Lorenz, Skinner and Maslow. On the question of whether moral judgements stem from emotions or reason, I agree with Hume. Writing well before the advent of genetic and neurobiological research, Hume argued that moral judgements were prompted by emotions rather than reason, which could not be viewed as the sole source of virtue and happiness and was, instead, a 'slave to the passions'. Thanks to advances in brain-imaging technologies, we now know that emotions are neurochemically mediated. In other words, emotions are not simply reactions initiated by thoughts. Indeed, all of our thoughts, emotions and behaviour are reducible to neurochemical processes which are genetically coded. This does not mean that emotions are not influenced in some way by the environment. Indeed, Hume himself argued that, while many moral judgements are initiated by emotions, some (such as justice) may require direction by society.

Like Darwin, Wilson, Dawkins, Pinker and de Waal, whose theories I analysed in Chapter 2.4, I believe that humankind's genetic make-up plays a fundamental role in shaping our psyche and behaviour. Since human beings, by and large, have the same genetic make-up, all of humankind is motivated by the same drives, the Neuro P5. Cultural arrogance, bias, injustice, exceptionalism and exclusion are, therefore, not only unfounded but misguided, and hinder humankind's potential for synergistic progress and prosperity. Indeed, cultural and ethnic diversity, which contributes to what I call 'cultural vigour', is an advantage to humankind's future survival, strength and excellence, just as molecular/genetic diversity in nature produces 'hybrid vigour' and, thus, strength, resilience and the potential for a future of fewer diseases.[577]

While acknowledging the role of nature, I also believe that the totality of our environment has a significant impact on our behaviour. Thus, in Chapter 3.2 I explained how a person's personal upbringing and education as well as social, cultural and global conditions all help to shape who he or she is. This associates my thinking closely with the likes of Locke, who believed that the human mind could be thought of as a clean slate or *tabula rasa* and that humankind possessed no innate ideas or principles. For Locke, the human psyche was shaped exclusively by experience. I do not share the view that human behaviour is entirely based on experience, given that we are driven by survival instincts which are largely genetically coded and expressed through emotions. In my view, it is more accurate to say that the human mind is a predisposed *tabula rasa*,[578] that is, predisposed through the presence of an in-built mechanism which dictates certain behaviour designed to ensure our survival. Human nature, in this sense, has a baseline in nature but is shaped through nurture. Like Locke, I attribute some importance to the human capacity for reason, although a comparatively small proportion of what drives humankind can be attributed to reason, as compared to genetically coded survival instincts. Recent findings of neuroscience show that we have free will and are, therefore, responsible for our actions. However, in no sense are we radically free to choose who we are in the sense described by existentialists such as Sartre and Kierkegaard, since we are by nature egoistic and non-rational beings.

In addition, and in the light of recent discoveries made by neuroscience, I argue that humankind is amoral. By amoral I mean that human beings lack an innate understanding of good and evil, as their moral judgements shift according to circumstances and have no objective validity. My conception of human nature differs in this respect from, for example, Hobbes' vision of human nature, as I assume psychological egoism to be the primary characteristic of humankind. I also depart from scholars (such as Hauser) who argue that morality is innate in human beings. As mentioned before, we have some pro-social emotions (such as empathy) from which moral codes can be developed through conscious reflection, as de Waal suggests. Yet this does not imply that morality is innate, especially as our pro-social affinities are often biased towards in-group members.

Often, what we may interpret as altruism is more likely to be 'pseudo-altruism'[579] – indeed, at some level, all apparently altruistic acts are related to a broadly defined idea of general self-interest. This does not necessarily mean that they do not serve the individual, society or the human species as a whole. However, only in conditions of relative political stability (which are, therefore, entirely different from the Hobbesian state of nature) where the individual's basic requirements for dignity are satisfied, can we expect moral behaviour to be widespread. Anarchy and situations of near anarchy must, therefore, be prevented at all costs. Such situations, in which one can only count on oneself and one's own actions in order to survive, engender a sense of fear which triggers aggression, brutality and injustice. These pre-emptive reactions are a function of the basic wiring of our emotional, amoral and egoistic nature, designed to alert us to danger, protect us from harm and ensure our survival, whatever the cost to anyone around us. Even in non-anarchic situations, survival instincts are very powerful and may be incited instantaneously, prompting aggressive behaviour. Indeed, very few human beings act selfishly or unfairly towards others out of sheer enjoyment, but rather do so out of fear for themselves or the people they care about the most. The next chapter explains how inclusiveness and confidence-building measures can avoid triggering these mechanisms which are so deeply ingrained in our neuropsychology.

Table 1 compares some of the most influential approaches which have been taken to theorising human nature. Again, the table is not intended to be comprehensive, but rather to provide a general overview of the central ideas of some of the key thinkers discussed earlier. A dash indicates that a particular facet of human nature or motivation is either not discussed or considered insignificant in a key thinker's theory, whereas one tick indicates that a specific facet is viewed as important. Two ticks mean that a facet is considered very important. I hope this table will help the reader to situate my ideas in relation to those from the past which have influenced them, and to compare and contrast my thoughts with that of other great thinkers.

Table 1: A Comparison of Approaches to Human Nature

	PLATO (472-347 BCE)	ARISTOTLE (384-322 BCE)	CONFUCIUS (551-479 BCE)	MACHIAVELLI (1469-1527)	HOBBES (1588-1679)	LOCKE (1632-1704)
1. MOTIVATIONS						
I Permanency	✓	—	✓	✓✓	✓✓	✓
II Power, Fear or Fear-Induced Aggression	✓	✓	—	✓✓	✓✓	—
III Pride	✓	✓	✓	✓✓	✓✓	—
IV Pleasure	✓	✓	✓	—	—	—
V Profit	✓	✓	✓	✓✓	✓✓	—
VI Specific Individual Inclinations	—	—	—	—	—	—
VII Reason	✓✓	✓✓	✓	—	✓	✓✓
VIII Reflection and Moral Sensitivity	✓✓	✓	✓	—	✓	✓
2. EMOTIONS	✓	✓	—	✓✓	✓✓	—
3. GENETIC MAKE-UP	Inherited Traits	—	—	—	—	—
4. HETEROGENEOUS VARIATIONS AND PERSONALITY TRAITS	—	—	—	—	—	—
5. NEUROCHEMISTRY	—	—	—	—	—	—
6. ENVIRONMENTAL INFLUENCES	✓	✓✓	✓	✓	✓	✓✓ Tabula Rasa
7. BEHAVIOURAL MODIFICATION	—	—	✓	—	✓	—
8. MORALITY	✓	✓	✓	—	—	✓

— Not mentioned or not significant
✓ Important
✓✓ Very important

The facets of human nature shown in the table do not necessarily represent the totality of the concepts as originally proposed by some of the thinkers. With this qualification in mind, the table should be read as a means of distinguishing the differences between thinkers, albeit according to the parameters of 'emotional amoral egoism'.

	HUME (1711-76)	ROUSSEAU (1712-78)	KANT (1724-04)	BENTHAM (1748-32)	DARWIN (1809-82)	KIERKEGAARD (1813-55)
1. MOTIVATIONS						
I Permanency	✓	✓	✓	✓	✓✓	—
II Power, Fear or Fear-Induced Aggression	✓✓	—	—	✓✓	✓✓	—
III Pride	—	—	—	✓✓	—	—
IV Pleasure	—	✓	—	✓✓	—	—
V Profit	—	✓	—	—	✓✓	—
VI Specific Individual Inclinations	✓✓	—	—	✓	✓✓	—
VII Reason	—	—	✓✓	✓	—	✓
VIII Reflection and Moral Sensitivity	✓	✓✓	✓	✓	—	✓✓
2. EMOTIONS	✓✓	✓	✓	✓✓	✓✓	✓✓
3. GENETIC MAKE-UP	—	✓	✓	—	Phenotype	—
4. HETEROGENEOUS VARIATIONS AND PERSONALITY TRAITS	—	—	—	—	✓✓	—
5. NEUROCHEMISTRY	—	—	—	—	—	—
6. ENVIRONMENTAL INFLUENCES	—	✓	✓✓	✓	✓	✓✓
7. BEHAVIOURAL MODIFICATION	—	—	—	—	—	—
8. MORALITY	✓	✓	✓	✓	✓	✓✓

—   Not mentioned or not significant
✓   Important
✓✓ Very important

	MARX (1818-83)	NIETZSCHE (1844-1900)	FREUD (1856-1939)	LORENZ (1903-89)	SKINNER (1904-90)	SARTRE (1905-80)
1. MOTIVATIONS						
I Permanency	—	—	✓✓	✓✓	—	—
II Power, Fear or Fear-Induced Aggression	—	—	✓✓	—	—	✓
III Pride	—	—	✓✓	—	—	—
IV Pleasure	—	—	✓✓	—	—	—
V Profit	✓	✓	✓	✓✓	✓✓	—
VI Specific Individual Inclinations	—	✓✓ Will to Power	✓✓	—	—	—
VII Reason	✓	—	—	✓✓	✓✓	—
VIII Reflection and Moral Sensitivity	—	✓	✓	✓✓	✓✓	✓✓
2. EMOTIONS	✓	—	✓✓	✓✓	✓✓	✓
3. GENETIC MAKE-UP	—	✓✓	✓✓	✓✓	—	—
4. HETEROGENEOUS VARIATIONS AND PERSONALITY TRAITS	—	—	✓✓	✓✓	—	—
5. NEUROCHEMISTRY	—	—	—	—	—	—
6. ENVIRONMENTAL INFLUENCES	✓✓	—	✓✓	✓✓	✓✓	—
7. BEHAVIOURAL MODIFICATION	—	—	✓✓	—	✓✓	—
8. MORALITY	—	—	✓	—	—	—

—   **Not mentioned or not significant**
✓   **Important**
✓✓   **Very important**

	MASLOW (1908-70)	RAWLS (1921-2002)	WILSON** (1975)	DAWKINS (1976)	PINKER (1997)	SINGER (2000)
1. MOTIVATIONS						
I Permanency	✓✓	✓	—	✓✓	✓	✓
II Power, Fear or Fear-Induced Aggression	✓✓	—	—	—	—	—
III Pride	✓✓	—	—	✓	—	—
IV Pleasure	✓✓	—	—	—	—	—
V Profit	✓	—	—	—	—	—
VI Specific Individual Inclinations	✓✓	—	—	—	—	—
VII Reason	✓✓	—	—	—	✓✓	—
VIII Reflection and Moral Sensitivity	✓	✓	✓	✓	✓	✓
2. EMOTIONS	✓✓	—	—	✓	—	—
3. GENETIC MAKE-UP	—	—	✓✓	✓✓	✓✓	—
4. HETEROGENEOUS VARIATIONS AND PERSONALITY TRAITS	—	—	✓✓	✓✓	—	—
5. NEUROCHEMISTRY	—	—	—	—	—	—
6. ENVIRONMENTAL INFLUENCES	✓✓	—	—	✓	—	—
7. BEHAVIOURAL MODIFICATION	✓✓	—	—	—	—	—
8. MORALITY	✓	✓✓ Justice as Fairness	—	—	—	✓

—   **Not mentioned or not significant**
✓   **Important**
✓✓ **Very important**

** from this point onwards, dates indicate key publications of contemporary thinkers

	DE WAAL (2006)	HAUSER (2006)	AL-RODHAN
1. MOTIVATIONS			
I Permanency	✓✓	✓	✓✓ Egoist (The Most Central Aspect of Human Nature)
II Power, Fear or Fear-Induced Aggression	✓✓	—	✓✓
III Pride	—	—	✓✓
IV Pleasure	—	—	✓✓
V Profit	✓	✓	✓
VI Specific Individual Inclinations	—	—	✓✓
VII Reason	—	✓	— Occasional Reason
VIII Reflection and Moral Sensitivity	✓✓	✓	— No Innate Morality and Infrequent Reflection
2. EMOTIONS	✓	✓	✓✓ Highly Emotional
3. GENETIC MAKE-UP	✓✓	✓✓	✓✓ In-Built Survival Code
4. HETEROGENEOUS VARIATIONS AND PERSONALITY TRAITS	✓✓	✓✓	✓✓ Highly Individualistic Differences
5. NEUROCHEMISTRY	—	—	✓✓ All Thoughts and Behaviour are Neurochemically Mediated
6. ENVIRONMENTAL INFLUENCES	—	—	✓ 'Predisposed *Tabula Rasa*'
7. BEHAVIOURAL MODIFICATION	—	—	✓ Highly Possible; Code of Ethics and Egalitarian Norms Required
8. MORALITY	✓✓	✓✓ Universal Moral Grammar	— 'Amoral' Individual, Societal and Global System are Collectively Responsible

—   **Not mentioned or not significant**
✓   **Important**
✓✓ **Very important**

Part 4

The Security Implications of the Theory of Emotional Amoral Egoism

Today's security landscape is shaped by unprecedented complexity. The ongoing Covid-19 pandemic, climate change, terrorism, cyber-crime and so much else pose global threats which bypass borders. Together, they create a multi-dimensional security environment which reaches well beyond the physical world into the virtual realm. In the coming decades, climate change, technological advances and shifts in population and power will profoundly reshape our world. Interdependencies between economies and countries will proliferate at an overwhelming pace.[580] The costs of the pandemic will be shouldered disproportionately by the economically disadvantaged. As a result, social grievances and tensions will rise and so will competition for resources. With this as the backdrop, the preservation of peace, security and prosperity will become increasingly challenging.

Understanding human nature is key to tackling today's and tomorrow's security challenges. However, how exactly can neuroscience be harnessed to improve domestic, global and technological security? Readers will remember that neurophilosophy draws on neuroscientific insights to address questions with which philosophy has traditionally concerned itself. The start of the neurophilosophy movement is commonly dated to 1986 with the publication of Patricia Churchland's pioneering *Neurophilosophy: Toward a Unified Science of the Mind-Brain*.[581] Churchland was among the first to feed neuroscientific findings into philosophical attempts to conceptualise and explain human behaviour. Whilst the field of neurophilosophy continues to define itself, I hope to push it into new territory by deploying a neurophilosophical lens to analyse the traditional objects of political discourse.

Acknowledging who we are and what we need to thrive is of paramount importance for knowing how to arrange our collective life to unlock humanity's positive potential. Whether people will act with regard for the well-being of others depends significantly on the prevailing norms and practices of their environment. As I argue in this section of the book, sustainable improvements in the human condition can only unfold in a context that reconciles the ever-present tension between the need for human dignity and the emotional amoral egoism innate within us all. By *dignity*, I do not refer to the mere absence of humiliation, nor do I exclusively mean the inherent worth of every human being. Rather, I use this term to describe a particular set of nine universal and timeless human needs: *reason, security, human rights, accountability, transparency, justice, opportunity, innovation* and *inclusiveness*. Part 4 begins by introducing a new good-governance paradigm, which I call dignity-based governance and which is capable of: (1) countering human amorality with justice, accountability and transparency; (2) channelling human egoism to benefit society through opportunity, inclusiveness and innovation; and (3) assuaging vitriolic human emotionality by providing security, safeguarding human rights and fostering a society based on reason. Dignity-based governance is the prerequisite of what I call *sustainable history*, that is, lasting improvement in the human condition (see Diagram 6).

The remainder of Part 4 uses my theory of emotional amoral egoism to pave the way for a richer understanding of some key issues for our current security landscape. Chief among them is the impact of globalisation on identity formation (see Chapter 4.2). Globalisation has generated significant shifts in social, ideological and cultural constellations, thus unsettling previously established identities, as well as increasing the number of people navigating between various and competing ones. This creates challenges for both individuals and societies. Today, most of us work or live in culturally diverse environments. At the same time, the fear of the 'other' is nestled in our brains. It is a powerful reflex triggered by encounters with the unfamiliar, making us susceptible to ethnocentrism, cultural arrogance, bias and a sense of exceptionalism. Further, our natural inclination towards us-versus-them thinking is often instrumentalised for political purposes and can easily degenerate into xenophobia, ethnic tension and violent conflict, as I discuss in Chapters 4.3 and 4.4. Other pressing security concerns

Diagram 6: A New Governance Paradigm:
Dignity-Based Governance

Sustainable History

SUSTAINABLE HISTORY
propelled by
GOOD GOVERNANCE
that balances the
ever-present tension between

human nature attributes VS. human dignity needs

EMOTIONALITY ⟷ REASON, SECURITY & HUMAN RIGHTS

AMORALITY ⟷ ACCOUNTABILITY, TRANSPARENCY & JUSTICE

EGOISM ⟷ OPPORTUNITY, INNOVATION & INCLUSIVENESS

© Nayef Al-Rodhan 2020

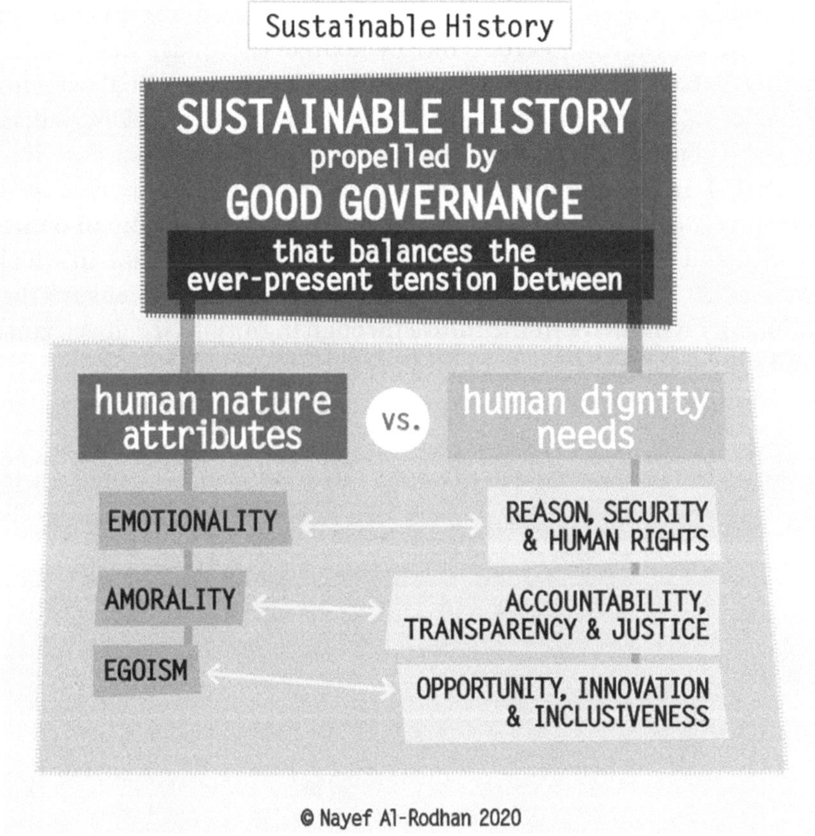

discussed in this section include fake news and big data, but also advances in synthetic biology and human enhancement technologies (see Chapter 4.5)

Dignity-based governance can help us address today's security challenges by unlocking the best in human behaviour and instilling in us greater concern for the welfare of others, distant as well as close. Global challenges, such as the worldwide spread of Sars-CoV-2, which is causing one of the worst pandemics in history,[582] remind us that we belong to a shared community of fate.[583] Yet, given that human beings have no inborn predisposition towards moral cosmopolitanism, dignity-based governance must extend our sense of moral obligation towards the distant 'other'. I explore this issue in greater detail in Chapter 4.6.

To shape history for the better, dignity-based governance must be ensured on both the domestic and global level and accompanied by harmonious interstate relations. These will be guided by the paradigm of *symbiotic realism*, which argues that, since states are interconnected and interdependent, in order to truly flourish they must seek absolute rather than relative gains in the way they conduct international relations. Chapter 4.7 sets out in more detail the implications of symbiotic realism in our turbulent international and interconnected world.

Part 4 illustrates the extent to which my theory of *emotional amoral egoism* provides a helpful lens to examine how human nature works, and how it is the architect of the security landscape in which we live. At the same time, it suggests a way forward to ensure that humanity will thrive in the future through dignity-based governance and symbiotic realism.

Dignity-Based Governance

The World Bank defines governance as:

> the traditions and institutions by which authority in a country is exercised. This includes the process by which governments are selected, monitored and replaced; the capacity of the government to effectively formulate and implement sound policies; and the respect of citizens and the state for the institutions that govern economic and social interactions among them.[584]

Governance as the term used in this chapter relates to both the domestic (within a nation or municipality) and the global levels. Global governance may be defined 'as a minimum framework of principles, rules and laws necessary to tackle global problems, which are upheld by a diverse set of institutions, including both international organisations and national governments'.[585] Gone are the days when security could be defined in state-centred terms. From climate change to the Covid-19 pandemic, today's major security threats respect no borders and require cooperation across countries and sectors.[586] Indeed, we are living in an era of instant connectivity and transnational dependencies. As David Held points out:

> [p]olitical events in one part of the world can rapidly acquire world-wide ramifications. Sites of political action can become embedded in extensive networks of political interaction involving states and nonstate actors. As a result,

developments at the local level – whether economic, social
or environmental – can acquire almost instantaneous global
consequences and vice versa.[587]

Globalisation has given rise to a security landscape of unprecedented
interconnectedness, blurring traditional distinctions between internal
and external threats. The Arab Spring is a case in point, highlighting
the complex interplay between domestic and international politics.
Among the grievances shared by many protesters was the general
frustration with foreign intervention in their domestic affairs (before
or during the protests) – or the complicity between their governments
and outside powers.[588]

Global problems are today not simply concerned with traditional
'high' politics of trade, power and security, but also with those which
have more often been thought of as 'low' political issues, such as
social, environmental and cultural concerns. Combating infectious
diseases, environmental degradation and managing relations between
diverse cultural groups, for instance, are now widely recognised as
global political issues which require increased communication and
cooperation.[589]

National governments alone cannot address many of today's security
challenges without supranational institutions. Only the latter can
establish frameworks for action which go beyond the narrow interests
of some states. Promoting good governance at the global level requires
active promotion of moral commitments towards people with whom
we have no direct contact. There are, of course, legal and regulatory
structures which have been shaped by moral duties in a broad sense, most
notably in the form of the United Nations' 1948 Universal Declaration
of Human Rights and the 1966 International Convention on Civil and
Political Rights, which hold that all people should be treated equally,
no matter where they reside or their origin.[590] However, with current
disparities in power, mechanisms for accountability at the international
level are still subject to the narrowly defined interests of powerful states
and geopolitical machinations.[591] In addition, the number of states and
agencies bound by the rule of law and international humanitarian law
needs to be enlarged.

As the line between domestic and international security challenges is
increasingly blurred, multiple levels of authority have been developing.
Indeed, although states retain legal sovereignty over their territories,
political power is shared between a variety of different actors, as well

as formal and informal institutionalised fora and networks. As a result, sites of political activity are proliferating, as are the number of people involved in shaping our security landscape.[592]

Prevailing global governance structures are frequently perceived to be suffering from an accountability deficit among states, and between state and non-state actors.[593] Arrangements to promote dialogue between non-state actors and states are also perceived to be inadequate. Multilateral bodies are often not representative of all the states which are members of them. The problem is not simply one of representation as such (although this is certainly something which has to be addressed) but also of *effective* representation. Some delegations may be more stretched as a result of having fewer resources, for instance.[594]

In light of this, systems of global governance need to be reformed to be more effective in addressing the major challenges of our age. A range of transnational security threats – climate change being the most momentous – have been building for years with disastrous consequences. Systems of domestic governance also need reform. According to the International Monetary Fund, over 50 per cent of countries and close to 90 per cent of advanced economies have witnessed a rise in income inequality over the past three decades.[595] Within numerous countries, populist politicians have exacerbated divisions through, for example, the securitisation of migration or religion, with nefarious implications for relations between cultural groups.[596] In effect, this has turned topics linked to migration, identity and culture, among others, into matters of (national) security. Artificial intelligence and other frontier technologies are likely to deepen existing inequalities, by offering opportunities only to those with the necessary capital, education, infrastructure or skills.[597] A global gender equality gap continues to deny women basic human rights, including access to education, healthcare and employment.[598] One in six children worldwide lives in a conflict zone.[599] The marginalisation of migrants and other minorities further hampers growth and creates socioeconomic grievances and political tensions. Such national, regional and global disparities are bound to have security and stability implications. They contribute to crime, terrorism and violence.[600] In addition, rapid change is unsettling people's identities and ways of life. For a safer world, we need to rethink our governance models, both domestically and globally.[601]

As previously stated, dignity-based governance brings with it the key to solving a variety of challenges facing humankind today, ranging from policy decisions concerning transformative technologies, fake news,

Big Data and even what we have come to know as social distancing to globalisation and radicalisation, as well as the rise in xenophobia, all of which I shall explore in more depth in the remaining chapters of the book. Before doing so, however, I shall use the remainder of this chapter to focus on the broader implications of dignity-based governance. Acknowledging our emotional nature provides us with a deeper understanding of the many security challenges we face. Indeed, it is often in contexts of fear and deprivation that politicians can easily manipulate us by capitalising on our negative emotions. The racist backlash against refugees, for example, illustrates how the fear of the unknown can swiftly induce responses in the form of pre-emptive aggression.[602] As a matter of fact, the fear of change, the challenge of evolving identities – be they national or cultural – is the root cause of many of the polarisation processes and tensions we are witnessing today.[603]

Yet, while humankind is predominantly driven by the dictates of self-interest, it also possesses the capacity for reason and conscious reflection. This enables us to develop codes of moral behaviour which oblige us to have regard for the well-being of others. For our capacity for reason to flourish, however, the right context is crucial. Circumstances largely determine whether our emotional amoral egoism is channelled into productive enterprises aimed at serving the public good, or whether our self-interest is pursued at the expense of others. Conditions of violence, fear, insecurity and poverty will induce more survival-oriented defensive or pre-emptive aggressive actions, as humans are genetically hardwired to pursue their survival at all costs. By contrast, good governance can unlock the positive potential found in our DNA.

What do I mean by good governance? First, I do *not* mean a uniform adoption of Western models of liberal democracy. Indeed, we should be careful not to idealise democracy in its current form, nor to hail it as the guarantor of human thriving or ultimate harbinger of peace. For all their merits, today's democracies face a gauntlet of economic, technological and cultural challenges resulting from policies devised with little understanding of human nature.[604] Even in the most mature liberal democracies, political freedom coexists with alienation, discrimination, injustice and marginalisation. For example, recent research has found that, within the United Kingdom, minority groups, such as the Asian and Black ethnic communities, are three times more likely to die of Covid-19.[605] Research of this kind, thus, highlights how, everywhere in the world, people can simultaneously have ample freedom and, at the same time, be severely disempowered. It was with this exact mindset that, in 1997, Arthur M. Schlesinger Jr. (1917–2007), rightly observed:

'Democracy has survived the twentieth century by the skin of its teeth. It will not enjoy a free ride through the century to come.'[606] Economic, technological and cultural pressures over the past few decades have provided fertile breeding ground for populist movements threatening the world's leading democracies.[607]

To rectify the shortcomings of today's democracies and foster the best in human behaviour, governance models must prioritise not just political freedom, but human dignity.[608] However, although dignity is, in fact, the single best predictor of sustainable improvements in the human condition, the vast majority of indexes and indicators of good governance fail to take it into account.[609] Human dignity as understood in this book is guaranteed by nine minimum criteria, specifically: *reason, security, human rights, accountability, transparency, justice, opportunity, innovation* and *inclusiveness*.[610] The definition of each criterion must be both universal and sensitive to cultural and historical specificities.

Of these nine dignity substrates, three in particular – reason, security and human rights – serve to curtail the destructive potential of human emotionality.[611] Reason, in this context, refers to the extent to which public institutions accept true facts and reasoned arguments, as opposed to regimes which deliberately spread false information and claim to hold an absolute monopoly on truth.[612] Indeed, not only are both of these essential for the promotion of democracy, but they are also a fundamental safeguard against regimes which try to rewrite history to suit their own policies and actions.[613] A good indicator for a reason-based society is the equal provision to all of access to education, especially when focussed on teaching critical thinking and newspaper and television literacy skills.

Another essential requirement for assuaging human emotionality is security, for it limits the possibility of fear-induced pre-emptive aggression which is likely to arise in a climate of insecurity where people face threats to their well-being.[614] Such threats may come from a variety of sources, including more traditional ones, such as terrorism, natural disasters and the state itself, as well as new kinds of threats ranging from pandemics to cyberattacks against critical infrastructure, to conflict in outer space,[615] to climate change.[616] Security must, therefore, be rethought in multi-sum and multi-dimensional terms. This means that global security and the security of any state cannot be achieved through zero-sum gains at the expense of others, nor can it be realised without good governance at the national, human, environmental, transnational and transcultural levels, all of which extend beyond the physical realm into the virtual space of the digital.[617]

Similarly, a commitment to human rights is key to satisfying basic physical and emotional needs, such as the need for a positive identity or freedom of thought, by protecting against degrading treatment and recognising the worth inherent in every person.[618]

Human amorality, in particular, must be countered with *accountability*, *transparency* and *justice*. Public institutions must be accountable and transparent in order to prevent abuses of power. Justice is ensured by a fair and well-governed judicial system which incentivises pro-social behaviour and establishes consequences to serve as deterrents for anti-social behaviour. Fundamentally, the judicial system must work equally for all sections of societies and must not function in a manner which applies justice relatively or discriminatively. Social injustices of any kind are antithetical to human dignity as they frustrate basic needs – access to health care, adequate food and clean water, for example. On the contrary, in a context in which public institutions prioritise the promotion of social cooperation, individuals are far more likely to evolve a moral compass which can steer them towards more altruistic and high-minded behaviour.[619] We also need actively to promote a cosmopolitan conception of morality, based on the assumption that all human beings possess equal moral worth, deserving of respect and concern by everyone.[620] The fact that we possess no innate morality, yet are prone to us-versus-them thinking, makes it all the more vital to promote the same rights and moral obligations for everyone.

Human egoism, on the other hand, must be channelled through opportunity, inclusiveness and innovation, all of which feed the individual's self-esteem and positive identity. Opportunity implies, above all, the provision of basic needs, including access to food, housing, clothing, health care, education and basic welfare. People from all segments of society should live in circumstances conducive to their positive physical, mental and social development. In addition, the natural egoism of all human beings can be productively harnessed through the kind of opportunities for professional, scientific and intellectual growth which foster an innovative society. Indeed, by enabling self-expression and the fulfilment of one's authenticity and ambition, innovation is able to constructively channel human egoism.[621]

The promotion of inclusiveness requires policy mechanisms which root out inequalities and marginalisation. By counteracting the resentment human beings experience when they feel 'left behind', inclusiveness reduces the risk of individuals giving into their egoism at the expense of others. It implies that all those affected by a public policy decision are part of the decision-making process. This is especially important as it confers ownership, consent and, therefore, legitimacy on the process, as well as enhances the appropriateness of the policy in meeting actual rather than perceived needs. Similarly, inclusiveness is a vital criterion for peace and security, because it offers the best chance of developing comprehensive approaches to problems. As explained previously, people have the need to feel a sense of belonging and the need for self-esteem. If the society in which they reside does not recognise their worth and does not respect them, it will be hard for the ego to reconcile the individual's inner needs with the social context, thus undermining both the needs for belonging and self-esteem. As a consequence, the individual is likely to seek comfort and refuge in other communities and to become alienated from the broader societal context. In the worst-case scenario, he or she may create the space needed to construct a 'self' which can only exist at the expense of others.[622] To avoid this, governments need to consciously promote national identities which embrace different cultural groups. Educational institutions arguably represent one of the best opportunities for promoting recognition of and respect for other cultures.[623] The newspapers, broadcasters and entertainment industry also play a crucial role in fostering respect for diversity, particularly in view of the advances made in information and communication technologies.

The connections between the nine dignity criteria and human nature can be operationalised and verified in practice. A few years ago, I proposed a 'dignity scale of sustainable governance', which broke down and quantified each of the nine basic requirements for dignity using a score from one to five, with one meaning the indicator is completely absent and five meaning which the particular indicator (i.e. the need for dignity) is fully integrated into society. To take one example, out of a sample of fifteen countries, Sweden was among those which fared best on this scale because it offers ample mechanisms for social integration and cohesion, extensive opportunities, accountable institutions and the rule of law.[624]

Great strides in improving the human condition can be made through the promotion of human dignity. Indeed, the circumstances we create domestically and globally will shape what gets enhanced or diminished in our nature. In conditions of instability and perceived vulnerability, our neurochemically-mediated emotions, as well as our amorality and especially our egoism, are more easily invoked to justify aggression, violence and narrow friend/enemy categorisations.[625] However, what I want the takeaway from this book to be is that we can work together on building a dignity-based environment where human beings are encouraged to act with concern not only for their own well-being, but also for the well-being of others and of the environment.

The remainder of Part 4 will illustrate what dignity-based governance means in practice. It will use the theory of emotional amoral egoism to advance understanding of some of the pressing security challenges we face today. In so doing, it will demonstrate how dignity-based governance can help us address these issues at both the national and global levels. It will begin by exploring the destabilising effects of globalisation on identity formation. In fact, many of the polarisation and radicalisation processes we are currently witnessing constitute in essence a revolt against globalisation. They are a desperate attempt by individuals to buttress their identities in an age of flux and uncertainty. The next section will explore this phenomenon in more detail, highlighting how dignity-based governance provides individuals with a positive and stable self-identity, thus reducing their susceptibility to extremist ideologies.

4.2

The Implications of the Theory of Emotional Amoral Egoism for Globalisation and Identity Construction

In the present era of globalisation, changes and transformations are underway which are disturbing people's habitual ways of making sense of the world. These changes, which began in the West and are now taking place elsewhere around the world, involve the restructuring of the global political economy and modifications to social constellations. These developments have been accompanied by shifts in ideological and cultural orientations. Against this backdrop, individuals are obliged to negotiate between their inner needs and a complex and fluid social world. In some instances, this may lead to unstable self-identities which fail to provide individuals with a sense of self-worth or of belonging, which are basic human requirements for success in any environment. Paradoxically, whilst globalisation knits the world together, rising levels of polarisation threaten to tear it apart. Many polarisation processes – such as those exacerbated by Brexit and Donald Trump – are widely perceived as a revolt against globalisation; they constitute an attempt by individuals and groups to buttress their identities and safeguard their culture.[626]

This chapter explores identity construction in the context of globalisation. It begins by briefly outlining how identities are constructed, in general. It then looks at identity formation in today's instant and interdependent world.[627] Whilst globalisation has exacerbated some of the socioeconomic factors which are conducive to radicalisation, support for extremist ideas cannot solely be explained by environmental factors. Nor is radicalisation the mere result of an individual pathology. There are certain mindsets which make individuals susceptible to extremist thinking, as I discuss further below. Finally, this chapter explores the ways dignity-based governance minimises people's susceptibility to extremist ideologies.

4.2.1. Identity Construction

In orthodox social science, knowledge is believed to be objective. In other words, it ought to be the product of reason and be free from values, politics and power.[628] This assumption began to be regarded as a problem, however, in the 1980s. It came to be recognised, as Robert Cox pointed out at the time, that 'theory is always for someone and for some purpose'.[629] Recent attempts to address the question of identity within the discipline emerged from discussions which took place in that decade.

Such attempts include social constructivist approaches arguing that individuals, groups and whole societies have malleable and multiple (cultural, racial, ethnic) identities which vary in salience across time and contexts.[630] These approaches stand in stark contrast to primordialism, which conceives of identity as fixed and pregiven.[631] Social constructivists reject the rationalist conception of knowledge and focus instead on discourse and practice. Human beings are taken to be, as Sheila Croucher has put it, 'socially embedded, communicatively constituted and culturally empowered'.[632] Therefore, social constructivists reject the notion that there are core or essential features of identity. For them, identity is something which is continually being constructed through linguistic exchange and social performance. They try to identify agents which sustain particular identity constructions, such as the family, schools and the mass media.[633]

Postmodernist scholars also see knowledge claims as intimately related to politics and power. Knowledge is not a purely cognitive process but a normative matter.[634] Discursive practices are thought to contribute to the production and reproduction of unequal power relations.[635] Many follow Foucault in using genealogy, which Richard Devetak explains is 'a style of historical thought which exposes and registers the significance of power–knowledge relations'.[636] This form of inquiry does not attempt to reveal an objective, timeless truth. Instead, a genealogical perspective emphasises that history is time- and place-specific. According to Foucault, history is plural, and sometimes contradictory, and the truth it tries to tell is not objective but is influenced by power dynamics. Genealogy is, therefore, used in an attempt to deconstruct particular representations of the past.[637]

Identity, for postmodernists, is not something stable to be discovered; instead, since it is fluid and dependent on where the self is located in history and culture, it is something to be explained. Postmodernists ask how identity is constructed. This implies a resistance to attributing essences to individuals or collectivities. Postmodernists explore how essentialist identity constructions take place. They deconstruct established identity categories and their related discourse. Discourse is not equated with truth, but may come to be established as truth, informing collective definitions, social arrangements and power relations. Postmodernists also identify variations within broad categories of identity (e.g. 'woman', 'indigenous group', 'scientist') as being as important as the variations between different categories, and focus on the discourses and practices which substitute a focus on threat for one on difference in the formation of political identity. As Devetak notes: 'There may be an irreducible possibility that difference will slide into opposition, danger, or threat, but there is no necessity.'[638]

Both approaches are useful in that they conceive of identity in non-essentialist terms: but what is identity? Identity is critical to how people make sense of the world and their experiences. It is implicated in self-representation and in social action. Manuel Castells defines identity as 'the process of construction of meaning on the basis of a cultural attribute, or related set of cultural attributes, which is given priority over other sources of meaning. For a given individual, or for a collective actor, there may be a plurality of identities.'[639] This definition is useful for its stress on multiple identities. If we think about our own identities, we should be able to discern that they comprise many elements.[640]

As Castells notes:

> The construction of identities uses building materials from history, from geography, from biology, from productive and reproductive institutions, from collective memory and from personal fantasies, from power apparatuses and religious revelations. But individuals, social groups, and societies process all these materials, and rearrange their meaning, according to social determination and cultural projects that are rooted in their social structure, and their space/time framework.[641]

Castells distinguishes between three types of identity construction: (1) legitimising identity, which helps to rationalise dominant institutions; (2) resistance identity, constructed by those who occupy devalued and/or stigmatised positions; and (3) project identity, generated by social actors who seek to transform the overall social structure.[642] Resistance identity, Castells suggests, may constitute the most important type of identity construction in today's societies. It provides a means of resisting what might otherwise be unbearable forms of oppression and of searching for a stable and independent identity. He suggests that it is likely to involve opposition to identities which have already been clearly defined by history, geography or biology, helping to essentialise this resistance identity.[643] Various kinds of radicalisms can be examples of resistance identities. The obvious risk associated with this kind of identity construction is the fragmentation of communities into 'tribes'. A resistance identity might, of course, in time become a process of legitimising identity or project identity construction. Exactly how and by whom different identities are constructed is dependent on the specificities of a social context, which means that identity politics must be situated historically.[644]

4.2.2. Identity in an Instant and Interdependent World

A number of scholars have been concerned with identity construction in the current era. Anthony Giddens, for example, speaks about identity construction in 'late modernity'. One of the key features of this historical period is viewed as the increasing linkage between two extremes: globalising tendencies, on the one hand, and personal dispositions, on the other. 'The more tradition loses its hold, and the more daily life is reconstituted in terms of the dialectical interplay of the local and the global, the more individuals are forced to negotiate lifestyle choices among a diversity of options.'[645]

Castells, while agreeing with some of Giddens' ideas about 'late modernity', argues that, for the majority of individuals in the age of globalisation, 'network society' is based on a disjuncture between the local and the global. This, he maintains, entails a loss of legitimising forms of identity construction and a disintegration of civil society. The search for meaning in this context largely takes place through the construction of resistance identities.[646]

Shmuel Noah Eisenstadt (1923–2010) identified a number of important changes which took place first in the West and are now under way in the rest of the world, which he linked to the idea of the existence of 'multiple modernities'.[647] First, there are 'structural, semi-liminal enclaves within which new cultural orientations – often couched in transcendental terms – tend to be developed and upheld, partially as counter-cultures, partly as components of new culture'.[648] These enclaves constitute spaces for often transitory radical movements, which may themselves become broader and more mainstream cultural orientations. Second, increased human mobility and changes related to global economic restructuring have resulted in new diasporic movements in the latter half of the twentieth century, such as Asian and Arab diasporas in Europe and the United States. Third, he identified a re-awakening and growth of self-consciousness in older diasporas, such as that of the Chinese across southeast Asia.[649]

Eisenstadt noted that these changes have been accompanied by a questioning of the Enlightenment belief in humankind's capacity to bring about continual progress and master nature through reason. In fact, as it has become increasingly clear, the belief in human rationality which recognises the value of plurality, whether in terms of cultural or moral systems, has been put to test over the past years.[650]

Eisenstadt's argument that globalisation gives rise to enclaves of cultural orientations may help to explain why more and more individuals create resistance identities around religion or ideological visions which seek to transform the present social order. Indeed, much has been written on radicalisation as both an individual and collective process of identity construction, as well as on the socioeconomic conditions motivating it. Much less well explored, however, is the mindset which makes individuals susceptible to certain kinds of extremism. After a brief discussion of environmental factors which propel radicalisation in the age of globalisation, I shall focus more narrowly on the neuroscience of extremism.

4.2.3. Globalisation and Radicalisation

Globalisation and corresponding changes in the global political economy are leading to profound changes for the role of religion and other institutions in society. According to Eisenstadt:

> This constellation was characterized by the paradoxical combination of, on the one hand, growing privatization of religious orientations and sensibilities, weakening of institutionalized religion and the official religious institutions,

with, on the other hand, the 'resurgence' of religious sensibilities, their move and transformation and transposition into the centres of national and international political activity, and in the constitution of collective identities.[651]

Significantly, Eisenstadt pointed out that this implied not simply a return to traditional society, but a far-reaching reconstitution of the religious dimension of culture and institutions.[652]

As I mentioned in Chapter 3.1.5, permanency constitutes a powerful drive. As a result, fear of death and the unknown, in addition to the pain of life – particularly if it is a life marked by loss, grief, and a lack of respect and recognition or hope – is likely to make extreme religion attractive, both because of its promise of transcendence and the sense it can provide of belonging to a broader community. Galina Soldatova suggests that, while we are continually constructing and experiencing the personal 'I' and the group 'We', transitional or crisis situations, as well as increased tensions in society, make it likely that an individual will seek refuge in a group identity as he or she seeks stability.[653] Promising belonging and stability, religious radicalism is likely to draw on what appear to be solid foundations (such as an eternal religious truth) to make the boundaries of identity more stable. For people living in contexts in which religion and familiar institutions appear to be losing their place, radicalism may, thus, seem appealing. Where the nation and state have lost ground, people may look to another broader community which offers a shared identity. For those outside the centres of power, the promise of not only a stable but also positive and empowering group identity is likely to be particularly appealing.

Radicalism has, of course, existed throughout much of human history but it appears to be particularly appealing in our present era.[654] It may start as an enclave for cultural/religious orientation, which enables a process of resistance identity formation, but it also has a project attached to it. Indeed, when we consider the basic needs of human beings, it is not surprising that continued inequality, injustice, alienation, fear and deprivation motivate some to satisfy their inner need for security and a sense of belonging and self-worth through a collective form of identity construction aimed initially at resistance and, later, at transformation of the self.

Thus, in an era which is marked by rapid change in political, socioeconomic and cultural spheres, unstable self-identities which fail to provide individuals with a sense of self-worth and belonging may lead to resistant forms of identity construction. These might take the form of radicalism, as people attempt to navigate between their inner ego needs and a fluid social context.

Dignity-based governance channels globalising forces in directions which minimise the extent of exclusion. At the national level, it ensures meaningful participation and representation of all citizens within a society, so that people from all cultural and religious backgrounds feel that they have a voice in society. In addition, it promotes inclusive national identities and combats discrimination by teaching tolerance and respect in schools, through the newspapers, broadasters and entertainment industry and political discourse. At the global level, dignity-based governance fosters greater inclusiveness through policies aimed at reducing structural inequalities between states and promoting inter-civilisational understanding and dialogue.

4.2.4. The Neuroscience of Radicalisation

Despite a wealth of research to the contrary, violent extremism still continues to be reduced by public discourse to either an individual pathology (such as a personality disorder or low IQ) or attributed to socioeconomic circumstances. The reality is much more complex, involving an interplay between internal and external factors.[655] An often-overlooked range of neurobiological predispositions underlies violent political extremism.

Diego Gambetta and Steffen Hertog argue, for example, that a particular mindset seeking cognitive closure (that is, seeking order and unambiguous truths) is a frequent trait among violent extremists. They also highlight the connection between political radicalisation and frustrated ambitions, the focus of relative deprivation theory, according to which, when people feel deprived of something which in their society is considered essential, they will organise or join movements aimed at obtaining it.[656] Our ambitions are a form of egoism and intimately linked to pride, one of the strongest motivators of human behaviour. Pride and permanency are, therefore, two powerful purveyors of neurochemical gratification which push terrorists to commit acts of violence in the quest for personal fulfilment and meaning.

Despite being born amoral, human beings create values for which we live and even die. Various studies stress the role of so-called sacred values in radicalisation processes. Sacred values are intrinsic to a person's identity and, thus, non-negotiable.[657] Research suggests that the propensity towards violence increases when extremist values become 'sacred'.[658] In the human brain, there are two areas which normally work in tandem: the dorsolateral prefrontal cortex, associated with deliberative reasoning and cost-benefit calculations, and the ventromedial prefrontal cortex, associated with subjective valuation. However, research shows that these two parts of the brain are disconnected in individuals who are ready to kill and die in the defence of their ideological and political views. In other words, such individuals no longer use decision control mechanisms which are normally involved in deliberative reasoning, including the dorsolateral prefrontal cortex's preference for the most equitable option against the temptation to maximise personal gain. Interestingly, social exclusion contributes to turning non-sacred values into sacred values, increasing the propensity for violence.[659] As mentioned before, when we feel vulnerable, excluded or marginalised, our egoism is more easily invoked to justify narrow friend/enemy categorisations. Feelings of exclusion are conducive to fear-induced pre-emptive aggression, as explained in Chapter 3.4.6.

In sum, radicalisation processes result from a complex interplay between neurobiological predispositions and social dynamics. Through its focus on inclusiveness, opportunity and reason, dignity-based governance allows vulnerable individuals to construct a positive identity through inclusion in the society they live in, thus minimising their susceptibility to violent extremist ideologies. In addition, by providing these individuals with the necessary education, it encourages critical thinking. All of these steps can, to a certain extent, disrupt the tendency towards cognitive closure.

Extremism is often associated with ethnocentrism, which describes the tendency to view one's own ethnic group as superior. Ethnocentrism merits closer attention as it is the root causes of many of today's security issues, including an increase in xenophobic sentiments which threaten to tear apart the fabric of our increasingly diverse societies. The next chapter will, therefore, focus on ethnocentrism, highlighting its neural basis and explaining how dignity-based governance can shape our innate in-group favouritism in a way which serves peaceful relations between people from different cultural backgrounds.

4.3

Xenophobia and Ethnocentrism

Today globalisation brings us more frequently into close contact with once-distant 'others'. If we are unaware of our innate fears and bias or the cultural systems which inform identity and behaviour, it can be all too easy to prejudge behaviour before we understand the basis for it. We may also be unaware of how some populist and nativist political leaders may choose to exploit these tendencies in order to drive division and hatred. This may lead to xenophobia and ethnocentrism. Both forms of behaviour may be the source of negative stereotypes, discrimination and the shaping of 'enemy others'. As such, xenophobia and ethnocentrism are related to some of our most serious social and security concerns. Populist leaders, for instance, often use the idea of 'the nation' as a marker of division and difference between human beings when trying to manipulate our predisposition for 'in-group favouritism' and 'out-group devaluation'.[660] As this chapter explores in greater depth, this tendency to distinguish between 'our' people and outsiders runs deep within us, being rooted in the neurochemical processes which underpin our capacity for empathy.[661]

As I have stressed, humankind is primarily driven by emotions, which are neurochemically mediated and derived largely from our genetic make-up. Indeed, human beings evolved specific emotions because they provided our ancestors with the best chance for survival. How we act on these instincts, however, depends on environmental factors, such as education and cultural orientations. A neurophilosophical understanding of human nature as shaped by the twin forces of nature and nurture helps explain the various forms our inborn in-group preferences may assume. This chapter discusses how xenophobia and ethnocentrism have been approached by others and then examines how we might understand these phenomena from a neurophilosophical perspective on human nature and how they may be counteracted through dignity-based governance.

4.3.1. Xenophobia

Soldatova writes that, historically, the arrival of strangers would have been considered an ill omen, since they would have been likely to have represented a threat to property and established ways of life. In modern society, xenophobia may relate to racial and ethnic phobias which lead to discrimination against members of a particular race or ethnic group, or religious phobias leading to fear of and prejudice towards believers in particular religions, or phobias against people who are different from the majority – for instance, against displaced groups and refugees. This human trait may be exploited for purposes of territorial gain, strengthening power or increasing capital and material resources.[662]

Xenophobia may be defined as a person's disposition to fear, or to deplore, other people or groups which are perceived as outsiders.[663] Indeed, although we always define ourselves through the metric of difference, this does not mean that difference has to be perceived as a threat or in other negative terms. When the differences between people are seen as a problem, they risk becoming a vector of discrimination, violence and conflict.[664] This is why xenophobia constitutes a security issue.

A number of approaches to xenophobia may be identified. From a functionalist perspective, it is the belief in the incapacity of immigrants and minorities to integrate into the host society which generates xenophobic behaviour on the part of the host population. This incapacity, it is argued, leads minorities to seek refuge in their own communities and to 'close ranks', which, in turn feeds xenophobia.[665] This view reflects what appears to be a widely held belief: that the problem lies with minorities. Here, people's identities are simply assumed to exist and to be so different from our own that we cannot even begin to understand them. A failure of this approach lies in the fact that it does not invite self- reflectivity or an effort to understand others through cultural lenses other than our own.

Postmodernist discourse analysis takes issue with static and essentialist views of culture. It considers xenophobia from the point of social identity. From this viewpoint, individual identity is intimately linked to collective meanings. The focus is on the discursive construction of cultural, ethnic and racial 'otherness', which may serve to exclude those considered outsiders from dominant structures in society and to contribute to establishing hierarchies of power between the host population and the relative newcomers. In this respect, postmodernist discourse argues that we should pay special attention to the discursive strategies of those who have the power to define social categories.[666] This latter element is particularly noteworthy in the context of dignity-based governance. In fact, the language used by representatives of the majority group and of the government often voluntarily or involuntarily labels minorities as an 'other' or a dangerous enemy. For dignity-based governance to be realised in practice, governments must, therefore, give special attention to such discursive strategies and to the definitions given to social categories, as I argue in Part 5.

Others draw on evolutionary theory as a source of explanation for xenophobia. Bradley A. Thayer, for example, maintains that the evolutionary foundation of behaviour can help to shed light on xenophobia. He argues that fear of strangers may have contributed to 'inclusive fitness', meaning the evolutionary currency of genes. He identifies four reasons why this may have been the case. First, people lived in family groups during the Pliocene, Pleistocene and Holocene eras and protected themselves from rival, and most likely unrelated, groups. These groups would have been competitors for territory and other scarce resources. As a result, they would probably have been viewed with hostility. Second, it may have served as a mechanism to protect communities against disease. Third, since human beings are the only species which kill conspecifics from a distance, fear of strangers may have been particularly pronounced among them as use of weaponry increased. Fourth, strangers may have been associated with threats to individuals' positions in the group hierarchy. Genotypes predisposing people to suspicion of strangers may consequently have been prevalent, since they would have ensured survival.[667]

Xenophobic reactions, according to Thayer, might be linked both to morphological and cultural differences. Genetic differences may lead to physical differences. However, because a great deal of our behaviour is culturally driven, cultural differences are also thought to have provided the means by which individuals belonging to one group may discriminate against those belonging to another group.[668]

An evolutionist argument is, therefore, premised on the notion that the looser the relationship, the stronger the chances are of negative suspicion and discrimination. It, thus, also highlights two possible strategies to counteract such tendencies. First, since they stem from our predisposition for survival, be it our own or that of our close kin, it is imperative that our more basic needs and requirements for dignity be fulfilled. When these needs are met, our behaviour is less likely to be steered by fears which are based, for example, on a sense of competition for resources or opportunities. This, in turn, enables us to employ our rationality and moral capacities, and to be less hostile towards those we consider outsiders. Similarly, the evolutionist argument also stresses the importance of government policies aimed at promoting greater tolerance and respect. As Part 5 will explore in depth, this can be achieved in four key ways. The education system, in particular, is an incredibly important means of combating xenophobia and ethnocentrism through, for example, the promotion of knowledge of the histories and cultures of peoples, as well as of cultural sensitivity and respect.[669] The adoption of inclusive and respectful language by the authorities also plays a key role in promoting tolerance. Further, the press, television industry, the film industry and even the gaming industry are also important for creating more inclusive definitions of the group, as well as for promoting new, multi-ethnic national identities which are also vital in culturally plural societies.[670]

4.3.2. Ethnocentrism

Ethnocentrism tends to have negative connotations. It may be described as a tendency to view one's own cultural ethnic group as superior to others, and to evaluate cultural ethnic groups from the standpoint of one's own. David Matsumoto defines ethnocentrism as 'viewing and interpreting the behaviour of others through our own cultural filters'.[671] He points out that, according to this definition, almost everyone qualifies as ethnocentric in that 'everyone learns a certain way of behaving, and in doing so, learns a certain way of perceiving and interpreting the behaviour of others. It is in this way which we first perceive and make interpretations about others, and is a normal consequence of growing up in a society.'[672]

As Matsumoto notes, we have not only developed particular expectations about behaviour, but also learnt ways of judging the behaviour of others. He points out that we have emotional reactions to other people's behaviour, which range from acceptance and pleasure to outrage, hostility and frustration. When people transgress against what we perceive to be socially appropriate behaviour, we typically react in a negative way. This entails emotions such as frustration or annoyance or even dismay. Often, these negative emotions lead us to make judgements about those who are transgressing our own cultural norms. We may judge those people to be ill-mannered, strange or stupid, for example.[673]

Ethnocentrism typically includes in-group favouritism. Ross Hammond and Robert Axelrod study ethnocentrism from an agent-based evolutionary model. They argue that in-group favouritism can emerge under a variety of conditions. They maintain that in-group favouritism can favour cooperation and, when cooperation is costly to individuals, ethnocentrism may be necessary to sustain it.[674]

Ethnocentrism may also affect how we understand the world. It causes us to analyse situations from the standpoint of our own cultures or from that of privileged social groups in the global economy. By doing so, we risk reifying power relations and inequalities which they (re)produce.[675] According to Charles McKelvey, Western social science is permeated by European ethnocentrism.[676]

Ethnocentrism is closely connected to stereotypes, which are generalisations of attitudes, beliefs or opinions about people who belong to cultures other than one's own. They may be employed when evaluating or interacting with people from different cultures. They can be pernicious when inflexible and applied to all people belonging to a cultural group, without being open to modification. The potential for misuse of stereotypes is evident when values such as 'inferior' are associated with behaviour which may not fit with what we judge (from within our own culture) to be appropriate.[677]

From an evolutionist's perspective, Thayer argues that inclusive fitness can also help to account for ethnocentrism. *Inclusive fitness* refers to behaviour which has evolved to increase an organism's survival and reproductive chances. As is mentioned above, ethnocentrism is usually defined as a belief in the superiority of one's own ethnicity. Yet, defined in this way, it is hard to see how it would contribute to inclusive fitness. Thayer redefines ethnocentrism as 'a collection of traits that predispose the individual to show discriminatory preferences for groups with the closest affinities to the self',[678] which allows him to argue that ethnocentrism has its origins not in beliefs, but in evolution – although he does allow for considerable environmental influence.[679]

For this reason, just as it can mitigate xenophobia, dignity-based governance can lessen the risks of ethnocentrism. Both educational institutions and the newspaper and broadcasting industry, for instance, can help to promote positive attitudes towards out-group members and to counteract negative stereotypes.

4.3.3. The Neural Basis of In-group Favouritism

Soldatova suggests that:

> [a]s identity takes shape, an individual becomes aware of
> his group affiliation and his position in society. He grows
> conscious of the continuity of his own existence within
> the system of generations and in the context of history. He
> accepts a certain way of life and submits to it, learning how
> to correlate his individuality within the system of values and
> norms. An individual looks for his Ego and almost always
> finds it in some or other group. Identity is, on the one hand,
> unity, sameness, and communion, while on the other, it is
> separation, opposition and confrontation: *I* and *Other*, *We*
> and *They*.[680]

The social psychologist Henri Tajfel (1919–82) concurred with the
idea that self-identification with a group tends to involve preferring and
valuing that group more than others. He investigated what minimal
conditions would cause out-group discrimination. According to Tajfel,
simply placing someone in a group is enough to do so. This is thought
to occur because the group effectively becomes a part of the self and is,
therefore, considered more positively than other groups.[681]

Thus, identity performs its functions by drawing boundaries,
normally based on a preference for one's own collective identity.
In-group favouritism is believed to be connected to the human need for
a positive identity, since the higher one's self-esteem, the higher one's
status and prestige, both of which are closely connected to our egoistic
nature. From a psychological perspective, positive group identity is an
important psychological requirement for stability and independence.[682]
During periods of turmoil or crisis, especially, the need to construct a
stable identity is likely to take on great significance.[683]

Recently it has become possible to explore the neural mechanisms
which underlie in-group favouritism, bias and xenophobia. Indeed,
modern neuroimaging has offered fascinating glimpses into how the
distinction between 'us' and 'them' (and, therefore, between in-group
and out-group) occurs in the prefrontal cortex when seeing another
human being.[684] This type of subconscious, instantaneous discrimination
is believed to have been necessary for survival during evolution.[685]
Further, neuroimaging studies have also shown that a wide range of
neural correlates involved in action perception, social categorisation,

empathy and face perception can influence our attitudes to in-group and out-group members.[686] Indeed, research has demonstrated how the ventromedial prefrontal cortex is activated when making judgements about similar people, whereas areas of the dorsomedial prefrontal cortex become active in the case of judgements about people who are dissimilar.[687] In other words, group membership affects various cognitive and emotional systems involved in information processing, meaning that we judge people differently based on whether they are known to us or not.[688] As a result, we perceive faces, words and actions of in-group and out-group members in a biased way. Importantly, group membership affects brain areas involved in empathising with the pain of others, such as the dorsal anterior cingulate cortex and anterior insula. Experiments in this area using fMRI have shown that, in the case of out-group perception, the so-called 'mirror neurons', normally responsible for mimicry and empathy, are 'switched off', which causes people to resist emotional connections. Group membership even affects brain areas involved in the reward system, encouraging *Schadenfreude* – taking pleasure in others' misfortune – in response to an out-group suffering harm and rejoicing when in-group members are rewarded.[689]

Most human attitudes are shaped by both genetic and environmental influences. This also holds true for our fear of the 'other', which is a reflex triggered by encounters with the unfamiliar. In premodern times, this neurochemical fear of the unfamiliar alerted humans to potential dangers coming from other groups who might steal their resources, be violent or introduce diseases to which they were not adapted. Beyond such genetic influences, however, culture can influence how we perceive others who are different from us.[690] On the one hand, divisive leaders have always tried to exploit these fundamental human predispositions in order to unleash our fears against each other, as is often the case through the use of 'electioneering sound-bites' which mock minorities or which label an entire minority group as criminals or as 'enemies of the nation'.[691] This type of discourse feeds xenophobia and ethnocentrism, as discussed earlier, and can lead to extreme forms of violence. This was the case, for instance, with the 1994 Rwandan genocide, in which Hutu extremists made use of the radio to urge their community to exterminate the 'cockroaches', their epithet for the Tutsi.[692]

On the other hand, numerous studies confirm our ability to mitigate the automatic process of out-group devaluation. These include studies conducted at Harvard and Yale analysing perceptions of race in the United States. They have shown that prejudicial responses will often occur where there is cognitive overload or when reflective processes are not well engaged. However, reflective processes, cultivated through positive messages and egalitarian norms, can counteract these automatic processes of devaluing the 'other'.[693] For this reason, through its focus on education and inclusiveness, dignity-based governance provides effective tools to positively influence our attitudes towards the 'other'.

Furthermore, it is important to note that having a positive group identity and self-identity does not have to imply denigrating difference, even if one's own group is ultimately preferred. The way group identity serves individual identity and vice versa may also serve peaceful relations by promoting stable and positive identities:

> In this case, identity should combine in its structure a positive and relatively preferred image of one's own group with a positive value attitude to other groups. A person possessing this kind of identity does not perceive the world as menacing; he feels tolerant towards other groups and is not characterised by xenophobic attitudes.[694]

In other words, while identity may be defined in relation to difference, this does not have to mean that difference is perceived as a problem, which typically enables identity to be used as a vector for relations of discrimination, violence and conflict, characteristically employing xenophobia to trigger such hostile feelings and behaviour.[695]

Since we have filters through which we perceive and interpret the world, whether ethnocentrism is harmful or not is likely to depend on whether we are aware of our own ethnocentrism. It becomes harmful when we do not recognise that we are judging others according to our own lifestyle and cultural context. It is, therefore, important to ensure that we develop flexibility when interacting with people who belong to cultures other than our own, and that we do not see them through our own rigid cultural lenses. Matsumoto suggests promoting 'flexible ethnocentrism', which does not imply that one must accept someone else's point of view, simply that one ought to employ new filters over existing cultural filters, helping us to see things from other perspectives.[696]

Dignity-based governance can play a large role in the development of this type of 'flexible ethnocentrism' and of what I refer to as *transcultural understanding* (more on this below). Policymakers should take account of the emotional aspects of human nature rather than simply assuming that people will act rationally when they perceive some dimension of their survival or existence to be threatened by an out-group member.

A number of measures may be taken to reduce irrational fears and the incidence of xenophobia. First, governments should adopt programmes aimed at fighting ethnic prejudice, which may include persuasive communication campaigns which highlight similarities between ethnic minorities and majority populations and promote increased exposure to ethnic minority groups. They should also adopt policies to monitor and regulate the language and forms of expression used by both public authorities and the private sector, as well as the aims of the communication.[697] Moreover, from an early age, children should be taught about the dangers of stereotypes when people try to comprehend the behaviour of others.[698] Again, the education system is a particularly important means of combating xenophobia and ethnocentrism by increasing awareness of other cultures. Interaction and exchange with those we consider different are also important means of breaking down stereotypes. Similarly, the press, TV industry and information and communication technologies are crucial vehicles not only for the diffusion of negative stereotyping and demonisation of the 'other', but also for increasing transcultural awareness, respect and recognition.

To this end, governments could require a code of conduct for journalists aimed at minimising the diffusion of xenophobic statements and images. Such a code of conduct would provide the necessary complement to global efforts to combat the spread of publications with violent and extremist content. The 2019 Christchurch Call to Eliminate Terrorist and Violent Extremist Content Online, for instance, represents an encouraging example of how it is possible to bring together governments, civil society and the corporate sector to voluntarily adopt ethical principles and codes of conduct to govern the publication of dangerous content.[699] Cultural minorities also need to be better represented within the broadcasting and newspaper establishment, so that they can establish effective strategies and responses to negative stereotyping.[700] For this same reason, policies should also be adopted regulating the conduct of the entertainment and gaming industries and their depictions of minority groups.

Creating national identities which embrace different ethnic groups is likely to be an important means of combating ethnocentrism. Given that group identity serves individual identity and vice versa, a positive identity may also serve peaceful relations, specifically by promoting independent and stable identities which are not defined by viewing difference as a threat. The promotion of inclusive national identities through dignity-based governance is, therefore, of paramount importance to the effort to combat xenophobia. Anti-racism legislation and the promotion of human rights are other positive measures which ought to be taken in support of this effort.

* * *

This chapter has explored the relationship between xenophobia and rigid forms of ethnocentrism. It briefly outlined the neurocognitive basis of our in-group preference, which may be a necessary consequence of the need for a positive identity. Our in-group bias is implicated in relations of discrimination and conflict. Understanding our innate predispositions is key to comprehending why conflicts and wars abound in human history. Alongside our in-group favouritism, fear-induced pre-emptive aggression plays a major role in leading people to forms of aggression and violence. The next section will show how the emotional-amoral-egoism view of human nature can advance understanding of a whole range of conflicts at the individual, intrastate and interstate levels. It will, likewise, illustrate the role of dignity-based governance for preventing conflict at these three levels.

4.4

The Implications of the Theory of Emotional Amoral Egoism for Understanding Conflict

The topic of conflict has garnered significant scholarly attention from a range of disciplines. Since many conflict analyses are inspired by insights from theories discussed in the first part of the book, we encounter once again the nature–nurture tension, which my own approach seeks to resolve. This chapter reviews some of the ways conflict has been explored at the individual, intrastate (particularly ethnic conflict) and interstate levels by prominent scholars from various disciplines and offers some insights from my approach to human nature. It particularly highlights the role of fear-induced pre-emptive aggression in conflict generation and challenges the 'clash of civilisations' narrative from a neurophilosophical perspective.

4.4.1. Conflict at the Individual Level

Among the realist philosophers, Hobbes is one of the most prominent figures to have discussed the causes of conflict at the individual level. He stressed the role of the biological determinants of human beings, who, in a state of anarchy (the absence of a government to enforce laws) are prone to egoism, aggression, pride and the desire for power and glory. Since all human beings possess such inclinations, Hobbes argued that the absence of a central government to check these tendencies is believed to result in fear, insecurity and conflict.[701] From a neo-realist perspective, Kenneth Waltz (1924–2013) also located the sources of conflict in the psychodynamics of human beings.[702]

The biological factors contributing to conflict also feature prominently in a number of other contributions to conflict analysis at the individual level. In evolutionary psychology, Lorenz claimed that selection pressure within the evolutionary process has resulted in an 'aggressive gene'.[703] Sociobiology, similarly, places emphasis on the notion of inclusive fitness – human behaviour which has adapted to the needs of evolution. Thus, sociobiologists emphasise the role of inherited instincts in predisposing humankind to act in particular ways. Essentially, behaviour which contributes to an organism's survival and chances of reproduction is passed on through generations.[704] To explain conflict, the above approaches point to our genetic predispositions and, in this sense, possess a strong materialism – that is, they focus on the biological factors influencing the human psyche and behaviour.

Despite their emphasis on our biological heritage, neither ethologists nor sociobiologists deny the contribution of environmental influences in shaping who we are. Clearly, the environment plays an important role in determining how human beings act on inner impulses. Some situations may provoke more aggressive behaviour than others.[705] Indeed, some see aggression and conflict as the result of a person's position in a particular societal context.[706]

4.4.2. Emotional Amoral Egoism and Conflict at the Individual Level

According to my theory of emotional amoral egoism, the human mind can aptly be described as a predisposed *tabula rasa* rather than the *tabula rasa* envisaged by Locke. As is explained above, it is influenced both by genes and environmental factors, comprising a person's personal state of affairs, upbringing and education as well as the societal, cultural and global state of affairs. Consequently, conflict at the individual level is likely to be the result of a complex interaction between biological and environmental factors.

A great deal of what may cause conflict between individuals is likely to be the result of our evolutionary survival instincts, which are manifested in neurochemically-mediated emotions: fear, anger, anxiety, jealousy, attachment and so on. Especially in circumstances of scarce resources and insecurity, our egoism pushes us to look out for our own welfare, even at terrible cost to others. Furthermore, our amorality may lead to irreconcilable divides over values. Across countries, the past few years have witnessed rising moral tribalism, as highlighted in the 2016 and 2020 US presidential elections, in which numerous Democrats and Republicans ascribed immorality to members of the other party.[707] Moreover, our continuous quest for neurochemical gratification may give rise to a variety of conflicts when the pursuit of the Neuro P5 (power, profit, pleasure, pride and permanency) assumes excessive dimensions. Desire for profit, for example, may result in greed, leading to criminal behaviour. Likewise, as explained before, unconstrained power may prompt undesirable distortions in judgements, causing toxic behaviour in leaders. Some conflicts may be the result of excessive pleasure-seeking, or the desire to maintain a sense of pride which is necessary for serving the needs of the ego. Others may be caused by specific individual inclinations, such as passionate commitment to ideologies which glorify violence.

As mentioned before, socialisation shapes, to a significant extent, what we perceive to be the sources of and legitimate ways of pursuing the Neuro P5. Through schooling, the press and television, or political discourse, dignity-based governance associates pro-social behaviour with 'feeling good' to prevent individuals from pursuing the Neuro P5 at the expense of other people. In addition, successful mediation and reconciliation between individuals requires awareness of the emotional forces which drive people's behaviour (such as their specific histories and painful memories). Underestimation of their importance will impede efforts to avoid or solve conflicts. Preventing conflict at the individual level also requires transparency, empathy, flexibility, humility, recognition of other 'truths', a lack of dogma and self-reflectivity – qualities which are not simply inborn but can actually be taught.

4.4.3. Intrastate Conflict

Intrastate conflict in the post-Cold War period has attracted an increasing amount of attention in the field of international relations (IR), particularly in security studies. This shift happened in the 1990s and is hardly surprising, given the tragic wars in the Balkans and the ethnic cleansing in Rwanda during this period. In the twenty-first century, episodes of ethnic-based violence, in some cases amounting to genocide, continue to occur around the world. Here I focus on ethnic conflict issues which affect interstate relations, generating foreign policy challenges, raising human rights issues and creating refugee situations, which can pose human, societal and interstate security challenges. Much of the most insightful work in this area has come from postmodernist scholars, who have focussed on the role of identity formation in their attempt to account for the dynamics of ethnic conflict. For this reason, my theory of symbiotic realism stresses the importance of inclusive global identities for securing peace, the topic to which I now turn.[708]

4.4.4. Approaches to Ethnic Conflict

In the field of international relations, attempts to understand ethnic conflict have tended to identify a number of its causes, including: (1) the trend towards 'democratisation' in formerly authoritarian regimes, which gives greater opportunity for ethnic groups to seek recognition; (2) increased international concern for human rights issues which now trump sovereignty; (3) uneven development; (4) differential modernisation; (5) relative regional deprivation; (6) internal colonialism; (7) failures of assimilation; and (8) cultural oppression.[709]

Ethnicity as a political force has not been examined in IR to the same extent as material forces such as power or class. The realist IR approach, for instance, has widely overlooked its existence. Instead, it has emphasised the state as the key political unit and the distribution of capabilities among states as an explanatory factor of stability. More recent attempts by realists to address the topic tend to view the ultimate cause of ethnic conflict in terms of international anarchy and the need to mobilise the population due to geopolitical developments. Realism assumes that states are unitary actors, and its continued dominance has, therefore, not helped further our understanding of ethnic conflict. Nor is it helpful to perceive internal and external security as separate, as traditional realist paradigms suggest. Neo-realism has also been unable to provide a more adequate understanding of ethnic conflict. It continues to assume that states are unitary actors and focusses on causal relations at the level of the system, without taking into consideration the role of individuals and smaller groups which make up the modern state.[710]

Liberal and Marxist-informed approaches to IR view ethnic conflicts as transitional phenomena. Such approaches tend to generalise from the Western experience and assume a linear, universal economic-political development. However, such assumptions have been radically called into question by the failure of nation-building which has resulted from the disassociation between national boundaries and ethnic groups caused by colonisation and decolonisation.

The distinction between interstate and intrastate conflict, however, is increasingly becoming regarded as a problem. According to some analysts, inter-group and intra-group dynamics may be intimately connected to larger strategic calculations. In Maheshwar Singh's view, when ethnicity becomes connected to the wider strategic situation in a problematic way, it becomes one of the lines along which societies disintegrate. He argues that anxieties about the future and about identity construction need to be understood at the micro *and* the macro levels.[711]

Singh emphasises the transnational dimensions of ethnic conflicts. Ethnic ties between people living in different countries must be taken into consideration, as alliances between these groups may be formed. He also points out that these kinds of ties may be used by elites to mobilise support for their political projects. Singh considers the constructivist approach is better suited to conceptualize global security, as it is able to link the international system with other security units, such as ethnic groups. Instead of focusing on outdated notions of security focused on the state alone, a constructivist approach defines threats in terms of the core values that various units (ethnic groups in this case) perceive as critical to protect. In his view, societal security defined in terms of identity is of greater use than state security defined in terms of sovereignty. In other words, when counteracting intrastate conflicts, states have to take into consideration how collective identity leads to threat perceptions.[712]

In *National Deconstruction* (2005), David Campbell examines the wars in the former Yugoslavia from a postmodernist perspective. As previously discussed, postmodernism does not attempt to understand the world by seeking objective truth. This is because, unlike orthodox approaches to social science, it does not assume that knowledge is free of politics, values and power. Instead, knowledge is seen as fundamentally political in the sense that dominant knowledge claims are always supportive of hierarchies of power. The aim of the postmodernist scholar is, therefore, to engage in the political act of deconstructing dominant knowledge forms.[713]

Campbell argues that a particular 'norm of community' has governed the wars in the former Yugoslavia. This norm generates a desire for a coherent, bounded community with a unified culture. The violence which occurred in Bosnia, he claims, was the result not of primordial hatreds, but of an intensification of this norm. Ethnic cleansing, in his view, is the product of the pursuit of a homogeneous political identity which represents a continuation of the political project implied in the construction of a modern nation state.[714] In short, bounded, homogeneous communities are likely to imply some degree of violence.[715]

The evolutionary model attempts to identify why people may respond to projects which aim to incite ethnic conflict. It is believed that under, certain conditions, distinctions made on the basis of ethnicity or nationality may be very appealing. Thayer argues that evolutionary theory helps explain why elites may be successful in manipulating the 'masses' by using the theme of ethnic or national identity. He maintains that such themes resonate with people because of the human capacity easily to generate ethnocentric distinctions. The evolutionary origin of ethnocentrism is thought to be related to inclusive fitness. In Thayer's view, ethnocentrism does not have its origin simply in symbolic representation linked to how we perceive and experience the world as a result of enculturation (the process by which individuals acquire the characteristics and norms of a specific culture). Instead, and as mentioned before, we evolved ethnocentric predispositions because caution in relation to strangers may have enabled people to avoid contracting diseases, or to prevent potential competitors from altering an established social hierarchy within a community. Thayer also suggests that fear of strangers may have evolved in response to the capacity which human beings have to develop weapons with which to kill at a distance.[716] As a result of the potential harm which strangers would have been able to inflict, people would have developed the capacity to recognise outsiders both visually and as a result of morphological, cultural and linguistic differences.[717]

While recognising ethnocentrism as an evolved and, therefore, basic genetic predisposition, Thayer acknowledges that the environment influences how people act on these predispositions: 'The ways in which humans determine their relations with unrelated individuals are complex, but key factors are physical resemblance, as well as environmental causes like shared culture, history, and language.'[718]

4.4.5. The Implications of the Theory of Emotional Amoral Egoism for Ethnic Conflict

Thayer seems to assume that ethnocentrism necessarily leads to ethnic conflict, but is this necessarily so? As already indicated, whilst our brains are wired to favour our own group over others, cultural education can help us move past inborn fears of the 'other'. This also requires counteracting the main sources of ethnic tensions which violate human dignity: inequality and injustice.

As Ted Robert Gurr (1936–2017) rightly observed, the cultural and political aspirations of minorities are typically linked to their right to exercise their human rights and fundamental freedoms without discrimination and with equality before the law. This is what he calls the 'quintessential bargain' that builds peace in heterogenous societies: governments must acknowledge the rights of subordinate and minority groups in 'exchange for civil peace and their acceptance of the state's superordinate political authority.'[719] Political and economic inequalities and minorities' unmet desire for recognition constitute the root causes of many ethnic conflicts, as they violate some of our most essential requirements for dignity. However, recognition and perpetuation of a group's distinctive culture is often essential in minority-majority relations, even if there are political and material inequalities.[720]

Because of the need for a positive identity, those who are outside the centres of power are likely to find an independent identity appealing. As Castells points out, 'Ethnicity has been a fundamental source of meaning and recognition throughout human history. It is a founding structure of social differentiation, and social recognition, as well as discrimination, in many contemporary societies, from the United States to Sub-Saharan Africa.'[721] Ethnic identity seems to offer a solid foundation for group identity, since it is supposedly based on timeless qualities and geographical and historical facts. Indeed, history has been an often-tapped resource for creating collective identities. Yet evocations of the past have rarely been free of ideological investments and, sadly, collective identities have often been instrumentalised to advance specific political agendas.

Evidence from neuroscience corroborates the view that ethnic conflict should be understood as a reaction to a group's unmet physiological, security and ego needs. This reaction is often motivated by the desire to protect something which people have invested in emotionally (such as ethnic heritage and pride) and which constitutes part of an individual's selfhood. In other words, protecting what one considers to be the interests of one's ethnic group is understood as a way of protecting the self from harm and from potential destruction. Ethnic conflict is, thus, linked to a defensive form of identity construction and, like radicalism, it is a form of resistance identity.

As Andreas Wimmer argues, ethnic politics have shaped modern societies to a far greater extent than is usually acknowledged.[722] In modern states, injustices (such as inequality before the law) are widely legitimised on the basis of ethnicity by a broader collective, namely a 'nation' which defines itself in homogeneous and, therefore, exclusionary terms. After all, our identities are not just the product of how we define *ourselves* in relation to *others*; they are also defined in relation to the way *others* define *us*. If I am not considered part of a collective identity, then it will be hard for me to think of myself as a member of that particular group.

Ethnic conflict, I would argue, is largely the result of political and socioeconomic inequality which has been legitimised along the fault lines of culture. It involves a defence, a resistance-based form of identity construction resulting from the experience of exclusion or marginalisation. Dignity-based governance prevents ethnic conflict through inclusive policies which ensure meaningful representation and participation by all those affected by decisions in policymaking and governance structures. In addition, it promotes a non-exclusive form of national identity, premised on the acceptance of multiple identities and respect for difference, which it entrenches in anti-racism legislation and through the protection of minority rights. It, therefore, not only recognises that constitutions should be such that laws cannot be changed at the whim of the popular 'mood'; it also places importance on the role of a truly independent newspaper, broadcasting and entertainment industry. In addition, it relies on representative, effective and accountable systems of government to fulfil the need for dignity of members of society. Furthermore, dignity-based governance also implies the promotion of equal opportunity as a means of preventing the rise of tensions between ethnic groups and the exploitation of the accompanying fear and insecurity. To ensure equal opportunities, the degree of ethnic polarisation and ethnic distribution of public sector posts should be regularly monitored.[723]

Globally, dignity-based governance prevents ethnic conflict through its unconditional defence of human rights, including basic survival needs. Furthermore, it recognises inclusive regional and global identities, political and social justice, inclusiveness, equality, respect and opportunity as conflict prevention measures and promotes them as such.

Where there has been ethnic conflict, with societies deeply divided and tensions still present, other measures are likely to be required to prevent violence from breaking out again. This involves post-conflict justice mechanisms which hold the instigators of conflict responsible for their actions, while allowing the population at large to overcome a sense of guilt and to reconcile.[724] Reconciliation requires that a post-conflict society reconstructs a collective memory which overcomes a divisive violent past and allows for the formation of inclusive identities.

Transnational justice processes, in the form of truth commissions and legal tribunals, may be a helpful means of creating such a new collective memory.[725] In sum, constructive measures can be taken in order to prevent the occurrence as well as the reoccurrence of ethnic conflict.

4.4.6. Approaches to Interstate Conflict

Within the field of IR, realists generally view the state as being a rational actor facing the world as if it were a hermetically sealed entity. States are believed to be selfish in the sense of pursuing their national interest above all else. As rational egoists, they are thought to be primarily concerned with maximising and employing their power – often defined in military terms, though sometimes in economic terms – in the interstate system. A state's survival is, therefore, believed to depend primarily on the accumulation and deployment of military power. Realists, such as Hobbes, have examined human nature as well as international anarchy as causes for interstate conflict. Others, including Waltz, have stressed the structure of the international system as a means of explaining the recurrence of interstate war.[726] In the absence of a world government, individual states are thought to be compelled to act in such a way as to ensure their own survival. One state's gain is believed to be another's loss. In this case, gains are thought to be absolute rather than relative.

In a seminal piece of work, Waltz argued that the distribution of power in the international system can account for the incidence of war. He considered bipolar systems to be the most stable, given that the two major powers in such a system are likely to be of equivalent power. This is thought to explain why the Cold War was 'stable'.[727] Mearsheimer had a similar view in that he considered bipolar systems inherently more stable and peaceful because they presented fewer possibilities of war. Multi-polar systems are, by contrast, believed to be the most unstable, since there are a number of dyads across which conflict may occur.[728] Mearsheimer used the term 'dyads' to refer to potential sources of conflict, or that which separates a situation from being conflictual or peaceful.

From Waltz's neo-realist perspective, the domestic or internal organisation of the state is less relevant as a cause for war.[729] By contrast, liberal IR theories which take their cue from Kant stress the centrality of a state's internal system of governance for explaining the likelihood of interstate conflict. Within this approach, liberal democracies are believed to be less prone to go to war with one another than non-liberal states.[730]

Other theorists argue that the domestic economic structure of states helps explain the incidence of interstate conflict. Marxist-oriented thinkers hold that the capitalist system as a whole is the cause of conflict between states. Others argue that particular groups, such as military-industrial complexes or foreign investors, may contribute to a state's expansionist foreign policies.[731] Theorists who seek to explain imperialism, such as John A. Hobson (1858–1940), claim that the social relations of production within capitalist states explain conflict. Great disparities of wealth and the growth of the poor meant that such countries experienced 'underconsumption' at home, which caused them to invest their capital abroad through imperialism. Competition for markets caused wars between states.[732]

A state's access to natural resources is also identified as a possible cause of conflict. Some resources, including timber, oil and minerals, contribute to a country's wealth. Intense competition for such resources can result in conflict, especially if there is a strong dependence on them for revenue. Historically, land has been one of the primary natural resources over which states have fought.[733] Over the past century, however, competition for other resources, especially oil, has played a role in triggering interstate conflicts, or at least in providing a reason for third-party states to get involved in conflicts between others or even in intrastate conflicts, as was alleged in the case of the US intervention in Iraq.[734] In the coming decades, other resources have the potential to ignite competition. Water is, in fact, already a growing source of conflict.[735] Competition for it represents a serious threat for global peace and security, which will only increase as climate change renders it an increasingly scarce resource.[736] Further, growing competition in outer space for access to and use of space resources, such as those found on the Moon, asteroids and, in the near future, Mars, also has the potential to rapidly escalate into a large-scale conflict.[737]

4.4.7. The Implications of the Theory of Emotional Amoral Egoism for Interstate Conflict

I certainly recognise the importance of the structure of the international system for the incidence of interstate conflict as a result of fear and insecurity. However, I place greater weight than realists do on the domestic factors contributing to conflict. The Neuro P5 are particularly important motivating factors which are likely to have a significant impact on the likelihood that a state will enter into conflict or go to war. Politicians often take particular courses of action because of the constraints imposed by a domestic audience. The quest for power, pride or permanency, for example, occurs not only on an individual level but also on a collective level. The domestic audience may, therefore, push a country's leadership to act in an uncooperative or antagonistic way to expand its power, for example. Wars may be declared in order to vindicate national pride or to provide a sense of national permanency. The latter may imply not only the survival of a nation but also the production of a collective memory stressing the role of a certain social group, family or class in the expansion and prosperity of a nation. The interest of strong political constituencies may also affect foreign policy stances. Economic and governance structures may contribute to sharpening the egoistic features of human nature. For example, the structure of the domestic economy, when lacking adequate checks and balances, may give particular economic groups the capacity to influence foreign policy choices in a way which only serves the narrow interests of certain economic lobbies.

The system of governance is, thus, an important factor for explaining the propensity for conflict. It is worth stressing that the issue of domestic 'interest groups' is as relevant to liberal democracies as to non-liberal states. Indeed, some of the most mature democracies are afflicted by this problem. Dignity-based governance implies representative and effective governance structures, as well as transparency, an independent press and broadcasting industry, and electoral and political systems which are sufficiently free from undue influence. It is committed to raising awareness of other people's histories, past and present pain and fears, as well as cultural symbolism, thus reducing the destructive potential of fear, pain, grief and ego as motivations of conflict.[738]

Increasing interdependence between states also means that absolute gains are possible, thereby reducing the likelihood that competition and greed will lead to conflict. Indeed, as I argue further below, *symbiotic realism* presents a viable and better alternative to zero-sum games. Symbiosis here refers to the idea that, due to the interconnected and interdependent nature of contemporary interstate relations, for these to be harmonious they must prioritise the goals of absolute gains and non-conflictual competition which allow all sides to benefit.[739]

4.4.8. Power, Fear-Induced Pre-emptive Aggression and Conflict

As I stated in Chapter 3.4.6, fear-induced pre-emptive aggression is the root cause of many conflicts and thus must also be addressed when discussing the relationship between dignity-based governance and conflict. In addition, it is often intertwined with the neurochemistry of power (see Chapter 3.4.5), which is key to understanding not only the wars and political decisions of the past, but also the conflicts we are experiencing today and the means of preventing future ones.

As I argued in Chapter 3.1, power is neurochemically mediated by a release of dopamine, the same chemical responsible for the feeling of pleasure and the activation of many reward neurocircuitries. Consequently, if we experience power, we shall most likely search for more power and for the 'highs' associated with the release of dopamine. Nevertheless, by ensuring accountability, dignity-based governance can limit the extremely dangerous search for more and more power. Conversely, if left unchecked, the hunt for power will know no boundary – and certainly will not be curtailed by any capacity or desire of the individual to limit himself or herself. In fact, power is not only highly intoxicating, but especially addictive, much like any drug. As I have pointed out, leaders who enjoy absolute power – as in dictatorships – will do literally anything to maintain it, including acts which in the long run may not even be in their own interest. When confronted with the fear – real or imagined – of losing this immense power, these leaders will at all costs seek to strengthen it and ensure it remains unchallenged.[740]

Two concepts, closely related to the Hobbesian framework introduced in Chapter 3.4.6, according to which fear and a perennial state of war prompt individuals to strike first, merit closer attention here. The first is the 'balance of power', a notion which has occupied the minds of theorists from Emmerich de Vattel (1714–67) to George Kennan (1904–2005). The basic concept is straightforward: regional (and, potentially, even global) powers hold one another in check simply by virtue of constituting formidable adversaries for one another. Theoretically and conceptually, this can be understood through the classical realist analogy of the 'man-state', which portrays states as a reflection of the character of human beings. Under this understanding, in the same way as human beings, states are selfish and strive to maximise their own power.[741]

In fact, balance-of-power considerations have historically been closely intertwined with fear-induced pre-emptive aggression. For example, in the War of the Spanish Succession (1701–14), the prospect of a large, united Franco-Spanish reign under King Philip led Britain and other regional powers to attack. Indeed, the only reason for this war was the fear of a dramatic shift in Europe's balance of power and, in particular, one which would lead to the consolidation of a single power which would be able to dominate all others. The collective fear of an outsized rival, which could pose an existential threat at some future date, motivated a 'preventive war' – widely characterised as an unjustified act of aggression – on the part of the allies. In this context, de Vattel's post-conflict commentary is of particular interest, as it acknowledges the role fear and suspicion played in the choice of the allies to attack.[742]

The ways in which fear affects multilateral political decision-making are no doubt complex, yet balance-of-power concerns represent a clear instance of the influence of fear on geopolitics. To take another example, following the years of Napoleon's reign and near-total domination of Europe, it was fear which motivated the great powers of Europe to endorse the balance-of-power paradigm at the Congress of Vienna in 1814–15, a paradigm which would influence Europe for the rest of the nineteenth century. Similarly, the efforts by Otto von Bismarck to achieve a balance of power later in the century were strongly motivated by a desire to discourage military expansion and domination for fear of reprisal.[743]

In a similar logic, fear of Hitler's attempts at hegemony pushed for the unlikely alliance between ideological competitors during the Second World War, thus bringing together Western democracies and the Soviet Union. The latter part of the twentieth century and the twenty-first century, however, have witnessed shifts in the balance of power. The most powerful actors in today's multi-polar system, the US and China, are currently in a 'symbiotic relation' in that their relationship is defined by an unprecedented amount of economic interdependence, despite the fact that they simultaneously remain ideologically incompatible and politically in competition for influence and hegemony.[744] On the one hand, these unique circumstances may assuage the fears of direct military confrontation – since both superpowers must regard their relationship with pragmatism (both of them having a lot to lose in the event of military escalation). On the other, competition and each government's fear of significant advances by the other are strong drivers of both countries' domestic and foreign policies.

The second concept meriting special attention is the 'security dilemma'.[745] A frequent trigger of fear-induced pre-emptive aggression, security dilemmas typically arise when one state perceives the increase in power of another state as a security threat. The consequent dilemma for the first state is either to do nothing, thus leaving itself open to potential domination by a superior power, or to militarise – with the likely consequence that the other state will perceive this activity as threatening, thus kicking off a cycle of mutual escalation. The least desirable, but also the most likely, outcome is a decrease in security for both parties as a consequence of the heightened threat, whether real or merely perceived. Arms races, including what is referred to in IR as 'mutual assured destruction', mostly originate in such security dilemmas.[746]

In short, fear can swiftly induce responses in the form of pre-emptive aggression, which, when taken to an extreme, results in conflict and war. Fear-induced pre-emptive aggression is a function of a basic wiring in our emotional, amoral and egoistic nature. It is designed to alert us to danger, protect us from harm and ensure our survival. Nevertheless, while this mechanism is ingrained in our neuropsychology, the existence of prolonged fear is a symptom of institutional failure because it implies that our need for dignity, particularly our need for security, is not being fulfilled. Dignity-based governance can help overcome fears and insecurity in a community or society. Conversely, the violation of the need for human dignity is likely to result in self-regarding behaviour on the part of groups of individuals aimed at maximising their chance of survival, often at catastrophic costs to others.

4.4.9. Conflict between Civilisations?

In his book *The Clash of Civilizations and the Remaking of World Order* (1996), Samuel Huntington (1927–2008) controversially argued that the world's civilisations are destined to clash.[747] Huntington identified eight civilisations: Sinic (Chinese), Japanese, Hindu, Islamic, Orthodox, Western, Latin American and African. He maintained that, in the post-Cold War era, civilisations would form the major fault lines of conflict. In his view, the West was on a collision course with the Sinic and Islamic civilisations.

The narrative of a 'clash of civilisations' is based on an essentialist view of cultures as finite projects which emerged *ex nihilo*. It widely overlooks the larger historical forces and power relations which created categories such as 'civilised' versus 'uncivilised'. In fact, the act of identifying multiple discrete civilisations is empirically unfounded and ahistorical. It establishes a hierarchy which directly or indirectly encourages preconceptions, alienation and the dehumanisation of the 'other'. In reality, narratives of divisions or 'incompatibility' among cultures are belied by undeniable evidence on our shared neuroanatomy and neurochemistry. They are also disproved by robust historical research, which reveals that there is only one human civilisation which prospered and evolved as a result of interactions between different geo-cultural domains, which have historically shaped one another. I have synthesised this fact in my 'ocean' model of civilisation: just as an ocean is fed by many rivers, so human civilisation is an accumulation of contributions from distinct yet intertwined geo-cultural domains. My model echoes some of the arguments made by revisionist currents of history, which advocate for a more inclusive narrative about cultures.[748]

The relationship between the West and the Arab-Islamic world provides a good example of the widely overlooked centuries of exchanges and mutual borrowings which tie together different geo-cultural domains. Too often, the Arab-Islamic world is portrayed as being in opposition to the West, and Islam in Europe is wrongly considered a recent and menacing phenomenon. This sadly vilifies and obliterates from collective memory the contributions of the Middle East to the rise of Western cultures in varied domains, such as the arts, mathematics, astronomy, medicine, architecture and philosophy. As I discussed at length in an edited volume on this subject, the dominant narrative on the rise of the West conventionally focusses on the Renaissance era, the Scientific Revolution and the Enlightenment, which propagates a Euro-centric, exclusionary and self-contained view of history.[749] As a result, there is a tendency to overlook the impact of the Arab-Islamic world on Europe's historical trajectory. In reality, however, Europe has thrived on borrowings from the Middle East and elsewhere, just as the Arab-Islamic world built upon the works of others while rising to its Golden Age.[750] It is crucial to recover this widely forgotten aspect of history to counteract perceptions of irreconcilable cultural differences, perceptions which lend themselves to instrumentalisation for political purposes. In fact, if cultural differences are securitised and given negative connotations for competing political agendas, we may indeed experience what appears to be a clash between civilisations.

Conversely, if we embrace cultural diversity, it will promote what I referred to in Chapter 3.8 as 'cultural vigour'. That is, diversity contributes to humankind's survival and prosperity, just as molecular/genetic diversity in nature produces 'hybrid vigour', and thus resilience and potential for a future free of disease.

4.4.10. Transcultural Understanding

As mentioned above, the greatest achievements in human history, albeit often wrongly attributed to one geo-cultural domain, are the result of transcultural synergies. By synergy I mean a situation in which two or more agents or influences together produce an effect which is greater than the net effect of each individual entity or force. Transcultural synergies presuppose transcultural understanding, the absence of which may exacerbate cultural prejudices at the expense of the progress of civilisation. It is, therefore, imperative to raise awareness of humanity's shared historical heritage to dispel misleading narratives of 'incompatibility' among cultures and disrupt our in-group bias. Indeed, we must move beyond the idea of homogenous cultures which are easily separable from one another and devoid of internal differentiation.[751] Importantly, it is crucial to teach and internalise equal respect for and recognition of all cultures. That is because human beings' need for dignity is both individual and collective: we expect dignified treatment both on a personal level and for the larger community with which we identify. Furthermore, transcultural understanding benefits from awareness of other people's histories, their past and present fears and cultural symbolism, the understanding of which is key to preventing pre-emptive aggression induced by fear and the survival instinct.

Through transcultural understanding and synergies, we can achieve what I call a *natural selection of ideas* (which is comparable to nature's way of selecting genetic traits). This will, in the long run, result in what I term the 'survival of the fittest ideas'. Thus, in the end, the best ideas and ideologies will prevail because they are the most 'just' and the most likely to reconcile our individual emotional amoral egoism with the need of others for dignity. If uninhibited by fear and prejudice, transcultural synergies are likely to give rise to ideas and views which result in some form of dignity-based governance.

4.4.11. *The Future of Conflicts*

Finally, a few remarks on a future, and unprecedented, kind of conflict. I discussed transhumanism in Chapters 2.5 and 4.2, so I shall only briefly recall here the potential for conflict brought about by trans- and post-humanism.

Interventions to enhance humans' physical and cognitive capacities beyond normal levels will deal a blow to the social contract and to the fundamental notion that we are entitled to inalienable rights by virtue of all being human. Since we can presume that the wealthy will have access to such enhancement techniques long before other people, at the very least, even milder forms of enhancement can widen the gap between the haves and have-nots. This growing divide between those who have more powers and capabilities and those who do not is likely to create tensions in the workplace and in academia. It will also give rise to a change in warfare as we know it today. Indeed, wealthy and more scientifically advanced states will have access to military technologies, with which others stand no chance of competing.[752]

Concerns of meritocracy and fairness, already compromised by other forms of inequality, will become even more acute. In a future when neurotechnologies permit more radical forms of intervention to the mind and body, the very essence of what it means to be human will be thrown into question, and with this will go the underlying presumption of the equal dignity of all human beings, grounded in their shared humanity. A hierarchical ordering of humanity along categories of enhanced and non-enhanced would most likely entail a denial of certain rights to some members of society, and thus increase the risks of social conflict. Readers will remember that our nature is driven by the powerful motivators which I refer to as the Neuro P5: power, profit, pleasure, pride and permanency. The Neuro P5 will push us to adopt technologies which promise to enhance one or more of these motivators. The only way to avoid bleak scenarios is to regulate the market for enhancements because we cannot leave it to our 'rationality' to prevent such outcomes.

* * *

This chapter has outlined some of the major approaches to understanding conflict at the individual, intrastate, interstate and inter-civilisational levels. It has suggested how a neurophilosophical perspective can contribute to a better understanding of conflict. Indeed, as demonstrated by my theory of emotional amoral egoism, the mechanisms which lie behind human psychodynamics and behaviour go far beyond nature–nurture dichotomies. As I have illustrated throughout this book, the human mind, in my view, is a predisposed *tabula rasa*, shaped by both genetic and environmental influences. The interaction of survival instincts – largely manifested as neurochemically-mediated emotions – and the environment, means that fear, pain, grief, ego, pride and greed are factors which contribute to conflict at all levels of analysis. Good governance, which ensures political and socioeconomic justice, human dignity, respect for diversity and recognition of other 'truths', is essential to all efforts to prevent conflict.

I hope to have illustrated, in the previous sections, how a neurophilosophical perspective widens the scope of our understanding of some of today's major security challenges, including radicalisation, xenophobia and various forms of conflict. The next chapter will give a brief overview of some other pressing security concerns which have received less scholarly attention than the security issues discussed above. The next chapter will demonstrate that the theory of emotional amoral egoism can be applied across a wide range of situations, showing how governance must be rethought to harness our innate tendencies for the greater good of life on this planet.

4.5

Analytic Neurophilosophy and Policy

The challenges shaping our current security landscape defy any brief summary. This chapter, nonetheless, offers a brief overview of some key trends from a neurophilosophical perspective. Using the theory of emotional amoral egoism, it will highlight the importance of meeting human dignity in order to circumvent the pitfalls associated with these trends.

4.5.1. Human Enhancement Technologies

Chapter 2.5 explored the various ways innovative technologies may radically change humankind's capabilities. Here, I wish to point out how dignity-based governance can help us reap the benefits of these technologies whilst minimising their risks.

Clearly, increased knowledge about the human brain, conjoint with technological advances, is opening up new possibilities for the enhancement of human faculties. In the future, an ever-increasing integration of human thought with AI and machine-learning could equip humankind with unprecedented decision-making potential, improved situational awareness and even new sensory experiences. Rapid developments in synthetic biology, in particular, make possible not only the alteration of biological systems, but also the creation of novel biological systems. As synthetic biology progresses on various fronts, biological super-intelligence, among much else, may soon become not a mere product of our imagination and science fiction fantasies, but a reality.[753] Human enhancement, which will rapidly extend far beyond current pharmaceutical adjustments to brain function, may soon set us on the path to trans- and post-humanism – a next phase of evolution in which innovations in technologies will alter our neurochemistry in radical ways. In this future world, the changes which may occur might be so dramatic that future 'humans' will no longer resemble past and present human beings.[754]

A neurophilosophical understanding of human nature as emotional, amoral and egoistic allows for specific predictions about how people will use the possibilities of human enhancement, and with what consequences. When left unchecked – whether by positive socialisation or institutional constraints – the egoistic character of human nature will entail a relentless search for the Neuro P5: power, profit, pleasure, pride and permanency.[755] The Neuro P5 activate the reward centres of the brain – delivering neurochemical satisfaction. The brain is pre-programmed to 'feel good' and it will push us to do everything it takes to attain this neurochemical gratification, maintain it and, if possible, enhance it. This is why we need to apply caution when dealing with technologies which promise to enhance neurochemical gratification far beyond therapeutic needs – this is a promise we are unlikely to resist, and we shall stop at nothing in order to make it become a reality. In other words, the increased abilities conferred by being biologically enhanced or super-intelligent will amplify issues of power addiction (see Chapter 3.1), so that the augmented elite would continuously increase its own power. A super-intelligent being, furthermore, could have greater opportunities to manufacture consent, remove checks on its power and engage in various activities which the political theorist Philip Pettit describes as 'domination'.[755] Indeed, the concept of domination is a useful framework through which to consider a number of challenges posed by human enhancement technologies and super-intelligence, which might be harnessed by the powerful to subvert the weak. Pettit's central contention is that the achievement of real freedom presupposes equality. He argues that the individual is 'free to the extent that others do not stand over him or her, able to interfere at will and with relative impunity in his or her affairs'.[756] Enhancement technologies, however, are likely not only to infringe upon our accepted norms of meritocracy and fairness, but also to call into question the authenticity of the human experience, and to create divisions and inequality between the enhanced and the non-enhanced.[757]

A neurophilosophical perspective dispels the illusion that our relationship with enhancement technologies will be driven by 'reason' or an appropriate sense of moderation. As we are driven by the quest for neurochemical gratification, enhancement technologies will require appropriate governance paradigms – domestic and global – to keep our egoism in check. Otherwise, emerging technologies will have the potential to lead to new forms of domination among social groups. A focus on human dignity can maximise the benefits brought about by innovative technologies whilst minimising their risks. Dignity, as I have argued, means much more than the mere absence of humiliation; it includes a comprehensive set of nine needs: *reason, security, human rights, accountability, transparency, justice, opportunity, innovation* and *inclusiveness.* All nine dimensions of human dignity must be safeguarded if we are to prevent advances in cutting-edge technologies from creating irreparable damage to individuals and societies. One way to pre-empt this damage would be to bring scientists, ethicists, civil society organisations and policymakers together to agree on ethical standards and regulatory frameworks for human enhancement technologies.[758]

4.5.2. Fake News

Recent years have seen a rapid growth in the phenomenon of fake news manipulating popular opinion and influencing politics and societies across the globe, as demonstrated by its extensive use during the 2016 US elections[759] and the Brexit referendum campaigns[760] and, more recently, during the Covid-19 pandemic.[761] Insights from neuroscience advance our understanding of human vulnerabilities to fake news, which is a prerequisite if we are to limit their nefarious effects.

Fake news exists in forms which vary in terms of their motivation and differ in their degree of falsity.[762] The falsehoods include disinformation, propaganda and, more recently, 'deepfakes' (i.e. highly realistic manipulations of video footage of individuals making statements which were never actually uttered or carrying out actions which never took place[763]). Although hardly a new phenomenon, advances in digital communication channels and the development of social media platforms have acted as accelerators for fake news, making it more difficult to contain and, ironically, radically 'democratised' – in the sense that anyone, anywhere can become a creator and messenger of fake news. For this reason, our age has often been described as a 'post-truth era' in which it is easy to cherry-pick information which corresponds to our own biases, with objective facts being less influential in shaping public opinion than appeals to strong emotions, such as fear, anger, or resentment, as well as personal convictions.[764] However, examples of spreading manipulated information can be found throughout human history. In ancient Rome, for example, it was a piece of fake news which helped Octavian defeat Marc Anthony in a fierce disinformation war. Capitalising on anti-eastern prejudices harboured by many ancient Romans, Octavian spread a probably fabricated document which allegedly disclosed Marc Anthony's intention to leave a sizable part of his legacy to his children with Cleopatra.[765]

Fake news preys on peoples' biases. It creates so-called echo chambers, in which the constant repetition of one-sided views amplifies pre-held prejudices and grievances. Without regulation, fake news has the capacity to sow discord, amplify polarisation, incite anger and even violence, undermining social harmony within democratic societies and thus weakening their overall functioning.[766] As Yale historian Timothy Snyder rightly remarks, a propaganda machine can be among the most effective forms of psychological warfare in history.[767]

Over the past few decades, psychology has made an important contribution to the understanding of human vulnerability to fake news. Among other things, it has highlighted the crucial role of what we refer to as 'confirmation bias' – our tendency to search for, interpret and retain information in a way which confirms our pre-existing convictions.[768] Neuroscience research has unveiled the neurochemical processes underlying our biases, as well as innate in-group tendencies which contribute to the allure of fake news.

In late 2019, a study published in *Nature* explored the neuroscience of confirmation bias, showing how existing judgements alter the neural representation of information strength, leading to reduced neural sensitivity to others' opinions (this occurs in the posterior medial prefrontal cortex) when such opinions do not confirm the ones we already held.[769] As previously stated, the idea of unbiased rationality, though long celebrated in many schools of philosophy, is simply not confirmed by neuroscience. Human emotionality is, therefore, key to understanding both the appeal of fake news and possible ways to fight it. Our feelings about people or ideas – be they negative or positive – arise unconsciously and much faster than our conscious thoughts, driving how information is processed by our brains.[770] The prefrontal cortex, which is responsible for our higher decision-making, is not always 'switched on' when reading the news; rather the social portion of the brain takes over. As shown by experiments with fMRI, the likelihood of sharing information with other people is significantly higher when reading news which activates the social parts of the brain. Additionally, the same brain regions which validate socially accepted messages are more resistant to new information which threatens to isolate the individual from the group.[771]

Another approach, explored both in psychology and neuroscience, has looked at a rudimentary mechanism known as 'fluency', which refers to the cognitive ease with which we process information. According to what is known as the 'illusory truth effect', information which is repeated again and again appears increasingly truer and, during this process, easier to comprehend and, thus, more comfortable to the brain.[772] Moreover, people interpret feelings, including ease of processing, as evidence of truth. This is how, in addition to hijacking our memory and learning neural circuitry, fake news appeals to our deep-seated emotions.[773]

Instruments to fight fake news have proliferated in recent years (including technical and algorithmic tools for better detection, fact-checking and removal of false content) and so have political and government actions and multilateral initiatives. For example, in 2018, the European Union introduced a Code of Practice on Disinformation as a voluntary mechanism of self-regulatory standards to fight disinformation. The code was signed, among others, by Facebook, Google and Twitter.[774] Yet, these efforts alone are unlikely to be sufficient. Research ranging from neuroscience to cognitive psychology is expanding our understanding of how humans are, on the one hand, guided by deep-seated emotions and, on the other, inhibited by cognitive biases in information processing. Countering fake news, therefore, requires enhanced efforts directed at equipping audiences with the critical literacy skills necessary to sort through the thicket of data, information and opinions which are thrown at us on a daily basis. Dignity-based governance fosters a reason-based society through high-quality education which enables us to separate facts from feelings. Neuroscience can help us devise better educational curricula and strategies for muting biased information processing, thereby shielding us from dangerous falsehoods. To fight fake news, it is also imperative that we promote transcultural understanding, stressing human civilisations' shared history and interconnectedness. In the absence of transcultural understanding, and given the globalised nature of our world, the perils of fake news are poised to exacerbate cultural prejudices and tensions.[775]

4.5.3. Divisive Politics, Inequality and Disempowerment

Our current times are characterised by rising levels of polarisation. Instead of seeking to create common ground, politicians around the world increasingly engage in divisive politics which aggravate tensions between people with different outlooks. As Barry Eichengreen points out, extreme partisanship is not a new phenomenon in Europe or the United States.[776] Yet, recent manifestations of political polarisation appear to be unprecedented in their intensity and simultaneity across various national contexts. Together, they pose a serious threat to global peace and security, one which policymakers must better understand and counteract. Divisive politics are fuelled by inequality.[777]

In this context, a neurophilosophical perspective on polarisation and its relationship with inequality and disempowerment is highly instructive. In conditions of instability and perceived vulnerability, populist politicians can easily capitalise on our innate in-group bias to strengthen their political power (Chapter 4.3.3 offers further details on this). Chief among the causes of popular feelings of insecurity is inequality. Moreover, inequality is rising, both within and between countries. Domestic inequalities are approaching near-all-time-highs in many of the major economies. As the World Inequality Report of 2018 observes, 'If established trends in wealth inequality were to continue, the top 0.1% alone will own more wealth than the global middle class by 2050.'[778]

Awareness of tremendous inequalities in wealth, income and power generates impressions of injustice and vulnerability. Given our strong survival instincts, these feelings of vulnerability are likely to translate into self-regarding behaviour and a lack of concern for the well-being of others. In fact, our egoism pushes us to do whatever it takes to ensure our survival and have our proportion of the cake, including acts which are illegal and harmful to others. Moreover, political disempowerment gives rise to fear and humiliation, feelings which are likely to consolidate learning mechanisms which promote mistrust and defensive and anti-social behaviour. On the other side, those doing well in circumstances of high economic disparity are likely to press their advantage. As a result, inequality contributes to polarisation along socioeconomic lines, which provides a fertile breeding ground for populist movements adept at instrumentalising economic grievances. This is why dignity-based governance promotes justice and inclusiveness for counteracting the forces which produce inequality.[779]

4.5.4. Big Data and the Social Contract

Pythagoras is said to have argued that numbers explain and control the world.[780] This observation holds true today more than ever before. Today's times are often referred to as the age of Big Data. Big Data and the related field of Big Data analytics refer to large datasets, which cannot be processed by traditional methods. The sources of Big Data are varied (driven, among others, by artificial intelligence, social media, the Internet of Things) and are generated continuously, often in real time. Big Data provides new methods to engage with data, outside structured models and paradigms, and it allows for (or so it promises) better and faster decision making, as well as modelling and predicting of future outcomes. This explains, for instance, its growing use in surveillance and policing. For all the possibilities it offers, Big Data poses various challenges to each of the nine basic requirements for dignity which are necessary for human beings to thrive and become the best versions of themselves, namely: reason, security, human rights, accountability, transparency, justice, opportunity, innovation and inclusiveness.

Reason, which broadly refers to the extent to which governments rely on facts, can be severely undermined by Big Data. Indeed, governments and public institutions may jump to conclusions on the basis of algorithmic data, losing sight of its inherent shortcomings, biases and even randomness. Similarly, Big Data brings about numerous security threats. Privacy risks are abundant and so is discrimination in data processing against certain social or ethnic groups. Human rights, such as the right to data protection, are also poised to be affected by Big Data. Above all, discrimination or biases in predictive analytics constitute a serious human rights violation.[781]

In addition, algorithms which operate on Big Data may weaken mechanisms for ensuring accountability and transparency, as algorithms are very complex and incomprehensible to the general public. In reality, even computer scientists at times struggle to understand them, given the possibility of algorithms behaving unpredictably.[782] Another requirement for dignity is justice, which may be compromised by unfair treatment resulting from computerised risks assessments which calculate the chances a convict will re-offend. These risk assessments may be imbued with the bias of their programmers.[783]

Furthermore, Big Data may curtail opportunity and inclusiveness, which are two of the requirements for dignity connected to our 'egoism', as they refer to access to essential resources for survival and self-fulfilment. Reflecting the bias of their programmers, predictive analytics tools may 'forecast' troublemakers, thus disqualifying certain individuals from, for example, employment opportunities.[784] Not only can Big Data reinforce existing discriminatory practices, such as those which affect ethnic, racial or religious minorities; it can also silence those wishing to report on injustices and discrimination. Another requirement for dignity linked to our egoism is innovation, which is key to enabling self-expression. However, the age of Big Data and mass surveillance increases the risk of self-censorship. In fact, following allegations of mass surveillance programmes carried out by the United States National Security Agency, a 2013 study found that a significant number of US writers chose some form of self-censorship.[785] Similar findings were reported in 2018 for Scotland-based writers.[786]

In sum, Big Data poses severe risks to human dignity, which may profoundly shift the meaning of the social contract. At its foundation, the social contract assumes equal stakes among the members of society. However, a private entity in possession of large amounts of personal data has predictive powers which enable it to have an unequal stake in the shared system.[787] Google, for instance, possesses enough data that would give it the capacity to accurately predict stock-market trends, if it chose to do so.[788] To avoid the risks associated with over-reliance on Big Data, regulatory frameworks are needed which ensure data protection, transparency and accountability and which prevent predictive models from reinforcing stereotypes and perpetuating inequalities. A growing sense of injustice will weaken the social contract and the voluntary social cooperation it brings with it, and no amount of data will be able to restore the trust necessary for the functioning of society.[789]

4.5.5. Social Distancing

At the time of the second edition of this book, the Covid-19 pandemic has started to profoundly alter our ways of life. To slow the spread of the virus, millions of people around the world have been asked to practise 'social distancing'. As one writer defined it on the eve of the public health shutdowns in 2020, social distancing is a 'public health practice which aims to prevent sick people from coming in close contact with healthy people in order to reduce opportunities for disease transmission'.[790] Typically, it requires both large-scale measures implemented by public authorities (such as the cancellation of public events) as well as conscious individual decisions to avoid gatherings.

Social distancing is perceived by most people as an excruciating imposition. In the twenty-first century, accustomed to an extraordinary degree of connectivity, frequent travel and liberty of movement, social distancing feels all the more dreadful. We have always been deeply social beings and neuroscientific research has shed new light on Aristotle's famous saying that man is a social animal.[791] Neuroscientific investigations have begun to unveil how social isolation and social interaction are expressed neurochemically, how they are connected to our primordial fears and how they affect our moral development, both collectively and individually.[792]

Prolonged periods of isolation affect mental and overall health in profound ways. A 2010 study, for example, showed that stronger social relations correlate with higher chances of survival. The study explored health risks in over 300,000 individuals, followed for an average of 7.5 years. The study group consisted of both healthy participants and patients with pre-existing conditions. It found that stronger social relations lead to at least 50 per cent increase in the odds of survival.[793]

Another study, published in 2019 in the *New England Journal of Medicine*, explored the impact of isolation on nine polar expeditioners working in remote parts of Antarctica. The study suggests that the brain shrinks as a result of environmental monotony and isolation, which leads to reductions in the hippocampal volume of the dentate gyrus – a part of the brain believed to be implicated in memory formation and special awareness. The study also found that the concentration of the protein BDNF (brain-derived neurotrophic factor) decreased after the first quarter of the expedition and had not recovered one and a half months after the end of the expedition. These reductions in dentate gyrus volume and BDNF concentration are associated with lower cognitive performance in spatial processing and selective attention.[794]

A cluster of cells located at the back of the brain, in an area called the dorsal raphe nucleus, is believed to be responsible for the feeling of loneliness.[795] Interestingly, numerous studies suggest that there are neuronal mechanisms which make us seek increased social contact after periods of isolation, or in anticipation of prolonged isolation.[796] Hence, our aversion to practising social distancing during the Covid-19 pandemic. Further, isolation makes us pay increased attention to social stimuli. This is confirmed by research showing how socially excluded individuals tend to display an enhanced selective memory for social events.[797] Research also suggests that the feeling of isolation is not experienced in the same way by all individuals but is dependent on a number of factors such as social rank.[798] In other words, there are differences in what social distancing means for different people, in neuroanatomic and neurochemical terms.[799]

Prolonged social isolation profoundly affects both our psyche and behaviour, as it provokes a number of neuropsychological and neuroendocrinological responses in brain regions responsible for threat surveillance and self-preservation. Despite its potential downsides (such as competition or the risks of pathogen transmission), sociality is critical to survival. A sense of isolation makes us focus more on negative social stimuli (e.g. threats, exclusion) and engage in behaviour centred on short-term self-preservation. This may result in sleep fragmentation, altered gene expression and immunity, decreased impulse control/ increased aggression, cognitive decline, risks of dementia and anxiety. In other words, when feeling isolated, the individual is more focussed on detecting threats and preparing to defend himself or herself.[800]

Whilst moments of serene solitude may be conducive to an individual's productivity or artistic creativity, externally imposed isolation is a straining experience which triggers a host of ancestral fears. A neurophilosophical perspective on social distancing helps explain why we cannot thrive in loneliness and why the older structures of our brain make us perceive prolonged isolation as distressing.[801]

The possibility of recurring pandemics represents one of the major global security risks of the twenty-first century.[802] In times of pandemic, dignity-based governance is well equipped to minimise harm to lives, livelihoods and mental health as it prioritises the human need for safety. Furthermore, its commitment to reason implies, first, a willingness to be led by expertise and science, which results in better crisis management. Second, it focusses on educating all segments of society not only about preventive measures, such as good hygiene practices, but also about how to mitigate the negative effects of social distancing through self-reflection and online engagement with others. After all, it might be helpful to recall the words of Seneca, who famously claimed that we tend to suffer more in our imagination than in reality.[803] In addition, the fears triggered by isolation can be assuaged by community support and effective and transparent communications from governments and health experts.[804]

4.5.6. *The Meaning of Existence*

A neurophilosophical perspective on human nature can even widen our perspective on a concept as elusive as the meaning of existence. Questions about fulfilment, the purpose of life and the achievement of happiness have accompanied inquiries into human nature since the beginning of human memory. How can we bestow meaning on our lives and what pushes us to engage in certain actions, beneficial or not? Whilst some aspects of these considerations remain shrouded in mystery, others have had light shed upon them by recent advances in neuroscience and our increasing understanding of neurochemistry. However, why am I discussing the meaning of life in a chapter devoted to exploring today's major security challenges? In fact, there is a strong correlation between the quest for meaning and radicalism, one of today's most pressing security challenges, as discussed above. An identity-relevant life goal is what many people are looking for when joining extremist groups. Moreover, happiness plays an important role in holistic approaches to development and politics. Bhutan, for example, has adopted Gross National Happiness (GNH) as a yardstick to measure success, in contrast to purely economic factors.[805] Gross National Happiness not only plays a major role in Bhutan's politics but is also recognised by the UN as key to a holistic approach to notions of progress.[806] In fact, every political, social and economic system should be conducive to promoting individual fulfilment. A neurophilosophical perspective helps to explain why the individual's quest for meaning and fulfilment is a key to peace and how it can be associated with productive enterprises.

As I have argued before, the human brain is pre-programmed to feel good. This tendency is 'encoded' in the neuronal reward systems of our brains, which seek to obtain – and maintain – a sense of well-being. In Chapter 3.1, I illustrated how, according to my Neuro P5 theory, there are five main drivers of human action through which that sense of well-being is sought: power, profit, pleasure, pride and permanency. Indeed, all human beings follow the sustainable neurochemical gratification principle, which implies that we tend to engage in, and repeat, activities which activate the reward centres of the brain, regardless of how constructive or destructive they may be. This principle also applies, *inter alia*, to various forms of faith, which fulfil our need for permanency, thus activating neurochemical mechanisms which sustain a sense of well-being. In other words, we are all addicts of some sort, sometimes to constructive activities, at other times to less useful or even destructive behaviour.[807]

Existence tends to be more meaningful for human beings when their attachments and pursuits deliver feelings of gratification. Importantly, this gratification is a result of engagement in these activities, rather than solely an end in itself. Therefore, orchestrating an undeserved victory in a sporting event or virtually simulating such a victory does not produce an equivalent feeling of euphoria to that of a hard-earned victory. It is also worth noting that the positive experience of gratification is far more motivating than the negative experience of punishment aiming at deterring particular behaviour.

Given our neuronal plasticity and susceptibility to socialising influences, sources of neurogratification can be influenced – both by other individuals and by existing institutional structures which encourage, or set limits to, the kind of behaviour we can engage in. Human beings in stable social and political circumstances can be encouraged to pursue forms of gratification which are beneficial to themselves and others. On the other hand, in circumstances of disregard for the needs of individuals or entire groups, power has proven to be among the most addictive forms of human gratification, with often nefarious consequences.[808]

The evolutionary inheritance of human beings – a suite of survival-oriented instincts – is not in any obvious way geared towards an objectively meaningful purpose. Yet, being aware of this, and understanding the neurochemical underpinnings of our sense of well-being, is empowering. It makes us realise that a meaningful existence must respect who we are, in terms of our neurobiology and our neurochemical and hormone motivations. Nevertheless, this understanding of the meaning of our existence leaves significant room for socialisation privileging the numerous positive forms which neurochemical gratification can take.[809] Through its focus on opportunity and innovation, dignity-based governance helps individuals to bestow meaning on their lives by giving them plentiful opportunities to pursue their talents, creativity and passions.

4.5.7. A Neurophilosophical Paradigm for a 'New Enlightenment'

A neurophilosophical perspective makes us rethink the legacy of the Enlightenment, calling into question the notion of 'progress through reason' associated with the movement. Recent neuroscientific insights into human nature disprove the classical divide between 'rationality' and 'emotionality' and, it is to be hoped, pave the way for a 'new Enlightenment'. By 'new Enlightenment' I refer to an ideological climate which recognises both the centrality of emotions in human experience and the shared biological and historical heritage of the human species. Being aware of our commonalities, shared by all people irrespective of culture or origin, is key to counteracting rigid forms of ethnocentrism which can easily lead to xenophobia and conflict, as discussed in Chapters 4.3 and 4.4.

In neuroscientific terms, we know that the Stoics' aversion to emotions as threats to reason was unfounded. We are all 'slaves' to emotions, but only insofar as it is through emotions that numerous learning mechanisms are consolidated in the brain, including fear-conditioned responses, which are crucial for survival.[810] Indeed, recent neuroscientific research has advanced our understanding of how knowledge and beliefs are acquired. It has revealed a close interplay between brain regions mediating sense experience – emotionality – and cognition. Against this background, I have elsewhere introduced a new knowledge paradigm called *neurorational physicalism* which more holistically explains the process of knowledge formation, with important conclusions for this discussion of Enlightenment. Neurorational physicalism recognises both sensory data and reason – both of which are filtered by interpretation – as sources of knowledge. It highlights the complex interplay of reason, emotionality and our built-in predilections (the most critical of which is the predisposition for survival). Knowledge is, therefore, hardly ever objective and complete because its sources are biased, being subject to interpretation and to inputs from prior assumptions which are shaped by one's surroundings, experience, education and cultural background.[811]

Neurorational physicalism acknowledges the neurobiological foundation of human nature, which means that thoughts and knowledge are always mediated through neurochemistry and, thus, have a physical basis. Although the idea of physicality of knowledge and mental processes has historically been a highly contentious issue in philosophy, most neuroscientists do support it.[812]

In the twenty-first century, as politics is increasingly defined by a resurgence of nationalistic bias, tribalism and exclusionary practices, it is common to decry an apparent estrangement from the legacy of the Enlightenment, which is often understood as being solely about individual autonomy and reason. This is, as Henry Martyn Lloyd rightly observes, a pathology of Western thought which has equated modernity with positivist science and cool-headed reason.[813] This conclusion about the Enlightenment is not merely simplistic. Whilst Enlightenment philosophers certainly valued reason, they did not take it to mean that humans could be perfectly rational. Nor did they dissociate emotions from good judgement.[814] This conclusion is also increasingly dangerous, as it is often used to pit a rational and secular West against irrational 'others'. Furthermore, neurophilosophical insights into human nature demonstrate the salience of emotions in our existence, as well as the malleability of our nature. Circumstances in our environment can push us to cruel deeds, or they can enhance our propensity for (pseudo)-altruistic acts.[815]

Our best chance of surviving and thriving is through dignity-based governance, which balances the ever-present tension between the three attributes of human nature (emotionality, amorality and egoism) with human dignity. Dignity-based governance is, in fact, the single best instrument of peace. The people of an enlightened twenty-first century (and those to follow) will, therefore, need to focus on human dignity in its holistic sense. One of the most valuable lessons from human history is that ideologies and regimes which have repeatedly ignored the need for human dignity have ultimately failed. For political ideas to pass the test of time, they must account for the emotional, amoral and egoistic nature of all human beings and balance these attributes with the corresponding nine requirements for dignity.[816]

Importantly, the need for dignity must be also upheld at the collective level. Dichotomising cultures as rational/secular versus traditional/irrational misreads the rich legacy of Enlightenment thought, which was heavily inspired by ancient and non-European works and ideas. A truly enlightened future for humanity will need to recognise the contribution of every geo-cultural domain. I previously referred to this as the ocean model of civilisation: just as an ocean is fed by many rivers, so human civilisation is an accumulation of contributions from distinct yet intertwined geo-cultural domains which, throughout the centuries, have interacted and shaped one another. This conception accounts for cultural influences of varying degrees, encompassing both the dominant cultural forces of the day as well as the cultural mixing we are increasingly experiencing today as a result of instant worldwide information sharing. By recognising all cultures as being constitutive of a single human civilisation, the 'ocean model' attributes value to them all. Everything in the Western world, from philosophy, astronomy, sciences, medicine and architecture to legal thought, is, in fact, a product of centuries of exchanges and interactions with the non-Western world, including China, India and the Arab-Islamic world, which were for long periods the epicentres of scientific discoveries and heavily influenced the European Enlightenment.[817] Through a concerted emphasis on the shared biological and historical heritage of the human species, a 'new Enlightenment' can undermine ethnocentric notions of progress and foster transcultural understanding and synergies.

4.5.8. A Neurophilosophy of Legitimacy

'The basis of every system of authority, and correspondingly of every kind of willingness to obey, is a belief, a belief by virtue of which those exercising authority are lent prestige.'[818] This common definition of political legitimacy – articulated by Max Weber – states that power structures are held in place by the popular belief that they are best suited for society.

Offering the basis for rule by consent, rather than coercion, legitimacy promotes constructive relations between the state and its citizens and is vital for keeping regimes in power. Legitimacy is the fulcrum around which debates on good governance turn. For this reason, a wealth of literature has investigated and continues to investigate the normative content of legitimacy, focussing on definitional issues, or justifications for the attribution of it. Whilst these approaches are instructive, they widely overlook neuroscientific insights. These include the role of individual and mass neuropsychology and the emotionality of states – which are directly traceable to neurocellular and neurochemical underpinnings – with respect to legitimacy. These insights are much needed as an increasing number of national governments and intergovernmental organisations appear to suffer from deficits of legitimacy.[819]

A useful definition of legitimacy is provided by Ian Hurd, who highlights that it is a consequence of intersubjectivity and is, therefore, directly linked to neuropsychological states. Legitimacy in this account consists of the belief that a rule ought to be followed or a purported authority 'ought to be obeyed'. Legitimacy is also 'relational between actor and institution, and defined by the actor's *perception* of the institution'.[820] Legitimacy is, thus, crucial to the survival of any regime, and regimes are likely to lose legitimacy as a consequence of (perceived) economic incompetence, mistreatment of citizens, or failures of representation.

As demonstrated above, human beings have egoist tendencies (the pursuit of survival is a basic form of egoism) but our emotionality, for good evolutionary reasons, also allows for social valuing and the recognition of benefits to group membership. These basic features of our biological nature enable the possibility of cooperative arrangements. It is, therefore, crucial to recognise that our genetic legacy (i.e. our emotional amoral egoism and need for dignity) informs our attribution of legitimacy. Given our egoistic tendencies, the legitimacy we attribute to an action or to an institution can be undermined by perceived threats to our survival and well-being. In addition to the provision of basic needs and security, governance which fulfils its constituents' need for human dignity is essential to the preservation of legitimacy. Indeed, the fulfilment of dignity is instrumental for stable conceptions of self-worth and is, thus, very close to our neurochemically mediated emotional core. When this need is systematically denied, populations begin to lose faith in their leadership (or analogously, in international organisations).[821]

Global politics, as manifested in intergovernmental organisations like the United Nations or the Bretton Woods institutions, must appeal to an incredibly diverse and multicultural constituency. The legitimacy of such global actors depends not only on their efficiency but also on the perception that they are representative in relevant ways, as demonstrated by the highly controversial existence of the so-called Permanent Five within the United Nations Security Council. The legitimacy of national politics, on the other hand, answers to a more narrowly circumscribed set of interests. Recalling Benedict Anderson's seminal work on nations, these entities are necessarily 'limited' in the sense that, by definition, they include some and exclude others.[822] In the language of evolutionary neuropsychology, nations differentiate in-groups and out-groups, first collectively imagining and then institutionalising them.[823] As a number of scholars in related fields have argued, these facts set up ethical conditions in which the treatment of those understood to possess membership of one's own group diverges from the treatment of outsiders. Only a long process of cultural education can ingrain within a group equal treatment of those whom they consider 'alien'.[824] Consequently, when it comes to national legitimacy, this implies that constituents must believe that their unique national interests are diligently pursued. Indeed, nearby looms the familiar danger of rabid nationalism, which subscribes to a kind of zero-sum thinking in which not merely the promotion of one's own nation is desirable but so is the denigration and possibly even the annihilation of others.[825]

Therefore, and in addition to the fulfilment of the need for dignity, specific programmes for historical and cultural education are required to soften perceived national or cultural boundaries. As mentioned before, education should focus on transcultural history, thus emphasising connections between different geo-cultural domains, connections which have frequently been cut from narratives which conceptualise different 'civilisations' as separate from one another or even incompatible.[826] This is often the case, for instance, with regard to relations between the West and the Arab-Islamic world, which have shared centuries of exchanges and mutual borrowings.[827] Indeed, with a more accurate account of history, domestic legitimacy would require fewer exclusionary practices.

To summarise, the legitimacy of both national and global politics depends on the ability to safeguard the fulfilment of the need for human dignity and to create inclusive national and global identities. In today's diverse and interdependent environments, I believe that the only sustainable form of power is *just* power, power which is non-discriminatory and which complies with the fundamental principle of the rule of law, according to which everyone, all states and nations, are equal before the law. Indeed, leadership in the twenty-first century must create cultures of belonging capable of uniting diverse people behind the shared vision of a safer and fairer world.[828]

4.5.9. Neurophilosophy of History

Policymakers must understand and learn from the past to be able to make the right decisions. From divine providence to inexorable evolution, the purveyors of historical change have been conceptualised in different ways by scholars from different disciplines. Often, they have considered history to follow a definite trajectory, moving towards some specified end-state. These end-states have been conceived in a variety of ways, ranging from idealised conceptions of social and political harmony to dystopian visions of anarchy. Yet, the underlying assumption has always been the same: that the seeds of future stages of history could be found in the present arrangement of things; and, with the right 'science' of history, we could foretell what would come next. Today, however, this idea of 'historical determinism' is strongly criticised.[829]

The tradition of interpreting history in patterned ways, whether linear or cyclical, has ancient roots. However, it was arguably later, with Hegel and Marx, that the phenomenon of 'directional' history reached its fully elaborated form in the Western canon. The two thinkers took very different stances on the direction and end-state of history. On the one side, Hegel viewed history as progressing towards the realisation of the 'modern' state, in which a truly ethical life, individual freedom and a strong community identity would arise and flourish.[830] Marx, on the other, supposed that the self-destructive nature of capitalism would inevitably culminate in revolution, allowing communism to prevail. At the close of the nineteenth century the ideas of both Hegel and Marx carried a significant degree of traction, but these predictive accounts of history were abruptly called into question by the First and the Second World Wars, which defined the first half of the twentieth century. The temptation remained, however, to incorporate the lessons of the twentieth century into a philosophy of history which focussed on explaining political events over a span of time.[831] In 1989, Fukuyama declared that the 'end of history' had been reached with the proliferation of democracy and the conclusion of the Cold War.[832] Nevertheless, the suppositions defended by *The End of History and the Last Man* have since been challenged by the events of the past three decades, as Fukuyama himself has acknowledged.[833]

Today, it is widely accepted that particular political arrangements are not ordained by nature but are, to the contrary, human creations and that, for this same reason, they need to respond to human needs.[834] Policymakers must take this insight into account when making decisions. An understanding of human nature as emotional, amoral and egoistic has important implications for making sense of history.

As human beings are subject to influences through socialisation, they are, to a large degree, at the mercy of circumstances. Where the need for dignity is met, human beings can flourish – and this flourishing, in turn, promotes social and political stability. A key consideration is, thus, that human nature is not static and can be shaped to either facilitate cooperation or to sharpen egoism at the expense of others. It is, therefore, critical to ensure the right context for humanity to thrive. To repeat, sustainable civilisational progress can only unfold in a context designed to enable the fulfilment of human dignity. Furthermore, and to build on the realist assumption that states reflect the behaviour of human beings, the emotional amoral egoism of individuals is also reflected at the state level (see Chapter 4.7.3 on symbiotic realism and the emotionality of states). Far from being rational actors, states, too, demand dignity and respect as collective entities on the international scene. This enables them to rationally set aside their emotionality and egoism and work towards absolute gains which benefit humanity as a whole.

For a better future, dignity in its holistic form must be placed at the core of governance. This is one of the lessons history teaches policymakers. Moreover, it is imperative to apply this lesson in the coming decades, as humanity will be faced with new frontiers, both in terms of its own biological limitations and, in a more literal sense, with the exploration of outer space.[835]

* * *

To conclude, this chapter has briefly outlined the relevance of my theories of emotional amoral egoism and dignity-based governance across a wide variety of imminent security challenges. It becomes obvious from the preceding overview that today's major security risks are immune to borders and require international collaboration. Moreover, as I shall argue in the next section, addressing them requires a moral cosmopolitanism which extends our sense of moral obligation to the whole of humanity. Whilst we possess no inborn predisposition towards moral cosmopolitanism, dignity-based governance can instil in us greater concern for the welfare of others, both close and distant.

Emotional Amoral Egoism and the Boundaries of Moral Communities

The nation and state have been the traditional projects of modernity. Yet, the organisation of human communities inside these rigid physical and conceptual boundaries no longer appears adequate in today's interdependent and interconnected world. In the twenty-first century, local occurrences can rapidly have an impact around the globe. Increased human mobility is combined with heightened awareness of events taking place elsewhere in the world; this has been made readily available to us by the advent of new technologies and revolutionary impact of social media on our lives. These developments have generated the sense that we belong to a common and global community. Furthermore, as has become increasingly clear, nationalism and statism provide 'inadequate political resources' to meet today's challenges.[836] Within this context, cosmopolitanism is appealing. Moral cosmopolitanism implies that individuals, rather than states or other political units, are the ultimate moral subjects. This means that, by virtue of being members of the human race, we belong to one common moral community, not multiple separate and different ones. It also holds that we have an obligation to recognise each individual's inherent worth, which leads to mutual respect. In addition, it stresses personal responsibility, which can only be realised in non-coercive and inclusive political processes, at both the local and global levels.[837]

In reality, however, anti-cosmopolitanism is pervasive, as highlighted by the recent resurgence of nationalism and nativism across countries. In our globalised world, our loyalties and duties seem to remain surprisingly parochial. How can we explain this apparent tension? This chapter explores the implications of the theory of emotional amoral egoism for the project of moral cosmopolitanism.

4.6.1. The Origins of Moral Cosmopolitanism

The word 'cosmopolitanism' derives from the Greek word *kosmopolitēs* ('citizen of the world') and has been deployed to describe a broad spectrum of positions in moral and sociopolitical philosophy.[838]

For Kant, for example, moral cosmopolitanism was an attitude of recognition, respect and concern for other human beings and cultures.[839] Kant's cosmopolitanism can be placed within the tradition of the Stoics who affirmed moral obligations towards everyone in the world. According to the Stoics, the human capacity for reason made all human beings worthy of moral concern.[840] Readers will recall that, for Kant, the human capacity for reason was the source of our morality. While we were at one time motivated by primitive impulses, cognitive rationality has enabled our species to develop into moral beings. True morality, in Kant's view, had to derive from good intentions (i.e. to derive from conscious choices)[841] and required a degree of emotional sensitivity and an understanding of social convention.[842] Some argue that Kant's moral cosmopolitanism was rather limited. For example, Lorraine Eliot and Graeme Cheeseman point out that Kant essentially recognised the moral right to hospitality, namely, the right of a stranger not to be treated as an enemy when entering the land which belongs to another. However, the kind of moral duties we may require today need to involve moral commitments to non-fellow nationals going well beyond this.[843] However, Kant's philosophical cosmopolitanism, as Pauline Kleingeld highlights, underwent a significant transformation in the mid-1790s, resulting in complex arguments about cultural diversity, global justice and the psychological dimension of the cosmopolitan ideal.[844]

In contrast to cosmopolitan positions, particularist views assume a limited scope for the application of moral principles.[845] Particularism can be associated with Hume. As mentioned before, Hume held that we know the world only through a collection of perceptions (of which there are two kinds, impressions and ideas) rather than as the result of reason.[846] From this perspective, we engage in moral behaviour merely because it feels good rather than as the result of a rational cognitive process.[847] Indeed, under this conception, reason itself is thought to be dominated by desires. In light of this, we cannot rely on our capacity for reason to ensure moral behaviour. On the contrary, in Hume's view, our moral judgements are the product of our emotions. We may choose to assist someone in need out of sympathy, for example.[848] However, given the bias inherent in emotions like sympathy, most people engage in moral judgement-making only when interacting with those closest to them. Nonetheless, Hume made an important distinction. He argued that, while some moral judgements may originate in innate emotions, such as self-esteem and benevolence, others, such as justice, may need to be deliberately fostered by society.[849] This arguably leaves some room for cosmopolitan socialisation.

Unlike Kant, Rawls does not presuppose that ordinary moral judgements are largely the result of reason alone but his position is not synonymous with Hume's either.[850] Rawls was concerned with challenging the dominance of utilitarianism in moral philosophy. He wanted to outline a theory of justice in which, under normal conditions of social life, all people were capable of conceiving of justice in the same way. Like Kant before him, Rawls aimed to identify the moral principles which inform reasoning and judgements about justice. He regarded people as having a moral nature and as being fully capable of treating others with respect and as equals. He did not consider human beings to be driven by rational calculations of self-interest.[851] Human nature, as Rawls portrayed it, appears to have cosmopolitan tendencies. Yet, despite endorsing many quintessentially cosmopolitan ideas and concerns, Rawls himself considered his position to be non-cosmopolitan. His personal view, however, did not prevent many scholars from developing a theory of cosmopolitan justice on the basis of his premises.[852]

In Hauser's account of the making of moral judgements, human beings are endowed with a universal moral grammar or innate moral capacity. If emotions may be said to be implicated in the moral judgements we make, they are so after the fact. In this view, emotions are stimulated by moral judgements.[853] Furthermore, our moral instincts do not necessarily coincide with the consciously devised moral systems under which we live.[854] Hauser, along with other evolutionists such as Wilson and de Waal, argues that morality has evolved over time as a consequence of natural selection, specifically as a means of survival for communities as a whole and not just for individuals, and that, consequently, it is not triggered to the same degree in all situations. The stronger our connection with specific others, the more willing we shall be to act altruistically towards them.[855] For example, if a loved one fell into a deep and fast-flowing river, the chances are that most individuals would risk their own life to save the life of their loved one. On the other hand, if the person who fell in were a stranger, we might be less likely to jump in without hesitation to save him or her. Moreover, if a cat fell in, it would be extremely unlikely that a human being would put his or her own life at risk to save it. Under Hauser's conception, human beings are not predisposed by nature to feel moral obligations towards distant others.

Advances in neuroscience shed new light on the old debate between moral cosmopolitanism and moral particularism. Indeed, recent insights provided by neuroscience suggest that human beings are born amoral. To repeat, I do not use *amoral* in the traditional sense to denote indifference to, or lack of awareness of, the notions of right and wrong. Instead, I mean that moral concepts are not innate in us but rather are highly context-sensitive. As Chapter 3 explained in depth, some emotions – such as empathy – play an important role in moral judgements, but they do not *per se* foster cosmopolitan moral reasoning or an innate morality. Instead, these emotions are often biased towards individuals who are spatio-temporally close (our family members, for example, or fellow nationals). This is because our emotions are largely biological in origin, reflecting the environment in which human beings evolved. Our ancestors lived in dispersed groups and our strongest relationships were with kin. Hence, as Hauser argues, it is most likely that our survival instincts and our desire for permanence produced forms of altruistic behaviour directed at people to whom we were close and not at members of some other distant group. Today, however, our interactions with people to whom we are neither related nor directly linked in some way or another have grown exponentially and require us to make moral decisions on an everyday basis. Therefore, the question we must ask ourselves is this: how can we expand our moral concern to every other individual in this world?

4.6.2. Deepening and Widening Our Moral Communities

Although we do not have an inborn predisposition towards moral cosmopolitanism, we can, through our capacity for reason, be charitable towards distant 'others' and assist them in times of need. Our self-awareness has endowed us with the capacity for occasional reflection and conscious moral judgements. There is a wealth of evidence suggesting that, under the influence of conscious reflection, we can override our innate biases and develop moral codes which may be applied to a much wider community than we instinctively tend to care for.[856] Indeed, being human also implies being able to recognise our moral and non-moral limits and to seek to exceed them through the use of reason. Another function of our humanity is being able to work towards shared goals to build a better future. In light of this, I believe that a higher form of morality can be taught. While we are naturally predisposed to egoism and survival, the fact that we are neither moral nor immoral, but rather amoral, implies that morality stems to a great extent from our experiences within a specific environment and, in simple terms, is actually learnt.

In other words, given that individuals at this stage of their evolution are unlikely to act instinctively in a moral way towards people in distant parts of the world, moral cosmopolitanism must be consciously promoted. Indeed, recognising that our genetic heritage may be responsible for these limitations does not mean that we have to accept them. We are, after all, capable of engaging in reflection and, thus, able to conceive what might be required to live a 'good' life. As long as we possess this faculty, we can conceive and promote moral cosmopolitanism.

The post-Second World War period witnessed a number of important attempts at expanding our range of moral obligations, such as the adoption in 1948 by the United Nations of the Universal Declaration of Human Rights or in 1966 of the International Covenant on Civil and Political Rights and the International Covenant on Economic, Social and Cultural Rights.[857] Still, sovereignty and geopolitical interests often take precedence. In the twenty-first century, for instance, we are witnessing a surge of populism in many countries, which is exacerbating in-group/out-group bias.[858] Nevertheless, I believe that it is possible to counteract this worrisome trend.

By taking active steps to foster emotional engagement and social integration among different communities and with people to whom we are not genetically and geographically close, we can expand our circles of morality.[859] Indeed, there is no better way for people to understand one another than through interaction and exchange. Education and culture play a fundamental role in shaping our contemporary understanding of moral obligations. This requires incentives for the promotion of high moral standards – those which foster equality, empathy and peace, for example – in schools as well as in the global entertainment industry and in the arts and local communities, since these entities are the primary conduits for the promotion of moral norms.

As I have stated in previous chapters, in accordance with their egoistic nature, human beings will do whatever they have to in order to preserve the self. If they have to do this in an immoral way, then they will. In situations of near anarchy, in which people fear for their survival and that of their loved ones, genetically coded survival motivations will most likely trump moral standards, such as concern for others, or fairness. Conscious moral judgements are, therefore, unlikely to transpire if people's basic needs go unfulfilled. These include survival needs (comprising basic sustenance and physical security) but also requirements for dignity. Conscious moral judgements depend on good governance to satisfy these needs – at both the national and global levels. Indeed, I believe that the answer to the achievement of moral behaviour lies in the specific type of governance which prioritises human dignity, the broader implications of which I illustrated in Chapter 4.1. The final part of this book (Part 5) will provide further insights into how dignity-based governance can be achieved in practice.

In sum, to foster moral cosmopolitanism, we have to consciously promote it and also to increase interaction and awareness between people beyond our immediate context. Ample evidence suggests that we do not have an inborn predisposition towards moral cosmopolitanism but are, instead, naturally biased in favour of our in-group and against those outside it. Our ability to reason can, nonetheless, enable us to overcome this bias and develop and live by moral values which affirm the dignity and equal value of every person everywhere in the world. To harness individuals' pro-social potential and extend their moral concern to the whole of humanity, dignity-based governance is required. Dignity-based governance must be ensured at both the domestic and global levels and accompanied by harmonious interstate relations. The latter are best ensured by what I have called *symbiotic realism*. The following chapter will explore how symbiotic realism contributes to reconciling the ever-present tension between our emotional, amoral and egoistic nature and the need of other people to enjoy dignity.

4.7

Dignity-Based Governance and International Relations

The preceding chapters have, I hope, illustrated the ways dignity-based governance can contribute to lasting improvements in the human condition. This type of governance requires us to rethink traditional approaches to IR. To ensure the fulfilment of the need for human dignity on a global scale, states must pursue symbiotic realism in their conduct of international affairs. Symbiotic realism stresses the critical importance of absolute gains, where win-win situations are possible. This chapter demonstrates how IR theory can benefit from neurophilosophical insights into human nature. It offers an alternative approach to international relations, one which is practical in orientation and aimed at resolving the tension between the need for human dignity and our human nature as emotional amoral egoists. This tension is present not only within but also between countries, as this chapter illustrates.

4.7.1. Traditional Approaches to International Relations

Connections between the field of neuroscience and the study of international relations and politics have historically been limited. The field of IR is generally understood to explore the relations between states, along with issues such as competition, power and resources. At first glance, the findings of neuroscience hold little relevance for IR. On closer inspection, though, we find that the philosophical interest in human nature has been a crucial driver in the development of IR studies since their inception. Yet, prior to the advent of neuroscience, the understanding of what drives humans and states had been more speculative than scientific. I shall argue that any discussion of human nature in IR studies which does not account for the role of neurochemistry is incomplete because it overlooks the deeper motives of our political decisions.

Let us briefly review some major approaches to IR and then illustrate how human nature has always been an important variable in explaining the behaviour of states. The study of IR is heavily influenced by the philosophical approaches discussed in Part 2. While many theories claim to be value-free and apolitical, theorists cannot divorce themselves from their social, cultural and political contexts. Not only the theory but also the practice of international relations, as we know them today, were significantly influenced by the dominance of realism in the Anglo-Saxon world in the latter part of the twentieth century. In this sense, realism helped shape the world that it was charged with analysing.

Realism is not a single theory but rather an orientation. In general, realists assume that states are rational unitary actors; as the central actors in international relations, they are presumed to be selfish. The principal concern of a state is assumed to be the accumulation and exercise of power in the international arena. For realists, military power remains the most effective means of ensuring a state's survival. Since realists view states as the main actors in the international realm, state sovereignty is perceived to be sacrosanct.[860]

Liberalism is widely believed to be realism's main competition as a theoretical approach.[861] Liberalism stresses the capacity for cooperation in international relations, where it occurs within the framework of shared norms and values which create relations of trust as a result of repeated interaction. From this perspective, states are interdependent and the boundaries between them are increasingly porous. Cooperation between states is believed to be facilitated through the spread of democratic institutions, economic liberalisation and the growth in importance of international institutions. Military power is considered important, but so too are economic, political and diplomatic tools.[862]

The end of the Cold War, however, opened up the field to a number of other approaches, such as constructivism, neo-Gramscianism and postmodernism. These approaches have considered how the established global order came into being, how it has evolved over time and how it is likely to change in the future. They focus more on the history of the global order and are less concerned with finding strategies to ensure its smooth functioning.[863]

The constructivist view is that international politics are socially constructed; that is, shaped by beliefs and cultures. Therefore, it focusses on the role played by ideas in constructing identities and giving meaning to the world. Norms and rules are also seen as shaping international relations, and they may be established just as much by international organisations and nongovernmental organisations as by states.[864]

Postmodernism is concerned, above all, with the relationship between power and knowledge. Instead of viewing knowledge as objective, postmodernist scholars view knowledge claims as conceptual constructs which are inseparable from values, interests and power. The principal task of the analyst is, therefore, to decipher how the workings of power are related to the wider social and political context, and to disturb dominant power relations by exposing the power–knowledge nexus.[865]

Neo-Gramscianism also attempts to provide a critical approach to the world order. Like Marxist theories, it departs from the state-centrism of traditional IR approaches to shift its central focus to the social relations of production: 'transnational historical materialism identifies state formation and international politics as moments of the transnational dynamics of capital accumulation and class formation'.[866] In this conception, state sovereignty is, thus, subjugated to a global and transnational economic system. International organisations, such as the World Bank and the International Monetary Fund, are considered important transmitters of the international norms associated with these historical configurations.

4.7.2. Concepts of Human Nature in International Relations Theories

The IR theories outlined above build on a range of conceptions of human nature.[867] I briefly review these and contrast them with my neurophilosophical account of emotional amoral egoism. The following overview cannot claim to be exhaustive but suffices to illustrate the extent to which IR theory is dependent on assumptions about human nature. These assumptions are rarely articulated and are often fundamentally incomplete or incorrect since they rest on unverified and speculative methods of theorising. In many instances, neuroscientific findings simply overturn the long-held assumptions which underlie many IR theories.[868]

Historical materialist approaches, such as neo-Marxism and neo-Gramscianism, seek to understand the world through an analysis of the relationship between human beings and the material world. In fact, they view human nature as conditioned by social relations of production, that is, all relations formed as a result of the (re)production of material life which exist within any particular economic system. Readers will recall that Marx argued that, within a capitalist system of production, human beings are alienated from their true selves and their true nature. Because they are obliged to sell their labour in order to meet their material needs, human beings are generally engaged in activities which do not make them happy. As a consequence, economic factors determine human consciousness and not the other way around. The human essence is given meaning through production. Free will is, therefore, significantly limited. Accordingly, morality is determined by the materialist basis of any particular economic system. As such, it is subject to change and so is human nature. Human nature and morality shift according to the social relations which predominate in an economic system.[869]

In Marxist thought, capitalism is a necessary evil on the path to socialism and contains the seeds of its own downfall.[870] Under socialism, unequal relations of production would cease to exist. In the resulting classless society, in which each person would contribute to production according to his or her ability and receive according to his or her needs, human beings would be free to develop themselves as they wished and to realise their true potential. Since morality is believed to be a product of the prevailing economic relations in a society, socialism would necessarily imply a change in the capacity of human beings to behave in a moral way and to live happily together in communities.[871] Thus, perfection is possible, though historically determined.

Liberal approaches to IR are based on a different account of human nature. Kant is one of the founding figures of this school. His conception of human nature has a particular trajectory, with human beings moving from being driven by instincts to being motivated by reason and eventually to becoming moral. Reason, rather than passion, is viewed as the central motivating force enabling people to reach a higher state of existence.[872] Indeed, as Part 2 discussed, the Kantian view of human nature sees morality as a function of reason.[873] While, in many instances, reason is employed in relation to the fulfilment of human desires, it is thought also to be used in the service of morality. Importantly, morality is conceived as a conscious choice.[874] These choices are not thought to have a physiological cause. However, this does not mean that liberal IR theory views human behaviour as being purely determined by rational thought. Some human actions are thought to be driven by desire, but moral duty is thought to be entirely a product of rationality.[875] In liberal IR theory, human nature is characterised by free will as a product of reason. It is the human capacity for reason which enables human beings to escape a Hobbesian world of insecurity and conflict.[876]

Neo-liberals similarly assume that human beings are rational but self-interested. Robert Keohane, for example, borrows from microeconomics, which assumes people to be highly rational beings, weighing alternatives and selecting the option which is optimal for them.[877] As with neo-realism, neo-liberal assumptions about human nature are transposed to the level of the state. This approach presupposes that states are the principal actors in international relations. International anarchy is not, however, viewed as inevitably leading to conflict. Regimes which regulate relations between states develop as a result of states' rational self-interest. Moreover, repeated and intense interaction can bring about cooperative relations.[878]

Approaches to IR which emphasise the social construction of meaning and identity hold that people are free to choose who they are. Such approaches tend to be sensitive to issues of ontology, ego and transcendence. A seminal figure in social constructivism is Alexander Wendt, who believes that human beings are capable of moving from an unenlightened state to a rational state of being. He identifies a number of human needs: physical security, ontological security, sociation, self-esteem and transcendence.[879] That he views reason as a means of reaching higher human ideals betrays his continued commitment to Enlightenment thinking.

For those who adopt an entirely post-positivist epistemology, humanity is believed to have no 'true' essence. Post-positivist scholars, such as postmodernists and postmodernist feminists, believe that knowledge is socially constructed. Transcendence from dominant knowledge structures comes not from the human capacity for reason, but from the capacity of human beings to produce and reproduce their identities, which are attributed a primary role in determining our nature. The focus on individual identity construction and subjectivity is particularly marked in feminist postmodernism.[880]

Postmodernist ethics derives from the belief that deconstructivism, which aims to dislodge concepts through critical discourse analysis, helps undermine social institutions which are implicated in maintaining unequal power relations. The latter are necessarily based on the exclusion of alternative forms of knowledge and, ultimately, other 'realities'. For example, postmodernists argue that, while the sovereign state may be a dominant actor in the international realm at present, its claim to be the principal and exclusive political subject in international relations is open to debate and has ethno-political costs in terms of limiting the possible political and moral communities we are able to imagine.[881]

Unlike materialist approaches, I do not see morality merely as a function of economic relations. Nor do I share the liberal view of morality as driven mainly by reason. Instead, in my view, it results from a complex interplay between our genetic predispositions, especially those gearing us towards survival, and our socialisation in a particular context. Likewise, values guiding foreign policy interests and strategies mainly result from a regime's survival strategies. Further, state behaviour is shaped, to varying degrees, by domestic and international pressures to conform to certain moral norms. Thus, unlike constructivist approaches, in my view, human beings are shaped by both inborn and learnt characteristics. By extension, state behaviour is, to a significant extent, driven by human beings' innate motivations.

My own approach has most in common with the realist approach, yet it seeks to refine it by infusing it with a neuroscientifically grounded view of human nature. Readers will recall that realists assume that human beings are primarily driven by ego, leading to selfishness, pride and the desire for glory, rather than higher aspirations.[882] Combined with international anarchy, understood as the lack of an overarching central government, human desires result in power struggles and conflict. A prime example of this is the Hobbesian concept of the state of nature, in which humankind is motivated exclusively by selfish desire.[883] According to realist theories, human behaviour:

> is to be understood primarily in terms of a mechanistic psychology of the passions, those forces in man, which, so to speak, push him from behind; it is not to be understood in terms of those things which could be thought of as attracting man from in front, the ends of man, or what for Hobbes would be the objects of the passions.[884]

Since egoism is given a central place in the Hobbesian conception of human nature, altruism is believed to be impossible, and insecurity endemic. This is because, in the context of anarchy, people have the same basic desires, limited resources and the same capacity to do good or bad and, therefore, have reason to fear each other.[885] Indeed, it is fear rather than love which is understood to be a primary motivating factor of human behaviour in a Hobbesian world.[886]

Hobbes is not optimistic about the ability to alter human behaviour.[887] Human nature, as envisaged by him, is fixed and not subject to significant modification through culture or education. It is reason, combined with fear, desire and hope, which are thought to prompt human beings to seek peaceful relations. The emphasis is, therefore, clearly placed on the constraints imposed by our more basic impulses.[888]

Self-preservation not only motivates people to seek peace but is also thought to be responsible for moral behaviour. Seeing others suffer may make us feel bad and, in order to feel better, we help them. We may also act in a virtuous way in order to save ourselves from harm.[889] Given the overriding characteristic of egoism, a strong central government is necessary in order to restrain individuals' pursuit of general self-interest.[890] Indeed, Hobbes believed that, in the absence of world government, the egoistic nature of humankind would lead to 'a war of every man against every man'.[891]

Neo-realism, too, which has been dominant since the 1970s, recognises the role of human nature but places greater emphasis on the qualities of the structure of the international system. International anarchy takes centre stage. For Waltz, a seminal figure of neo-realism, international anarchy determines the regularities of international relations. In short, the very existence of states, and the absence of any international enforcement mechanism, make conflict and even large-scale war inevitable.[892]

In sum, my own approach to international relations shares many tenets of realist IR theories, including the emphasis on the central motivating forces of self-interest and the quest for power. However, realist IR theories fail to either spell out a precise and comprehensive definition of human nature or offer a consistent analysis of its role in steering state behaviour.[893] I seek to remedy this gap by turning to neuroscience for a fresh account of human nature and state behaviour. Advocating for a symbiotic realism, I seek to offer a refined framework for understanding how the conduct of international relations can serve the ultimate goal of ensuring human dignity. At the heart of symbiotic realism lies my neurophilosophical account of emotional amoral egoism.

4.7.3. Symbiotic Realism and the Emotionality of States

As I have explained, human beings are far more emotional than rational. In addition, we are amoral, coming into the world as largely blank slates which are, however, endowed by nature with a drive for survival – a basic form of egoism. Because our brains are neurochemically impacted by everything in our environment, our moral compass shifts according to conditions around us. A fear-laden environment, for example, profoundly affects our decision-making abilities. Chronic stress has been shown to cause neural atrophy in the medial prefrontal cortex and the dorsal striatum, with far-reaching implications for how we set goals, leading to a focus on short-term, immediate needs, as opposed to long-term goals and gratification.[894] Nevertheless, how are these neuroscientific insights relevant to our understanding of international relations?

Realists *are* right to describe conflict as a reflection of the competitive and dominating nature of man. Generally, however, they focus too heavily on rational calculations to the neglect of the role played by emotions. In light of the more complex picture of human nature provided by neuroscience, the tenets of realism must be fundamentally revisited. This is necessary because realists, in general, fail to address the many instances when conflict is less 'rational'. While there is an element of eternal truth in the realist analogy of the man-state, insofar as institutions and states are human enterprises, that analogy is informed by a view of human nature which is often far too simplistic. Indeed, the realist account of rational statecraft has been called into question by evidence from neuroscience, which has demonstrated the key role of emotions in human behaviour.

I believe that states too, like humans, change as a result of evolving circumstances.[895] I also contend that, in the same way as individuals, states are emotional, amoral and egoistic beings and that, contrary to the realist tradition, they act primarily out of emotion rather than mere rational self-interest.[896] Their behaviour will, thus, fluctuate significantly, on the basis of interests, perceptions and many other variables.[897] This is evident through countries' distinct strategic cultures, which are reflections of national identity, collective memory and geopolitical experiences, as well as other emotion-filled behavioural patterns (including habits) and responses to perceived or real fears. Chapter 4.4.8 demonstrated in detail how the behaviour of states has time and again been driven by fear-induced pre-emptive aggression. Further examples of the influence of emotion on state policies include China's behaviour in the South China Sea and the United States' national and global narrative, in which it sees itself as exceptional. The sense of exceptionalism is not restricted to the American hemisphere but shared widely among states. In fact, nationalism is an ideology grounded in emotions and symbols.[898] Similarly, the Neuro P5 play a crucial role in determining relations between states. As mentioned before, wars are often declared in order to vindicate national pride or bolster national permanency. The latter often implies not only the quest for survival but also the production of a collective memory which stresses the superiority of a certain nation.

To make sense of these factors, I propose a more comprehensive theoretical framework for understanding international relations in the twenty-first century: symbiotic realism. As I detail in my book on the subject, my theory shares with realism the view that human nature must be at the centre of theorising about the state and the global system of states.[899] It departs from realism, however, in the definition it gives to human nature. Symbiotic realism is premised on four main elements: (1) my general theory of human nature, emotional amoral egoism, (2) *global anarchy* – a persistent reality of the international system, which is defined by the absence of a superior authority, which in our century simultaneously coexists with (3) *unprecedented interdependence* and (4) *instant connectivity*.

Symbiotic realism stresses the critical importance of absolute gains, where win-win situations are possible. This is in contrast to the realist notion of relative gains related to zero-sum games and premised on the notion of gains at the expense of others. The pursuit of absolute gains is key to guaranteeing human dignity for the whole of humanity. Emotional amoral egoism, therefore, pushes not only individuals but also states to seek their own welfare, even at disastrous cost to other individuals and countries. Herein lies a major source of exploitation and inequalities which have reduced relations between countries to zero-sum games. Emotional amoral egoism leads to a perpetual clash of national interests, even in areas which require global collaboration and absolute gains, such as climate change. Zero-sum games wreak havoc in poor countries, robbing many people of their right to a dignified life and their opportunities to thrive. Refugees fleeing from war-torn countries epitomise the costs of zero-sum games and the incapacity of global governance structures to provide human dignity at the global level.

Symbiotic realism is to be understood not as utopian thinking but as anchored in the pragmatic understanding of what enables sustainable progress in today's interconnected world. In the age of globalisation, security can no longer be thought of as a zero-sum game involving states alone.[900] Further, security in the global age moves beyond the merely national dimension to encompass human, environmental, transnational and transcultural security.[901] Globalisation is giving rise to more and more mutual goals and interests (e.g. environmental protection), making international cooperation which maximises collective gains for all a greater necessity. For years, international trade and cooperation in areas such as culture and environment have been creating win-win situations for all parties concerned. 'Economic growth, education, and health – the three key drivers of the Human Development Index (HDI) – are all positive sum', the World Economic Forum rightly observes.[902]

Still, many states refuse to pursue symbiotic realism in the way they conduct international relations. This is not because win-win situations are impossible to achieve in most instances. Rather, hegemonic aspirations and national egoism transform what could be a multi-sum into a zero-sum game. For the world to evolve towards win-win situations, these aspirations must be abandoned in recognition of the fact that, in today's interdependent world, no geo-cultural domain can excel in isolation from others.[903]

Part 5

The Way Forward

How to Unlock the Best in Human Nature

What neuroscience has recently discovered about the human brain sheds new light on issues long thought unanswerable – issues which we have traditionally pondered within the realms of the humanities and social sciences. Do we possess an innate moral compass? If so, how can we explain the evils perpetrated by human beings? Do we have any scope for free will, or is our future predetermined by our genes or environment? Whilst modern neuroscience still has far to go before it can unlock all of the mysteries surrounding human nature, it has drastically advanced our understanding of how the human mind works, as I hope to have demonstrated in this book. Neurophilosophy takes these neuroscientific insights and subjects them to careful philosophical scrutiny. This book has, therefore, explored human nature from a neurophilosophical vantage point. Indeed, no single disciplinary lens can capture so complex and intangible a phenomenon as human nature. Being cognizant of this fact, neurophilosophy integrates neuroscientific findings with insights from other disciplines which, over the course of millennia, have sought to elucidate the human mind, ranging from philosophy and psychology to evolutionary sciences.

5.1

Casting Light on the Mysteries
of Human Nature

5.1.1. Who We Are

In this book I have embarked on the task of formulating a neurophilosophical theory of human nature, which I call emotional amoral egoism. As I have illustrated, different though we all may be, exhibited in all of us are three fundamental features in which lies the key to disclosing the true nature of humankind. Chief among them is our emotionality. A wealth of research has confirmed the centrality of emotions in human experience and their close interaction with key cognitive functions. In fact, the processes in our brains which govern how we interact with one another and with the surrounding world are largely mediated by emotions and not by reason.

Furthermore, and equally importantly, we are all born 'amoral', by which I refer to the preponderance of evidence suggesting that human beings possess no innate understandings of good and evil, and that their moral judgements shift according to circumstances. In this book I have demonstrated how our moral compass is largely shaped by our environment (both personal and political). Still, we do not enter this world as entirely blank slates. On the contrary, we are endowed by nature with a number of predispositions gearing us towards, first and foremost, survival (and all those acts which maximise our chances of survival). One way to illustrate this fact is through the notion of a predisposed *tabula rasa*, which highlights how theorists such as Locke failed to account for humankind's inborn tendencies and survival instincts.

While largely 'written upon' by experience, human nature is also – critically – predisposed in a basic sense, insofar as, when confronted with threats to life and basic security, we seek to pursue our survival.

No matter how selfless an act may appear, some form of self-interest is likely to be lurking beneath the veneer of altruism. It is in this sense that human nature is fundamentally egoistic: this is the third commonality we all share. Our 'egoism' pushes us not only into pursuing and fighting for our biological survival, but also towards striving for the attainment of our life goals and the opportunity to express our authenticity.

Despite being predominantly driven by the dictates of self-interest, humankind also possesses the capacity for reason and conscious reflection. Under the influence of conscious reflection, we can override our innate biases and develop moral codes of behaviour which oblige us to have regard for the well-being of others, and not only for ourselves. For our capacity for reason to flourish, however, the right sociopolitical context is crucial.

5.1.2. What We Want

At the heart of my general theory of human nature lies my specific theory of human motivation. As this book has demonstrated, comparatively little of what drives us is generated by reason alone. On the contrary, our emotions have the upper hand in shaping our behaviour and in motivating us to pursue certain goals. At the fundamental level, the human brain is pre-programmed to want to feel good, neurochemically speaking, and seeks this type of neurochemical gratification through five main drivers of human action. I have referred to these as the Neuro P5: *power, profit, pleasure, pride* and *permanency*. The latter, in particular, is closely linked to our egoism and our instinct for survival, since it also encompasses our desire to survive death, be it through the transmission of our genes or through our cultural, literary or historical legacy. Given our neuronal plasticity and receptivity to socialising influence, the sources of our neurochemical gratification are not predetermined but largely shaped by our environment. However, and as discussed at length, social circumstances and neurochemical predispositions interact in highly complex ways, often leading individuals towards what we may describe as addictive traps, as is the case in the pursuit of power. The experience of power, particularly in non-accountable systems, generates a quest for ever-more power. Power's addictive high is truly intoxicating and associated with a host of specific neurobehavioral responses that cannot be reversed by 'reason' alone. I have long advocated for institutions that limit the abuses of power, and the excesses of our nature generally, as the only viable pathway for limiting our darker impulses. Accountability, transparency-monitoring institutions and regulatory frameworks are especially important in the context of the galloping development of human enhancement technologies.

5.1.3. Taking Charge of Evolution: Possible Futures

The three primordial features of human nature – emotionality, amorality and egoism – are genetically coded into our DNA, yet they are modified and impacted by the totality of our environment. Contrary to many long-revered beliefs, we are, as such, products of both nature and nurture, which interact so closely with one another that, in the light of today's neuroscientific discoveries, the nature–nurture dichotomy loses its meaning. On the one hand, individual variations in genotypes and phenotypes account for our varied behaviour, tendencies and predispositions. Importantly, there are as many variations within ethnic groups as between them and these differences should never be misused for reasons of ethnic profiling and discrimination. On the other hand, human nature is malleable and its development is informed by a wide range of external factors. It can, thus, be subject to significant influences from drugs, psychotherapy and enhancement technologies, the therapeutic and non-therapeutic potential of which we are only now beginning to truly explore.

Enhancement technologies, in particular, could ultimately alter what it means to be human. Could we soon even have the capacity to take our biological evolution into our own hands? The growing possibilities of manipulating human nature are giving rise to fundamental ethical and existential questions about how to reap the benefits and minimise the risks of innovative technologies. These risks include inequalities reinforced along lines of social class and nationality, and the erosion of meritocratic systems, as enhancement technologies are, and will likely remain, very expensive.

Beyond considerations of costs, they bring about truly existential risks, threatening to erode parts of our identity and reflexes developed over the course of millennia of evolution. They are also a direct affront to the notion of authenticity of the human experience. Although we could reduce the sense of sadness or anxiety by means of neurochemical interventions, having such means readily at our disposal eliminates the drive to seek happiness and relief from fear and grief by methods that have long undergirded human relations, including friendship and companionship. Moreover, a future of wide availability of neuroenhancers will likely lower the threshold for interventions to 'fix' suboptimal moods: will we resist employing that enhancer at the slightest sense of sadness if it is easily within reach? I argued that the answer is no. Given our Neuro P5 motivators, we shall find it increasingly hard to resist such promises of enhancement and we cannot count on reason alone to prevent us from an irresponsible engagement with these technologies.

To a significant extent, the reins of our destiny are within our grasp. How we can move the world in the right direction is a question which neurophilosophy can help to answer by showing us how to unlock the best in human behaviour.

5.1.4. Redefining the Contours of Neurophilosophy

What is of fundamental importance is that in the malleability and amorality of our nature lies the answer to the riddle surrounding our capacity for both good and evil: circumstances in our environment can push us towards acts of unspeakable cruelty, or they can cultivate a propensity for virtuous behaviour. Indeed, such malleability and amorality explain how human beings are capable of the perpetration of mass atrocities as well as of acts of immense solidarity and care for other members of their community and beyond.

Understanding the governance structures needed for humanity to thrive requires an appreciation of how our brains work. Yet, existing neurophilosophical literature largely ignores the implications of neuroscientific discoveries for geopolitics, international relations and global security. My book has sought to fill this gap by exploring how neuroscience research can advance our understanding of our global order and how it might change. At its heart, it has focussed on identifying the governance responses needed to foster the best in human behaviour. This book has made use of neurophilosophy not only as a lens through which to examine the complexity of human nature, but also as the key to harnessing it for the greater good of humanity in its entirety. I have thus pushed the field of neurophilosophy into widely uncharted territory by incorporating it into the study of politics and policy, both domestically and globally.

Maurizio Meloni posits that the attempt to bring light to questions of politics via neuroscience was made possible in the intellectual context of the post-1989 world, a world no longer defined by the dichotomy between the liberal and capitalist tradition of the United States and the socialist and communist one which had defined the Soviet Union. According to Meloni, neuroscience helps to fill the void left behind by some of the leading theories which had shaped the twentieth century, including Marxism but also the Kantian rationalism in political theory.[904] This shift coincided with the gradual admission of explanations from biology and related fields, which had been avoided for a long time by those involved in the social and political sciences as a result of the exploitation by the Nazis of the natural sciences during the Second World War. By the end of the 1970s, we could already witness a closer scrutiny and revival of biological arguments about what makes us human. This interdisciplinary dialogue remains, in my opinion, still underdeveloped as social and bio/neurosciences continue to operate mostly in silos.

In fact, throughout this book I have endeavoured to fill in the blanks in existing approaches to politics and security, which too often have failed to recognise that human beings are driven by emotions and that rational and abstract entities are not at the centre of decision-making. I have thereby departed from the classical and widely speculative accounts of the driving forces of human behaviour as well as from the classical theories of international relations.

5.1.5. What Humanity Needs to Thrive

Acknowledging who we are most fundamentally, and what we want and, therefore, instinctively strive towards, is of paramount importance to knowing how to devise public and global policies and arrange our collective life in order to realise peace, security and prosperity for all. Part 4, in particular, has illustrated the various ways my neurophilosophical theory of emotional amoral egoism advances our understanding of political phenomena. From transformative technologies and human enhancement to Big Data, from xenophobia and other forms of inequality to the challenges presented by pandemics, my theory helps to deepen comprehension of key trends which are shaping not only peace and prosperity but also how we perceive ourselves in relation to each other and to the world.

Indeed, since human beings are, by nature, born neither good nor bad, their instincts can be harnessed for the better. My account of human nature as malleable and subject to external influences highlights the fundamental role of conscious efforts in shaping who we are. Good governance, in particular, plays a critical function in enabling or obstructing our propensity for moral acts.

Importantly, whilst moral concepts are not part of our genetic endowment, we are innately programmed with some pro-social affinities, which provide fertile ground for the teaching and development of regard for the well-being of others, both close and distant. The emergence and consolidation of pro-social behaviour is dependent on egalitarian norms and good governance, which can ensure human dignity – in the absence of which, the 'worst', least cooperative and, at times, pre-emptively aggressive facets of human nature emerge, prompted by our survival instincts and by a fear of everyone and everything who is 'other'. More concretely, for human nature to flourish, governance models must mediate between our emotional, amoral and egoistic nature and what I have referred to as nine critical needs, specifically: reason, security, human rights, accountability, transparency, justice, opportunity, innovation and inclusiveness. Dignity-based governance is the pre-requisite of what I call 'sustainable history', which posits that fulfilling the need for human dignity is the only way to ensure a lasting improvement in the human condition.[905]

Dignity-Based Governance in Practice: Policy Recommendations

Having demonstrated how dignity-based governance provides the key to unlocking humanity's positive potential, in this final section of the book I shall make some policy recommendations for the realisation of dignity-based governance.

5.2.1. Balance Emotionality with Reason, Security and Human Rights

Policymakers must recognise that individuals are highly emotional actors and devise policies accordingly. Of the nine dignity substrates I identified, three in particular help to mitigate vitriolic human emotionality: *reason*, *security* and *human rights*. A reason-based society depends on high-quality education for all. Another requirement is that political discourse should be based on true facts and reasoned arguments, rather than populist appeals to emotion. Education should, therefore, be focussed on teaching critical thinking and newspaper and television literacy skills, thus enabling the population to distinguish between facts and disinformation. Furthermore, education should also encourage self-reflection and self-regulation.

Security is another important requirement for dignity, which means that governments must be committed to protecting society as a whole against violence, hunger, disease and the effects of natural disasters. To this end, security must be rethought in multi-sum and multi-dimensional terms. In other words, global security and the security of any state cannot be achieved through gains at the expense of others, nor can it be realised without good governance at five separate, yet intertwined, levels, namely, at the *human, national, environmental, transnational* and *transcultural* level. Human security, for instance, encompasses not only protecting people from disadvantages resulting from disability, sickness and old age, but also respecting data protection regulations, including during desperate and challenging times such as the coronavirus pandemic.[906] Environmental protection, on the other hand, and the associated threats of natural disaster and climate change, constitutes one of the most difficult existential challenges we are facing today. It requires international collaboration on a large scale, both in terms of policy and scientific research. Technological transformation also presents numerous challenges across the various security dimensions and calls for strategic short-term and long-term thinking in both the public and the private sectors. Since security on all five levels cannot be achieved in a relative manner, international cooperation is required – as well as early warning mechanisms to detect and prevent violence and brutality in situations of near anarchy (e.g. natural disaster) and within failing or failed states.

Equally important for dignity-based governance is the promotion of human rights, which include civil, political, social and cultural rights. Governments must, therefore, ensure, for example, that individuals' rights to privacy are respected in the context of Big Data. In addition, they must guarantee freedom of expression, whilst prohibiting incitement to religious, racial or national hatred, which is fundamental when addressing issues of fake news or 'state truths'. Human beings must be allowed to voice their political opinions and must simultaneously be encouraged to develop values of tolerance and non-discrimination through education. Indeed, guaranteeing access to education for all plays a fundamental role in the promotion and protection of cultural rights which, as I have illustrated in previous chapters, is necessary to counteract humankind's in-group tendency. The promotion of social rights, such as healthcare or housing, by fulfilling our most basic needs will help to balance our emotionality and allow us to move beyond mere survival mode to being able to apply reason and logic in our everyday life.

5.2.2. Counter Amorality with Accountability, Transparency and Justice

In arranging our collective lives, we must recognise that self-interest will usually trump morality – unless we have undergone a socialisation process which has inculcated specific values which make us act with regard to the well-being of others. There should, therefore, be incentives for the promotion of high moral standards in schools as well as in the global economic, entertainment, literature and arts communities.

In countering human amorality, *justice*, *accountability* and *transparency* play a vital role. Public institutions must be accountable and transparent in order to limit the misuse and abuse of power. This is particularly important because unconstrained power blinds those in authority to the needs of others. Private bodies must also be held accountable for their policy decisions and practices, particularly in the case of those which can infringe on individuals' rights, be they civil, political, social or cultural, or those which could present challenges for global security, such as those developing new technologies.

Justice should be ensured by impartial, well-functioning and transparent judicial systems which are fully independent from the executive and which focus on rehabilitation and not just punishment. A strong constitution, in a liberal democracy, can prevent laws from being changed at the whim of people with a particular political belief. However, as has often been the case in non-democratic systems, another constitution may not ensure that the law is applied fairly and equally to all human beings. For dignity-based governance to truly favour the development of a morality which embraces all human beings, justice systems must, therefore, be truly impartial and fair in their practices and apply the law equally to all, independently of their nationality, religion, ethnic origin or gender.

5.2.3. Channel Egoism through Opportunity, Inclusiveness and Innovation

Good governance channels human egoism to benefit society through *opportunity*, *inclusiveness* and *innovation*. As I have previously stated, survival instincts and the egoistic nature of human beings are very closely connected. In light of this, and for dignity-based governance to flourish, people from all segments of society should live in circumstances conducive to their positive physical, mental and social development. This implies, among other things, the provision of adequate housing and nutrition, sanitation, education and health services, including widely available and affordable psychotherapeutic and psychoeducational care.

Moreover, human egoism can be harnessed productively through opportunities for professional, scientific and intellectual growth, which result not only in the fulfilment of the individual's ego, but also in an innovative society. Since innovation can play a key role in the economic growth and stability of a state, its promotion also fosters prosperity across all sectors. States should, therefore, increase funding for research and development (R&D) in all areas, focussing especially on new technologies and the environment, two of the most important challenges for humanity in the twenty-first century.

It is equally important for opportunities to be fairly and evenly distributed among the population. This type of fairness and equality requires proactive efforts to reduce income gaps, focussing especially on women, minority groups and migrants. Inclusiveness also requires sustained policy efforts to eliminate all forms of discrimination and marginalisation which fuel social divisions, be they on the basis of race, ethnicity, religion, nationality or gender orientation. As I have mentioned above, educational institutions arguably represent one of the best venues for promoting inclusive national and global identities and transcultural understanding.

In light of these considerations, I believe that, at the very least, states must take the following steps to discourage human beings' emotional, amoral and egoistic tendencies. First, governments should prioritise the right to *education* in their policy agendas, and recognise that access to education for all, and especially to higher education, is one of the simplest ways through which we can counteract the negative traits of human nature. Indeed, educational institutions can play a key role in the promotion of *egalitarian norms* within society. Second, governments should also take care to ensure that their representatives use a *language* which fosters respect and inclusion, and not give in to the temptation towards demagogic sound-bites which, whether intentionally or not, can trigger division, xenophobia and fear of the 'other'. Similarly, the *entertainment industry* must comply with stricter rules so as to avoid denigration of other groups and not be another source of out-group propaganda, as has happened on countless occasions in recent history.[907] Extra care should also be taken to move away from the long tradition in Western culture of using colours such as black to identify evil, which may also contribute to racial stereotyping. On the contrary, the press and broadcasters can be an important means of fostering respect for diversity since it spreads messages to large audiences and can encourage reflection. The *gaming industry* should also be placed under scrutiny, especially at a time of easy access, and as full adult supervision is simply not always possible. If not only adults but even young children are instructed in games on a daily basis to 'fight against' or 'kill' enemies who closely resemble other human beings, they may normalise such behaviour and might consider those people enemies when they encounter them face to face.[908] All of these elements combined can contribute to channelling positively the egoism of human beings and to counteracting it by encouraging people to look beyond the narrow contours of in-group/out-group dynamics and to feel that they belong to a larger community, that of humanity as a whole.

What Does Dignity-Based Governance Mean for All of Us?

When it privileges the requirements of human dignity, governance creates an environment which channels our quest for sustainable neurochemical gratification, or the Neuro P5, into productive enterprises. Normatively (through parenting, schooling, societal and global influences), it associates 'feeling good' with constructive behaviour. Neuronal craving mediated through neurochemistry (e.g. the 'dopamine rush') will then ensure the repetition of 'feel-good' behaviour which is beneficial to the individual, social cooperation and humanity as a whole. It steers our pride, for example, in a positive direction, by encouraging personal development and feelings of achievement arising from innovations which benefit our communities and not just ourselves. In addition, when our nine requirements for dignity are met, we are more likely to employ reason and engage in reflection and conscious moral behaviour.

For a safer world, dignity-based governance must be ensured at both the domestic and global level and take into account the implications of technological developments for the future of humankind and for human nature. It needs to recognise that our relationship with enhancement technologies is unlikely to be driven by reason or an appropriate sense of moderation, and that such technologies are likely to infringe on meritocracy, authenticity and fairness, creating hierarchies and divisions between the enhanced and the non-enhanced. Scientists, ethicists, civil society organisations and policymakers must, therefore, agree on ethical and safety standards regulating emerging technologies.

5.4

Where are we Going?

'Only that which has no history is definable', Nietzsche famously remarked.[909] Indeed, one of the difficulties in conceiving of human nature lies in its historically contingent variability. Since human nature is the result of biological evolution and is, at least partly, shaped by external influences, it is highly mutable and has, over time, demonstrated its capacity for extremely different and even contradictory behaviour. Normally, when we speak of evolution, we consider very long periods of time. This sense of *longue durée* may be conducive to the misleading impression that, whatever innovations in life sciences and other fields are being developed now, their impact on our nature and evolution will be painstakingly slow. That is not the case with the current type of innovations, particularly in genetic engineering, synthetic biology and interdisciplinary domains, such as nanobiotechnology, to name a few. This is an important consideration to bear in mind going forward. Most importantly, we must not stay reassured that such technologies, given their extraordinary potential to interfere with biological processes at the cellular level, will not impact both our biology and our identity in the not-too-distant future. Simultaneously, we must not be complacent about the virtues of our nature when faced with technologies that promise in one way or another to 'enhance' us.

As I have illustrated, through the discovery of new techniques, such as fMRI, the twenty-first century witnessed a brain-imaging revolution, as well as the emergence of numerous technologies which previously we could only have conceived of in the realm of science fiction. Together, not only do they overturn many long-revered beliefs about our species, but their combined impact may also transform some of the features which have long been considered most timeless in human nature, shifting our physical, cognitive and emotional limitations. Our best hope for the progress of humankind, thus, depends on how we use our increased understanding of the human brain, and how we harness the positive potential of emerging technologies – for instance, their therapeutic uses – while simultaneously mitigating their risks.

Whilst acknowledging the malleability of human nature, this book has sought to describe what is, and will likely remain in the foreseeable future, most unchangeable and universal: our emotional amoral egoism and our five most powerful motivators: power, pride, pleasure, profit and permanency. I believe, however, that we must never be complacent about the virtues and vices of human nature. Indeed, more than a mere description of who we are, emotional amoral egoism is a useful theoretical lens through which to examine how human nature is the architect of the world in which we live. My key takeaway is that, far from being totally determined by our neurochemistry and by our genetic heritage, we are free to work together to build a dignity-based world which can nurture us and bring out the best in every single human being. On this cautiously optimistic note, I hope to leave the reader with a sense of agency through which he or she can contribute to the fostering of a thriving humanity and a world in which all people can live with the dignity, peace and security we deserve.

Notes

1. J. Bickle, *The Oxford Handbook of Philosophy and Neuroscience* (Oxford: Oxford University Press, 2009), p. 3.
2. L.P. Pojman, *Who Are We? Theories of Human Nature* (New York: Oxford University Press, 2006), p. xiv.
3. L. Berns, 'Thomas Hobbes', in L. Strauss and J. Cropsey (eds), *History of Political Philosophy*, 3rd edn (Chicago: Chicago University Press, 1987), p. 399.
4. Pojman, *Who Are We?*, pp. 6–7.
5. M.D. Hauser, *Moral Minds: How Nature Designed Our Universal Sense of Right and Wrong* (New York: HarperCollins, 2006), p. 23.
6. A.W. Price, *Virtue and Reason in Plato and Aristotle* (Oxford: Oxford University Press, 2011), p. 190.
7. R. Barrow, *Plato* (London: Bloomsbury Academic, 2014), p. 102.
8. A. Damasio, *Descartes' Error: Emotion, Reason and the Human Brain* (London: Vintage, 2006), pp. 39–40.
9. J.-P. Sartre, *Jean-Paul Sartre: Basic Writings*, ed. Stephen Priest (New York: Routledge, 2001), p. 32.
10. Pojman, *Who Are We?*, p. 2.
11. Pojman, *Who Are We?*, pp. 252–53, 255.
12. R. Kane, *The Oxford Handbook of Free Will*, 2nd edn (New York: Oxford University Press, 2011), p. 8.
13. L. Barrett, R. Dunbar and J. Lycett, *Human Evolutionary Psychology* (Basingstoke: Palgrave, 2002), p. 25.
14. F. de Waal, *Primates and Philosophers: How Morality Evolved* (Princeton, NJ: Princeton University Press, 2006); E.O. Wilson, *Sociobiology: The New Synthesis* (Cambridge, MA: Harvard University Press, 1975).
15. See Hauser, *Moral Minds*.
16. See D. Sankey, 'Can the Synaptic Self Have Values and Make Choices?', paper presented at the 33rd Annual Philosophy of Education Society of Australia Conference, Melbourne, 26–27 November 2004, p. 1, www.pesa.org.au.

17. R. Carter, *The Human Brain Book: An Illustrated Guide to its Structure, Function, and Disorders* (London: DK Publishing, 2019), p. 6.

18. W.R. Uttal, *Neural Theories of Mind: Why the Mind-Brain Problem May Never Be Solved* (New York: Psychology Press, 2020), p. 95.

19. Carter, *The Human Brain Book*, p. 7.

20. A. Shackman and T. Wager, 'The Emotional Brain: Fundamental Questions and Strategies for Future Research', *Neuroscience Letters* 693 (2019), pp. 68–74, https://doi.org/10.1016/j.neulet.2018.10.012.

21. Nayef R.F. Al-Rodhan, 'A Neurophilosophy of Human Nature: Emotional Amoral Egoism and the Five Motivators of Humankind', *Blog of the American Philosophical Association*, 4 April 2019, https://blog.apaonline. org/2019/04/04/a-neuro-philosophy-of-human-nature-emotional-amoral -egoism-and-the-five-motivators-of-humankind; Nayef R.F. Al-Rodhan, 'Predisposed Tabula Rasa', *The Oxford University Politics Blog*, 15 May 2015, https://blog.politics.ox.ac.uk/predisposed-tabula-rasa.

22. S.D. Pitlik, 'COVID-19 Compared to Other Pandemic Diseases', *Rambam Maimonides Medical Journal* 11, no. 3 (2020), pp. 1–17, https:// doi.org/10.5041/RMMJ.10418.

23. F. Bound Alberti, 'Coronavirus Is Revitalising the Concept of Community for the 21st Century', *The Conversation*, 29 April 2020, https://theconversation.com/coronavirus-is-revitalising-the-concept-of -community-for-the-21st-century-135750.

24. Pojman, *Who Are We?*, p. 27.

25. Pojman, *Who Are We?*, pp. 27–30.

26. Plato, *The Republic*, ed. T. Griffith, trans. G.R.F. Ferrari (Cambridge: Cambridge University Press, 2000).

27. Pojman, *Who Are We?*, p. xiv.

28. See Pojman, *Who Are We?*, ch. 1.

29. See Pojman, *Who Are We?*, ch. 6.

30. J.D. Fowler *et al.*, *World Religions: An Introduction for Students* (Eastbourne: Sussex Academic Press, 1997), p. 184.

31. D. Sarma, 'A Hindu Perspective', in Scott J. Fitzpatrick *et al.*, 'Religious Perspectives on Human Suffering: Implications for Medicine and Bioethics', *Journal of Religion and Health* 55 (2015), pp. 169–70.

32. Fowler *et al.*, *World Religions*; J. Fowler, *Perspectives of Reality: An Introduction to the Philosophy of Hinduism* (Eastbourne: Sussex Academic Press, 2002).

33. Fowler *et al.*, *World Religions*, p. 35; Encyclopaedia Britannica, 'Hinduism: Religion', by A.L. Basham *et al.*, esp. 'Karma, Samsara, and Moksha', https://www.britannica.com/topic/Hinduism/Karma-samsara -and-moksha (accessed 13 March 2021).

34. S. Jhingran, *Aspects of Hindu Morality* (Delhi: Motilal Banarsidass, 1989), p. 131.

35. L. Stevenson and D.L. Haberman, *Ten Theories of Human Nature*, 4th edn (New York: Oxford University Press, 2004), pp. 13–14.

36. Ibid., pp. 21–24.

37. F. Braudel, *A History of Civilizations* (New York: Penguin Books, 1993), pp. 41, 47.

38. A. Sachedina, 'An Islamic Perspective', in Fitzpatrick *et al.*, 'Religious Perspectives on Human Suffering: Implications for Medicine and Bioethics', pp. 167–69.

39. M. Cillis, *Free Will and Predestination in Islamic Thought: Theoretical Compromises in the Works of Avicenna, al-Ghazālī and Ibn 'Arabī* (New York: Routledge, 2014), p. 1.

40. Josép Puig Montada, 'Ibn Rushd's Natural Philosophy', in *Stanford Encyclopedia of Philosophy* (Stanford University, 1997-), article pub. 17 August 2018, https://plato.stanford.edu/entries/ibn-rushd-natural.

41. Ibid.

42. P. Adamson, *A History of Philosophy without Any Gaps: Volume 3: Philosophy in the Islamic World* (Oxford: Oxford University Press, 2016), p. 188.

43. Muhammad ibn Abd al-Malik Ibn Tufayl, *Ibn Tufayl's Hayy ibn Yaqdhan: A Philosophical Tale*, trans. L.E. Goodman (New York: Twayne, 1972).

44. Encyclopaedia Britannica, 'Ibn Tufayl: Moorish Philosopher and Physician', by the Editors of Encyclopaedia Britannica, https://www.britannica.com/biography/Ibn-Tufayl (accessed 14 January 2021).

45. Stevenson and Haberman, *Ten Theories of Human Nature*, p. 113.

46. Ibid., p. 116.

47. J.-J. Rousseau, *On the Social Contract*, trans. D.A. Cress (Indianapolis: Hackett Publishing, 1998), p. 5; S. On, 'Kant and Nietzsche on Human Rights: A Theoretical Approach', paper presented at the International Studies Association, 41st Annual Convention, Los Angeles, CA, 14–18 March 2000.

48. Immanuel Kant, *Kant: Political Writings*, ed. H. Reiss, trans. N.B. Nisbet, 2nd enlarged edn (Cambridge: Cambridge University Press, 1991), pp. 19–20, 42–43.

49. Ibid., pp. 129–31.

50. Karl Marx, *Capital: Volume III: A Critique of Political Economy* (London: Penguin Books, 1993).

51. See L.A. Coser, 'Alienation', in L.A. Coser, *Masters of Sociological Thought: Ideas of Historical and Social Context*, 2nd edn (Fort Worth, TX: Harcourt Brace Jovanovich, 1977), pp. 50–53.

52. Pojman, *Who Are We?*, pp. 211, 213–14.

53. Nayef R.F. Al-Rodhan, 'The "Sustainable History" Thesis: A Guide for Regulating Trans- and Post-Humanism', *E-International Relations*, 24 April 2018, https://www.e-ir.info/2018/04/24/the-sustainable-history-thesis-a-guide-for-regulating-trans-and-post-humanism.

54. B. Lemma, 'CRISPR Dreams: The Potential for Gene Editing', *Harvard International Review* 40, no. 1 (2019), pp. 6–7.

55. Nayef R.F. Al-Rodhan, 'Neurophilosophy and Transhumanism', *Blog of the American Philosophical Association*, 19 February 2019, https://blog.apaonline.org/2019/02/19/neurophilosophy-and-transhumanism.

56. Nayef R.F. Al-Rodhan, 'A Neurophilosophy of Two Technological Game-Changers: Synthetic Biology and Superintelligence', *Blog of the American Philosophical Association*, 29 June 2020, https://blog.apaonline.org/2020/06/29/a-neurophilosophy-of-two-technological-game-changers-synthetic-biology-superintelligence.
57. Pojman, *Who Are We?*, p. 5.
58. Encyclopaedia Britannica, 'Christianity', by Matt Stefon *et al.*, esp. 'The Human as the Image of God', https://www.britannica.com/topic/Christianity (accessed 11 March 2021).
59. Pojman, *Who Are We?*, p. 6.
60. Encyclopaedia Britannica, 'Christianity', by Matt Stefon *et al.*, esp. 'The Human as a Creature', https://www.britannica.com/topic/Christianity (accessed 11 March 2021).
61. Stevenson and Haberman, *Ten Theories of Human Nature*, p. 63.
62. Ibid.; Encyclopaedia Britannica, 'Sin', by the Editors of Encyclopaedia Britannica, https://www.britannica.com/topic/sin-religion (accessed 11 March 2021).
63. Encyclopaedia Britannica, 'Sin'.
64. Stevenson and Haberman, *Ten Theories of Human Nature*, p. 63.
65. H. Küng, *Islam: Past, Present and Future* (Oxford: Oneworld, 2007), p. 25.
66. R. Dogan, 'The Position of Human Being in the Universe according to Islam', *Sociology and Anthropology* 1, no. 3 (2013), pp. 142–43.
67. A. Guillaume, 'Some Remarks on Free Will and Predestination in Islam, Together with a Translation of the Kitabu-l Qadar from Sahih of al-Bukhari', *The Journal of the Royal Asiatic Society of Great Britain and Ireland*, no. 1 (1924), esp. pp. 61–62.
68. Pojman, *Who Are We?*, p. xiv.
69. Pojman, *Who Are We?*, p. 84.
70. Pojman, *Who Are We?*, p. 88.
71. R.P. Hayes, 'Buddhist Philosophy, Indian', in E. Craig (ed.), *The Shorter Routledge Encyclopedia of Philosophy* (London: Routledge, 2005), pp. 112 ff. For the online version, see R.P. Hayes, 'Buddhist Philosophy, Indian', *Routledge Encyclopedia of Philosophy Online*, https://doi.org/10.4324/9780415249126-F001-1 (accessed 13 January 2021).
72. Ibid.
73. Pojman, *Who Are We?*, pp. 90–91.
74. Ibid., pp. 94–98; Hayes, 'Buddhist Philosophy, Indian'.
75. K. Swancutt, 'Animism', in *The Cambridge Encyclopedia of Anthropology*, initially published 25 June 2019, http://doi.org/10.29164/19anim (accessed 11 March 2021).
76. N. Whitten, 'Animism', in M.C. Horowitz (ed.), *New Dictionary of the History of Ideas*, Vol. 1 (Detroit: Charles Scribner's Sons, 2005), pp. 72–73.
77. E. Craig (ed.), *Routledge Encyclopedia of Philosophy: Volume 4: Genealogy to Iqbal* (London: Routledge, 1998), p. 521.

78. T. Hurka, 'Perfectionism', in E. Craig (ed.) *Routledge Encyclopedia of Philosophy* (London: Routledge, 1998). For the online version, see T. Hurka, 'Perfectionism', *Routledge Encyclopedia of Philosophy Online*, http://doi.org/10.4324/9780415249126-L070-1 (accessed 13 January 2021).
79. Aristotle, *The Politics*, trans. Carnes Lord (Chicago: University of Chicago Press, 1984).
80. Pojman, *Who Are We?*, pp. xiv, 68.
81. Ibid., pp. 68–69.
82. Ibid., p. 69.
83. Ibid., p. 165.
84. K. Marx, *Capital: Volume III: A Critique of Political Economy* (London: Penguin Books, 1993), p. 178.
85. Coser, 'Alienation'.
86. Pojman, *Who Are We?*, p. 162.
87. Ibid., p. 65.
88. D. Hume, 'Of the Origin of Our Ideas', in D. Hume, *A Treatise of Human Nature* (Cambridge: Cambridge University Press, 2009), section I, part I, book i. Emphasis in original.
89. Ibid.
90. Pojman, *Who Are We?*, p. 116.
91. Hauser, *Moral Minds*, p. 23.
92. Hume, quoted in ibid., p. 24.
93. Pojman, *Who Are We?*, p. 127.
94. Hume, *A Treatise of Human Nature*, III, I, i.
95. Hauser, *Moral Minds*, p. 25.
96. Ibid., p. 24.
97. See T. Fuller, 'Jeremy Bentham and James Mill', in Strauss and Cropsey (eds), *History of Political Philosophy*, pp. 710–31.
98. Ibid., p. 714.
99. I. Adams and R.W. Dyson, *Fifty Major Political Thinkers* (London: Routledge, 2003), pp. 39–45.
100. Pojman, *Who Are We?*, pp. 105–7.
101. Ibid., pp. 111, 117.
102. Ibid., p. 106.
103. T. Hobbes, *Leviathan* (Ware, Herts: Wordsworth Editions, 2014 [1651]).
104. J. Locke, *An Essay Concerning Human Understanding, with the Notes and Illustrations of the Author and An Analysis of His Doctrine of Ideas*, 13th edn (London: William Tegg & Co., 1849), p. 10.
105. Ibid.
106. Ibid., p. 13.
107. J. Seigel, *The Idea of the Self: Thought and Experience in Western Europe since the Seventeenth Century* (Cambridge: Cambridge University Press, 2005), pp. 90–92.
108. Pojman, *Who Are We?*, pp. 117, 119, 267; Seigel, *The Idea of the Self*, pp. 88–89.

109. J.-J. Rousseau, *The Social Contract and Discourses*, trans. G.D.H. Cole (New York: E. P. Dutton, 1950 [1750–62]).

110. Pojman, *Who Are We?*, p. 112.

111. Rousseau, *The Social Contract and Discourses*.

112. Ibid., pp. 9–10.

113. Ibid., p. 3.

114. Pojman, *Who Are We?*, p. 117.

115. I. Kant, 'Idea for a Universal History with a Cosmopolitan Purpose', in Kant, *Kant: Political Writings*, p. 42.

116. Stevenson and Haberman, *Ten Theories of Human Nature*, p. 120.

117. Ibid., pp. 124–25, 129.

118. I. Kant, *The Metaphysics of Morals*, trans. M.J. Gregor (Cambridge: Cambridge University Press, 1996), p 57.

119. Stevenson and Haberman, *Ten Theories of Human Nature*, p. 126.

120. Ibid., p. 152.

121. Ibid., pp. 127–29.

122. Ibid., p. 130.

123. Plato, *The Republic*, pp. 36–46.

124. Ibid, p 332.

125. Stevenson and Haberman, *Ten Theories of Human Nature*, p. 76.

126. Pojman, *Who Are We?*, p. 51.

127. Stevenson and Haberman, *Ten Theories of Human Nature*, pp. 77–79.

128. Ibid., pp. 82–83.

129. Pojman, *Who Are We?*, p. 48.

130. Hauser, *Moral Minds*, p. 65.

131. Ibid., p. 42.

132. Ibid., p. 251.

133. J. Rawls, *A Theory of Justice*, rev. edn (Oxford: Oxford University Press, 1999), p. 11.

134. S. Pinker, *The Blank Slate: The Modern Denial of Human Nature* (London: Penguin Books, 2002), pp. 150–51.

135. Rawls, *A Theory of Justice*, p. 11.

136. Ibid., pp. xii, 11.

137. De Waal, *Primates and Philosophers*.

138. Ibid., p. 57.

139. Ibid., pp. 52, 55.

140. Ibid., pp. 53–54.

141. Ibid., pp. 6–7, 10.

142. A. Subramanian, 'Born to Kill? The Story of "Serial Killer" Genes', *Berkeley Scientific Journal*, 21 July 2020, https://bsj.berkeley.edu/born-to-kill-the-story-of-serial-killer-genes.

143. See, for example, M.K. Xu *et al.*, 'Monoamine Oxidase A (MAOA) Gene and Personality Traits from Late Adolescence through Early Adulthood: A Latent Variable Investigation', *Frontiers in Psychology* 8 (2017), pp. 1–13, https://doi.org/10.3389/fpsyg.2017.01736; L.M. Williams *et al.*,

'A Polymorphism of the MAOA Gene Is Associated with Emotional Brain Markers and Personality Traits on an Antisocial Index', *Neuropsychopharmacology* 34 (2009), pp. 1797–1809.

144. Subramanian, 'Born to Kill?'
145. Ibid.; Xu *et al.*, 'Monoamine Oxidase A'.
146. Subramanian, 'Born to Kill?'
147. Ibid.
148. Pojman, *Who Are We?*, pp. 187, 189, 190.
149. G. Marino, 'Introduction', in G. Marino (ed.), *Basic Writings of Existentialism* (New York: Modern Library, 2004), p. xiv.
150. C.B. Guignon, 'Existentialism', in E. Craig (ed.), *The Shorter Routledge Encyclopedia of Philosophy* (London: Routledge, 2005), pp. 252–60.
151. Marino, 'Introduction', p. xi.
152. Stevenson and Haberman, *Ten Theories of Human Nature*, p. 176.
153. Guignon, 'Existentialism'.
154. Pojman, *Who Are We?*, p. 200.
155. Ibid., pp. 190–91.
156. Ibid., p. 194.
157. P. Gardiner, 'Kierkegaard, Søren Aabye', in E. Craig (ed.), *The Shorter Routledge Encyclopedia of Philosophy* (London: Routledge, 2005). For the online version, see P. Gardiner, 'Kierkegaard, Søren Aabye', *Routledge Encyclopedia of Philosophy Online*, https://www.rep.routledge.com/articles/biographical/kierkegaard-s-ren-aabye-1813-55/v-1 (accessed 13 January 2021).
158. Ibid.
159. S. Kierkegaard, *Fear and Trembling*, trans. H.V. and E.H. Hong (Princeton, NJ: Princeton University Press, 1983), excerpted in Marino, *Basic Writings of Existentialism*, pp. 11–12.
160. Ibid., p. 15.
161. Seigel, *The Idea of the Self*, p. 538.
162. Ibid.
163. Pojman, *Who Are We?*, pp. 185–86; F. Nietzsche, *The Gay Science: With a Prelude in Rhymes and an Appendix of Songs*, ed. and trans. W. Kaufmann (New York: Vintage Books, 1974).
164. B. Russell, *History of Western Philosophy* (London: Routledge, 2006), pp. 690–91.
165. Pojman, *Who Are We?*, pp. 186–87.
166. F. Nietzsche, *Basic Writings of Nietzsche*, trans. W. Kauffmann (New York: Modern Library, 2000), excerpted in Marino, *Basic Writings of Existentialism*, p. 167. Emphasis in original.
167. Pojman, *Who Are We?*, pp. 195, 197.
168. J.-P. Sartre, *Being and Nothingness*, trans. H. Barnes (New York: Philosophical Publishers, Inc., 1956), excerpted in Marino, *Basic Writings of Existentialism*, p. 369.
169. Guignon, 'Existentialism', p. 254.

170. P.R. Robbins, *Understanding Psychology*, 3rd edn (Portland, ME: J. Weston Walch, 2003), p. 4.
171. Pojman, *Who Are We?*, p. 168.
172. Stevenson and Haberman, *Ten Theories of Human Nature*, pp. 157, 160.
173. See, for example, S. Freud, *The Interpretation of Dreams*, trans. and ed. J. Strachey (New York: Basic Books, 1955); S. Freud, *The Psychopathology of Everyday Life*, standard edn, with a bibliographical introduction by P. Gay (New York: W.W. Norton & Co., 1990); S. Freud, *Three Essays on the Theory Sexuality*, trans. J. Strachey (New York: Basic Books, 1975).
174. Stevenson and Haberman, *Ten Theories of Human Nature*, pp. 157, 161.
175. See S. Freud, *The Ego and the Id* (London: Hogarth Press, 1949).
176. Pojman, *Who Are We?*, p. 171.
177. Stevenson and Haberman, *Ten Theories of Human Nature*, p. 162.
178. Pojman, *Who Are We?*, p. 170; Stevenson and Haberman, *Ten Theories of Human Nature*, p. 164.
179. Stevenson and Haberman, *Ten Theories of Human Nature*, p. 163.
180. E. Gellner, *The Psychoanalytic Movement: The Cunning of Unreason* (Oxford: Blackwell Publishing, 2003), p. xvii.
181. R.H. Blank, 'Neuroscience, Free Will, and Individual Responsibility: Implications for Addictive Behaviour', in A. Somit and S. Peterson (eds), *Human Nature and Public Policy: An Evolutionary Approach* (New York: Palgrave Macmillan, 2003), p. 59; A.P. Demorest, *Psychology's Grand Theorists: How Personal Experiences Shaped Professional Ideas* (Mahwah, NJ: Lawrence Erlbaum Associates, 2005), p. 75.
182. R.A. Moxley, 'B.F. Skinner's Other Positivistic Book: "Walden Two"', *Behavior and Philosophy* 34 (2006), pp. 24–26.
183. B.F. Skinner, 'The Behaviour of Organisms at Fifty', in J.T. Todd and E.K. Morris (eds), *Modern Perspectives on B.F. Skinner and Contemporary Behaviorism*, Contributions in Psychology, No. 28, foreword by E.R. Hilgard (Westport, CT: Greenwood Press, 1995), p. 159.
184. See Skinner, 'The Behaviour of Organisms at Fifty'.
185. Demorest, *Psychology's Grand Theorists*, p. 80.
186. N. Sheehy, *Fifty Key Thinkers in Psychology* (London: Routledge, 2003), p. 206.
187. Demorest, *Psychology's Grand Theorists*, p. 88.
188. Ibid., p. 92.
189. Sheehy, *Fifty Key Thinkers in Psychology*, p. 206.
190. S.S. Sengupta, 'Growth in Human Motivation: Beyond Maslow', *Indian Journal of Industrial Relations* 47, no. 1 (2011), p. 103.
191. Ibid., p. 104.
192. R.J. Zalenski and R. Raspa, 'Maslow's Hierarchy of Human Needs: A Framework for Achieving Human Potential in Hospice', *Journal of Palliative Medicine* 9, no. 5 (2006), p. 1121.
193. Ibid., p. 1122.

194. See K. Lorenz, *On Aggression*, trans. M. Latzke (New York: Bantham Books, 1963).

195. Encyclopaedia Britannica, 'Konrad Lorenz: Austrian Zoologist', by Eckhard H. Hess, https://www.britannica.com/biography/Konrad -Lorenz (accessed 13 January 2021).

196. J.D. Singer, 'Genetic and Cultural Evolution: Implications for International Security Policies', in Somit and Peterson, *Human Nature and Public Policy*, pp. 244–45.

197. Stevenson and Haberman, *Ten Theories of Human Nature*, p. 227.

198. Ibid., pp. 227–28.

199. Singer, 'Genetic and Cultural Evolution' pp. 245–46.

200. Pojman, *Who Are We?*, pp. 219–20.

201. A. Somit and S. Peterson, 'From Human Nature to Public Policy: Evolutionary Theory Challenges the "Standard Model"', in Somit and Peterson, *Human Nature and Public Policy*, p. 13.

202. Ibid., pp. 13–14.

203. R. Winston, *Human Instinct: How Our Primeval Impulses Shape Our Modern Lives* (London: Bantam Books, 2003), p. 28.

204. Ibid., pp. 28–29.

205. G. Chancellor, 'Levels of Selection in Darwin's "Origin of Species"', *History and Philosophy of the Life Sciences* 37, no. 2 (2015), pp. 131–32.

206. C. Darwin, *The Expression of the Emotions in Man and Animals* (London: John Murray, 1872); S. Walton, *Humanity: An Emotional History* (London: Atlantic Books, 2004), p. xiii.

207. Walton, *Humanity*, p. xxii.

208. T. Dobzhansky, *Genetics and the Origins of Species*, 3rd edn (New York: Columbia University Press, 1951); E. Mayr, *Animal Species and Evolution* (Cambridge, MA: Belknap Press, 1963); S.J. Gould, *The Structure of Evolutionary Theory* (Cambridge, MA: Harvard University Press, 2002).

209. De Waal, *Primates and Philosophers*, p. 16.

210. Pojman, *Who Are We?*, p. 219.

211. Hauser, *Moral Minds*, p. 60.

212. Somit and Peterson, 'From Human Nature to Public Policy', pp. 14–15.

213. G.C. Williams, *Adaptation and Natural Selection* (Princeton, NJ: Princeton University Press, 1966).

214. Wilson, *Sociobiology,* Chapters 1, Chapter 5, Chapter 27.

215. P.N. Furbank, 'Altruism, Selfishness, and Genes', *The Threepenny Review*, no. 114 (Summer 2008), p. 6.

216. Pojman, *Who Are We?*, pp. 214–15.

217. T.J. Bouchard Jr, D.T. Lykken, M. McGue, N.L. Segal, A. Tellegen, 'Sources of Human Psychological Differences: The Minnesota Study of Twins Reared Apart', *Science* 250, no. 4978 (1990), pp. 223–28, https:// doi.org/10.1126/science.2218526; Nayef R.F. Al-Rodhan,

'Socio-Neuro-Biology and Prospects for Our Collective Global Future', *E-International Relations*, 30 July 2015, https://www.e-ir.info/2015/07/30/socio-neuro-biology-and-prospects-for-our-collective-global-future.
218. Pojman, *Who Are We?*, p. 217.
219. Hauser, *Moral Minds*, p. 60.
220. Hauser, *Moral Minds*, 60; R. Dawkins, *The God Delusion* (London: Transworld Publishers, 2006), pp. 245–54.
221. Pojman, *Who Are We?*, p. 219.
222. Hauser, *Moral Minds*, p. xvii.
223. S. Pinker, *The Language Instinct* (New York: HarperCollins, 1994).
224. See T.W. Clark, 'Materialism and Morality: The Problem with Pinker', *The Humanist* 58, no. 6 (1998), p. 20–25.
225. Hauser, *Moral Minds*, p. xviii.
226. Ibid., p. 12.
227. Ibid., pp. xviii, 13, 15.
228. Ibid., pp. 13, 15, 23.
229. Ibid., pp. 17–18.
230. Ibid., p. 222.
231. Ibid., pp. 46, 229, 235, 250.
232. Ibid., p. xviii.
233. De Waal, *Primates and Philosophers*.
234. Ibid., pp. 52, 55.
235. Ibid., p. 4.
236. Ibid.
237. Ibid., p. 5.
238. Ibid., p. 57.
239. Ibid.
240. Ibid., pp. 6–7, 10.
241. Ibid., pp. 14, 16.
242. Ibid., p. 23.
243. Ibid., pp. 23, 25.
244. Ibid., pp. 53–54.
245. Ibid., p. 54.
246. P.A.D. Singer, *A Darwinian Left: Politics, Evolution, and Cooperation* (New Haven, CT: Yale University Press, 2000).
247. Pinker, *The Blank Slate*, p. 167.
248. Carter, *The Human Brain Book*, p. 7.
249. C.D. Salzman and S. Fusi, 'Emotion, Cognition, and Mental State Representation in Amygdala and Prefrontal Cortex', *Annual Review of Neuroscience* 33 (2010), pp. 173–202, https://doi.org/10.1146/annurev.neuro.051508.135256.
250. Uttal, *Neural Theories of Mind*, p. 95.
251. S.M. Liao, 'Morality and Neuroscience: Past and Present', in S.M. Liao (ed.), *Moral Brains: The Neuroscience of Morality* (Oxford: Oxford University Press, 2016), p. 2.

252. Al-Rodhan, 'Neurophilosophy and Transhumanism'.
253. See, for example, E. Klein *et al.*, 'Brain-Computer Interface-based Control of Closed-loop Brain Stimulation: Attitudes and Ethical Considerations', *Brain-Computer Interfaces* 3, no. 3 (2016), pp. 140–48, https://doi.org/10.1080/2326263X.2016.1207497.
254. Nayef R.F. Al-Rodhan, 'A Neurophilosophy of Governance of Artificial Intelligence and Brain-Computer Interface', *Blog of the American Philosophical Association*, 1 June 2020, https://blog.apaonline.org/2020/06/01/a-neurophilosophy-of-governance-of-artificial-intelligence-and-brain-computer-interface; L. Drew, 'The Ethics of Brain-Computer Interfaces', *Nature* 571 (2019), p. S19, https://doi.org/10.1038/d41586-019-02214-2.
255. S. Aas and D. Wasserman, 'Brain-Computer Interfaces and Disability: Extending Embodiment, Reducing Stigma?', *Journal of Medical Ethics* 42, no. 1 (2016), p. 37.
256. A. P. Alivisatos *et al.*, 'The Brain Activity Map', *Science* 339, no. 6125 (2013), pp. 1284–85.
257. A. van Mil, H. Hopkins and S. Kinsella, 'From Our Brain to the World: Views on the Future of Neural Interfaces; A Public Research Programme Conducted on Behalf of the Royal Society: Findings Report', The Royal Society, July 2019, https://royalsociety.org/-/media/policy/projects/ihuman/public-engagement-full-report.pdf.
258. D. Plass-Oude Bos *et al.*, 'Brain Computer Interfacing and Games', in D.S. Tan and A. Nijholt (eds), *Brain Computer Interfaces* (London: Springer, 2010), pp. 150–51.
259. S. Steinert and O. Friedrich, 'Wired Emotions: Ethical Issues of Affective Brain-Computer Interfaces', *Science and Engineering Ethics* 26 (2020), p. 357.
260. Al-Rodhan, 'A Neurophilosophy of Governance of Artificial Intelligence and Brain-Computer Interface'; C. MacKellar (ed.), *Cyborg Mind: What Brain-Computer and Mind-Cyberspace Interfaces Mean for Cyberneuroethics* (New York: Berghahn Books, 2019), pp. 46–47.
261. Steinert and Friedrich, 'Wired Emotions', pp. 354–55.
262. Ibid., pp. 358–60.
263. L. Pycroft *et al.*, 'Brainjacking: Implant Security Issues in Invasive Neuromodulation', *World Neurosurgery* 92 (August 2016) pp. 454–62, https://doi.org/10.1016/j.wneu.2016.05.010; Al-Rodhan, 'A Neurophilosophy of Governance of Artificial Intelligence and Brain-Computer Interface'.
264. L. Pycroft, 'Brainjacking – A New Cyber-Security Threat', *The Conversation*, 23 August 2016, https://theconversation.com/brainjacking-a-new-cyber-security-threat-64315.
265. J.A. Alegría-Torres, A. Baccarelli, and V. Bollati, 'Epigenetics and Lifestyle', *Epigenomics* 3, no. 3 (2011), pp. 267–77, https://doi.org/10.2217/epi.11.22; Al-Rodhan, 'A Neurophilosophy of Governance of Artificial Intelligence and Brain-Computer Interface'.
266. Ibid.

267. Al-Rodhan, 'A Neurophilosophy of Two Technological Game-Changers'.
268. Nayef R.F. Al-Rodhan, *The Politics of Emerging Strategic Technologies: Implications for Geopolitics, Human Enhancement and Human Destiny* (London: Palgrave Macmillan, 2011), p. 178.
269. Al-Rodhan, 'Neurophilosophy and Transhumanism'; P. Scharre and L. Fish, *Human Performance Enhancement* (Washington, DC: Center for a New American Security, 2018), p. 8, https://s3.us-east-1.amazonaws.com/files .cnas.org/documents/CNAS_Super-Soldiers_6_Human-Performance -Enhancement-FINAL.pdf?mtime=20180917103621&focal=none.
270. Al-Rodhan, 'Neurophilosophy and Transhumanism'; N.J. Davis, 'Brain Stimulation for Cognitive Enhancement in the Older Person: State of the Art and Future Directions', *Journal of Cognitive Enhancement* 1 (2017), p. 338.
271. M.W. Vahle, 'The Future', in M.W. Vahle, *Opportunities and Implications of Brain-Computer Interface Technology*, Wright Flyer Paper No. 75 (Maxwell Air Force Base, Alabama: Air University Press, 1 July 2020), p. 13, https://www.airuniversity.af.edu/Portals/10/AUPress/Papers/WF _0075_VAHLE_OPPORTUNITIES_AND_IMPLICATIONS_OF_BRAIN _COMPUTER_INTERFACE_TECHNOLOGY.PDF.
272. Al-Rodhan, 'A Neurophilosophy of Two Technological Game-Changers'; see also M. El Karoui, M. Hoyos-Flight and Liz Fletcher, 'Future Trends in Synthetic Biology – A Report', *Frontiers in Bioengineering and Biotechnology* 7 (2019), p. 1, https://doi.org/10.3389/fbioe.2019.00175.
273. See M.-S. Roell and M.D. Zurbriggen, 'The Impact of Synthetic Biology for Future Agriculture and Nutrition', *Current Opinion in Biotechnology* 61 (2020), pp. 102–9, https://doi.org/10.1016/j.copbio.2019.10.004.
274. Al-Rodhan, 'A Neurophilosophy of Two Technological Game-Changers'; see also J. Dou and M.R. Bennett, 'Synthetic Biology and the Gut Microbiome', *Biotechnology Journal* 13, no. 5 (2018), p. 1700159, https:// doi.org/10.1002/biot.201700159.
275. Al-Rodhan, 'A Neurophilosophy of Two Technological Game-Changers'; P. Nouvel, 'De la biologie synthétique à l'homme synthétique', *Comptes Rendus Biologies* 338, nos. 8–9 (2015), pp. 559–65, https://doi.org/10.1016 /j.crvi.2015.06.015.
276. S. Stevens, 'Synthetic Biology in Cell and Organ Transplantation', *Cold Spring Harbor Perspectives in Biology* 9, no. 2 (2017), pp. 3–4, https://doi .org/10.1101/cshperspect.a029561.
277. Ibid., p. 5.
278. See Center of Excellence for Engineering Biology, *GP-Write FAQ: 8. Does this Project Propose the Creation of So-called Parentless Babies?*, http://engineeringbiologycenter.org/faq/#8 (accessed 13 January 2021); Al-Rodhan, 'A Neurophilosophy of Two Technological Game-Changers'.
279. Al-Rodhan, 'A Neurophilosophy of Two Technological Game-Changers'; N. Bostrom, 'Five Ways the Superintelligence Revolution Might Happen', *The Conversation*, 25 September 2014, https://theconversation. com/five-ways-the-superintelligence-revolution-might-happen-32124.

280. Bostrom, 'Five Ways the Superintelligence Revolution Might Happen'.
281. Al-Rodhan, 'A Neurophilosophy of Two Technological Game-Changers'.
282. H. Okon-Singer *et al.*, 'The Neurobiology of Emotion-Cognition Interactions', *Frontiers in Human Neuroscience* 9 (2015), p. 6, https://doi.org/10.3389/fnhum.2015.00058.
283. E.A. Phelps, K.M. Lempert and P. Sokol-Hessner, 'Emotion and Decision Making: Multiple Modulatory Neural Circuits', *Annual Review of Neuroscience* 37 (2014), pp. 263–87, https://doi.org/10.1146/annurev-neuro-071013-014119.
284. Liao, 'Morality and Neuroscience', p. 8.
285. Ibid., p. 2.
286. D. Vertsberger, S. Israel and A. Knafo-Noam, 'Genetics, Parenting, and Moral Development', in D. Laible, G. Carlo and L.M. Padilla-Walker (eds), *The Oxford Handbook of Parenting and Moral Development* (Oxford: Oxford University Press, 2019), pp. 107–28.
287. See M. Buades-Rotger and D. Gallardo-Pujol, 'The Role of the Monoamine Oxidase A Gene in Moderating the Response to Adversity and Associated Antisocial Behavior: A Review', *Psychology Research and Behavior Management* 7 (2014), pp. 187–89, https://doi.org/10.2147/PRBM.S40458.
288. Phelps, Lempert and Sokol-Hessner, 'Emotion and Decision Making', pp. 267–68.
289. Liao, 'Morality and Neuroscience', p. 13.
290. T. Wheatley and J. Haidt, 'Hypnotic Disgust Makes Moral Judgments More Severe', *Psychological Science* 16, no. 10 (2005), pp. 780–84, https://doi.org/10.1111/j.1467-9280.2005.01614.x.
291. See J.D. Greene *et al.*, 'An fMRI Investigation of Emotional Engagement in Moral Judgment', *Science* 293, no. 5537 (2001), pp. 2105–8, https://doi.org/10.1126/science.1062872.
292. Ibid.
293. Ibid.
294. Liao, 'Morality and Neuroscience', p. 6.
295. T. Kühne, 'Nazi Morality', in S. Baranowski, Armin Nolzen, Claus-Christian W. Szejnmann (eds), *A Companion to Nazi Germany* (Oxford: Wiley-Blackwell, 2018), p. 216.
296. J. Prinz, 'The Emotional Basis of Moral Judgments', *Philosophical Explorations* 9, no. 1 (2006), p. 33, quoted in Liao, 'Morality and Neuroscience', p. 9.
297. Liao, 'Morality and Neuroscience', p. 20.
298. J. Decety *et al.*, 'Empathy as a Driver of Prosocial Behaviour: Highly Conserved Neurobehavioural Mechanisms across Species', *Philosophical Transactions: Biological Sciences* 371, no. 1686 (2016), p. 6.
299. T. Malti *et al.*, 'Children's Moral Motivation, Sympathy and Prosocial Behaviour', *Child Development* 80, no. 2 (2009), p. 443.

300. J. Decety and J.M. Cowell, 'Friends or Foes: Is Empathy Necessary for Moral Behavior?', *Perspectives on Psychological Science* 9, no. 4 (2014), pp. 525–37, https://doi.org/10.1177/1745691614545130.

301. I. Persson and J. Savulescu, 'The Moral Importance of Reflective Empathy', *Neuroethics* 11, no. 2 (2018), pp. 183–93, https://doi.org/10.1007/s12152-017-9350-7.

302. M. Bernhard, T. Fernandes and R. Branco, 'Introduction: Civil Society and Democracy in an Era of Inequality', *Comparative Politics* 49, no. 3 (2017), p. 300.

303. D.J. Hosken, J. Hunt and N. Wedell (eds), *Genes and Behaviour: Beyond Nature–Nurture* (Chichester: John Wiley & Sons Ltd, 2019), p. 9.

304. D. Banks, 'What Is Brain Plasticity and Why Is It So Important?', *The Conversation*, 4 April 2016, https://theconversation.com/what-is-brain-plasticity-and-why-is-it-so-important-55967.

305. See Nayef R.F. Al-Rodhan, *Sustainable History and the Dignity of Man: A Philosophy of History and Civilisational Triumph* (Berlin: LIT Verlag, 2009).

306. Liao, 'Morality and Neuroscience', p. 16.

307. R.M. Ryan (ed.), *The Oxford Handbook of Human Motivation* (Oxford: Oxford University Press, 2019), pp. 1–2.

308. D. Wrong, *Power: Its Forms, Bases and Uses* (Abingdon: Routledge, 2017), p. 2.

308. B.A. Dobratz, L.K. Waldner and T. Buzzell, *Power, Politics, and Society: An Introduction to Political Sociology*, 2nd edn (London: Routledge, 2019), p. 2.

309. Weber, quoted in ibid., p. 2.

310. Ibid., p. 3.

311. B. Russell, *Power: A New Social Analysis* (London: George Allen & Unwin, 1938), pp. 278, 308.

312. Nayef R.F. Al-Rodhan, 'The Neurochemistry of Power: Implications for Political Change', *The Oxford University Politics Blog*, 27 February 2014, https://blog.politics.ox.ac.uk/neurochemistry-power-implications-political-change.

313. Bertrand Russell, 'What Desires Are Politically Important?', Nobel Lecture, The Nobel Prize, 11 December 1950, www.nobelprize.org/prizes/literature/1950/russell/lecture.

314. C. Camerer, G. Loewenstein and D. Prelec, 'Neuroeconomics: How Neuroscience Can Inform Economics', *Journal of Economic Literature* 43, no. 1 (2005), pp. 39–40.

315. Stevenson and Haberman, *Ten Theories of Human Nature*, p. 172; S. Freud, *Civilization and Its Discontents*, reissue edn (New York: W.W. Norton & Co., 1989); James E. Crimmins, 'Jeremy Bentham', in *Stanford Encyclopedia of Philosophy* (Stanford University, 1997-), article pub. 17 March 2015, substantive rev. 28 January 2019, https://plato.stanford.edu/entries/bentham.

316. E. Winner, *How Art Works: A Psychological Exploration* (Oxford: Oxford University Press, 2019), p. 11.

317. L. Moccia *et al.*, 'The Experience of Pleasure: A Perspective between Neuroscience and Psychoanalysis', *Frontiers in Human Neuroscience* 12 (2018), pp. 1–10, https://doi.org/10.3389/fnhum.2018.00359.

318. D. Sander and K. Scherer (eds), *Oxford Companion to Emotion and the Affective Sciences* (Oxford: Oxford University Press, 2014), p. 141.

319. L. Roth *et al.*, 'Brain Activation Associated with Pride and Shame', *Neuropsychobiology* 69, no. 2 (2014), p. 96, https://doi.org/10.1159/000358090.

320. See G. Northoff *et al.*, 'Self-Referential Processing in Our Brain: A Meta-Analysis of Imaging Studies on the Self', *Neuroimage* 31 (2006), pp. 440–57.

321. J.L. Tracy and R.W. Robins, 'The Psychological Structure of Pride: A Tale of Two Facets', *Journal of Personality and Social Psychology* 92, no. 3 (2007), p. 506.

322. Ibid., p. 507.

323. D.A. Reinhard *et al.*, 'Expensive Egos: Narcissistic Males Have Higher Cortisol', *PLOS One* 7, no. 1 (2012), p. 1, https://doi.org/10.1371/journal.pone.0030858.

324. D.S. Chester *et al.*, 'Narcissism Is Associated with Weakened Frontostriatal Connectivity: A DTI Study', *Social Cognitive and Affective Neuroscience* 11, no. 7 (2016), pp. 1036–40, https://doi.org/10.1093/scan/nsv069.

325. F.R. George and D. Short, 'The Cognitive Neuroscience of Narcissism', *Journal of Brain Behaviour and Cognitive Sciences* 1, no. 1 (2018), p. 6, http://www.imedpub.com/articles/the-cognitive-neuroscience-of-narcissism.php?aid=22149

326. A. Carter and E. Gordon, *The Moral Psychology of Pride* (London: Rowman & Littlefield, 2017), p. 21.

327. Roth *et al.*, 'Brain Activation Associated with Pride and Shame', p. 96.

328. See S. Freud, *The Complete Psychological Works of Sigmund Freud*, trans. and ed. J. Strachey (London: Hogarth Press, 1953–74).

329. G. Murphy, *Personality: A Biosocial Approach to Origins and Structure* (New York: Harper & Brothers, 1947), ch. 22.

330. P.M. Symonds, *The Ego and the Self* (New York: Appleton-Century-Crofts, 1951), p. 4.

331. Ibid., p. 164.

332. Ibid., pp. 121–24, 126.

333. Nayef R.F. Al-Rodhan, *Symbiotic Realism: A Theory of International Relations in an Instant and an Interdependent World* (Berlin: LIT Verlag, 2007), 71.

334. Ibid., p. 71.

335. J.L. Tracy and R.W. Robins, 'Emerging Insights into the Nature and Function of Pride', *Current Directions in Psychological Science* 16, no. 3 (2007), p. 149.

336. M.J.J. Wubben, D. De Cremer, and E. van Dijk, 'Is Pride a Prosocial Emotion? Interpersonal Effects of Authentic and Hubristic Pride', *Cognition and Emotion* 26, no. 6 (2012), pp. 1084–1985.
337. S. Trip *et al.*, 'Psychological Mechanisms Involved in Radicalization and Extremism: A Rational Emotive Behavioral Conceptualization', *Frontiers in Psychology* 10 (2019), p. 3, https://doi.org/10.3389/fpsyg.2019.00437.
338. C. Zuber and A. Conzelmann, 'Achievement-Motivated Behavior in Individual Sports (AMBIS-I) – Coach Rating Scale', *German Journal of Exercise and Sport Research* 49 (2019), p. 410.
339. S. Cunningham, B. Engelstätter and M.R. Ward, 'Violent Video Games and Violent Crime', *Southern Economic Journal* 82, no. 4 (2016), p. 1247.
340. Stevenson and Haberman, *Ten Theories of Human Nature*, pp. 71–72.
341. Ibid., pp. 125, 157.
342. For a discussion of reason without emotion, see D.J. Stein, 'The Neurobiology of Evil: Psychiatric Perspectives on Perpetrators', *Ethnicity and Health* 5, nos 3–4 (2000), pp. 303–15.
343. Hobbes, *Leviathan*.
344. Al-Rodhan, *Symbiotic Realism*, p. 68.
345. See, for instance, R. Dawkins, *The Selfish Gene*, 30th anniversary edn (Oxford: Oxford University Press, 2006); Hauser, *Moral Minds*.
346. Barrett, Dunbar and Lycett, *Human Evolutionary Psychology*, p. 3.
347. Dawkins, *The Selfish Gene*, pp. 12–13.
348. Ibid., pp. 14–15, 17.
349. Ibid., p. 17.
350. Ibid., pp. 19–20.
351. Ibid., p. 22.
352. Ibid., p. 23.
353. H. Pearson, 'Genetics: What Is a Gene?', *Nature* 441, no. 7092 (2006), pp. 398–401.
354. Winston, *Human Instinct*, p. 22.
355. Dawkins, *The Selfish Gene*, pp. 22–24.
356. Ibid., pp. 24–25, 27, 31, 36.
357. Nayef R.F. Al-Rodhan and L. Watanabe, *A Proposal for Inclusive Peace and Security* (Genève: Éditions Slatkine, 2007), p. 92.
358. Nayef R.F. Al-Rodhan, *The Role of Education in Global Security* (Genève: Éditions Slatkine, 2007), p. 54.
359. Ibid., p. 51.
360. See Al-Rodhan, *Symbiotic Realism*, esp. ch. 3.
361. Al-Rodhan, *The Role of Education in Global Security*, p. 55.
362. A. Maalouf, *In the Name of Identity: Violence and the Need to Belong*, trans. B. Bray (New York: Penguin Books, 2003).
363. Al-Rodhan, *Symbiotic Realism*, p. 123.
364. C. Jenks, *Culture* (New York: Routledge, 2004), p. 9.
365. Ibid., pp. 8, 11–12.

366. R.W. Cox and M.G. Schechter, *The Political Economy of a Plural World: Critical Reflections on Power, Morals and Civilization* (London: Routledge, 2002), p. 157.
367. Dawkins, *The Selfish Gene*, p. 191.
368. Ibid., p. 189.
369. Ibid., p. 192.
370. Ibid., p. 193.
371. Ibid., pp 192–193. See the rest of Chapter 11 ("Memes: the new replicators").
372. Ibid., pp. 199–200.
373. Ibid., pp. 200–1.
374. R. Dessí, 'Collective Memory, Cultural Transmission, and Investments', *The American Economic Review* 98, no. 1 (2008), p. 534.
375. Somit and Peterson, 'From Human Nature to Public Policy', p. 6.
376. Al-Rodhan, *The Role of Education in Global Security*, p. 57.
377. Ibid., p. 53.
378. Ibid., p. 57.
379. Al-Rodhan, *Symbiotic Realism*, p. 124.
380. Phelps, Lempert and Sokol-Hessner, 'Emotion and Decision Making'.
381. Winston, *Human Instinct*, p. xiv.
382. A.J. Zautra, *Emotions, Stress, and Health* (Oxford: Oxford University Press, 2003), p. 12.
383. S.S. Pattwell, B.J. Casey and F.S. Lee, 'The Teenage Brain: Altered Fear in Humans and Mice', *Current Directions in Psychological Science* 22, no. 2 (2013), p. 146, https://doi.org/10.1177/0963721412471323.
384. Darwin, *The Expression of Emotions in Man and Animals*.
385. Walton, *Humanity*, p. xiii.
386. Ibid., p. xiv.
387. D. Goleman, *Destructive Emotions and How We Can Overcome Them: A Dialogue with the Dalai Lama* (London: Bloomsbury, 2004), p. 120.
388. Ibid., pp. 123, 125–26.
389. P. Ekman, E.R. Sorenson and W.V. Friesen, 'Pan-Cultural Elements in Facial Displays of Emotion', *Science* 164, no. 3875 (1969), pp. 86–88, https://doi.org/10.1126/science.164.3875.86; P. Ekman *et al.*, 'Universals and Cultural Differences in the Judgments of Facial Expressions of Emotions', *Journal of Personal and Social Psychology* 53, no. 4 (1987), pp. 712–17, https://doi.org/10.1037//0022-3514.53.4.712.
390. C. Crivelli *et al.*, 'Reading Emotions from Faces in Two Indigenous Societies', *Journal of Experimental Psychology: General* 145, no. 7 (2016), pp. 830–43, https://doi.org/10.1037/xge0000172.
391. C. Crivelli *et al.*, 'The Fear Gasping Face as a Threat Display in a Melanesian Society', *Proceedings of the National Academy of Sciences of the United States of America* 113, no. 44 (2016), pp. 12404–6, https://doi.org/10.1073/pnas.1611622113.
392. Walton, *Humanity*, p. xviii.

393. Ibid., p. xiv.
394. Zautra, *Emotions, Stress, and Health*, pp. 384, 13.
395. Catherine Soanes, Sara Hawker and Julia Elliott (eds), *Paperback Oxford English Dictionary* (2006), s.v. 'fear'.
396. Walton, *Humanity*, p. 3.
397. Ibid., p. 25.
398. A. Javanbakht, 'The Politics of Fear: How Fear Goes Tribal, Allowing Us to Be Manipulated', *The Conversation*, 11 January 2019, https://the conversation.com/the-politics-of-fear-how-fear-goes-tribal-allowing-us -to-be-manipulated-109626.
399. For more information on the debate concerning the fear of falling, see K.E. Adolph, K.S. Kretch and V. LoBue, 'Fear of Heights in Infants?', *Current Directions in Psychological Science* 23, no. 1 (2014), pp. 60–66, https://doi.org/10.1177/0963721413498895; R.D. Walk and E.J. Gibson, 'The "Visual Cliff"', *Scientific American* 202, no. 4 (1960), pp. 64–71, https://doi.org/10.1038/scientificamerican0460-64. For information on the fear of loud noises, see N. Erlich, O.V. Lipp and V. Slaughter, 'Of Hissing Snakes and Angry Voices: Human Infants Are Differentially Responsive to Evolutionary Fear-Relevant Sounds', *Developmental Science* 16, no. 6 (2013), pp. 894–904, https:// doi.org/10.1111/desc.12091. For information on the neuroscience behind fear, see R. Adolphs, 'The Biology of Fear', *Current Biology* 23, no. 2 (2013), pp. R79-R93, https://doi.org/10.1016/j. cub.2012.11.055.
400. See Hobbes, *Leviathan*, ch. 11 ('Of the difference of Manners').
401. Ibid., ch. 11.
402. Nayef R.F. Al-Rodhan, 'A Neurophilosophy of Fear-Induced Pre-emptive Aggression and Pseudo-Altruism', *Blog of the American Philosophical Association*, 4 August 2020, https://blog.apaonline.org /2020/08/04/a-neurophilosophy-of-fear-induced-pre-emptive-aggression -pseudo-altruism/#:~:text=Fear%20can%20swiftly%20induce%20 responses,harm%20and%20ensure%20our%20survival.
403. M.A. Lumley *et al.*, 'Pain and Emotion: A Biopsychosocial Review of Recent Research', *Journal of Clinical Psychology* 67, no. 9 (2011), pp. 5–6, https://doi.org/10.1002/jclp.20816.
404. Ibid.
405. Ibid.
406. J. Archer, *The Nature of Grief: The Evolution and Psychology of Reactions to Loss* (London: Routledge, 1999), p. 1.
407. Ibid., p. 2.
408. Ibid., p. 3.
409. Ibid., p. 5.
410. Ibid., pp. 179–80.
411. Ibid., p. 8.
412. Walton, *Humanity*, p. 45.

413. See C. Tavris, *Anger: The Misunderstood Emotion*, rev. edn (New York: Touchstone, 1989).

414. Walton, *Humanity*, p. 173.

415. Winston, *Human Instinct*, p. 143.

416. Walton, *Humanity*, pp. 143–46.

417. Ibid., pp. 247–48, 259.

418. Ibid., pp. 286–87.

419. C. Bastin *et al.*, 'Feelings of Shame, Embarrassment and Guilt and Their Neural Correlates: A Systematic Review', *Neuroscience & Biobehavioral Reviews* 71 (2016), pp. 455–71, https://doi.org/10.1016/j. neubiorev.2016.09.019.

420. Ibid.

421. A. Barto, M. Mirolli and G. Baldassarre, 'Novelty or Surprise', *Frontiers in Psychology* 4 (2013), pp. 1–15, https://doi.org/10.3389/ fpsyg.2013.00907.

422. Nayef R.F. Al-Rodhan, 'A Neurophilosophy of "Sustainable Neurochemical Gratification" and the Meaning of Existence', *Blog of the American Philosophical Association*, 13 July 2020, https://blog.apaonline .org/2020/07/13/a-neurophilosophy-of-sustainable-neurochemical-grati fication-and-the-meaning-of-existence.

423. Ibid.

424. Walton, *Humanity*, p. 378.

425. Stevenson and Haberman, *Ten Theories of Human Nature*, pp. 95–97.

426. Walton, *Humanity*, p. 4.

427. Ibid., p. 89.

428. Ibid., pp. 207, 221.

429. C.E. Izard, *Human Emotions* (New York: Springer, 2013), p. 337.

430. J. LeDoux, *The Emotional Brain* (New York: Simon & Schuster, 1996); P. Brodal, *Neurological Anatomy in Relation to Clinical Medicine*, 3rd edn (New York: Oxford University Press, 1981).

431. Zautra, *Emotions, Stress, and Health*, p. 9; LeDoux, *The Emotional Brain*.

432. LeDoux, *The Emotional Brain*, p. 12.

433. Ibid., p. 9.

434. W. Wittling and R. Roschmann, 'Emotion-Related Hemisphere Asymmetry: Subjective Emotional Responses to Laterally Presented Films', *Cortex* 29, no. 3 (1993), pp. 431–48, https://doi.org/10.1016 /s0010-9452(13)80252-3.

435. Ibid., pp. 434–435.

436. Zautra, *Emotions, Stress, and Health*, p. 29.

437. Winston, *Human Instinct*, p. 49.

438. Ibid., p. 51.

439. Ibid., pp. 37–39.

440. W.R. Stauffer *et al.*, 'Components and Characteristics of the Dopamine Reward Utility Signal', *Journal of Comparative Neurology* 524, no. 8 (2016), pp. 1699–1711, https://doi.org/10.1002/cne.23880.

441. P.J. Cowen and M. Browning, 'What Has Serotonin to Do with Depression?', *World Psychiatry* 14, no. 2 (2015), pp. 158–59, https://doi .org/10.1002/wps.20229.
442. D. Seo, C.J. Patrick and P.J. Kennealy, 'Role of Serotonin and Dopamine System Interactions in the Neurobiology of Impulsive Aggression and Its Comorbidity with Other Clinical Disorders', *Aggressive and Violent Behavior* 13, no. 5 (2008), pp. 2–3, https://doi.org/10.1016/j.avb.2008 .06.003.
443. A.A. Duke *et al.*, 'Revisiting the Serotonin-Aggression Relation in Humans: A Meta-Analysis', *Psychological Bulletin* 139, no. 5 (2013), p. 2, https://doi.org/10.1037/a0031544.
444. W. Gallagher, 'How We Become What We Are', *The Atlantic Monthly* 274, no. 3 (1994), p. 38.
445. Ibid.
446. S. An *et al.*, 'Two Sides of Emotion: Exploring Positivity and Negativity in Six Basic Emotions across Cultures', *Frontiers of Psychology* 8 (2017), p. 2, https://doi.org/10.3389/fpsyg.2017.00610.
447. Gallagher, 'How We Become What We Are', p. 38.
448. S.C. Tanaka, Bernard W. Balleine and John P. O'Doherty, 'Calculating Consequences: Brain Systems that Encode the Causal Effects of Actions', *The Journal of Neuroscience* 28, no. 26 (2008), pp. 6753–54.
449. Blank, 'Neuroscience, Free Will, and Individual Responsibility', p. 64; M.P. Paulus, S.F. Tapert and M.A. Schuckit, 'Neural Activation Patterns of Methamphetamine-Dependent Subjects during Decision Making Predict Relapse', *Archives of General Psychiatry* 62, no. 7 (2005), pp. 761–68. https://doi.org/10.1001/archpsyc.62.7.761.
450. Blank, 'Neuroscience, Free Will, and Individual Responsibility', p. 65.
451. Ibid., pp. 65–66. See also R. West and M. Gossop, 'Overview: A Comparison of Withdrawal Symptoms from Different Drug Classes', *Addiction* 89, no. 11 (1994), pp. 1483–89, https://doi.org/10.1111/j.1360 -0443.1994.tb03747.x.
452. Blank, 'Neuroscience, Free Will, and Individual Responsibility', p. 66.
453. E.J. Nestler, 'The Neurobiology of Cocaine Addiction', *Science & Practice Perspectives* 3, no. 1 (2005), pp. 5–6, https://doi.org/10.1151/spp05314, available at: https://www.ncbi.nlm.nih.gov/pmc/articles/PMC2851032/.
454. D.S. Levine, 'Angels, Devils, and Censors in the Brain', *Complexus*, no. 2 (2004–05), pp. 42–43, https://doi.org/10.1159/000089747.
455. R.A. Lanius *et al.*, 'The Dissociative Subtype of Posttraumatic Stress Disorder: Rationale, Clinical and Neurobiological Evidence, and Implications', *Depression and Anxiety* 29, no. 8 (2012), pp. 701–8, https:// doi.org/10.1002/da.21889; H. Bækkelund *et al.*, 'Trauma-related Altered States of Consciousness in Post-Traumatic Stress Disorder Patients with or without Comorbid Dissociative Disorders', *European Journal of Psychotraumatology* 9, no. 1 (2018), p. 2, https://doi.org/10.1080/2000819 8.2018.1544025.

456. H.E. Fisher *et al.*, 'Defining the Brain Systems of Lust, Romantic Attraction, and Attachment', *Archives of Sexual Behavior* 31, no. 5 (2002), pp. 413–19, https://doi.org/10.1023/a:1019888024255.

457. For the role of oxytocin in female attachment towards sexual partners, see A. Campbell, 'Attachment, Aggression and Affiliation: The Role of Oxytocin in Female Behavior', *Biological Psychology* 77, no. 1 (2008), pp. 1–10, https://doi.org/10.1016/j.biopsycho.2007.09.001; for the role of oxytocin in mother-child attachment, see C.K.D. de Dreu, 'Oxytocin Modulates the Link between Adult Attachment and Cooperation through Reduced Betrayal Aversion', *Psychoneuroendocrinology* 37, no. 7 (2012), pp. 871–80, https://doi.org/10.1016/j.psyneuen.2011.10.003; S. Krause *et al.*, 'Effects of the Adult Attachment Projective Picture System on Oxytocin and Cortisol Blood Levels in Mothers', *Frontiers in Human Neuroscience* 10 (2016), pp. 1–12, https://doi.org/10.3389/fnhum.2016.00627; M. Nagasawa *et al.*, 'Oxytocin and Mutual Communication in Mother-Infant Bonding', *Frontiers in Human Neuroscience* 6 (2012), pp. 2–3, https://doi.org/10.3389/fnhum.2012.00031.

458. Levine, 'Angels, Devils, and Censors in the Brain', p. 44; see also C.S. Carter, 'The Oxytocin-Vasopressin Pathway in the Context of Love and Fear', *Frontiers in Endocrinology* 8 (2017), pp. 1–12, https://doi.org/10.3389/fendo.2017.00356; C.S. Carter, 'Neuroendocrine Perspectives on Social Attachment and Love', *Psychoneuroendocrinology* 23, no. 8 (1998), pp. 779–818, https://doi.org/10.1016/S0306-4530(98)00055-9.

459. R. Feldman, 'The Neurobiology of Human Attachments', *Trends in Cognitive Sciences* 21, no. 2 (2017), pp. 80–81, https://doi.org/10.1016/j.tics.2016.11.007.

460. Fisher *et al.*, 'Defining the Brain Systems of Lust, Romantic Attraction, and Attachment'.

461. Ibid.

462. Al-Rodhan, 'The Neurochemistry of Power: Implications for Political Change'.

463. Al-Rodhan, 'A Neurophilosophy of "Sustainable Neurochemical Gratification" and the Meaning of Existence'.

464. Al-Rodhan, 'The Neurochemistry of Power'.

465. Ibid.

466. Ibid.

467. R.D. Rogers, 'The Roles of Dopamine and Serotonin in Decision-Making: Evidence from Pharmacological Experiments in Humans', *Neuropsychopharmacology* 36, no. 1 (2011), pp. 116–18, https://doi.org/10.1038/npp.2010.165.

468. Al-Rodhan, 'The Neurochemistry of Power'.

469. Ibid.

470. Ibid.

471. Ibid.

472. Al-Rodhan, 'A Neurophilosophy of Fear-Induced Pre-emptive Aggression and Pseudo-Altruism'.

473. Ibid.
474. Ibid.
475. Adolphs, 'The Biology of Fear', pp. 3–4, 5–7.
476. Al-Rodhan, 'A Neurophilosophy of Fear-Induced Pre-emptive Aggression and Pseudo-Altruism'.
477. Ibid., p. 37.
478. Barrett, Dunbar and Lycett, *Human Evolutionary Psychology*, pp. 3–4.
479. Dawkins, *The Selfish Gene*, pp. 49–50.
480. Ibid., p. 59.
481. Ibid., p. 60.
482. Winston, *Human Instinct*, p. 201.
483. Ibid., p. 200.
484. Ibid., pp. 201–2.
485. Barrett, Dunbar and Lycett, *Human Evolutionary Psychology*, p. 25.
486. Ibid., p. 26.
487. Dawkins, *The Selfish Gene*, pp. 36–37, 39.
488. Ibid., pp. 2–4.
489. Ibid., p. 5.
490. Ibid., pp. 5–6.
491. T.H. Goldsmith, *The Biological Roots of Human Nature: Forging Links between Evolution and Behaviour* (New York: Oxford University Press, 1991), pp. 105–6.
492. Ibid., pp. 107–8.
493. Ibid., p. 34.
494. Winston, *Human Instinct*, p. 22.
495. T.A. Shannon, 'Human Nature in a Post-Human Genome Project World', in H.W. Baillie and T.K. Casey (eds), *Is Human Nature Obsolete? Genetics, Bioengineering, and the Future of the Human Condition* (Cambridge, MA: MIT Press, 2005), p. 269.
496. L. Sperry, 'Psychopharmacology as an Adjunct to Psychotherapy in the Treatment of Personality Disorders', *Journal of Individual Psychology* 62, no. 3 (2006), p. 324.
497. M. Gerlach *et al.*, 'A Robust Data-Driven Approach Identifies Four Personality Types across Four Large Data Sets', *Nature Human Behaviour* 2 (2018), pp. 735–42, https://doi.org/10.1038/s41562-018-0419-z.
498. Ibid.
499. Personality Disorders Foundation (University of Connecticut), *What Are the Personality Disorders? A Summary from the Personality Disorders Foundation*, updated 15 February 2016, https://mhreference.org/person ality-disorder/foundation/summary.
500. Personality Disorders Foundation, *What Are the Personality Disorders?*; Sperry, 'Psychopharmacology as an Adjunct to Psychotherapy', pp. 326, 332; A.D.P. Mak and L.C.W. Lam, 'Neurocognitive Profiles of People with Borderline Personality Disorder', *Current Opinion in Psychiatry* 26, no. 1 (2013), pp. 91–92, https://doi.org/10.1097/YCO.0b013e32835b57a9.

501. Sperry, 'Psychopharmacology as an Adjunct to Psychotherapy', pp. 327–28.
502. Personality Disorders Foundation, *What Are the Personality Disorders?*
503. Sperry, 'Psychopharmacology as an Adjunct to Psychotherapy', p. 325.
504. Ibid., p. 329.
505. Ibid., p. 331.
506. Ibid., p. 334.
507. Encyclopaedia Britannica, 'Nanotechnology', by S. Tom Picraux, https://www.britannica.com/technology/nanotechnology (accessed 12 March 2021).
508. Al-Rodhan, 'Neurophilosophy and Transhumanism'.
509. Ibid.
510. See M. More, 'On Becoming Posthuman', *Free Inquiry* 1, no. 4 (1994), pp. 38–41.
511. More, 'On Becoming Posthuman'.
512. N. Bostrom, 'Transhumanist Values', *Review of Contemporary Philosophy* 4 (2005), pp. 87–101.
513. Nayef R.F. Al-Rodhan, 'Free Will in the Age of Neuromodulation', *Philosophy Now*, no. 127 (2018), pp. 28–30, https://philosophynow.org /issues/127/Free_Will_in_the_Age_of_Neuromodulation.
514. E. Waltz, 'Electronic Pump Delivers Drugs to the Brain to Stop Seizures', *IEEE Spectrum*, 30 August 2018, https://spectrum.ieee.org/the-human-os /biomedical/devices/electronic-pump-delivers-drugs-to-the-brain-to-stop -seizures.
515. More, 'On Becoming Posthuman'.
516. Bostrom, 'Transhumanist Values'.
517. M. Zimmer, 'Nobel Prize for CRISPR Honors Two Great Scientists – and Leaves Out Many Others', *The Conversation*, 8 October 2020, https:// theconversation.com/nobel-prize-for-crispr-honors-two-great-scientists -and-leaves-out-many-others-147730.
518. H. Frangoul *et al.*, 'CRISPR-Cas9 Gene Editing for Sickle Cell Disease and β-Thalassemia', *The New England Journal of Medicine* 384 (2021), pp. 252–60, https://doi.org/10.1056/NEJMoa2031054.
519. D.B. Paul, 'Genetic Engineering and Eugenics: The Use of History', in Baillie and Casey (eds), *Is Human Nature Obsolete?*, pp. 123–24.
520. Bostrom, 'Transhumanist Values'.
521. For more information, see G.A.R. Gonçalves and R. de Melo Alves Paiva, 'Gene Therapy: Advances, Challenges and Perspectives', *Einstein* (São Paulo) 15, no. 3 (2017), pp. 369–75, https://doi.org/10.1590/S1679 -45082017RB4024.
522. G. Feng *et al.*, 'Opportunities and Limitations of Genetically Modified Nonhuman Primate Models for Neuroscience Research', *Proceedings of the National Academy of Sciences of the United States of America* 117, no. 39 (2020), p. 24024, https://doi.org/10.1073/pnas .2006515117.

523. A. Boggio *et al.*, 'The Human Right to Science and the Regulation of Human Germline Engineering', *The CRISPR Journal* 2, no. 3 (2019), p. 134, https://doi.org/10.1089/crispr.2018.0053.

524. Ibid., p. 137.

525. Ibid., p. 134.

526. L. Walters, 'Human Genetic Intervention: Past, Present, and Future', in Baillie and Casey (eds), *Is Human Nature Obsolete?*, pp. 380–81.

527. K.E. Drexler, C. Peterson and G. Pergamit, *Unbounding the Future: The Nanotechnology Revolution* (Indianapolis, IN: Quill, 1993), ch. 1.

528. More, 'On Becoming Posthuman'.

529. C. Peterson, 'Nanotechnology: From Feynman to the Grand Challenge of Molecular Manufacturing', *IEEE Technology and Society* 23, no. 4 (2004), pp. 9–15, http://doi.org/10.1109/MTAS.2004.1371633.

530. C. Peterson, 'Taking Technology to the Molecular Level', *Computer* 33, no. 1 (2000), pp. 46–53, https://doi.org/10.1109/2.816268.

531. N. Bostrom, 'What is Transhumanism?', updated 2001, https://www.nickbostrom.com/old/transhumanism.html.

532. Bostrom, 'Transhumanist Values'.

533. Encyclopaedia Britannica, 'Bernard Feringa: Dutch Chemist', by Erik Gregersen, https://www.britannica.com/biography/Bernard-Feringa (accessed 12 March 2021).

534. More, 'On Becoming Posthuman'.

535. Bostrom, 'Transhumanist Values'.

536. A. Renton, 'Neuralink Put a Chip in Gertrude the Pig's Brain. It Might Be Useful One Day', *The Conversation*, 1 September 2020, https://theconversation.com/neuralink-put-a-chip-in-gertrude-the-pigs-brain-it-might-be-useful-one-day-145383.

537. Nayef R.F. Al-Rodhan, "Will Technology Change What It Means to Be Human," World Economic Forum Agenda, 10 November 2014, https://www.weforum.org/agenda/2014/11/synthetic-biology-designing-our-existence.

538. Al-Rodhan, 'A Neurophilosophy of Two Technological Game-Changers'.

539. T.K. Casey, 'Nature, Technology, and the Emergence of Cybernetic Humanity', in H.W. Baillie and T.K. Casey (eds), *Is Human Nature Obsolete? Genetics, Bioengineering, and the Future of the Human Condition* (Cambridge, MA: MIT Press, 2005), p. 36.

540. Ibid., pp. 46–48.

541. Ibid., pp. 50–53.

542. M.S.A. Abdel-Mottaleb, J.A. Byrne and D. Chakarov, 'Nanotechnology and Solar Energy', *International Journal of Photoenergy*, Special Issue (2011), pp. 1–2, https://doi.org/10.1155/2011/194146.

543. Y. Zhang *et al.*, 'Nanotechnology in Cancer Diagnosis: Progress, Challenges and Opportunities', *Journal of Hematology and Oncology* 12, no. 137 (2019), p. 2, https://doi.org/10.1186/s13045-019-0833-3.

544. J. Moor, 'Issues: Health and Environment', in F. Allhoff *et al.* (eds), *Nanoethics. The Ethical and Social Implications of Nanotechnology* (Hoboken, NJ: John Wiley & Sons, 2007), pp 150–152.
545. Ibid., pp 151–152.
546. T. Peters, 'Are We Playing God with Nanoenhancement?', in Allhoff *et al* (eds), *Nanoethics*, pp 174–176.
547. For more information, see National Human Genome Institute, *What is the Human Genome Project?*, https://www.genome.gov/human-genome-project/What (accessed 13 January 2021).
548. Shannon, 'Human Nature in a Post-Human Genome Project World', p. 405.
549. Seigel, *The Idea of the Self*, p. 12.
550. Ibid., p. 298.
551. Ibid., p 298.
552. Ibid., p. 537.
553. R.S. Hill, 'David Hume', in Strauss and Cropsey (eds), *History of Political Philosophy*, pp. 535–36.
554. Pojman, *Who Are We?*, p. 128.
555. Ibid., p. 129.
556. Ibid., p. 129; Hill, 'David Hume', p. 543.
557. Hauser, *Moral Minds*, p. 419.
558. Ibid., p. 420.
559. Ibid., p. 423.
560. Ibid., p. 426.
561. Ibid., p. 425.
562. N. Smith and A. Law, 'On Parametric (and Non-Parametric) Variation', *Biolinguistics* 3, no. 4 (2009), p. 333.
563. J. Moll *et al.*, 'The Self as a Moral Agent: Linking the Neural Bases of Social Agency and Moral Sensitivity', *Social Neuroscience* 2, nos 3–4 (2007), pp. 336–52, https://doi.org/10.1080/17470910701392024.
564. A.E. Vélez Garcia and F. Ostrosky-Solis, 'From Morality to Moral Emotions', *International Journal of Psychology* 41, no. 5 (2006), pp. 348–54; J. Blair *et al.*, 'Neuro-cognitive Systems Involved in Morality', *Philosophical Explorations* 9, no. 1 (2006), pp. 12–27.
565. J. Prinz, 'The Emotional Basis of Moral Judgments', pp. 29–43.
566. J. Moll *et al.*, 'The Neural Correlates of Moral Sensitivity: A Functional Magnetic Resonance Imaging Investigation of Basic and Moral Emotions', *The Journal of Neuroscience* 22, no. 7 (2002), pp. 2730–36.
567. A. Raine and Y. Yang, 'Neural Foundations to Moral Reasoning and Antisocial Behavior', *Social Cognitive and Affective Neuroscience* 1, no. 3 (2006), pp. 203–13, https://doi.org/10.1093/scan/nsl033.
568. A.S. Gönül, 'Where is Human Morality? Is it in Brain or Heart?', *New Yeni Symposium Journal* 44, no. 2 (2006), pp. 107–8.
569. Liao, 'Morality and Neuroscience', p. 2.

570. Ibid., p. 9.
571. Phelps *et al.*, 'Emotion and Decision Making', pp. 267–68.
572. Moll *et al.*, 'The Self as a Moral Agent'.
573. Person and Savulescu, 'The Moral Importance of Reflective Empathy', p. 183.
574. Al-Rodhan, *Symbiotic Realism*, p. 70.
575. Ibid., p. 72.
576. Liao, 'Morality and Neuroscience', p. 16.
577. J.A. Birchler, H. Yao and S. Chudalayandi, 'Unraveling the Genetic Basis of Hybrid Vigor', *Proceedings of the National Academy of Sciences of the United States of America* 103, no. 35 (2006), p. 12957.
578. Al-Rodhan, 'Predisposed Tabula Rasa'.
579. Al-Rodhan, 'A Neurophilosophy of Fear-Induced Pre-Emptive Aggression and Pseudo-Altruism'.
580. Development, Concepts and Doctrine Centre, *Global Strategic Trends: The Future Starts Today (Sixth Edition)*, UK Ministry of Defence Website, October 2018, https://assets.publishing.service.gov.uk/govern ment/uploads/system/uploads/attachment_data/file/771309/Global_Stra tegic_Trends_-_The_Future_Starts_Today.pdf.
581. P.S. Churchland, *Neurophilosophy: Toward a Unified Science of the Mind-Brain* (Cambridge, MA: MIT Press, 1986).
582. See Pitlik, 'COVID-19 Compared to Other Pandemic Diseases'.
583. Alberti, 'Coronavirus Is Revitalising the Concept of Community for the 21st Century'.
584. World Bank, *Worldwide Governance Indicators*, https://datacatalog. worldbank.org/dataset/worldwide-governance-indicators (accessed 3 May 2021).
585. The Centre for the Study of Global Governance of the London School of Economics defines global governance in this way. See W.D. Drake and E.J. Wilson III (eds), *Governing Global Electronic Networks: International Perspectives on Policy and Power* (Cambridge, MA: MIT Press, 2008), p. 6.
586. Nayef R.F. Al-Rodhan, '3 Disruptive Frontier Risks that Could Strike by 2040', World Economic Forum Agenda, 18 December 2020, https://www .weforum.org/agenda/2020/12/3-disruptive-frontier-risks-that-could -strike-by-2040.
587. D. Held, 'Democratic Accountability and Political Effectiveness from a Cosmopolitan Perspective', *Government and Opposition* 39, no. 2 (2004), pp. 364–65, https://doi.org/10.1111/j.1477-7053.2004.00127.x.
588. See R. Alcaro and M. Haubrich-Seco (eds), *Re-thinking Western Policies in Light of the Arab Uprisings* (Rome: Edizioni Nuova Cultura, 2012).
589. Nayef R.F. Al-Rodhan, 'Why Agile Governance Should Be Human-Centred Governance', World Economic Forum Agenda, 14 September 2020, https://www.weforum.org/agenda/2020/09/technology -data-security-agile-governance.

590. See UN General Assembly, Universal Declaration of Human Rights, Article 1, https://www.un.org/en/about-us/universal-declaration-of-human-rights (accessed 29 April 2021); UN General Assembly, International Covenant on Civil and Political Rights (adopted 16 December 1966, came into force 23 March 1976), Articles 2 and 3, https://treaties.un.org/doc/publication/unts/volume%20999/volume-999-i-14668-english.pdf (accessed 29 April 2021).

591. See, for example, S.M. Akram, 'US Punishes International Criminal Court for Investigating Potential War Crimes in Afghanistan', *The Conversation*, 2 September 2020, https://theconversation.com/us-punishes-international-criminal-court-for-investigating-potential-war-crimes-in-afghanistan-143886.

592. See, for example, S. Stockwell, 'Legal "Black Holes" in Outer Space: The Regulation of Private Space Companies', *E-International Relations*, 20 July 2020, https://www.e-ir.info/2020/07/20/legal-black-holes-in-outer-space-the-regulation-of-private-space-companies.

593. See, for example, K.E. Boon and F. Mégret, 'New Approaches to the Accountability of International Organisations', *International Organizations Law Review* 16, no. 1 (2019), pp. 1–10.

594. See, for example, Held, 'Democratic Accountability and Political Effectiveness from a Cosmopolitan Perspective', pp. 371–72.

595. International Monetary Fund, *The IMF and Income Inequality: Introduction to Inequality*, https://www.imf.org/en/Topics/Inequality/introduction-to-inequality (accessed 13 January 2021).

596. On the securitisation of migration, see K. Jaskulowski, 'The Securitisation of Migration: Its Limits and Consequences', *International Political Review* 40, no. 5 (2018), pp. 710–20; on the securitisation of religion, see W. Vancutsem, 'Freedom of Religion and the Securitisation of Religious Identity: An Analysis of Proposals Impacting on Freedom of Religion Following Terrorist Attacks in Flanders', *Global Campus Human Rights Journal* 2 (2018), pp. 41–58.

597. United Nations Economic and Social Commission for Asia and the Pacific, *Inequality in Asia and the Pacific in the Era of the 2030 Agenda for Sustainable Development* (New York: United Nations Publication, 2018), p. 64, https://www.unescap.org/publications/inequality-asia-and-pacific-era-2030-agenda-sustainable-development.

598. The World Bank, Gender Data Portal, https://www.worldbank.org/en/data/datatopics/gender (accessed 28 April 2021).

599. G. Østby, S.A. Rustad and A.F. Tollefsen, 'Children Affected by Armed Conflict, 1990–2019', PRIO *Conflict Trends*, no. 6 (Oslo: Peace Research Institute, 2020), p. 1, https://www.prio.org/Publications/Publication/?x=12527.

600. See, for example, R. Ezcurra and D. Palacios, 'Terrorism and Spatial Disparities: Does Interregional Inequality Matter?', *European Journal of Political Economy* 42 (2016), pp. 60–74, https://doi.org/10.1016/j.ejpoleco.2016.01.004.

601. Al-Rodhan, 'Why Agile Governance Should Be Human-Centred Governance'.
602. F. Georgie, 'The Role of Racism in the European "Migration Crisis": A Historical Materialist Perspective', in V. Satgar (ed.), *Racism After Apartheid: Challenges for Marxism and Anti-Racism* (Johannesburg: Wits University Press, 2019), pp. 96–117, https://doi. org/10.18772/22019033061.
603. S. Croucher, *Globalization and Belonging: The Politics of Identity in a Changing World* (Lanham, MD: Rowman & Littlefield, 2018), p. 2.
604. Nayef R.F. Al-Rodhan, 'Reforming Democracy and the Future of History', Center for Security Studies, ETH Zürich, 24 June 2014, https:// css.ethz.ch/content/specialinterest/gess/cis/center-for-securities-studies /en/services/digital-library/articles/article.html/180942.
605. Office for National Statistics, *Why Have Black and South Asian People Been Hit Hardest by COVID-19?*, 14 December 2020, https://www.ons.gov .uk/peoplepopulationandcommunity/healthandsocialcare/condition sanddiseases/articles/whyhaveblackandsouthasianpeoplebeenhithardest bycovid19/2020-12-14.
606. A. Schlesinger Jr, 'Has Democracy a Future?', *Foreign Affairs* 76, no. 5 (1997), pp. 2–12.
607. See, for example, K. Weyland, 'Populism's Threat to Democracy: Comparative Lessons for the United States', *Perspectives on Politics* 18, no. 2 (2020), pp. 389–406.
608. Nayef R.F. Al-Rodhan, 'Proposal of a Dignity Scale for Sustainable Governance', *The Journal of Public Policy*, 29 November 2015, https:// jpublicpolicy.wordpress.com/2015/11/29/proposal-of-a-dignity-scale -for-sustainable-governance; Nayef R. F. Al-Rodhan, 'A Neuro-Philosophy of Dignity-Based Governance', *Blog of the American Philosophical Association*, 16 October 2018, https://blog.apaonline. org/2018/10/16/a-neuro-philosophy-of-dignity-based-governance.
609. Al-Rodhan, 'A Neuro-Philosophy of Dignity-Based Governance'.
610. Ibid.
611. Al-Rodhan, 'Proposal of a Dignity Scale for Sustainable Governance'; Al-Rodhan, 'A Neuro-Philosophy of Dignity-Based Governance'.
612. Al-Rodhan, 'A Neuro-Philosophy of Dignity-Based Governance'.
613. R. Halévi, 'The New Truth Regime', *Le Débat* 197, no. 5 (2017), p. 29.
614. Al-Rodhan, 'A Neuro-Philosophy of Dignity-Based Governance'.
615. Al-Rodhan, '3 Disruptive Frontier Risks that Could Strike by 2040'.
616. F. Sindico, 'Climate Change and Security', *Carbon & Climate Law Review* 11, no. 3 (2017), pp. 187–90.
617. Al-Rodhan, 'Why Agile Governance Should Be Human-Centred Governance'.
618. Al-Rodhan, 'A Neuro-Philosophy of Dignity-Based Governance'.
619. Ibid.

620. R. Pierik and W. Werner (eds), *Cosmopolitanism in Context: Perspectives from International Law and Political Theory* (Cambridge: Cambridge University Press, 2010), p. 3.

621. Al-Rodhan, 'A Neuro-Philosophy of Dignity-Based Governance'.

622. Ibid.

623. Al-Rodhan, 'Proposal of a Dignity Scale for Sustainable Governance'.

624. Ibid.

625. Al-Rodhan, 'A Neurophilosophy of Fear-Induced Pre-emptive Aggression and Pseudo-Altruism'.

626. Croucher, *Globalization and Belonging*, p. 2.

627. See Croucher, *Globalization and Belonging*.

628. R. Devetak, 'Postmodernism', in S. Burchill, A. Linklater, R. Devetak, J. Donnelly, M. Paterson, C. Reus-Smit, and J. True (eds), *Theories of International Relations*, 3rd edn (Basingstoke: Palgrave Macmillan, 2005), p. 162.

629. R.W. Cox, 'Social Forces, States and World Order: Beyond International Relations Theory', *Millennium* 10, no. 2 (1981), p. 128.

630. C. Reus-Smit, 'Constructivism', in Burchill *et al.* (eds), *Theories of International Relations*, p. 188.

631. Croucher, *Globalization and Belonging*, p. 42.

632. Ibid., p. 195.

633. K.A. Cerulo, 'Identity Construction: New Issues, New Directions', *Annual Review of Sociology* 23 (1997), pp. 385–409.

634. Devetak, 'Postmodernism', p. 162.

635. M. Jørgensen and L.J. Phillips, *Discourse Analysis as Theory and Method* (London: Sage Publications, 2002), p. 63.

636. Devetak, 'Postmodernism', p. 163; Foucault discussed genealogy in 'Nietzsche, Genealogy, History', in D.F. Bouchard (ed.), *Language, Counter-Memory, Practice: Selected Essays and Interviews* (Ithaca, NY: Cornell University Press, 1977), pp. 139–64.

637. Devetak, 'Postmodernism', p. 163.

638. Cerulo, 'Identity Construction: New Issues, New Directions'; Devetak, 'Postmodernism', p. 178.

639. M. Castells, *The Information Age: Economy, Society and Culture: Volume 2: The Power of Identity*, 2nd edn (Malden, MA: Blackwell Publishing Ltd, 2004), p. 6.

640. Maalouf, *In the Name of Identity*, p. 16.

641. Castells, *The Power of Identity*, p. 7.

642. Ibid., p. 8.

643. Ibid., p. 9.

644. Ibid., p. 10.

645. A. Giddens, *Modernity and Self-Identity* (Cambridge: Polity Press, 1991), p. 5.

646. Castells, *The Power of Identity*, p. 11.

647. S.N. Eisenstadt, 'Multiple Modernities', *Daedalus* 129, no. 1 (2000), p. 3.
648. S.N. Eisenstadt, 'The Reconstitution of Collective Identities and Inter-Civilizational Relations in the Age of Globalization', *Canadian Journal of Sociology/Cahiers canadiens de sociologie* 32, no. 1 (2007), p. 115.
649. Ibid.
650. Ibid., pp. 115–16.
651. Ibid., p. 116.
652. Ibid., p. 117.
653. G. Soldatova, 'Psychological Mechanisms of Xenophobia', *Social Sciences* 38, no. 2 (2007), p. 107.
654. Castells, *The Power of Identity*, p. 13.
655. N. Hamid and C. Pretus, 'The Neuroscience of Terrorism: How We Convinced a Group of Radicals to Let Us Scan Their Brains', *The Conversation*, 12 June 2019, https://theconversation.com/the-neuro science-of-terrorism-how-we-convinced-a-group-of-radicals-to-let-us -scan-their-brains-114855.
656. D. Gambetta and S. Hertog, *Engineers of Jihad: The Curious Connection between Violent Extremism and Education* (Princeton, NJ: Princeton University Press, 2016), p. 34.
657. S. Canna, C. St Clair and A. Desjardins, *Neuroscience Insights on Radicalization and Mobilization to Violence: A Review (Second Edition)*, NSI, 14 December 2012, https://nsiteam.com/social/wp-content/uploads /2016/01/Neuroscience-Insights-on-Radicalization-and-Mobilization -to-Violence-November-2012.pdf.
658. Hamid and Pretus, 'The Neuroscience of Terrorism: How We Convinced a Group of Radicals to Let Us Scan Their Brains'.
659. Ibid.
660. Nayef R.F Al-Rodhan, 'Us versus Them: How Neurophilosophy Explains Our Divided Politics', World Economic Forum Agenda, 3 October 2016, https://www.weforum.org/agenda/2016/10/us-versus-them-how-neurophilosophy-explains-populism-racism-and-extremism.
661. See D.A. Vaughn *et al.*, 'Empathic Neural Responses Predict Group Allegiance', *Frontiers in Human Neuroscience* 12 (2018), pp. 8–9, https://doi.org/10.3389/fnhum.2018.00302; M. Tarrant, S. Dazeley and T. Cottom, 'Social Categorization and Empathy for Outgroup Members', *British Journal of Social Psychology* 48, no. 3 (2009), pp. 427–46, https://doi.org/10.1348/014466608X373589.
662. Soldatova, 'Psychological Mechanisms of Xenophobia', p. 106.
663. E. Cashmore, 'Xenophobia', in E. Cashmore (ed.), *Dictionary of Race and Ethnic Relations* (London: Routledge, 1994), p. 346.
664. Soldatova, 'Psychological Mechanisms of Xenophobia', p. 116.
665. A. Wimmer, *Nationalist Exclusion and Ethnic Conflict: Shadows of Modernity* (Cambridge: Cambridge University Press, 2002), p. 206.
666. Ibid., pp. 209–10.

667. B.A. Thayer, 'Ethnic Conflict and State Building', in Somit and Peterson (eds), *Human Nature and Public Policy*, pp. 227–30.

668. Ibid., pp. 230–31.

669. See Al-Rodhan, *The Role of Education in Global Security*.

670. Ibid., pp. 232, 236.

671. D. Matsumoto, *Culture and Psychology: People around the World*, 2nd edn (Belmont, CA: Wadsworth, 2000), p. 38.

672. Ibid., p. 77.

673. Ibid., p. 78.

674. R.A. Hammond and R. Axelrod, 'The Evolution of Ethnocentrism', *Journal of Conflict Resolution* 50, no. 6 (2006), pp. 926–36.

675. C. McKelvey, *Beyond Ethnocentrism: A Reconstruction of Marx's Concept of Science* (Westport, CT: Greenwood Press, 1991), p. 24.

676. Ibid., p. 173.

677. Matsumoto, *Culture and Psychology*, p. 38.

678. Thayer, 'Ethnic Conflict and State Building', p. 232.

679. Ibid., p. 233.

680. Soldatova, 'Psychological Mechanisms of Xenophobia', p. 107.

681. See H.E. Tajfel, 'Experiments in Intergroup Discrimination', *Scientific American* 223, no. 5 (1970), pp. 96–102; H.E. Tajfel, 'Social Categorization, Social Identity and Social Comparison', in H.E. Tajfel (ed.), *Differentiation between Social Groups: Studies in the Social Psychology of Intergroup Relations* (London: Academic Press, 1978), pp. 61–76.

682. Soldatova, 'Psychological Mechanisms of Xenophobia', pp. 107–8.

683. Ibid., p. 107.

684. J. Yang *et al.*, 'Within-group Synchronization in the Prefrontal Cortex Associates with Intergroup Conflict', *Nature Neuroscience* 23, no. 6 (2020), pp. 754–60, https://doi.org/10.1038/s41593-020-0630-x.

685. Ibid.

686. P. Molenberghs, 'The Neuroscience of In-Group Bias', *Neuroscience & Biobehavioral Reviews* 37, no. 8 (2013), pp. 1530–36, https://doi.org/10.1016/j.neubiorev.2013.06.002.

687. Al-Rodhan, 'Us versus Them'.

688. Ibid.

689. R. Eres and P. Molenberghs, 'The Influence of Group Membership on the Neural Correlates Involved in Empathy', *Frontiers in Human Neuroscience* 7 (2013), pp. 1–6, https://doi.org/10.3389/fnhum.2013.00176.

690. T. Oliver, 'Why Overcoming Racism Is Essential for Humanity's Survival', *The Conversation BBC Future*, 6 April 2020, https://www.bbc.com/future/article/20200403-how-to-overcome-racism-and-tribalism.

691. Al-Rodhan, 'Us versus Them'.

692. J. McCoy, 'Making Violence Ordinary: Radio, Music and the Rwandan Genocide', *African Music* 8, no. 3 (2009), p. 87.

693. W. Cunningham *et al.*, 'Separable Neural Components in the Processing of Black and White Faces', *Psychological Science* 15, no. 12 (2004), pp. 806–13, https://doi.org/10.1111/j.0956-7976.2004.00760.x.
694. Soldatova, 'Psychological Mechanisms of Xenophobia', p. 108.
695. Ibid., p. 116.
696. Matsumoto, *Culture and Psychology*, p. 80.
697. A. Vrij, E. van Schie and J. Cherryman, 'Reducing Ethnic Prejudice through Public Communication Programs: A Social-Psychological Perspective', *Journal of Psychology* 130, no. 4 (1996), pp. 413–20.
698. Matsumoto, *Culture and Psychology*, p. 38.
699. See New Zealand Ministry of Foreign Affairs and Trade, Christchurch Call to Eliminate Terrorist and Extremist Content Online, signed at the Christchurch Call to Action Summit in Paris, 15 May 2019, https://www.christchurchcall.com/call.html.
700. Nayef R.F. Al-Rodhan, 'Editorial of Policy Brief on Xenophobia, Media Stereotyping, and Their Role in Global Security', in Nayef R.F. Al-Rodhan (ed.), *Policy Briefs on the Transcultural Aspects of Security and Stability* (Berlin: LIT Verlag, 2006), pp. 39–40.
701. Hobbes, *Leviathan*.
702. K. Waltz, *Man, the State and War: A Theoretical Analysis* (New York: Columbia University Press, 1959).
703. Lorenz, *On Aggression*.
704. Hauser, *Moral Minds*; Somit and Peterson, 'From Human Nature to Public Policy'.
705. B. Russett, H. Starr and D. Kinsella, *World Politics: The Menu for Choice*, 7th edn (Belmont, CA: Thomson Wadsworth, 2004), p. 198.
706. T.R. Gurr, *Why Men Rebel* (Princeton, NJ: Princeton University Press, 1970).
707. M. Schulson, 'The Moral Tribalism of Contemporary Politics', *Religion and Politics*, 15 August 2016, https://religionandpolitics.org/2016/08/15/the-moral-tribalism-of-contemporary-politics.
708. Al-Rodhan, *Symbiotic Realism*, pp. 107–10.
709. See M. Singh, 'Ethnic Conflict and International Security: Theoretical Considerations', *World Affairs* 6, no. 4 (2002), pp. 72–89.
710. Thayer, 'Ethnic Conflict and State Building', p. 232.
711. Singh, 'Ethnic Conflict and International Security'., pp. 88–89.
712. Ibid., p. 89.
713. D. Campbell, *National Deconstruction: Violence, Identity, and Justice in Bosnia* (Minneapolis: University of Minnesota Press, 1998); for a good overview of Campbell's argument, see Devetak, 'Postmodernism', p. 177.
714. Campbell, *National Deconstruction*, pp 25–31.
715. Devetak, 'Postmodernism'.
716. Thayer, 'Ethnic Conflict and State Building', pp. 232–34.
717. Ibid., pp. 233–34.

718. Ibid., p. 234.

719. T.R. Gurr, 'Democratic Governance and Strategies of Accommodation in Plural Societies', T.R. Gurr (ed.), *Peoples versus States. Minorities at Risk in the New Century* (Washington, DC: United States Institute of Peace Press, 2002), p. 151.

720. Gurr, 'Democratic Governance', p. 165.

721. Castells, *The Power of Identity*, p. 56.

722. Wimmer, *Nationalist Exclusion and Ethnic Conflict*, p. 1.

723. I.W. Zartman, 'Managing Ethnic Conflict', First Perlmutter Lecture on Ethnic Conflict, *Foreign Policy Research Institute Wire* 6, no. 5 (September 1998), pp. 1–2.

724. Ibid.

725. M. Andrews, 'Grand National Narratives and the Project of Truth Commissions: A Comparative Analysis', *Media, Culture & Society* 25, no. 1 (2003), p. 48; E.A. Cole and J. Barsalou, *Unite or Divide? The Challenges of Teaching History in Societies Emerging from Violent Conflict*, Special Report 163 (Washington, DC: United States Institute of Peace, June 2006), p. 2.

726. See Al-Rodhan, *Symbiotic Realism*.

727. J.L. Gaddis, *The Long Peace: Inquiries into the History of the Cold War* (New York: Oxford University Press, 1989).

728. J. Mearsheimer, 'Back to the Future: Instability in Europe after the Cold War', *International Security* 15, no. 1 (1990), pp. 5–56.

729. Waltz, *Man, the State and War: A Theoretical Analysis*, pp 120–123.

730. M.W. Doyle, 'Kant, Liberal Legacies, and Foreign Affairs', *Philosophy & Public Affairs* 12, no. 3 (1983), pp. 205–35.

731. Russett, Starr and Kinsella, *World Politics*, p. 208.

732. Ibid., p. 209.

733. See United States Institute of Peace, *Natural Resources, Conflict, and Conflict Resolution: A Study Guide Series on Peace and Conflict for Independent Learners and Classroom Instructors* (Washington, DC: United States Institute of Peace, 2007), https://www.usip.org/sites/default/files/file/08sg.pdf; see also Al-Rodhan and Watanabe, *A Proposal for Inclusive Peace and Security*, esp. ch. 2.

734. N.J. Jhaveri, 'Petroimperialism: US Oil Interests and the Iraq War', *Antipode* 36, no. 1 (2004), p. 2, https://doi.org/10.1111/j.1467-8330.2004.00378.x.

735. D. Michel, 'Water Insecurity and Conflict Risks', in D. Michel, *Water Conflict Pathways and Peacebuilding Strategies*, Peaceworks Research Report No. 164 (Washington, DC: United States Institute of Peace, 2020), p. 3.

736. Ibid.

737. See Nayef R.F. Al-Rodhan, *The Meta-Geopolitics of Outer Space: An Analysis of Space Power, Security and Governance* (London: Palgrave Macmillan, 2012).

738. See Al-Rodhan and Watanabe, *A Proposal for Inclusive Peace and Security*, esp. ch. 2.
739. See Al-Rodhan, *Symbiotic Realism*, esp. p. 119.
740. Al-Rodhan, *Symbiotic Realism*.
741. See H. Bull, 'The Balance of Power and International Order', in H. Bull, *The Anarchical Society: A Study of Order in World Politics* (London: Palgrave, 1977), pp. 101–26.
742. Al-Rodhan, 'A Neurophilosophy of Fear-Induced Pre-emptive Aggression and Pseudo-Altruism'.
743. Ibid.
744. Nayef R.F. Al-Rodhan, 'China and the United States: A Symbiosis', *The National Interest*, 27 September 2013, https://nationalinterest.org/commen tary/china-the-united-states-symbiosis-9143.
745. J.H. Herz, 'Idealist Internationalism and the Security Dilemma', *World Politics* 2, no. 2 (1950), p. 157.
746. Encyclopaedia Britannica, 'Mutual Assured Destruction', by the Editors of Encyclopaedia Britannica, https://www.britannica.com/topic/mutual -assured-destruction (accessed 15 March 2021).
747. S. Huntington, *The Clash of Civilizations and the Remaking of World Order* (London: Simon & Schuster, 1996).
748. Nayef R.F. Al-Rodhan, 'The "Ocean Model of Civilisation", Sustainable History Theory, and Global Cultural Understanding', *The Oxford University Politics Blog*, 1 June 2017, https://blog.politics.ox.ac.uk /ocean-model-civilization-sustainable-history-theory-global-cultural -understanding.
749. See Nayef R.F. Al-Rodhan, *The Role of the Arab-Islamic World in the Rise of the West: Implications for Contemporary Trans-Cultural Relations* (London: Palgrave Macmillan, 2012).
750. Ibid.
751. C. Brumann, 'Writing for Culture: Why a Successful Concept Should Not Be Discarded', *Current Anthropology* 40, Supplement (1999), p. S1.
752. Nayef R.F. Al-Rodhan, 'Major Transformative Technologies and the Five Dimensions of Security', *Oxford Political Review*, 23 June 2020, https:// oxfordpoliticalreview.com/2020/06/23/major-transformative-technologies -and-the-five-dimensions-of-security.
753. Bostrom, 'Five Ways the Superintelligence Revolution Might Happen'.
754. See Chapter 3.6 for further details on how these technologies may change human nature.
755. See, for example, P. Pettit, 'The Globalized Republican Ideal', *Global Justice and Non-Domination* 9, no. 1 (2016), pp. 47–68, https://doi.org /10.21248/gjn.9.1.101.
756. P. Pettit, 'The Domination Complaint', *Nomos* 46 (2005), p. 87.
757. Al-Rodhan, 'A Neurophilosophy of Two Technological Game-Changers'.
758. Al-Rodhan, 'Major Transformative Technologies and the Five Dimensions of Security'.

759. A. Bovet and H.A. Makse, 'Influence of Fake News in Twitter during the 2016 US Presidential Election', *Nature Communications* 10, no. 1 (2019), p. 2, https://doi.org/10.1038/s41467-018-07761-2.

760. J. Rose, 'Brexit, Trump, and Post-Truth Politics', *Public Integrity* 19, no. 6 (2017), p. 557, https://doi.org/10.1080/10999922.2017.1285540.

761. S. van der Linden, J. Roozenbeek and J. Compton, 'Inoculating against Fake News about COVID-19', *Frontiers in Psychology* 11 (2020), pp. 1–2, https://doi.org/10.3389/fpsyg.2020.566790.

762. I. Linkov, L. Roslycky and B.D. Trump, *Resilience and Hybrid Threats: Security and Integrity for the Digital World. Security and Integrity for the Digital World* (Amsterdam: IOS Press, 2018), p. 188.

763. H. Jahankhani *et al.* (eds), *Cyber Defence in the Age of AI, Smart Societies and Augmented Humanity* (Cham: Springer, 2020), p. 43.

764. L. McIntyre, *Post-Truth* (Cambridge, MA: MIT Press, 2018), p. 10.

765. J. Sifuentes, 'The Propaganda of Octavian and Marc Anthony's Civil War', *Ancient History Encyclopedia*, 20 November 2019, https://www.ancient.eu /article/1474/the-propaganda-of-octavian-and-mark-antonys-civil.

766. See I. Manor and C. Bjola, 'Public Diplomacy in the Age of Post-reality', in P. Surowiec and I. Manor (eds), *Public Diplomacy and the Politics of Uncertainty* (Cham: Palgrave Macmillan, 2020), p. 111–44.

767. T. Snyder, *The Road to Unfreedom: Russia, Europe, America* (New York: Penguin Random House, 2018), p 224.

768. D. Star (ed.), *The Oxford Handbook of Reasons and Normativity* (Oxford: Oxford University Press, 2018), p. 950.

769. A. Kappes *et al.*, 'Confirmation Bias in the Utilization of Others' Opinion Strength', *Nature Neuroscience* 23 (2019), pp. 130–37, https:// doi.org/10.1038/s41593-019-0549-2.

770. E. Winter, 'Feelings: What's the Point of Rational Thought If Emotions Always Take Over?', *The Conversation*, 21 February 2020, https:// theconversation.com/feelings-whats-the-point-of-rational-thought-if -emotions-always-take-over-128592.

771. S.M. Burns *et al.*, 'Making Social Neuroscience Less WEIRD: Using fNIRS to Measure Neural Signatures of Persuasive Influence in a Middle East Participant Sample', *Journal of Personality and Social Psychology: Attitudes and Social Cognition* 116, no. 3 (2019), pp. 1–11.

772. G. Pennycook, T.D. Cannon and D.G. Rand, 'Prior Exposure Increases Perceived Accuracy of Fake News', *Journal of Experimental Psychology: General* 147, no. 12 (2018), pp. 1865–80, https://doi.org/10.1037/xge0000465.

773. R.A. Barr, 'Fake News Grabs Our Attention, Produces False Memories and Appeals to Our Emotions', *The Conversation*, 17 November 2019, https://theconversation.com/fake-news-grabs-our-attention-produces -false-memories-and-appeals-to-our-emotions-124842.

774. European Commission, Code of Practice on Disinformation, first published 26 September 2018, updated 7 July 2020, https://ec.europa.eu /digital-single-market/en/news/code-practice-disinformation.

775. Nayef R.F. Al-Rodhan, 'A Neurophilosophy of Fake News, Disinformation and Digital Citizenship', *Blog of the American Philosophical Association*, 25 August 2020, https://blog.apaonline .org/2020/08/25/a-neurophilosophy-of-fake-news-disinformation -and-digital-citizenship.

776. B. Eichengreen, *The Populist Temptation: Economic Grievance and Political Reaction in the Modern Era* (Oxford: Oxford University Press, 2018).

777. Nayef R.F. Al-Rodhan, 'A Neurophilosophy of Divisive Politics, Inequality and Disempowerment', Geneva Centre for Security Policy Op-Ed, 26 June 2020, https://www.gcsp.ch/global-insights/ neurophilosophy-divisive-politics-inequality-and-disempowerment.

778. F. Alvaredo *et al.*, *World Inequality Report 2018: Part IV – Trends in Global Wealth Inequality*, World Inequality Lab, accessed 13 January 2021, https:// wir2018.wid.world/part-4.html (accessed 13 January 2021).

779. Al-Rodhan, 'A Neurophilosophy of Divisive Politics, Inequality and Disempowerment'.

780. Carl Huffman, 'Pythagoras', in *Stanford Encyclopedia of Philosophy* (Stanford University, 1997-), article pub. 23 February 2005, substantive rev. 17 October 2018, https://plato.stanford.edu/entries/pythagoras.

781. Nayef R.F. Al-Rodhan, 'A Neurophilosophy of Big Data & Civil Liberties, and the Need for a New Social Contract', *Blog of the American Philosophical Association*, 21 May 2020, https://blog.apaonline. org/2020/05/21/a-neurophilosophy-of-big-data-civil-liberties-and-the -need-for-a-new-social-contract.

782. W. Knight, 'The Dark Secret at the Heart of AI', *MIT Technology Review*, 11 April 2017, https://www.technologyreview.com/2017/04/11/5113/the -dark-secret-at-the-heart-of-ai.

783. Al-Rodhan, 'A Neurophilosophy of Big Data & Civil Liberties, and the Need for a New Social Contract'.

784. Ibid.

785. The FDR Group, *Chilling Effects: NSA Surveillance Drives U.S. Writers to Self-Censor* (New York: PEN American Center, 2013), https://pen.org /sites/default/files/Chilling%20Effects_PEN%20American.pdf.

786. D. McMenemy, L. Smith and N. Williams, *Scottish Chilling: Impact of Government and Corporate Surveillance on Writers*, Report of research conducted by Scottish PEN and the University of Strathclyde, Glasgow, November 2018, https://strathprints.strath.ac.uk/66291/8/Williams_etal _PEN_2018_Scottish_chilling_impact_of_government_and_corporate _surveillance_on_writers.pdf.

787. Nayef R.F. Al-Rodhan, 'The Social Contract 2.0: Big Data and the Need to Guarantee Privacy and Civil Liberties', *The Oxford University Politics Blog*, 22 September 2014, https://blog.politics.ox.ac.uk/social-contract-2 -0-big-data-need-guarantee-privacy-civil-liberties.

788. Al-Rodhan, 'A Neurophilosophy of Big Data & Civil Liberties, and the Need for a New Social Contract'.

789. Ibid.

790. K. Pearce, 'What is Social Distancing and How Can It Slow the Spread of Covid-19?', *Johns Hopkins Magazine*, 13 March 2020, https://hub.jhu .edu/2020/03/13/what-is-social-distancing.

791. Nayef R.F. Al-Rodhan, 'A Neurophilosophical Perspective on Social Distancing', Geneva Centre for Security Policy Op-Ed, 10 April 2020, https://www.gcsp.ch/global-insights/neurophilosophical-perspective -social-distancing.

792. Ibid.

793. J. Holt-Lunstad, T.B. Smith and J.B. Layton, 'Social Relationships and Mortality Risk: A Meta-analytic Review', *PLOS Medicine* 7, no. 7 (2010), pp. 1–2, https://doi.org/10.1371/journal.pmed.1000316.

794. A.C. Stahn *et al.*, 'Brain Changes in Response to Long Antarctic Expeditions', *The New England Journal of Medicine*, no. 381 (2019), pp. 2273–75, https://doi.org/10.1056/NEJMc1904905.

795. G.A. Matthews *et al.*, 'Dorsal Raphe Dopamine Neurons Represent the Experience of Social Isolation', *Cell* 164, no. 4 (2016), pp. 626–27, https:// doi.org/10.1016/j.cell.2015.12.040.

796. Ibid., p. 617.

797. W.L. Gardner, C.L. Pickett and M.B. Brewer, 'Social Exclusion and Selective Memory: How the Need to Belong Influences Memory for Social Events', *Personality and Social Psychology Bulletin* 26, no. 4 (2000), pp. 486–96, https://doi.org/10.1177/0146167200266007.

798. Matthews *et al.*, 'Dorsal Raphe Dopamine Neurons Represent the Experience of Social Isolation', p. 618.

799. Ibid.

800. G. Pietrabissa and S.G. Simpson, 'Psychological Consequences of Social Isolation during Covid-19 Outbreak', *Frontiers in Psychology* 11 (2020), p. 2, https://doi.org/10.3389/fpsyg.2020.02201.

801. R.G. Arzate-Mejía *et al.*, 'Long-Term Impact of Social Isolation and Molecular Underpinnings', *Frontiers in Genetics* 11 (2020), p. 9, https:// doi.org/10.3389/fgene.2020.589621.

802. Nayef R.F. Al-Rodhan, 'Meta-Geopolitics of Pandemics: The Case of COVID-19', *Global Policy*, 8 May 2020, https://www.globalpolicyjournal .com/blog/08/05/2020/meta-geopolitics-pandemics-case-covid-19.

803. L.A. Seneca, 'Letter 13: On Groundless Fears', in L.A. Seneca, *Seneca: Letters from a Stoic: Epistulae Morales ad Lucilium*, ed. and with an introduction by R. Campbell (London: Harper Collins, 2020).

804. Al-Rodhan, 'A Neurophilosophical Perspective on Social Distancing'.

805. D. Bok, *The Politics of Happiness: What Government Can Learn from the New Research on Well-Being* (Princeton, NJ: Princeton University Press, 2010), p. 1.

806. Gross National Happiness Index, United Nations Department of Economic and Social Affairs Sustainable Development, https://sustainabledevelopment.un.org/index.php?page=view&type=99&nr=266&menu=1449 (accessed 10 March 2021).
807. Al-Rodhan, 'A Neurophilosophy of "Sustainable Neurochemical Gratification" and the Meaning of Existence'.
808. Ibid.
809. Ibid.
810. Nayef R.F. Al-Rodhan, 'A Neurophilosophical Paradigm for a New Enlightenment', *Blog of the American Philosophical Association*, 24 March 2020, https://blog.apaonline.org/2020/03/24/a-neurophilosophical-paradigm-for-a-new-enlightenment.
811. Al-Rodhan, *Sustainable History and the Dignity of Man*.
812. Al-Rodhan, 'A Neurophilosophical Paradigm for a New Enlightenment'.
813. Ibid.; H. M. Lloyd, 'Why the Enlightenment was not the age of reason', *Aeon*, 16 November 2018, https://aeon.co/ideas/why-the-enlightenment-was-not-the-age-of-reason.
814. Ibid.
815. Ibid.
816. Ibid.
817. Al-Rodhan, *Sustainable History and the Dignity of Man*, p. 37; see also Nayef R.F. Al-Rodhan, 'A Neuro-Philosophy of History: "Sustainable History"; with Dignity, and without Directionality', *Blog of the American Philosophical Association*, 20 August 2018, https://blog.apaonline.org/2018/08/20/a-neuro-philosophy-of-history-sustainable-history-with-dignity-and-without-directionality; Al-Rodhan, 'The "Ocean Model of Civilisation", Sustainable History Theory, and Global Cultural Understanding'.
818. Max Weber, *The Theory of Social and Economic Organization*, ed. Talcott Parsons (New York: Free Press, 1964), quoted in Fabienne Peter, 'Political Legitimacy', in *Stanford Encyclopedia of Philosophy* (Stanford University, 1997-), article pub. 29 April 2010, substantive rev. 24 April 2017, https://plato.stanford.edu/entries/legitimacy.
819. Nayef R.F. Al-Rodhan, 'A Neurophilosophy of Legitimacy in National and Global Politics', *Blog of the American Philosophical Association*, 4 May 2020, https://blog.apaonline.org/2020/05/04/a-neurophilosophy-of-legitimacy-in-national-and-global-politics.
820. I. Hurd, 'Legitimacy and Authority in International Politics', *International Organization* 53, no. 2 (1999), p. 381. Emphasis in original.
821. Al-Rodhan, 'A Neurophilosophy of Legitimacy in National and Global Politics'.
822. B. Anderson, *Imagined Communities: Reflections on the Origin and Spread of Nationalism* (New York: Verso, 1983).
823. Al-Rodhan, 'Us versus Them'.

824. J. Greene, *Moral Tribes: Emotion, Reason and the Gap Between Us and Them* (London: Penguin Press, 2013).

825. Al-Rodhan, 'A Neurophilosophy of Legitimacy in National and Global Politics'.

826. Ibid.

827. See, in particular, Nayef R.F. Al-Rodhan, *The Role of the Arab-Islamic World in the Rise of the West: Implications for Contemporary Trans-Cultural Relations* (London: Palgrave Macmillan, 2012).

828. Ibid.

829. Al-Rodhan, 'A Neuro-Philosophy of History'.

830. G. Browning, *A History of Modern Political Thought: The Question of Interpretation* (Oxford: Oxford University Press, 2016), p. 263.

831. Ibid.[SHOULD THERE BE A PAGE NUMBER HERE? E.G.: Ibid., p. XXX.]

832. F. Fukuyama, *The End of History and the Last Man* (New York: Free Press, 1992).

833. Al-Rodhan, 'A Neuro-Philosophy of History'.

834. Ibid.

835. Al-Rodhan, 'Why Agile Governance Should Be Human-Centred Governance'.

836. D. Held, 'Cosmopolitanism: Globalisation Tamed?', *Review of International Studies* 29 (2003), pp. 465–69.

837. Al-Rodhan and Watanabe, *A Proposal for Inclusive Peace and Security*, pp. 116–17.

838. Pauline Kleingeld and Eric Brown, 'Cosmopolitanism', in *Stanford Encyclopedia of Philosophy* (Stanford University, 1997-), article pub. 23 February 2002, substantive rev. 17 October 2019, https://plato.stanford.edu/entries/cosmopolitanism/#HistCosm.

839. P. Kleingeld, *Kant and Cosmopolitanism: The Philosophical Ideal of World Citizenship* (Cambridge: Cambridge University Press, 2012), p. 2.

840. Kleingeld and Brown, 'Cosmopolitanism'.

841. Pojman, *Who Are We?*, p. 128.

842. Eric Entrican Wilson and Lara Denis, 'Kant and Hume on Morality', in *Stanford Encyclopedia of Philosophy* (Stanford University, 1997-), article pub. 26 March 2008, substantive rev. 29 March 2018, https://plato.stanford.edu/archives/sum2018/entries/kant-hume-morality.

843. L. Elliott and G. Cheeseman, *Cosmopolitanism Theory, Militaries and the Deployment of Force*, Working Paper 2002/8 (Canberra: Department of International Relations, Australian National University, November 2002), p. 11.

844. Kleingeld, *Kant and Cosmopolitanism*, p. 8.

845. J.-C. Heilinger, *Cosmopolitan Responsibility: Global Injustice, Relational Equality, and Individual Agency* (Berlin/Boston: De Gruyter, 2019), p. 47, https://doi.org/10.1515/9783110612271.

846. Pojman, *Who Are We?*, p. 116.

847. Hauser, *Moral Minds*, p. 23.
848. Pojman, *Who Are We?*, p. 127.
849. Hauser, *Moral Minds*, p. 24.
850. S. Freeman, *The Cambridge Companion to Rawls* (Cambridge: Cambridge University Press, 2003), pp. 1–2.
851. R. Jackson, *Classical and Modern Thought on International Relations: From Anarchy to Cosmopolis* (New York: Palgrave Macmillan, 2005), p. 160.
852. G.W. Brown and D. Held (eds), *The Cosmopolitanism Reader* (Cambridge: Polity Press, 2010), p. 452.
853. Hauser, *Moral Minds*, p. 46.
854. Ibid., p. xviii.
855. Ibid., p. 309.
856. Liao, 'Morality and Neuroscience', p. 16.
857. D. Levy and N. Sznaider, 'The Institutionalization of Cosmopolitan Morality: The Holocaust and Human Rights', *Journal of Human Rights* 3, no. 2 (2004), pp. 147, 150.
858. P. Norris and R. Inglehart, *Cultural Backlash: Trump, Brexit, and Authoritarian Populism* (Cambridge: Cambridge University Press, 2019), p. 2.
859. U. Beck and N. Sznaider, 'Unpacking Cosmopolitanism for the Social Sciences: A Research Agenda', *The British Journal of Sociology* 57, no. 1 (2006), p. 8.
860. Nayef R.F. Al-Rodhan, 'The Neuro-Philosophy of International Relations', *The Oxford University Politics Blog*, 3 August 2016, https://blog.politics.ox.ac.uk/neuro-philosophy-international-relations.
861. E.A. Heinze and B.J. Jolliff, 'Idealism and Liberalism', in J.T. Ishiyama and M Breuning (eds), *21st Century Political Science: A Reference Handbook*, Vol. 1 (London: SAGE Publications, 2011), p. 312.
862. See Al-Rodhan, 'The Neuro-Philosophy of International Relations'.
863. B. Teschke, 'Marxism', in C. Reus-Smit and D. Snidal (eds), *The Oxford Handbook of International Relations* (Oxford: Oxford University Press: 2010), pp. 163–200.
864. Ibid.
865. Devetak, 'Postmodernism', pp. 162–63.
866. H. Overbeek, 'Transnational Historical Materialism: Theories of Transnational Class Formation and World Order', in R. Palan (ed.), *Global Political Economy: Contemporary Theories* (London: Routledge, 2000), p. 169.
867. D. Jacobi and A. Freyberg-Inan, *Human Beings in International Relations* (Cambridge: Cambridge University Press, 2015), p. 9.
868. D. Llyod, 'Functional MRI and the Study of Human Consciousness', *Journal of Cognitive Neuroscience* 14, no. 6 (2002), pp. 818–31, https://doi.org/10.1162/089892902760191027.
869. Pojman, *Who Are We?*, ch. 10.

870. Ibid., p. 162.

871. Ibid., p. 165.

872. Stevenson and Haberman, *Ten Theories of Human Nature*, p. 120.

873. Pojman, *Who Are We?*, p. 128.

874. Stevenson and Haberman, *Ten Theories of Human Nature*, p. 126.

875. Ibid., pp. 127–29.

876. See Al-Rodhan, *Symbiotic Realism*, p. 68.

877. Ibid., p. 69; R. Keohane, *After Hegemony: Cooperation and Discord in the World Political Economy* (Princeton: Princeton University Press, 1984), pp. 110–135.

878. Ibid., p. 31.

879. Ibid., p. 69; A. Wendt, *Social Theory of International Politics* (Cambridge: Cambridge University Press, 1999), pp. 119–135.

880. See ibid., chs 7 and 8.

881. See Devetak, 'Postmodernism'.

882. J. Donnelly, 'Realism', in Burchill *et al.* (eds), *Theories of International Relations*, p. 30.

883. Berns, 'Thomas Hobbes', pp. 396–97.

884. Ibid., p. 398.

885. Pojman, *Who Are We?*, pp. 105–7.

886. Donnelly, 'Realism', p. 41.

887. Ibid., p. 34.

888. Pojman, *Who Are We?*, pp. 111, 117.

889. Ibid., p. 106.

890. Ibid., p. 110.

891. Hobbes, *Leviathan*, ch. 13.

892. Al-Rodhan, *Symbiotic Realism*, p. 22.

893. A. Freyberg-Inan, *What Moves Man: The Realist Theory of International Relations and Its Judgment of Human Nature* (New York: State University of New York, 2004), p. 4.

894. K. Starcke *et al.*, 'Does Stress Alter Everyday Moral Decision-Making?', *Psychoneuroendocrinology* 36, no. 2 (2011), pp. 210–19, https://doi.org/10.1016/j.psyneuen.2010.07.010.

895. Nayef R.F. Al-Rodhan, 'The Emotional Amoral Egoism of States', *The Oxford University Politics Blog*, 25 June 2015, https://blog.politics.ox.ac.uk/the-emotional-amoral-egoism-of-states.

896. Ibid.

897. Nayef R.F. Al-Rodhan, 'Strategic Culture and Pragmatic National Interest', *Global Policy*, 22 July 2015, https://www.globalpolicyjournal.com/blog/22/07/2015/strategic-culture-and-pragmatic-national-interest.

898. Ibid.

899. See Al-Rodhan, *Symbiotic Realism*.

900. Nayef R.F. Al-Rodhan, 'Symbiotic Realism, Multi-Sum Security and Just Power', *Open Mind*, 19 June 2019, https://www.bbvaopenmind.com/en/humanities/beliefs/symbiotic-realism-multi-sum-security-and-just-power.

901. Al-Rodhan, *Sustainable History and the Dignity of Man*.
902. R. Greenhill, 'Is the World Zero-Sum or Win-Win?', World Economic Forum Agenda, 20 January 2015, https://www.weforum.org/agenda/2015/01/win-win-world.
903. Ibid.
904. M. Meloni, 'On the Growing Intellectual Authority of Neuroscience for Political and Moral Theory', in F. Vander Valk, *Essays on Neuroscience and Political Theory: Thinking the Body Politic* (Abingdon: Routledge, 2012), pp. 25–49.
905. Al-Rodhan, 'The "Sustainable History" Thesis: A Guide for Regulating Trans- and Post-Humanism'.
906. Al-Rodhan, 'Why Agile Governance Should Be Human-Centred Governance'.
907. See X. Wang, 'Movies without Mercy: Race, War, and Images of Japanese People in American Films, 1942–1945', *The Journal of American-East Asian Relations* 18, no. 1 (2011), pp. 13–15; T. Shaw and D.J. Youngblood, 'American Cinema and the Cold War', in T. Shaw and D.J. Youngblood, *Cinematic Cold War: The American and Soviet Struggle for Hearts and Minds* (Lawrence, KS: University Press of Kansas, 2010), p. 17–36.
908. For the debate on the possible correlates between violent video games and aggressive behaviour, see R. Shao and Y. Wang, 'The Relation of Violent Video Games to Adolescent Aggression: An Examination of Moderated Mediation Effect', *Frontiers in Psychology* 10 (2019), pp. 1–9, https://doi.org/10.3389/fpsyg.2019.00384; S. Kühn *et al.*, 'Does Playing Violent Video Games Cause Aggression? A Longitudinal Intervention Study', *Molecular Psychiatry* 24, no. 8 (2019), pp. 1220–34, https://doi.org/10.1038/s41380-018-0031-7.
909. F. Nietzsche, *On the Genealogy of Morals and Ecce Homo*, ed. and trans. W. Kaufmann (New York: Vintage Books, 1989 [1887]), p. 80.

Bibliography

Aas, S., and D. Wasserman, 'Brain-Computer Interfaces and Disability: Extending Embodiment, Reducing Stigma?', *Journal of Medical Ethics* 42, no. 1 (2016), pp. 37–40

Abdel-Mottaleb, M.S.A., J.A. Byrne and D. Chakarov, 'Nanotechnology and Solar Energy', *International Journal of Photoenergy*, Special Issue (2011), pp. 1–2. https://doi.org/10.1155/2011/194146

Adams, I., and R.W. Dyson, *Fifty Major Political Thinkers* (London: Routledge, 2003)

Adamson, P., *A History of Philosophy without Any Gaps: Volume 3: Philosophy in the Islamic World* (Oxford: Oxford University Press, 2016)

Adolph, K.E., K.S. Kretch and V. LoBue, 'Fear of Heights in Infants', *Current Directions in Psychological Science* 23, no. 1 (2014), pp. 60–66, https://doi.org/10.1177/0963721413498895

Adolphs, R., 'The Biology of Fear', *Current Biology* 23, no. 2 (2013), pp. R79-R93, doi:10.1016/j.cub.2012.11.055

Akram, S.M., 'US Punishes International Criminal Court for Investigating Potential War Crimes in Afghanistan', *The Conversation*, 2 September 2020, https://theconversation.com/us-punishes-international-criminal-court-for-investigating-potential-war-crimes-in-afghanistan-143886

Alberti, F. Bound, 'Coronavirus Is Revitalising the Concept of Community for the 21st Century', *The Conversation*, 29 April 2020, https://theconversation.com/coronavirus-is-revitalising-the-concept-of-community-for-the-21st-century-135750

Alcaro, R.M., and M. Haubrich-Seco (eds), *Re-thinking Western Policies in Light of the Arab Uprisings* (Rome: Edizioni Nuova Cultura, 2012)

Alegría-Torres, J.A., A. Baccarelli and V. Bollati, 'Epigenetics and Lifestyle', *Epigenomics* 3, no. 3 (2011), pp. 267–77, https://doi.org/10.2217/epi.11.22

Alivisatos, A.P., M. Chun, G.M. Church, K. Deisseroth, J.P. Donoghue, R.J. Greenspan, P.L. McEuen, M.L. Roukes, T.J. Sejnowski, P.S. Weiss, R. Yuste, 'The Brain Activity Map', *Science* 339, no. 6125 (2013), pp. 1284–85.

Allhoff, F., Lin, P., Moor, J., Weckert, J. (eds), *Nanoethics. The Ethical and Social Implications of Nanotechnology* (Hoboken, NJ: John Wiley & Sons, 2007).

Al-Rodhan, Nayef R.F., *Meta-Geopolitics of Outer Space: An Analysis of Space Power, Security and Governance* (London: Palgrave Macmillan, 2012)

———, *Sustainable History and the Dignity of Man: A Philosophy of History and Civilisational Triumph* (Berlin: LIT Verlag, 2009)

———, *Symbiotic Realism: A Theory of International Relations in an Instant and an Interdependent World* (Berlin: LIT Verlag, 2007)

———, *The Politics of Emerging Strategic Technologies: Implications for Geopolitics, Human Enhancement and Human Destiny* (London: Palgrave Macmillan, 2011)

———, *The Role of Education in Global Security* (Genève: Éditions Slatkine, 2007)

———, *The Role of the Arab-Islamic World in the Rise of the West: Implications for Contemporary Trans-Cultural Relations* (London: Palgrave Macmillan, 2012)

———, '3 Disruptive Frontier Risks that Could Strike by 2040', World Economic Forum Agenda, 18 December 2020, https://www.weforum.org/agenda/2020/12/3-disruptive-frontier-risks-that-could-strike-by-2040

———, 'A Neurophilosophical Paradigm for a New Enlightenment', *Blog of the American Philosophical Association*, 24 March 2020, https://blog.apaonline.org/2020/03/24/a-neurophilosophical-paradigm-for-a-new-enlightenment

———, 'A Neurophilosophical Perspective on Social Distancing', Geneva Centre for Security Policy Op-Ed, 10 April 2020, https://www.gcsp.ch/global-insights/neurophilosophical-perspective-social-distancing

———, 'A Neurophilosophy of Big Data & Civil Liberties, and the Need for a New Social Contract', *Blog of the American Philosophical Association*, 21 May 2020, https://blog.apaonline.org/2020/05/21/a-neurophilosophy-of-big-data-civil-liberties-and-the-need-for-a-new-social-contract

———, 'A Neuro-Philosophy of Dignity-Based Governance', *Blog of the American Philosophical Association*, 16 October 2018, https://blog.apaonline.org/2018/10/16/a-neuro-philosophy-of-dignity-based-governance

———, 'A Neurophilosophy of Divisive Politics, Inequality and Disempowerment', Geneva Centre for Security Policy Op-Ed, 26 June 2020, https://www.gcsp.ch/global-insights/neurophilosophy-divisive-politics-inequality-and-disempowerment

———, 'A Neurophilosophy of Fake News, Disinformation and Digital Citizenship', *Blog of the American Philosophical Association*, 25 August 2020, https://blog.apaonline.org/2020/08/25/a-neurophilosophy-of-fake-news-disinformation-and-digital-citizenship

———, 'A Neurophilosophy of Fear-Induced Pre-emptive Aggression and Pseudo-Altruism', *Blog of the American Philosophical Association*, 4 August 2020, https://blog.apaonline.org/2020/08/04/a-neurophilosophy

-of-fear-induced-pre-emptive-aggression-pseudo-altruism/#:~:text=Fear%20
can%20swiftly%20induce%20responses,harm%20and%20ensure%20our%20
survival

——, 'A Neurophilosophy of Governance of Artificial Intelligence and
Brain-Computer Interface', *Blog of the American Philosophical Association*,
1 June 2020, https://blog.apaonline.org/2020/06/01/a-neurophilosophy-of
-governance-of-artificial-intelligence-and-brain-computer-interface

——, 'A Neuro-Philosophy of History: "Sustainable History"; with Dignity,
and without Directionality', *Blog of the American Philosophical Association*,
20 August 2018, https://blog.apaonline.org/2018/08/20/a-neuro-philosophy
-of-history-sustainable-history-with-dignity-and-without-directionality

——, 'A Neurophilosophy of Human Nature: Emotional Amoral Egoism
and the Five Motivators of Humankind', *Blog of the American Philosophical
Association*, 4 April 2019, https://blog.apaonline.org/2019/04/04/a-neuro
-philosophy-of-human-nature-emotional-amoral-egoism-and-the-five
-motivators-of-humankind

——, 'A Neurophilosophy of Legitimacy in National and Global Politics',
Blog of the American Philosophical Association, 4 May 2020, https://blog
.apaonline.org/2020/05/04/a-neurophilosophy-of-legitimacy-in-national
-and-global-politics

——, 'A Neurophilosophy of "Sustainable Neurochemical Gratification"
and the Meaning of Existence', *Blog of the American Philosophical
Association*, 13 July 2020, https://blog.apaonline.org/2020/07/13/a
-neurophilosophy-of-sustainable-neurochemical-gratification-and-the
-meaning-of-existence

——, 'A Neurophilosophy of Two Technological Game-Changers: Synthetic
Biology and Superintelligence', *Blog of the American Philosophical
Association*, 29 June 2020, https://blog.apaonline.org/2020/06/29/a-neuro
philosophy-of-two-technological-game-changers-synthetic-biology-super
intelligence

——, 'China and the United States: A Symbiosis', *The National Interest*,
27 September 2013, https://nationalinterest.org/commentary/china-the
-united-states-symbiosis-9143

——, 'Editorial of Policy Brief on Xenophobia, Media Stereotyping, and
Their Role in Global Security', in N.R.F. Al-Rodhan (ed.), *Policy Briefs
on the Transcultural Aspects of Security and Stability* (Berlin: LIT Verlag,
2006), pp. 37–42

——, 'Free Will in the Age of Neuromodulation', *Philosophy Now*, no. 127
(2018), pp. 28–30, https://philosophynow.org/issues/127/Free_Will_in_the
_Age_of_Neuromodulation

——, 'Major Transformative Technologies and the Five Dimensions of
Security', *Oxford Political Review*, 23 June 2020, https://oxfordpolitical
review.com/2020/06/23/major-transformative-technologies-and-the-five
-dimensions-of-security

———, 'Meta-Geopolitics of Pandemics: The Case of Covid-19', *Global Policy*, 8 May 2020, https://www.globalpolicyjournal.com/blog/08/05/2020/meta -geopolitics-pandemics-case-covid-19

———, 'Neurophilosophy and Transhumanism', *Blog of the American Philosophical Association*, 19 February 2019, https://blog.apaonline.org /2019/02/19/neurophilosophy-and-transhumanism

———, 'Predisposed Tabula Rasa', *The Oxford University Politics Blog*, 15 May 2015, https://blog.politics.ox.ac.uk/predisposed-tabula-rasa

———, 'Proposal of a Dignity Scale for Sustainable Governance', *The Journal of Public Policy*, 29 November 2015, https://jpublicpolicy.wordpress. com/2015/11/29/proposal-of-a-dignity-scale-for-sustainable-governance

———, 'Reforming Democracy and the Future of History', Center for Security Studies, ETH Zürich, 24 June 2014, https://css.ethz.ch/content /specialinterest/gess/cis/center-for-securities-studies/en/services/digital -library/articles/article.html/180942

———, 'Socio-Neuro-Biology and Prospects for Our Collective Global Future', *E-International Relations*, 30 July 2015, https://www.e-ir.info/2015/07/30/socio -neuro-biology-and-prospects-for-our-collective-global-future

———, 'Strategic Culture and Pragmatic National Interest', *Global Policy*, 22 July 2015, https://www.globalpolicyjournal.com/blog/22/07/2015/strategic -culture-and-pragmatic-national-interest

———, 'Symbiotic Realism, Multi-Sum Security and Just Power', *Open Mind*, 19 June 2019, https://www.bbvaopenmind.com/en/humanities/beliefs /symbiotic-realism-multi-sum-security-and-just-power

———, 'The Emotional Amoral Egoism of States', *The Oxford University Politics Blog*, 25 June 2015, https://blog.politics.ox.ac.uk/the-emotional -amoral-egoism-of-states

———, 'The Neurochemistry of Power: Implications for Political Change', *The Oxford University Politics Blog*, 27 February 2014, https://blog.politics.ox.ac .uk/neurochemistry-power-implications-political-change

———, 'The Neuro-Philosophy of International Relations', *The Oxford University Politics Blog*, 3 August 2016, https://blog.politics.ox.ac.uk/neuro -philosophy-international-relations

———, 'The "Ocean Model of Civilisation", Sustainable History Theory, and Global Cultural Understanding', *The Oxford University Politics Blog*, 1 June 2017, https://blog.politics.ox.ac.uk/ocean-model-civilization-susta inable-history-theory-global-cultural-understanding

———, 'The Social Contract 2.0: Big Data and the Need to Guarantee Privacy and Civil Liberties', *The Oxford University Politics Blog*, 22 September 2014, https://blog.politics.ox.ac.uk/social-contract-2-0-big-data-need-guarantee -privacy-civil-liberties

———, 'The "Sustainable History" Thesis: A Guide for Regulating Trans- and Post-Humanism', *E-International Relations*, 24 April 2018, https://www.e-ir .info/2018/04/24/the-sustainable-history-thesis-a-guide-for-regulating-trans -and-post-humanism

———, 'Us versus Them: How Neurophilosophy Explains Our Divided
Politics', World Economic Forum Agenda, 3 October 2016, https://www
.weforum.org/agenda/2016/10/us-versus-them-how-neurophilosophy-explains
-populism-racism-and-extremism

———, 'Why Agile Governance Should Be Human-Centred Governance',
World Economic Forum Agenda, 14 September 2020, https://www
.weforum.org/agenda/2020/09/technology-data-security-agile-governance

———, 'Will Technology Change What It Means to be Human', World
Economic Forum Agenda, 10 November 2014, https://www.weforum.org
/agenda/2014/11/synthetic-biology-designing-our-existence

Al-Rodhan, N.R.F., and L. Watanabe, A Proposal for Inclusive Peace and
Security (Genève: Éditions Slatkine, 2007)

Alvaredo, F., L. Chancel, T. Piketty, E. Saez and G. Zucman, World
Inequality Report 2018: Part IV – Trends in Global Wealth Inequality,
World Inequality Lab, https://wir2018.wid.world/part-4.html (accessed 13
January 2021)

An, S., L.-J. Ji, M. Marks and Z. Zhang, 'Two Sides of Emotion: Exploring
Positivity and Negativity in Six Basic Emotions across Cultures',
Frontiers of Psychology 8 (2017), pp. 1–14, https://doi.org/10.3389/fpsyg
.2017.00610

Anderson, B., Imagined Communities: Reflections on the Origin and Spread of
Nationalism (New York: Verso, 1983)

Andrews, M., 'Grand National Narratives and the Project of Truth
Commissions: A Comparative Analysis', Media, Culture & Society 25, no. 1
(2003), pp. 45–65.

Archer, J., The Nature of Grief: The Evolution and Psychology of Reactions to
Loss (London: Routledge, 1999)

Aristotle, The Politics, trans. by Carnes Lord (Chicago: University of Chicago
Press, 1984)

Arzate-Mejía, R.G., Z. Lottenbach, V. Schindler, A. Jawaid and I.M. Mansuy,
'Long-Term Impact of Social Isolation and Molecular Underpinnings',
Frontiers in Genetics 11 (2020), pp. 1–13, https://doi.org/10.3389/fgene.2020
.589621

Bækkelund, H., P. Frewen, R. Lanius, A. Ottesen Berg and E.A. Arnevik,
'Trauma-Related Altered States of Consciousness in Post-Traumatic Stress
Disorder Patients with or without Comorbid Dissociative Disorders',
European Journal of Psychotraumatology 9, no. 1 (2018), pp. 1–11, https://doi
.org/10.1080/20008198.2018.1544025

Banks, D., 'What Is Brain Plasticity and Why Is It So Important?', The
Conversation, 4 April 2016, https://theconversation.com/what-is-brain
-plasticity-and-why-is-it-so-important-55967

Barr, R.A., 'Fake News Grabs Our Attention, Produces False Memories and
Appeals to Our Emotions', The Conversation, 17 November 2019, https://
theconversation.com/fake-news-grabs-our-attention-produces-false
-memories-and-appeals-to-our-emotions-124842

Barrett, L., R. Dunbar and J. Lycett, *Human Evolutionary Psychology* (Basingstoke: Palgrave, 2002)

Barrow, R., *Plato* (London: Bloomsbury Academic, 2014)

Barto, A., M. Mirolli and G. Baldassarre, 'Novelty or Surprise', *Frontiers in Psychology* 4 (2013), pp. 1–15, https://doi.org/10.3389/fpsyg.2013.00907

Bastin, C., B.J. Harrison, C.G. Davey, J. Moll and S. Whittle, 'Feelings of Shame, Embarrassment and Guilt and Their Neural Correlates: A Systematic Review', *Neuroscience & Biobehavioral Reviews* 71 (2016), pp. 455–71, https://doi.org/10.1016/j.neubiorev.2016.09.019

Beck, U., and N. Sznaider, 'Unpacking Cosmopolitanism for the Social Sciences: A Research Agenda', *The British Journal of Sociology* 57, no. 1 (2006), pp. 1–23

Bernhard, M., T. Fernandes and R. Branco, 'Introduction: Civil Society and Democracy in an Era of Inequality', *Comparative Politics* 49, no. 3 (2017), pp. 297–309

Berns, L., 'Thomas Hobbes', in L. Strauss and J. Cropsey (eds), *History of Political Philosophy*, 3rd edn (Chicago: Chicago University Press, 1987), pp. XXX-XXX

Bickle, J., *The Oxford Handbook of Philosophy and Neuroscience* (Oxford: Oxford University Press, 2009)

Birchler, J.A., H. Yao and S. Chudalayandi, 'Unraveling the Genetic Basis of Hybrid Vigor', *Proceedings of the National Academy of Sciences of the United States of America* 103, no. 35 (2006), pp. 12957–58

Blair, J., A.A. Marsh, E. Finger, K.S. Blair and J. Luo, 'Neuro-cognitive Systems Involved in Morality', *Philosophical Explorations* 9, no. 1 (2006), pp. 13–27

Blank, R.H., 'Neuroscience, Free Will, and Individual Responsibility: Implications for Addictive Behaviour', in A. Somit and S. Peterson (eds), *Human Nature and Public Policy: An Evolutionary Approach* (New York: Palgrave Macmillan, 2003), pp. 55–76

Boggio, A., B.M. Knoppers, J. Almqvist and C.P.R. Romano, 'The Human Right to Science and the Regulation of Human Germline Engineering', *The CRISPR Journal* 2, no. 3 (2019), pp. 134–42, https://doi.org/10.1089/crispr.2018.0053

Bok, D., *The Politics of Happiness: What Government Can Learn from the New Research on Well-Being* (Princeton, NJ: Princeton University Press, 2010)

Boon, K.E., and F. Mégret, 'New Approaches to the Accountability of International Organisations', *International Organizations Law Review* 16, no. 1 (2019), pp. 1–10

Bostrom, N., 'Five Ways the Superintelligence Revolution Might Happen', *The Conversation*, 25 September 2014, https://theconversation.com/five-ways-the-superintelligence-revolution-might-happen-32124

——, 'Transhumanist Values', *Review of Contemporary Philosophy* 4 (2005), pp. 87–101

———, 'What is Transhumanism?', updated 2001, https://www.nickbostrom
  .com/old/transhumanism.html

Bouchard Jr, T.J., D.T. Lykken, M. McGue, N.L. Segal and A. Tellegen,
  'Sources of Human Psychological Differences: The Minnesota Study of
  Twins Reared Apart', *Science* 250, no. 4978 (1990), pp. 223–28, https://doi
  .org/10.1126/science.2218526

Bovet, A., and H.A. Makse, 'Influence of Fake News in Twitter during the
  2016 US Presidential Election', *Nature Communications* 10, no. 1 (2019),
  pp. 1–14, https://doi.org/10.1038/s41467-018-07761-2

Braudel, F., *A History of Civilizations* (New York: Penguin Books, 1993)

Brodal, P., *Neurological Anatomy in Relation to Clinical Medicine*, 3rd edn
  (New York: Oxford University Press, 1981)

Brown, G.W., and D. Held (eds), *The Cosmopolitanism Reader* (Cambridge:
  Polity Press, 2010)

Browning, G., *A History of Modern Political Thought: The Question of
  Interpretation* (Oxford: Oxford University Press, 2016)

Brumann, C., 'Writing for Culture: Why a Successful Concept Should Not Be
  Discarded', *Current Anthropology* 40, Supplement (1999), pp. S1-S27

Buades-Rotger, M., and D. Gallardo-Pujol, 'The Role of the Monoamine
  Oxidase A Gene in Moderating the Response to Adversity and Associated
  Antisocial Behavior: A Review', *Psychology Research and Behavior
  Management* 7 (2014), pp. 185–200, https://doi.org/10.2147/PRBM.S40458

Bull, H., *The Anarchical Society: A Study of Order in World Politics* (London:
  Palgrave, 1977)

Burns, S.M., L.N. Barnes, I.A. McCulloh, M.M. Dagher, E.B. Falk, J.D. Storey
  and M.D. Lieberman, 'Making Social Neuroscience Less WEIRD: Using
  fNIRS to Measure Neural Signatures of Persuasive Influence in a Middle
  East Participant Sample', *Journal of Personality and Social Psychology:
  Attitudes and Social Cognition* 116, no. 3 (2019), pp. 1–11

Camerer, C., G. Loewenstein and D. Prelec, 'Neuroeconomics: How
  Neuroscience Can Inform Economics', *Journal of Economic Literature* 43,
  no. 1 (2005), pp. 9–64

Campbell, A., 'Attachment, Aggression and Affiliation: The Role of Oxytocin
  in Female Behavior', *Biological Psychology* 77, no. 1 (2008), pp. 1–10, https://
  doi.org/10.1016/j.biopsycho.2007.09.001

Campbell, D., *National Deconstruction: Violence, Identity, and Justice in
  Bosnia* (Minneapolis: University of Minnesota Press, 1998)

Canna, S., C. St Clair and A. Desjardins, *Neuroscience Insights on
  Radicalization and Mobilization to Violence: A Review (Second Edition)*,
  NSI, 14 December 2012, https://nsiteam.com/social/wp-content/uploads
  /2016/01/Neuroscience-Insights-on-Radicalization-and-Mobilization
  -to-Violence-November-2012.pdf

Carter, A., and E. Gordon, *The Moral Psychology of Pride* (London: Rowman
  & Littlefield, 2017)

Carter, C.S., 'Neuroendocrine Perspectives on Social Attachment and Love', *Psychoneuroendocrinology* 23, no. 8 (1998), pp. 779–818, https://doi .org/10.1016/S0306-4530(98)00055-9

——, 'The Oxytocin-Vasopressin Pathway in the Context of Love and Fear', *Frontiers in Endocrinology* 8 (2017), pp. 1–12, https://doi.org/10.3389 /fendo.2017.00356

Carter, R., *The Human Brain Book: An Illustrated Guide to Its Structure, Function, and Disorders* (London: DK Publishing, 2019)

Casey, T.K., 'Nature, Technology, and the Emergence of Cybernetic Humanity', in H.W. Baillie and T.K. Casey (eds), *Is Human Nature Obsolete? Genetics, Bioengineering, and the Future of the Human Condition* (Cambridge, MA: MIT Press, 2005)

Cashmore, E., 'Xenophobia', in E. Cashmore (ed.), *Dictionary of Race and Ethnic Relations* (London: Routledge, 1994)

Castells, M., *The Information Age: Economy, Society and Culture: Volume 2: The Power of Identity*, 2nd edn (Malden, MA: Blackwell Publishing Ltd, 2004)

Center of Excellence for Engineering Biology, *GP-Write FAQ: 8. Does this Project Propose the Creation of So-called Parentless Babies?*, http:// engineeringbiologycenter.org/faq/#8 (accessed 13 January 2021)

Cerulo, K.A., 'Identity Construction: New Issues, New Directions', *Annual Review of Sociology* 23 (1997), pp. 385–409

Chancellor, G., 'Levels of Selection in Darwin's "Origin of Species"', *History and Philosophy of the Life Sciences* 37, no. 2 (2015), pp. 131–57

Chester, D.S., D.R. Lynam, D.K. Powell and C.N. DeWall, 'Narcissism Is Associated with Weakened Frontostriatal Connectivity: A DTI Study', *Social Cognitive and Affective Neuroscience* 11, no. 7 (2016), pp. 1036–40, https://doi.org/10.1093/scan/nsv069

Churchland, P.S., *Neurophilosophy: Toward a Unified Science of the Mind-Brain* (Cambridge, MA: MIT Press, 1986)

Cillis, M., *Free Will and Predestination in Islamic Thought: Theoretical Compromises in the Works of Avicenna, al-Ghazālī and Ibn 'Arabī* (New York: Routledge, 2014)

Clark, T.W., 'Materialism and Morality: The Problem with Pinker', *The Humanist* 58, no. 6 (1998), pp. 20–25

Cole, E.A., and J. Barsalou, *Unite or Divide? The Challenges of Teaching History in Societies Emerging from Violent Conflict*, Special Report 163 (Washington, DC: United States Institute of Peace, June 2006)

Coser, L.A., *Masters of Sociological Thought: Ideas of Historical and Social Context*, 2nd edn (Fort Worth, TX: Harcourt Brace Jovanovich, 1977)

Cowen, P.J., and M. Browning, 'What Has Serotonin to Do with Depression?', *World Psychiatry* 14, no. 2 (2015), pp. 158–60, https://doi.org/10.1002/wps .20229

Cox, R.W., 'Social Forces, States and World Order: Beyond International Relations Theory', *Millennium* 10, no. 2 (1981), pp. 126–55

Cox, R.W., and M.G. Schechter, *The Political Economy of a Plural World: Critical Reflections on Power, Morals and Civilization* (London: Routledge, 2002)

Craig, E. (ed.), *Routledge Encyclopedia of Philosophy: Volume 4: Genealogy to Iqbal* (London: Routledge, 1998)

Crimmins, James E., 'Jeremy Bentham', in *Stanford Encyclopedia of Philosophy* (Stanford University, 1997-), article pub. 17 March 2015, substantive rev. 28 January 2019, https://plato.stanford.edu/entries/bentham

Crivelli, C., J.A. Russell, S. Jarillo and J.-M. Fernández-Dols, 'The Fear Gasping Face as a Threat Display in a Melanesian Society', *Proceedings of the National Academy of Sciences of the United States of America* 113, no. 44 (2016), pp. 12404–7, https://doi.org/10.1073/pnas.1611622113

Crivelli, C., S. Jarillo, J.A. Russell and J.-M. Fernàndez-Dols, 'Reading Emotions from Faces in Two Indigenous Societies', *Journal of Experimental Psychology: General* 145, no. 7 (2016), pp. 830–43, https://doi.org/10.1037/xge0000172

Croucher, S., *Globalization and Belonging: The Politics of Identity in a Changing World* (Lanham, MD: Rowman & Littlefield, 2018)

Cunningham, S., B. Engelstätter and M.R. Ward, 'Violent Video Games and Violent Crime', *Southern Economic Journal* 82, no. 4 (2016), pp. 1247–65

Cunningham, W., M.K. Johnson, C.L. Raye, J.C. Gatenby, J.C. Gore and M.R. Banaji, 'Separable Neural Components in the Processing of Black and White Faces', *Psychological Science* 15, no. 12 (2004), pp. 806–13, http://www.people.fas.harvard.edu/~banaji/research/publications/articles/2004_Cunningham_PS.pdf

Damasio, A., *Descartes' Error: Emotion, Reason and the Human Brain* (London: Vintage, 2006)

Darwin, C., *The Expression of Emotions in Man and Animals* (London: John Murray, 1872)

Davis, N.J., 'Brain Stimulation for Cognitive Enhancement in the Older Person: State of the Art and Future Directions', *Journal of Cognitive Enhancement* 1 (2017), pp. 337–44

Dawkins, R., *The God Delusion* (London: Transworld Publishers, 2006)
——, *The Selfish Gene*, 30th anniversary ed. (Oxford: Oxford University Press, 2006)

Decety, J., and J.M. Cowell, 'Friends or Foes: Is Empathy Necessary for Moral Behavior?', *Perspectives on Psychological Science* 9, no. 4 (2014), pp. 525–37, https://doi.org/10.1177/1745691614545130

Decety, J., I.B.-A. Bartal, F. Uzefovsky and A. Knafo-Noam, 'Empathy as a Driver of Prosocial Behaviour: Highly Conserved Neurobehavioural Mechanisms across Species', *Philosophical Transactions: Biological Sciences* 371, no. 1686 (2016), pp. 1–11

Demorest, A.P., *Psychology's Grand Theorists: How Personal Experiences Shaped Professional Ideas* (Mahwah, NJ: Lawrence Erlbaum Associates, 2005)

Dessí, R., 'Collective Memory, Cultural Transmission, and Investments', *The American Economic Review* 98, no. 1 (2008), pp. 534–60

Development, Concepts and Doctrine Centre, *Global Strategic Trends: The Future Starts Today (Sixth Edition)*, UK Ministry of Defence Website, October 2018, https://assets.publishing.service.gov.uk/government/uploads /system/uploads/attachment_data/file/771309/Global_Strategic_Trends _-_The_Future_Starts_Today.pdf

Devetak, R., 'Postmodernism', in S. Burchill, A. Linklater, R. Devetak, J. Donnelly, M. Paterson, C. Reus-Smit and J. True (eds), *Theories of International Relations*, 3rd edn (Basingstoke: Palgrave Macmillan, 2005), pp. 161–87

Dobratz, B.A., L.K. Waldner and T. Buzzell, *Power, Politics, and Society: An Introduction to Political Sociology*, 2nd edn (London: Routledge, 2019)

Dobzhansky, T., *Genetics and the Origins of Species*, 3rd edn (New York: Columbia University Press, 1951)

Dogan, R., 'The Position of Human Being in the Universe according to Islam', *Sociology and Anthropology* 1, no. 3 (2013), pp. 141–48

Donnelly, J., 'Realism', in S. Burchill, A. Linklater, R. Devetak, J. Donnelly, M. Paterson, C. Reus-Smit and J. True (eds), *Theories of International Relations*, 3rd edn (Basingstoke: Palgrave Macmillan, 2005), pp. 29–54

Dou, J., and M.R. Bennett, 'Synthetic Biology and the Gut Microbiome', *Biotechnology Journal* 13, no. 5 (2018), e1700159, https://doi.org/10.1002/biot .201700159

Doyle, M.W., 'Kant, Liberal Legacies, and Foreign Affairs', *Philosophy & Public Affairs* 12, no. 3 (1983), pp. 205–35

Drake, W.D., and E.J. Wilson III (eds), *Governing Global Electronic Networks: International Perspectives on Policy and Power* (Cambridge, MA: MIT Press, 2008)

Dreu, C.K.D. de, 'Oxytocin Modulates the Link between Adult Attachment and Cooperation through Reduced Betrayal Aversion', *Psychoneuroendocrinology* 37, no. 7 (2012), pp. 871–80, https://doi.org/10 .1016/j.psyneuen.2011.10.003

Drew, L., 'The Ethics of Brain–Computer Interfaces', *Nature* 571 (2019), S19-S21, https://doi.org/10.1038/d41586-019-02214-2

Drexler, K.E., C. Peterson and G. Pergamit, *Unbounding the Future: The Nanotechnology Revolution* (Indianapolis, IN: Quill, 1993)

Duke, A.A., L. Bègue, R. Bell and T. Eisenlohr-Moul, 'Revisiting the Serotonin-Aggression Relation in Humans: A Meta-Analysis', *Psychological Bulletin* 139, no. 5 (2013), pp. 1148–72, https://doi.org/10.1037/a0031544

Eichengreen, B., *The Populist Temptation: Economic Grievance and Political Reaction in the Modern Era* (Oxford: Oxford University Press, 2018)

Eisenstadt, S.N., 'Multiple Modernities', *Daedalus* 129, no. 1 (2000), pp. 1–29

———, 'The Reconstitution of Collective Identities and Inter-Civilizational Relations in the Age of Globalization', *Canadian Journal of Sociology/Cahiers canadiens de sociologie* 32, no. 1 (2007), pp. 113–26

Ekman, P., E.R. Sorenson and W.V. Friesen, 'Pan-Cultural Elements in Facial Displays of Emotion', *Science* 164, no. 3875 (1969), pp. 86–88, https://doi.org/10.1126/science.164.3875.86

Ekman, P., W.V. Friesen, M. O'Sullivan, A. Chan, I. Diacoyanni-Tarlatzis, K. Heider, R. Krause, W.A. LeCompte, T. Pitcairn, P.E. Ricci-Bitti, K. Scherer, M. Tomita and A. Tzavaras, 'Universals and Cultural Differences in the Judgments of Facial Expressions of Emotions', *Journal of Personality and Social Psychology* 53, no. 4 (1987), pp. 712–17, https://doi.org/10.1037//0022-3514.53.4.712

El Karoui, M., M. Hoyos-Flight and Liz Fletcher, 'Future Trends in Synthetic Biology – A Report', *Frontiers in Bioengineering and Biotechnology* 7 (2019), pp. 1–8, https://doi.org/10.3389/fbioe.2019.00175

Elliott, L., and G. Cheeseman, *Cosmopolitanism Theory, Militaries and the Deployment of Force*, Working Paper 2002/8 (Canberra: Department of International Relations, Australian National University, November 2002)

Encyclopaedia Britannica, 'Bernard Feringa: Dutch Chemist', by Erik Gregersen, https://www.britannica.com/biography/Bernard-Feringa (accessed 12 March 2021)

Encyclopaedia Britannica, 'Christianity', by Matt Stefon *et al.*, https://www.britannica.com/topic/Christianity (accessed 11 March 2021)

Encyclopaedia Britannica, 'Hinduism: Religion', by A.L. Basham *et al.*, https://www.britannica.com/topic/Hinduism/Karma-samsara-and-moksha (accessed 13 March 2021)

Encyclopaedia Britannica, 'Ibn Tufayl: Moorish Philosopher and Physician', by the Editors of Encyclopaedia Britannica, https://www.britannica.com/biography/Ibn-Tufayl (accessed 14 January 2021)

Encyclopaedia Britannica, 'Konrad Lorenz: Austrian Zoologist', by Eckhard H. Hess, https://www.britannica.com/biography/Konrad-Lorenz (accessed 13 January 2021)

Encyclopaedia Britannica, 'Mutual Assured Destruction', by the Editors of Encyclopaedia Britannica, https://www.britannica.com/topic/mutual-assured-destruction (accessed 15 March 2021)

Encyclopaedia Britannica, 'Nanotechnology', by S. Tom Picraux, https://www.britannica.com/technology/nanotechnology (12 March 2021)

Encyclopaedia Britannica, 'Sin', by the Editors of Encyclopaedia Britannica, https://www.britannica.com/topic/sin-religion (accessed 11 March 2021)

Eres, R., and P. Molenberghs, 'The Influence of Group Membership on the Neural Correlates Involved in Empathy', *Frontiers in Human Neuroscience* 7 (2013), pp. 1–6, https://doi.org/10.3389/fnhum.2013.00176

Erlich, N., O.V. Lipp and V. Slaughter, 'Of Hissing Snakes and Angry Voices: Human Infants Are Differentially Responsive to Evolutionary Fear-Relevant Sounds', *Developmental Science* 16, no. 6 (2013), pp. 894–904, https://doi.org/10.1111/desc.12091

European Commission, Code of Practice on Disinformation, first published 26 September 2018, updated 7 July 2020, https://ec.europa.eu /digital-single-market/en/news/code-practice-disinformation

Ezcurra, R., and D. Palacios, 'Terrorism and Spatial Disparities: Does Interregional Inequality Matter?', *European Journal of Political Economy* 42 (2016), pp. 60–74, https://doi.org/10.1016/j.ejpoleco.2016.01.004

FDR Group, *Chilling Effects: NSA Surveillance Drives U.S. Writers to Self-Censor* (New York: PEN American Center, 2013), https://pen.org/sites/default/files /Chilling%20Effects_PEN%20American.pdf

Feldman, R., 'The Neurobiology of Human Attachments', *Trends in Cognitive Sciences* 21, no. 2 (2017), pp. 80–99, https://doi.org/10.1016/j.tics.2016.11.007

Feng, G., F.E. Jensen, H.T. Greely, H. Okano, S. Treue, A.C. Roberts, J.G. Fox *et al.*, 'Opportunities and Limitations of Genetically Modified Nonhuman Primate Models for Neuroscience Research', *Proceedings of the National Academy of Sciences of the United States of America* 117, no. 39 (2020), pp. 24022–31, https://doi.org/10.1073/pnas.2006515117

Fisher, H.E., A. Aron, D. Mashek, H. Li and L.L. Brown, 'Defining the Brain Systems of Lust, Romantic Attraction, and Attachment', *Archives of Sexual Behavior* 31, no. 5 (2002), pp. 413–19, https://doi.org/10.1023/a:101 9888024255

Foucault, M., 'Nietzsche, Genealogy, History', in D.F. Bouchard (ed.), *Language, Counter-Memory, Practice: Selected Essays and Interviews* (Ithaca, NY: Cornell University Press, 1977), pp. 139–64

Fowler, J., *Perspectives of Reality: An Introduction to the Philosophy of Hinduism* (Brighton: Sussex Academic Press, 2002)

Fowler, J., M. Fowler, D. Norcliffe, N. Hill and D. Watkins, *World Religions: An Introduction for Students* (Brighton: Sussex Academic Press, 1997)

Frangoul, H., D. Altshuler, M.D. Cappellini, Y.-S. Chen, J. Domm, B.K. Eustace, J. Foell *et al.*, 'CRISPR-Cas9 Gene Editing for Sickle Cell Disease and β-Thalassemia', *The New England Journal of Medicine* 384 (2021), pp. 252–260, https://doi.org/10.1056/NEJMoa2031054

Freeman, S., *The Cambridge Companion to Rawls* (Cambridge: Cambridge University Press, 2003)

Freud, S., *Civilization and Its Discontents*, reissue edn (New York: W.W. Norton & Co., 1989)

———, *Complete Psychological Works of Sigmund Freud*, trans. and ed. J. Strachey (London: Hogarth Press, 1953–74)

———, *The Ego and the Id* (London: Hogarth Press, 1949)

———, *The Interpretation of Dreams*, trans. and ed. J. Strachey (New York: Basic Books, 1955)

———, *The Psychopathology of Everyday Life*, standard ed. with a bibliographical introduction by P. Gay (New York: W.W. Norton & Co., 1990)

———, *Three Essays on the Theory Sexuality*, trans. J. Strachey (New York: Basic Books, 1975)

Freyberg-Inan, A., *What Moves Man: The Realist Theory of International Relations and Its Judgment of Human Nature* (Albany: State University of New York, 2004)

Fukuyama, F., *The End of History and the Last Man* (New York: Free Press, 1992)

Fuller, T., 'Jeremy Bentham and James Mill', in L. Strauss and J. Cropsey (eds), *History of Political Philosophy*, 3rd edn (Chicago: University of Chicago Press, 1987), pp. 710–31

Furbank, P.N., 'Altruism, Selfishness, and Genes', *The Threepenny Review*, no. 114 (Summer 2008), pp. 6–9

Gaddis, J.L., *The Long Peace: Inquiries into the History of the Cold War* (New York: Oxford University Press, 1989)

Gallagher, W., 'How We Become What We Are', *The Atlantic Monthly* 274, no. 3 (1994), pp. 38–60

Gambetta, D., and S. Hertog, *Engineers of Jihad: The Curious Connection between Violent Extremism and Education* (Princeton, NJ: Princeton University Press, 2016)

Gardiner, P., 'Kierkegaard, Søren Aabye', in E. Craig (ed.), *The Shorter Routledge Encyclopedia of Philosophy* (London: Routledge, 2005), pp. 511–18

Gardner, W.L., C.L. Pickett and M.B. Brewer, 'Social Exclusion and Selective Memory: How the Need to Belong Influences Memory for Social Events', *Personality and Social Psychology Bulletin* 26, no. 4 (2000), pp. 486–96, https://doi.org/10.1177/0146167200266007

Gellner, E., *The Psychoanalytic Movement: The Cunning of Unreason* (Oxford: Blackwell Publishing, 2003)

George, F.R., and D. Short. 'The Cognitive Neuroscience of Narcissism', *Journal of Brain Behaviour and Cognitive Sciences* 1, no. 1 (2018), pp. 1–9, http://www.imedpub.com/articles/the-cognitive-neuroscience-of-narcissism.php?aid=22149

Georgie, F., 'The Role of Racism in the European "Migration Crisis": A Historical Materialist Perspective', in V. Satgar (ed.), *Racism After Apartheid: Challenges for Marxism and Anti-Racism* (Johannesburg: Wits University Press, 2019), pp. 96–117, https://doi.org/10.18772/22019033061

Gerlach, M., B. Farb, W. Revelle and L.A. Nunes Amaral, 'A Robust Data-Driven Approach Identifies Four Personality Types across Four Large Data Sets', *Nature Human Behaviour* 2 (2018), pp. 735–42, https://doi.org/10.1038/s41562-018-0419-z

Giddens, A., *Modernity and Self-Identity* (Cambridge: Polity Press, 1991)

Goethe, J.W. von, *Elective Affinities* (1809), in *Novels and Tales by Goethe*, trans. by R.D. Boylan (London: Henry G. Bohn, 1854), pp. 1–245

Goldsmith, T.H., *The Biological Roots of Human Nature: Forging Links between Evolution and Behaviour* (New York: Oxford University Press, 1991)

Goleman, D., *Destructive Emotions and How We Can Overcome Them: A Dialogue with the Dalai Lama* (London: Bloomsbury, 2004)

Gonçalves, G.A.R., and R. de Melo Alves Paiva, 'Gene Therapy: Advances, Challenges and Perspectives', *Einstein* (São Paulo) 15, no. 3 (2017), pp. 369–75, https://doi.org/10.1590/S1679-45082017RB4024

Gönül, A.S., 'Where is Human Morality? Is It in Brain or Heart?', *New Yeni Symposium Journal* 44, no. 2 (2006), pp. 107–8

Gould, S.J., *The Structure of Evolutionary Theory* (Cambridge, MA: Harvard University Press, 2002)

Greene, J.D., R.B. Sommerville, L.E. Nystrom, J.M. Darley and J.D. Cohen, 'An fMRI Investigation of Emotional Engagement in Moral Judgment', *Science* 293, no. 5537 (2001), pp. 2105–8, https://doi.org/10.1126/science.1062872

Greene, J., *Moral Tribes: Emotion, Reason and the Gap Between Us and Them* (London: Penguin Press, 2013)

Greenhill, R., 'Is the World Zero-Sum or Win-Win?', World Economic Forum Agenda, 20 January 2015, https://www.weforum.org/agenda/2015/01/win-win-world

Gross National Happiness Index, United Nations Department of Economic and Social Affairs Sustainable Development, https://sustainabledevelopment.un.org/index.php?page=view&type=99&nr=266&menu=1449 (accessed 10 March 2021)

Guignon, C.B., 'Existentialism', in E. Craig (ed.), *The Shorter Routledge Encyclopedia of Philosophy* (London: Routledge, 2005), pp. 252–60

Guillaume, A., 'Some Remarks on Free Will and Predestination in Islam, Together with a Translation of the Kitabu-l Qadar from Sahih of al-Bukhari', *The Journal of the Royal Asiatic Society of Great Britain and Ireland*, no. 1 (1924), pp. 43–63

Gurr, T.R. (ed.), *Peoples versus States. Minorities at Risk in the New Century* (Washington, DC: United States Institute of Peace Press, 2002)

——, *Why Men Rebel* (Princeton, NJ: Princeton University Press, 1970)

Halévi, R., 'The New Truth Regime', *Le Débat* 197, no. 5 (2017), pp. 28–41

Hamid, N., and C. Pretus, 'The Neuroscience of Terrorism: How We Convinced a Group of Radicals to Let Us Scan Their Brains', *The Conversation*, 12 June 2019, https://theconversation.com/the-neuroscience-of-terrorism-how-we-convinced-a-group-of-radicals-to-let-us-scan-their-brains-114855

Hammond, R.A., and R. Axelrod, 'The Evolution of Ethnocentrism', *Journal of Conflict Resolution* 50, no. 6 (2006), pp. 926–36

Hauser, M.D., *Moral Minds: How Nature Designed Our Universal Sense of Right and Wrong* (New York: HarperCollins, 2006)

Hayes, R.P., 'Buddhist Philosophy, Indian', in E. Craig (ed.), *The Shorter Routledge Encyclopedia of Philosophy* (London: Routledge, 2005), pp. 112 ff.

Heilinger, J.-C., *Cosmopolitan Responsibility: Global Injustice, Relational Equality, and Individual Agency* (Berlin/Boston: De Gruyter, 2019), https://doi.org/10.1515/9783110612271

Heinze, E.A., and B.J. Jolliff, 'Idealism and Liberalism', in J.T. Ishiyama and M. Breuning (eds), *21st Century Political Science: A Reference Handbook*, Vol. 1 (London: SAGE Publications, 2011), pp. 319–26

Held, D., 'Cosmopolitanism: Globalisation Tamed?', *Review of International Studies* 29 (2003), pp. 465–80

——, 'Democratic Accountability and Political Effectiveness from a Cosmopolitan Perspective', *Government and Opposition* 39, no. 2 (2004), pp. 364–91, https://doi.org/10.1111/j.1477-7053.2004.00127.x

Herz, J.H., 'Idealist Internationalism and the Security Dilemma', *World Politics* 2, no. 2 (1950), pp. 157–80

Hill, R.S., 'David Hume', in L. Strauss and J. Cropsey (eds), *History of Political Philosophy*, 3rd edn (Chicago: University of Chicago Press, 1987), pp. 535–36

Hobbes, T., *Leviathan* (Ware, Herts: Wordsworth Editions, 2014 [1651])

Holt-Lunstad, J., T.B. Smith and J.B. Layton, 'Social Relationships and Mortality Risk: A Meta-analytic Review', *PLOS Medicine* 7, no. 7 (2010), pp. 1–2, https://doi.org/10.1371/journal.pmed.1000316

Hosken, D.J., J. Hunt and N. Wedell (eds), *Genes and Behaviour: Beyond Nature–Nurture* (Chichester: John Wiley & Sons Ltd, 2019)

Huffman, C., 'Pythagoras', in *Stanford Encyclopedia of Philosophy* (Stanford University, 1997-), article pub. 23 February 2005, substantive rev. 17 October 2018, https://plato.stanford.edu/entries/pythagoras

Hume, D., *A Treatise of Human Nature* (Cambridge: Cambridge University Press, 2009)

Huntington, S., *The Clash of Civilizations and the Remaking of World Order* (London: Simon & Schuster, 1996)

Hurd, I., 'Legitimacy and Authority in International Politics', *International Organization* 53, no. 2 (1999), pp. 379–408

Hurka, T., 'Perfectionism', in E. Craig (ed.), *Routledge Encyclopedia of Philosophy* (London: Routledge, 1998)

Ibn Tufayl, Muhammad ibn Abd al-Malik. *Ibn Tufayl's Hayy ibn Yaqdhan: A Philosophical Tale*, trans. L.E. Goodman (New York: Twayne, 1972)

International Monetary Fund, *The IMF and Income Inequality: Introduction to Inequality*, https://www.imf.org/en/Topics/Inequality/introduction-to-inequality (accessed 13 January 2021)

Izard, C.E., *Human Emotions* (New York: Springer, 2013)

Jackson, R., *Classical and Modern Thought on International Relations: From Anarchy to Cosmopolis* (New York: Palgrave Macmillan, 2005)

Jacobi, D., and A. Freyberg-Inan, *Human Beings in International Relations* (Cambridge: Cambridge University Press, 2015)

Jahankhani, H., S. Kendzierskyj, N. Chelvachandran and J. Ibarra (eds), *Cyber Defence in the Age of AI, Smart Societies and Augmented Humanity* (Cham: Springer, 2020)

Jaskulowski, K., 'The Securitisation of Migration: Its Limits and Consequences', *International Political Review* 40, no. 5 (2018), pp. 710–20

Javanbakht, A., 'The Politics of Fear: How Fear Goes Tribal, Allowing Us to Be Manipulated', *The Conversation*, 11 January 2019, https://theconversation.com/the-politics-of-fear-how-fear-goes-tribal-allowing-us-to-be-manipulated-109626

Jenks, C., *Culture* (New York: Routledge, 2004)

Jhaveri, N.J., 'Petroimperialism: US Oil Interests and the Iraq War',
 Antipode 36, no. 1 (2004), pp. 2–11, https://doi.org/10.1111/j.1467-8330.2004
 .00378.x

Jhingran, S., *Aspects of Hindu Morality* (Delhi: Motilal Banarsidass, 1989)

Jørgensen, M., and L.J. Phillips, *Discourse Analysis as Theory and Method*
 (London: Sage Publications, 2002)

Kane, R., *The Oxford Handbook of Free Will*, 2nd edn (New York: Oxford
 University Press, 2011)

Kant, I., *Kant: Political Writings*, ed. H. Reiss, trans. N.B. Nisbet,
 2nd enlarged edn (Cambridge: Cambridge University Press, 1991)

——, *The Metaphysics of Morals*, trans. M.J. Gregor (Cambridge: Cambridge
 University Press, 1996)

Kappes, A., A.H. Harvey, T. Lohrenz, P.R. Montague and T. Sharot,
 'Confirmation Bias in the Utilization of Others' Opinion Strength', *Nature
 Neuroscience* 23 (2020), pp. 130–37, https://doi.org/10.1038/s41593-019
 -0549-2

Keohane, R., *After Hegemony: Cooperation and Discord in the World Political
 Economy* (Princeton: Princeton University Press, 1984). Kierkegaard, S.,
 Fear and Trembling, trans. H.V. and E.H. Hong (Princeton, NJ: Princeton
 University Press, 1983)

Klein, E., S. Goering, J. Gagne, C.V. Shea, R. Franklin, S. Zorowitz, D.D.
 Dougherty and A.S. Widge, 'Brain-Computer Interface-based Control
 of Closed-loop Brain Stimulation: Attitudes and Ethical Considerations',
 Brain-Computer Interfaces 3, no. 3 (2016), pp. 140–48, https://doi.org/10.1080
 /2326263X.2016.1207497

Kleingeld, P., *Kant and Cosmopolitanism: The Philosophical Ideal of World
 Citizenship* (Cambridge: Cambridge University Press, 2012)

Kleingeld, P., and E. Brown, 'Cosmopolitanism', in *Stanford Encyclopedia
 of Philosophy* (Stanford University, 1997-), article pub. 23 February 2002,
 substantive rev. 17 October 2019, https://plato.stanford.edu/entries/cos
 mopolitanism/#HistCosm

Knight, W., 'The Dark Secret at the Heart of AI', *MIT Technology Review*, 11
 April 2017, https://www.technologyreview.com/2017/04/11/5113/the-dark
 -secret-at-the-heart-of-ai

Krause, S., D. Pokorny, K. Schury, C. Doyen-Waldecker, A.-L. Hulbert,
 A. Karabatsiakis, I.-T. Kolassa, H. Gündel, C. Waller and A. Buchheim,
 'Effects of the Adult Attachment Projective Picture System on Oxytocin
 and Cortisol Blood Levels in Mothers', *Frontiers in Human Neuroscience* 10
 (2016), pp. 1–12, https://doi.org/10.3389/fnhum.2016.00627

Kühn, S., D.T. Kugler, K. Schmalen, M. Weichenberger, C. Witt and J.
 Gallinat, 'Does Playing Violent Video Games Cause Aggression? A
 Longitudinal Intervention Study', *Molecular Psychiatry* 24, no. 8 (2019),
 pp. 1220–34, https://doi.org/10.1038/s41380-018-0031-7

Kühne, T., 'Nazi Morality', in S. Baranowski, A. Nolzen and C.-C.W. Szejnmann (eds), *A Companion to Nazi Germany* (Oxford: Wiley-Blackwell, 2018), pp. 215–29

Küng, H., *Islam: Past, Present and Future*, trans. J. Bowden (Oxford: Oneworld, 2007)

Lanius, R.A., B. Brand, E. Vermetten, P.A. Frewen and D. Spiegel, 'The Dissociative Subtype of Posttraumatic Stress Disorder: Rationale, Clinical and Neurobiological Evidence, and Implications', *Depression and Anxiety* 29, no. 8 (2012), pp. 701–8 https://doi.org/10.1002/da.21889

LeDoux, J. *The Emotional Brain* (New York: Simon & Schuster, 1996)

Lemma, B., 'CRISPR Dreams: The Potential for Gene Editing', *Harvard International Review* 40, no. 1 (2019), pp. 6–7

Levine, D.S., 'Angels, Devils, and Censors in the Brain', *ComPlexUs*, no. 2 (2004–5), pp. 35–59, https://doi.org/10.1159/000089747

Levy, D., and N. Sznaider, 'The Institutionalization of Cosmopolitan Morality: The Holocaust and Human Rights', *Journal of Human Rights* 3, no. 2 (2004), pp. 143–57

Liao, S.M., 'Morality and Neuroscience: Past and Present', in S.M. Liao (ed.), *Moral Brains: The Neuroscience of Morality* (Oxford: Oxford University Press, 2016), pp. 1–42

Linden, S. van der, J. Roozenbeek and J. Compton, 'Inoculating against Fake News about COVID-19', *Frontiers in Psychology* 11 (2020), pp. 1–7, https://doi.org/10.3389/fpsyg.2020.566790

Linkov, I., L. Roslycky and B.D. Trump, *Resilience and Hybrid Threats: Security and Integrity for the Digital World* (Amsterdam: IOS Press, 2018)

Lloyd, H.M., 'Why the Enlightenment was not the age of reason', *Aeon*, 16 November 2018, https://aeon.co/ideas/why-the-enlightenment-was-not-the-age-of-reason.

Lloyd, D., 'Functional MRI and the Study of Human Consciousness', *Journal of Cognitive Neuroscience* 14, no. 6 (2002), pp. 818–31, https://doi.org/10.1162/089892902760191027

Locke, J., *An Essay Concerning Human Understanding, with the Notes and Illustrations of the Author and an Analysis of His Doctrine of Ideas*, 13th edn (London: William Tegg & Co., 1849)

Lorenz, K., *On Aggression*, trans. M. Latzke (New York: Bantam Books, 1963)

Lumley, M.A., J.L. Cohen, G.S. Borszcz, A. Cano, A.M. Radcliffe, L.S. Porter, H. Schubiner and F.J. Keefe, 'Pain and Emotion: A Biopsychosocial Review of Recent Research', *Journal of Clinical Psychology* 67, no. 9 (2011), pp. 942–68, https://doi.org/10.1002/jclp.20816

Maalouf, A., *In the Name of Identity: Violence and the Need to Belong*, trans. B. Bray (New York: Penguin Books, 2003)

MacKellar, C., (ed.), *Cyborg Mind: What Brain-Computer and Mind-Cyberspace Interfaces Mean for Cyberneuroethics* (New York: Berghahn Books, 2019)

Mak, A.D.P., and L.C.W. Lam, 'Neurocognitive Profiles of People with
Borderline Personality Disorder', *Current Opinion in Psychiatry* 26, no. 1
(2013), pp. 90–96, https://doi.org/10.1097/YCO.0b013e32835b57a9

Malti, T., M. Gummerum, M. Keller and M. Buchmann, 'Children's Moral
Motivation, Sympathy and Prosocial Behaviour', *Child Development* 80,
no. 2 (2009), pp. 442–60

Manor, I., and C. Bjola, 'Public Diplomacy in the Age of Post-Reality',
in P. Surowiec and I. Manor (eds), *Public Diplomacy and the Politics of
Uncertainty* (Cham: Palgrave Macmillan, 2020), pp. 111–44

Marino, G., (ed.), *Basic Writings of Existentialism* (New York: Modern
Library, 2004)

Marx, K., *Capital: Volume III: A Critique of Political Economy* (London:
Penguin Books, 1993)

Matsumoto, D., *Culture and Psychology: People around the World*, 2nd edn
(Belmont, CA: Wadsworth, 2000)

Matthews, G.A., E.H. Nieh, C.M. Vander Weele, S.A. Halbert, R.V. Pradhan,
A.S. Yosafat, G.F. Glober *et al.*, 'Dorsal Raphe Dopamine Neurons Represent
the Experience of Social Isolation', *Cell* 164, no. 4 (2016), pp. 617–31, https://
doi.org/10.1016/j.cell.2015.12.040

Mayr, E., *Animal Species and Evolution* (Cambridge, MA: Belknap Press, 1963)

McCoy, J., 'Making Violence Ordinary: Radio, Music and the Rwandan
Genocide', *African Music* 8, no. 3 (2009), pp. 85–96

McIntyre, L., *Post-Truth* (Cambridge, MA: MIT Press, 2018)

McKelvey, C., *Beyond Ethnocentrism: A Reconstruction of Marx's Concept of
Science* (Westport, CT: Greenwood Press, 1991)

McMenemy, D., L. Smith and N. Williams, *Scottish Chilling: Impact of
Government and Corporate Surveillance on Writers*, Report of research
conducted by Scottish PEN and the University of Strathclyde, Glasgow,
November 2018, https://strathprints.strath.ac.uk/66291/8/Williams_etal_PEN
_2018_Scottish_chilling_impact_of_government_and_corporate_surveill
ance_on_writers.pdf

Mearsheimer, J., 'Back to the Future: Instability in Europe after the Cold
War', *International Security* 15, no. 1 (1990), pp. 5–56

Meloni, M., 'On the Growing Intellectual Authority of Neuroscience for
Political and Moral Theory', in F. Vander Valk (ed.), *Essays on Neuroscience
and Political Theory: Thinking the Body Politic* (Abingdon: Routledge, 2012),
pp. 25–49

Michel, D., *Water Conflict Pathways and Peacebuilding Strategies*, Peaceworks
Research Report No. 164 (Washington DC: United States Institute of Peace,
2020)

Mil, A. van, H. Hopkins and S. Kinsella, *From Our Brain to the World: Views
on the Future of Neural Interfaces; A Public Research Programme Conducted
on Behalf of the Royal Society: Findings Report*, The Royal Society,
July 2019, https://royalsociety.org/-/media/policy/projects/ihuman/public
-engagement-full-report.pdf

Moccia, L., M. Mazza, M. Di Nicola and L. Janiri, 'The Experience of Pleasure: A Perspective between Neuroscience and Psychoanalysis', *Frontiers in Human Neuroscience* 12 (2018), pp. 1–10, https://doi.org/10.3389/fnhum.2018.00359

Molenberghs, P., 'The Neuroscience of In-Group Bias', *Neuroscience & Biobehavioral Reviews* 37, no. 8 (2013), pp. 1530–36, https://doi.org/10.1016/j.neubiorev.2013.06.002

Moll, J., R. de Oliviera-Souza, G.J. Garrido, I.E. Bramati, E.M. Caparelli-Dáquer, M.L.M.F. Paiva, R. Zahn and J. Grafman, 'The Self as a Moral Agent: Linking the Neural Bases of Social Agency and Moral Sensitivity', *Social Neuroscience* 2, nos. 3–4 (2007), pp. 336–52, https://doi.org/10.1080/17470910701392024

Moll, J., R. de Oliviera-Souza, P.J. Eslinger, I.E. Bramati, J. Mourão-Miranda, P.A. Andreiuolo and L. Pessoa, 'The Neural Correlates of Moral Sensitivity: A Functional Magnetic Resonance Imaging Investigation of Basic and Moral Emotions', *The Journal of Neuroscience* 22, no. 7 (2002), pp. 2730–36

Montada, Josép Puig, 'Ibn Rushd's Natural Philosophy', in *Stanford Encyclopedia of Philosophy* (Stanford University, 1997-), article pub. 17 August 2018, https://plato.stanford.edu/entries/ibn-rushd-natural

More, M., 'On Becoming Posthuman', *Free Inquiry* 1, no. 4 (1994), pp. 38–41

Moxley, R.A., 'B.F. Skinner's Other Positivistic Book: "Walden Two"', *Behavior and Philosophy* 34 (2006), pp. 19–37

Murphy, G., *Personality: A Biosocial Approach to Origins and Structure* (New York: Harper & Brothers, 1947)

Nagasawa, M., S. Okabe, K. Mogi and T. Kikusui, 'Oxytocin and Mutual Communication in Mother-Infant Bonding', *Frontiers in Human Neuroscience* 6 (2012), pp. 1–10, https://doi.org/10.3389/fnhum.2012.00031

National Human Genome Institute, *What is the Human Genome Project?*, https://www.genome.gov/human-genome-project/What (accessed 13 January 2021)

Nestler, E.J., 'The Neurobiology of Cocaine Addiction', *Science & Practice Perspectives* 3, no. 1 (2005), pp. 4–10, https://doi.org/10.1151/spp05314, available at: https://www.ncbi.nlm.nih.gov/pmc/articles/PMC2851032/

New Zealand Ministry of Foreign Affairs and Trade, Christchurch Call to Eliminate Terrorist and Extremist Content Online, Signed at the Christchurch Call to Action Summit in Paris, 15 May 2019, https://www.christchurchcall.com/call.html

Nietzsche, F., *Basic Writings of Nietzsche*, trans. W. Kaufmann (New York: Modern Library, 2000)

——, *On the Genealogy of Morals and Ecce Homo*, ed. and trans. W. Kaufmann (New York: Vintage Books, 1989 [1887])

——, *The Gay Science: With a Prelude in Rhymes and an Appendix of Songs*, ed. and trans. W. Kaufmann (New York: Vintage Books, 1974)

Norris, P., and R. Inglehart, *Cultural Backlash: Trump, Brexit, and Authoritarian Populism* (Cambridge: Cambridge University Press, 2019)

Northoff, G., A. Heinzel, M. de Greck, F. Bermpohl, H. Dobrowolny and J. Panksepp, 'Self-Referential Processing in Our Brain: A Meta-Analysis of Imaging Studies on the Self', *Neuroimage* 31, no. 1 (2006), pp. 440–57

Nouvel, P., 'De la biologie synthétique à l'homme synthétique', *Comptes Rendus Biologies* 338, nos. 8–9 (2015), pp. 559–65, https://doi.org/10.1016/j.crvi.2015.06.015

Office for National Statistics, *Why Have Black and South Asian People Been Hit Hardest by COVID-19?*, 14 December 2020, https://www.ons.gov.uk/peoplepopulationandcommunity/healthandsocialcare/conditionsand diseases/articles/whyhaveblackandsouthasianpeoplebeenhithardestby covid19/2020-12-14

Okon-Singer, H., T. Hendler, L. Pessoa and A.J. Shackman, 'The Neurobiology of Emotion-Cognition Interactions', *Frontiers in Human Neuroscience* 9 (2015), pp. 1–14, https://doi.org/10.3389/fnhum.2015.00058

Oliver, T., 'Why Overcoming Racism Is Essential for Humanity's Survival', *The Conversation BBC Future*, 6 April 2020, https://www.bbc.com/future/article/20200403-how-to-overcome-racism-and-tribalism

On, S., 'Kant and Nietzsche on Human Rights: A Theoretical Approach', Paper presented at the International Studies Association, 41st Annual Convention, Los Angeles, CA, 14–18 March 2000

Østby, G., S.A. Rustad and A.F. Tollefsen, 'Children Affected by Armed Conflict, 1990–2019', PRIO *Conflict Trends*, no. 6 (Oslo: Peace Research Institute, 2020), https://www.prio.org/Publications/Publication/?x=12527

Overbeek, H., 'Transnational Historical Materialism: Theories of Transnational Class Formation and World Order', in R. Palan (ed.), *Global Political Economy: Contemporary Theories* (London: Routledge, 2000), pp. 162–76

Pattwell, S.S., B.J. Casey and F.S. Lee, 'The Teenage Brain: Altered Fear in Humans and Mice', *Current Directions in Psychological Science* 22, no. 2 (2013), pp. 146–51, https://doi.org/10.1177/0963721412471323

Paul, D.B., 'Genetic Engineering and Eugenics: The Use of History', in H.W. Baillie and T.K. Casey (eds), *Is Human Nature Obsolete? Genetics, Bioengineering, and the Future of the Human Condition* (Cambridge, MA: MIT Press, 2005), pp. 123–51

Paulus, M.P., S.F. Tapert and M.A. Schuckit, 'Neural Activation Patterns of Methamphetamine-Dependent Subjects during Decision Making Predict Relapse', *Archives of General Psychiatry* 62, no. 7 (2005), pp. 761–68, https://doi.org/10.1001/archpsyc.62.7.761

Pearce, K., 'What is Social Distancing and How Can It Slow the Spread of Covid-19?', *Johns Hopkins Magazine*, 13 March 2020, https://hub.jhu.edu/2020/03/13/what-is-social-distancing

Pearson, H., 'Genetics: What Is a Gene?', *Nature* 441, no. 7092 (2006), p. 398–401

Pennycook, G., T.D. Cannon and D.G. Rand, 'Prior Exposure Increases Perceived Accuracy of Fake News', *Journal of Experimental Psychology: General* 147, no. 12 (2018), pp. 1865–80, https://doi.org/10.1037/xge0000465

Personality Disorders Foundation (University of Connecticut), *What Are the Personality Disorders? A Summary from the Personality Disorders Foundation*, updated 15 February 2016, https://mhreference.org/personality -disorder/foundation/summary

Persson, I., and J. Savulescu, 'The Moral Importance of Reflective Empathy', *Neuroethics* 11, no. 2 (2018), pp. 183–93, https://doi.org/10.1007/s12152-017 -9350-7

Peter, Fabienne, 'Political Legitimacy', in *Stanford Encyclopedia of Philosophy* (Stanford University, 1997-), article pub. 29 April 2010, substantive rev. 24 April 2017, https://plato.stanford.edu/entries/legitimacy

Peterson, C., 'Nanotechnology: From Feynman to the Grand Challenge of Molecular Manufacturing', *IEEE Technology and Society* 23, no. 4 (2004), pp. 9–15, http://doi.org/10.1109/MTAS.2004.1371633

——, 'Taking Technology to the Molecular Level', *Computer* 33, no. 1 (2000), pp. 46–53, https://doi.org/10.1109/2.816268

Pettit, P., 'The Domination Complaint', in M. Williams and S. Macedo (eds), *Political Exclusion and Domination*, NOMOS 46, Special Issue (2005), pp, 87–117

——, 'The Globalized Republican Ideal', *Global Justice and Non-Domination* 9, no. 1 (2016), pp. 47–68, https://doi.org/10.21248/gjn.9.1.101

Phelps, E.A., K.M. Lempert and P. Sokol-Hessner, 'Emotion and Decision Making: Multiple Modulatory Neural Circuits', *Annual Review of Neuroscience* 37 (2014), pp. 263–87, https://doi.org/10.1146/annurev-neuro -071013-014119

Pierik, R., and W. Werner (eds), *Cosmopolitanism in Context: Perspectives from International Law and Political Theory* (Cambridge: Cambridge University Press, 2010)

Pietrabissa, G., and S.G. Simpson, 'Psychological Consequences of Social Isolation during Covid-19 Outbreak', *Frontiers in Psychology* 11 (2020), pp. 1–4, https://doi.org/10.3389/fpsyg.2020.02201

Pinker, S., *How the Mind Works* (New York: W.W. Norton & Co., 1997)

——, *The Blank Slate: The Modern Denial of Human Nature* (London: Penguin Books, 2002)

——, *The Language Instinct* (New York: HarperCollins, 1994)

Pitlik, S.D., 'COVID-19 Compared to Other Pandemic Diseases', *Rambam Maimonides Medical Journal* 11, no. 3 (2020), pp. 1–17, https://doi.org/10 .5041/RMMJ.10418

Plass-Oude Bos, D., B. Reuderink, B. van de Laar, H. Gürkök, C. Mühl, M. Poel, A. Nijholt and D Heylen, 'Brain Computer Interfacing and Games', in D.S. Tan and A. Nijholt (eds), *Brain Computer Interfaces* (London: Springer, 2010), pp. 149–78

Plato, *The Republic*, ed. T. Griffith, trans. G.R.F. Ferrari (Cambridge: Cambridge University Press, 2000)

Pojman, L.P., *Who Are We? Theories of Human Nature* (New York: Oxford University Press, 2006)

Price, A.W., *Virtue and Reason in Plato and Aristotle* (Oxford: Oxford University Press, 2011)

Prinz, J., 'The Emotional Basis of Moral Judgments', *Philosophical Explorations* 9, no. 1 (2006), pp. 29–43

Pycroft, L., 'Brainjacking – A New Cyber-Security Threat', *The Conversation*, 23 August 2016, https://theconversation.com/brainjacking-a-new-cyber-security-threat-64315

Pycroft, L., S.G. Boccard, S.L.F. Owen, J.F. Stein, J.J. Fitzgerald, A.L. Green and T.Z. Aziz, 'Brainjacking: Implant Security Issues in Invasive Neuromodulation', *World Neurosurgery* 92 (August 2016), pp. 454–62, https://doi.org/10.1016/j.wneu.2016.05.010

Raine, A., and Y. Yang, 'Neural Foundations to Moral Reasoning and Antisocial Behavior', *Social Cognitive and Affective Neuroscience* 1, no. 3 (2006), pp. 203–13, https://doi.org/10.1093/scan/nsl033

Rawls, J., *A Theory of Justice*, rev. edn (Oxford: Oxford University Press, 1999)

Reinhard, D.A., S.H. Konrath, W.D. Lopez and H.G. Cameron, 'Expensive Egos: Narcissistic Males Have Higher Cortisol', *PLOS One* 7, no. 1 (2012), pp. 1–8, https://doi.org/10.1371/journal.pone.0030858

Renton, A., 'Neuralink Put a Chip in Gertrude the Pig's Brain. It Might Be Useful One Day', *The Conversation*, 1 September 2020, https://theconversation.com/neuralink-put-a-chip-in-gertrude-the-pigs-brain-it-might-be-useful-one-day-145383

Reus-Smit, C., 'Constructivism', in S. Burchill, A. Linklater, R. Devetak, J. Donnelly, M. Paterson, C. Reus-Smit, and J. True (eds), *Theories of International Relations*, 3rd edn (Basingstoke: Palgrave Macmillan, 2005), pp. 188–212

Robbins, P.R., *Understanding Psychology*, 3rd edn (Portland, ME: J. Weston Walch, 2003)

Roell, M.-S., and M.D. Zurbriggen, 'The Impact of Synthetic Biology for Future Agriculture and Nutrition', *Current Opinion in Biotechnology* 61 (2020), pp. 102–9, https://doi.org/10.1016/j.copbio.2019.10.004

Rogers, R.D., 'The Roles of Dopamine and Serotonin in Decision-Making: Evidence from Pharmacological Experiments in Humans', *Neuropsychopharmacology* 36, no. 1 (2011), pp. 114–32, https://doi.org/10.1038/npp.2010.165

Rose, J., 'Brexit, Trump, and Post-Truth Politics', *Public Integrity* 19, no. 6 (2017), pp. 555–58, https://doi.org/10.1080/10999922.2017.1285540

Roth, L., T. Kaffenberger, U. Herwig and A.B. Brühl, 'Brain Activation Associated with Pride and Shame', *Neuropsychobiology* 69, no. 2 (2014), pp. 95–106, https://doi.org/10.1159/000358090

Rousseau, J.-J., *On the Social Contract*, trans. D.A. Cress (Indianapolis: Hackett Publishing, 1998)

———, *The Social Contract and Discourses*, trans. G.D.H. Cole (New York: E.P. Dutton, 1950 [1750–62])

Russell, B., *History of Western Philosophy* (London: Routledge, 2006)

———, *Power: A New Social Analysis* (London: George Allen & Unwin, 1938)

———, 'What Desires Are Politically Important?', Nobel Lecture, The Nobel Prize, 11 December 1950, www.nobelprize.org/prizes/literature/1950/russell /lecture

Russett, B., H. Starr and D. Kinsella, *World Politics: The Menu for Choice*, 7th edn (Belmont, CA: Thomson Wadsworth, 2004)

Ryan, R.M., (ed.), *The Oxford Handbook of Human Motivation* (Oxford: Oxford University Press, 2019)

Sachedina, A., 'An Islamic Perspective', in S.J. Fitzpatrick, I.H. Kerridge, C.F.C. Jordens, L. Zoloth, C. Tollefsen, K.L. Tsomo, M.P. Jensen, A. Sachedina and D. Sarma, 'Religious Perspectives on Human Suffering: Implications for Medicine and Bioethics', *Journal of Religion and Health* 55 (2015), pp. 167–69

Salzman, C.D., and S. Fusi, 'Emotion, Cognition, and Mental State Representation in Amygdala and Prefrontal Cortex', *Annual Review of Neuroscience* 33 (2010), pp. 173–202, https://doi.org/10.1146/annurev.neuro .051508.135256

Sander, D., and K. Scherer (eds), *Oxford Companion to Emotion and the Affective Sciences* (Oxford: Oxford University Press, 2014)

Sankey, D., 'Can the Synaptic Self Have Values and Make Choices?', paper presented at the 33rd Annual Philosophy of Education Society of Australia Conference, Melbourne, 26–27 November 2004, p. 1, www.pesa.org.au

Sarma, D., 'A Hindu Perspective', in S.J. Fitzpatrick, I.H. Kerridge, C.F.C. Jordens, L. Zoloth, C. Tollefsen, K.L. Tsomo, M.P. Jensen, A. Sachedina and D. Sarma, 'Religious Perspectives on Human Suffering: Implications for Medicine and Bioethics', *Journal of Religion and Health* 55 (2015), pp. 159–73

Sartre, J.-P., *Being and Nothingness*, trans. H. Barnes (New York: Philosophical Library, 1956)

———, *Jean-Paul Sartre: Basic Writings*, ed. Stephen Priest (New York: Routledge, 2001)

Scharre, P., and L. Fish, *Human Performance Enhancement* (Washington, DC: Center for a New American Security, 2018), p. 8, https://s3.us-east-1 .amazonaws.com/files.cnas.org/documents/CNAS_Super-Soldiers_6 _Human-Performance-Enhancement-FINAL.pdf?mtime=20180917103621 &focal=none

Schlesinger Jr, A., 'Has Democracy a Future?', *Foreign Affairs* 76, no. 5 (1997), pp. 2–12

Schulson, M., 'The Moral Tribalism of Contemporary Politics', *Religion and Politics*, 15 August 2016, https://religionandpolitics.org/2016/08/15/the-moral -tribalism-of-contemporary-politics

Seigel, J., *The Idea of the Self: Thought and Experience in Western Europe since the Seventeenth Century* (New York: Cambridge University Press, 2005)

Seneca, L.A., 'Letter 13: On Groundless Fears', in L.A. Seneca, *Seneca: Letters from a Stoic: Epistulae Morales ad Lucilium*, ed. and with an introduction by R. Campbell (London: Harper Collins, 2020)

Sengupta, S.S., 'Growth in Human Motivation: Beyond Maslow', *Indian Journal of Industrial Relations* 47, no. 1 (2011), pp. 102–16

Seo, D., C.J. Patrick and P.J. Kennealy, 'Role of Serotonin and Dopamine System Interactions in the Neurobiology of Impulsive Aggression and Its Comorbidity with Other Clinical Disorders', *Aggressive and Violent Behavior* 13, no. 5 (2008), pp. 383–95, https://doi.org/10.1016/j.avb.2008.06.003

Shackman, A., and T. Wager, 'The Emotional Brain: Fundamental Questions and Strategies for Future Research', *Neuroscience Letters* 693 (2019), pp. 68–74, https://doi.org/10.1016/j.neulet.2018.10.012

Shannon, T.A., 'Human Nature in a Post-Human Genome Project World', in H.W. Baillie and T.K. Casey (eds), *Is Human Nature Obsolete? Genetics, Bioengineering, and the Future of the Human Condition* (Cambridge, MA: MIT Press, 2005), pp. 269–316

Shao, R., and Y. Wang, 'The Relation of Violent Video Games to Adolescent Aggression: An Examination of Moderated Mediation Effect', *Frontiers in Psychology* 10 (2019), pp. 1–9, https://doi.org/10.3389/fpsyg.2019.00384

Shaw, T., and D.J. Youngblood, *Cinematic Cold War: The American and Soviet Struggle for Hearts and Minds* (Lawrence, KS: University Press of Kansas, 2010)

Sheehy, N., *Fifty Key Thinkers in Psychology* (London: Routledge, 2003)

Sifuentes, J., 'The Propaganda of Octavian and Marc Anthony's Civil War', *Ancient History Encyclopedia*, 20 November 2019, https://www.ancient.eu /article/1474/the-propaganda-of-octavian-and-mark-antonys-civil

Sindico, F., 'Climate Change and Security', *Carbon & Climate Law Review* 11, no. 3 (2017), pp. 187–90

Singer, J.D., 'Genetic and Cultural Evolution: Implications for International Security Policies', in A. Somit and S. Peterson (eds), *Human Nature and Public Policy: An Evolutionary Approach* (New York: Palgrave Macmillan, 2003), pp. 243–61

Singer, P.A.D., *A Darwinian Left: Politics, Evolution, and Cooperation* (New Haven, CT: Yale University Press, 2000)

Singh, M., 'Ethnic Conflict and International Security: Theoretical Considerations', *World Affairs* 6, no. 4 (2002), pp. 72–89

Skinner, B.F., 'The Behaviour of Organisms at Fifty', in J.T. Todd and E.K. Morris (eds), *Modern Perspectives on B. F. Skinner and Contemporary Behaviorism*, Contributions in Psychology, No. 28 (Westport, CT: Greenwood Press, 1995)

Smith, N., and A. Law, 'On Parametric (and Non-Parametric) Variation', *Biolinguistics* 3, no. 4 (2009), pp. 332–43

Snyder, T., *The Road to Unfreedom: Russia, Europe, America* (New York: Penguin Random House, 2018)

Soanes, C., S. Hawker and J. Elliott (eds), *Paperback Oxford English Dictionary* (Oxford: Oxford University Press, 2006)

Soldatova, G., 'Psychological Mechanisms of Xenophobia', *Social Sciences* 38, no. 2 (2007), pp. 105–21

Somit, A., and S. Peterson, 'From Human Nature to Public Policy: Evolutionary Theory Challenges the "Standard Model"', in A. Somit and S. Peterson (eds), *Human Nature and Public Policy: An Evolutionary Approach* (New York: Palgrave Macmillan, 2003), pp. 3–18

Sperry, L., 'Psychopharmacology as an Adjunct to Psychotherapy in the Treatment of Personality Disorders', *Journal of Individual Psychology* 62, no. 3 (2006), pp. 324–37

Stahn, A.C., H.-C. Gunga, E. Kohlberg, J. Gallinat, D.F. Dinges and S. Kühn, 'Brain Changes in Response to Long Antarctic Expeditions', *The New England Journal of Medicine*, no. 381 (2019), pp. 2273–75, https://doi .org/10.1056/NEJMc1904905

Star, D., (ed.), *The Oxford Handbook of Reasons and Normativity* (Oxford: Oxford University Press, 2018)

Starcke, K., C. Polzer, O.T. Wolf and M. Brand, 'Does Stress Alter Everyday Moral Decision-Making?', *Psychoneuroendocrinology* 36, no. 2 (2011), pp. 210–19, https://doi.org/10.1016/j.psyneuen.2010.07.010

Stauffer, W.R., A. Lak, S. Kobayashi and W. Schultz, 'Components and Characteristics of the Dopamine Reward Utility Signal', *Journal of Comparative Neurology* 524, no. 8 (2016), pp. 1699–1711, https://doi.org /10.1002/cne.23880

Stein, D.J., 'The Neurobiology of Evil: Psychiatric Perspectives on Perpetrators', *Ethnicity and Health* 5, nos 3–4 (2000), pp. 303–15

Steinert, S., and O. Friedrich, 'Wired Emotions: Ethical Issues of Affective Brain-Computer Interfaces', *Science and Engineering Ethics* 26 (2020), pp. 351–67

Stevens, S., 'Synthetic Biology in Cell and Organ Transplantation', *Cold Spring Harbor Perspectives in Biology* 9, no. 2 (2017), pp. 1–12, https://doi.org /10.1101/cshperspect.a029561

Stevenson, L., and D.L. Haberman, *Ten Theories of Human Nature*, 4th edn (New York: Oxford University Press, 2004)

Stockwell, S., 'Legal "Black Holes" in Outer Space: The Regulation of Private Space Companies', *E-International Relations*, 20 July 2020, https://www.e-ir .info/2020/07/20/legal-black-holes-in-outer-space-the-regulation-of-private -space-companies

Subramanian, A., 'Born to Kill? The Story of "Serial Killer" Genes', *Berkeley Scientific Journal*, 21 July 2020, https://bsj.berkeley.edu/born-to-kill-the -story-of-serial-killer-genes

Swancutt, K., 'Animism', in *The Cambridge Encyclopedia of Anthropology*, initially pub. 25 June 2019, http://doi.org/10.29164/19anim (accessed 11 March 2021)

Symonds, P.M., *The Ego and the Self* (New York: Appleton-Century-Crofts, 1951)

Tajfel, H.E., 'Experiments in Intergroup Discrimination', *Scientific American* 223, no. 5 (1970), pp. 96–102

———, 'Social Categorization, Social Identity and Social Comparison', in H.E. Tajfel (ed.), *Differentiation between Social Groups: Studies in the Social Psychology of Intergroup Relations* (London: Academic Press, 1978), pp. 61–76

Tanaka, S.C., B.W. Balleine and J.P. O'Doherty, 'Calculating Consequences: Brain Systems that Encode the Causal Effects of Actions', *The Journal of Neuroscience* 28, no. 26 (2008), pp. 6750–55

Tarrant, M., S. Dazeley and T. Cottom, 'Social Categorization and Empathy for Outgroup Members', *British Journal of Social Psychology* 48, no. 3 (2009), pp. 427–46, https://doi.org/10.1348/014466608X373589

Tavris, C., *Anger: The Misunderstood Emotion*, rev. edn (New York: Touchstone, 1989)

Teschke, B., 'Marxism', in C. Reus-Smit and D. Snidal (eds), *The Oxford Handbook of International Relations* (Oxford: Oxford University Press: 2010), pp. 163–200

Thayer, B.A., 'Ethnic Conflict and State Building', in A. Somit and S. Peterson (eds), *Human Nature and Public Policy: An Evolutionary Approach* (New York: Palgrave Macmillan, 2003), pp. 225–42

Tracy, J.L., and R.W. Robins, 'Emerging Insights into the Nature and Function of Pride', *Current Directions in Psychological Science* 16, no. 3 (2007), pp. 147–50

———, 'The Psychological Structure of Pride: A Tale of Two Facets', *Journal of Personality and Social Psychology* 92, no. 3 (2007), pp. 506–25

Trip, S., C.H., Bora, M. Marian, A. Halmajan and M.I. Drugas, 'Psychological Mechanisms Involved in Radicalization and Extremism: A Rational Emotive Behavioral Conceptualization', *Frontiers in Psychology* 10 (2019), pp. 1–8, https://doi.org/10.3389/fpsyg.2019.00437

UN Economic and Social Commission for Asia and the Pacific, *Inequality in Asia and the Pacific in the Era of the 2030 Agenda for Sustainable Development* (New York: United Nations Publication, 2018), https://www.unescap.org/publications/inequality-asia-and-pacific-era-2030-agenda-sustainable-development

UN General Assembly, International Covenant on Civil and Political Rights, https://treaties.un.org/doc/publication/unts/volume%20999/volume-999-i-14668-english.pdf (accessed 29 April 2021)

———, Universal Declaration of Human Rights, https://www.un.org/en/about-us/universal-declaration-of-human-rights (accessed 29 April 2021)

United States Institute of Peace, *Natural Resources, Conflict, and Conflict Resolution: A Study Guide Series on Peace and Conflict for Independent Learners and Classroom Instructors* (Washington, DC: United States Institute of Peace, 2007), https://www.usip.org/sites/default/files/file/08sg.pdf

Uttal, W.R., *Neural Theories of Mind: Why the Mind-Brain Problem May Never Be Solved* (New York: Psychology Press, 2020)

Vahle, M.W., *Opportunities and Implications of Brain-Computer Interface Technology*, Wright Flyer Paper No. 75 (Maxwell Air Force Base, AL: Air University Press, 2020), https://www.airuniversity.af.edu/Portals/10 /AUPress/Papers/WF_0075_VAHLE_OPPORTUNITIES_AND_IMPLI CATIONS_OF_BRAIN_COMPUTER_INTERFACE_TECHNOLOGY .PDF

Vancutsem, W., 'Freedom of Religion and the Securitisation of Religious Identity: An Analysis of Proposals Impacting on Freedom of Religion Following Terrorist Attacks in Flanders', *Global Campus Human Rights Journal* 2 (2018), pp. 41–58

Vaughn, D.A., R.R. Savjani, M.S. Cohen and D.M. Eagleman, 'Empathic Neural Responses Predict Group Allegiance', *Frontiers in Human Neuroscience* 12 (2018), pp. 1–10, https://doi.org/10.3389/fnhum.2018.00302

Vélez Garcia, A.E., and F. Ostrosky-Solis, 'From Morality to Moral Emotions', *International Journal of Psychology* 41, no. 5 (2006), pp. 348–54

Vertsberger, D., S. Israel and A. Knafo-Noam, 'Genetics, Parenting, and Moral Development', in D. Laible, G. Carlo and L.M. Padilla-Walker (eds), *The Oxford Handbook of Parenting and Moral Development* (Oxford: Oxford University Press, 2019), pp. 107–28

Vrij, A., E. van Schie and J. Cherryman, 'Reducing Ethnic Prejudice through Public Communication Programs: A Social-Psychological Perspective', *Journal of Psychology* 130, no. 4 (1996), pp. 413–20

Waal, F. de, *Primates and Philosophers: How Morality Evolved* (Princeton, NJ: Princeton University Press, 2006)

Walk, R.D., and E.J. Gibson, 'The "Visual Cliff"', *Scientific American* 202, no. 4 (1960), pp. 64–71, https://doi.org/10.1038/scientificamerican0460-64

Walters, L., 'Human Genetic Intervention: Past, Present, and Future', in H.W. Baillie and T.K. Casey (eds), *Is Human Nature Obsolete? Genetics, Bioengineering, and the Future of the Human Condition* (Cambridge, MA: MIT Press, 2005), pp. 380–81

Walton, S., *Humanity: An Emotional* History (London: Atlantic Books, 2004)

Waltz, E., 'Electronic Pump Delivers Drugs to the Brain to Stop Seizures', *IEEE Spectrum*, 30 August 2018, https://spectrum.ieee.org/the-human-os /biomedical/devices/electronic-pump-delivers-drugs-to-the-brain-to-stop -seizures

Waltz, K., *Man, the State and War: A Theoretical Analysis* (New York: Columbia University Press, 1959)

Wang, X., 'Movies without Mercy: Race, War, and Images of Japanese People in American Films, 1942–1945', *The Journal of American-East Asian Relations* 18, no. 1 (2011), pp. 11–36

Wendt, A., *Social Theory of International Politics* (Cambridge: Cambridge University Press, 1999).

West, R., and M. Gossop, 'Overview: A Comparison of Withdrawal Symptoms from Different Drug Classes', *Addiction* 89, no. 11 (1994), pp. 1483–89, https://doi.org/10.1111/j.1360-0443.1994.tb03747.x

Weyland, K., 'Populism's Threat to Democracy: Comparative Lessons for the United States', *Perspectives on Politics* 18, no. 2 (2020), pp. 389–406

Wheatley, T., and J. Haidt, 'Hypnotic Disgust Makes Moral Judgments More Severe', *Psychological Science* 16, no. 10 (2005), pp. 780–84, https://doi.org /10.1111/j.1467-9280.2005.01614.x

Whitten, N., 'Animism', in M.C. Horowitz (ed.), *New Dictionary of the History of Ideas*, Vol. 1 (Detroit: Charles Scribner's Sons, 2005)

Williams, G.C., *Adaptation and Natural Selection* (Princeton, NJ: Princeton University Press, 1966)

Williams, L.M., J.M. Gatt, S.A. Kuan, C. Dobson-Stone, D.M. Palmer, R.H. Paul, L. Song, P.T. Costa, P.R. Schofield and E. Gordon, 'A Polymorphism of the MAOA Gene is Associated with Emotional Brain Markers and Personality Traits on an Antisocial Index', *Neuropsychopharmacology* 34 (2009), pp. 1797–1809

Wilson, E.E., and L. Denis, 'Kant and Hume on Morality', in *Stanford Encyclopedia of Philosophy* (Stanford University, 1997-), article pub. 26 March 2008, substantive rev. 29 March 2018, https://plato.stanford.edu /archives/sum2018/entries/kant-hume-morality

Wilson, E.O., *On Human Nature* (Cambridge, MA: Harvard University Press, 1978)

———, *Sociobiology: The New Synthesis* (Cambridge, MA: Harvard University Press, 1975)

Wimmer, A., *Nationalist Exclusion and Ethnic Conflict: Shadows of Modernity* (Cambridge: Cambridge University Press, 2002)

Winner, E., *How Art Works: A Psychological Exploration* (Oxford: Oxford University Press, 2019)

Winston, R., *Human Instinct: How Our Primeval Impulses Shape Our Modern Lives* (London: Bantam Books, 2003)

Winter, E., 'Feelings: What's the Point of Rational Thought If Emotions Always Take Over?', *The Conversation*, 21 February 2020, https://the conversation.com/feelings-whats-the-point-of-rational-thought-if-emotions -always-take-over-128592

Wittling, W., and R. Roschmann, 'Emotion-Related Hemisphere Asymmetry: Subjective Emotional Responses to Laterally Presented Films', *Cortex* 29, no. 3 (1993), pp. 431–48, https://doi.org/10.1016/s0010 -9452(13)80252-3

World Bank, Gender Data Portal, https://www.worldbank.org/en/data/datat opics/gender (accessed 28 April 2021)

World Bank, *Worldwide Governance Indicators*, https://datacatalog. worldbank.org/dataset/worldwide-governance-indicators (accessed 3 May 2021)

Wrong, D. *Power: Its Forms, Bases and Uses*. Abingdon: Routledge, 2017.

Wubben, M.J.J., D. De Cremer and E. van Dijk 'Is Pride a Prosocial Emotion? Interpersonal Effects of Authentic and Hubristic Pride', *Cognition and Emotion* 26, no. 6 (2012), pp. 1084–1097.

Xu, M.K., D. Gaysina, R. Tsonaka, A.J.S. Morin, T.J. Croudace, J.H. Barnett, J. Houwing-Duistermaat, M. Richards, P.B. Jones and LHA Genetics Group, 'Monoamine Oxidase A (MAOA) Gene and Personality Traits from Late Adolescence through Early Adulthood: A Latent Variable Investigation', *Frontiers in Psychology* 8 (2017), pp. 1–13, https://doi.org/10.3389/fpsyg.2017.01736

Yang, J., H. Zhang, J. Ni, C.K.W. de Dreu and Y. Ma, 'Within-group Synchronization in the Prefrontal Cortex Associates with Intergroup Conflict', *Nature Neuroscience* 23, no. 6 (2020), pp. 754–60, https://doi.org/10.1038/s41593-020-0630-x

Zalenski, R.J., and R. Raspa, 'Maslow's Hierarchy of Human Needs: A Framework for Achieving Human Potential in Hospice', *Journal of Palliative Medicine* 9, no. 5 (2006), pp. 1120–27

Zartman, I.W., 'Managing Ethnic Conflict', First Perlmutter Lecture on Ethnic Conflict, *Foreign Policy Research Institute Wire* 6, no. 5 (September 1998), pp. 1–2

Zautra, A.J., *Emotions, Stress, and Health* (Oxford: Oxford University Press, 2003)

Zhang, Y., M. Li, X. Gao, Y. Chen and T. Liu, 'Nanotechnology in Cancer Diagnosis: Progress, Challenges and Opportunities', *Journal of Hematology and Oncology* 12, no. 137 (2019), pp. 1–13. https://doi.org/10.1186/s13045-019-0833-3

Zimmer, M., 'Nobel Prize for CRISPR Honors Two Great Scientists – and Leaves Out Many Others', *The Conversation*, 8 October 2020, https://theconversation.com/nobel-prize-for-crispr-honors-two-great-scientists-and-leaves-out-many-others-147730

Zuber, C., and A. Conzelmann, 'Achievement-Motivated Behavior in Individual Sports (AMBIS-I) – Coach Rating Scale', *German Journal of Exercise and Sport Research* 49 (2019), pp. 410–23

Index

You may also be interested in:

Sustainable History and Human Dignity:
A Neurophilosophy of History and the
Future of Civilisation

Nayef R.F. Al-Rodhan

In *Sustainable History and Human Dignity*, Professor Nayef Al-Rodhan shows that it is the human quest for sustainable governance, balancing the ever-present tension between nine human dignity needs and three human nature attributes (emotionality, amorality & egoism), that has and will most profoundly shape the course of history. Beginning with an 'Ocean Model' of a single collective human civilisation, Al-Rodhan constructs a common human story comprised of multiple geo-cultural domains and sub-cultures with a history of mutual borrowing and synergies. If humanity as a whole is to flourish, all of these diverse geo-cultural domains must succeed. Only thus can lasting peace and prosperity be achieved for all, especially in the face of 'Civilisational Frontier Risks' and highly disruptive technologies in the twenty-first century.

Dr. Nayef R.F. Al-Rodhan challenges us to grapple with the meaning of history and how it could lead to the improvement of the human condition. This book presents his views on how a sustainable history based on human dignity could be achieved. In his opinion, this requires good governance, based on 'reason, security, human rights, accountability, transparency, justice, opportunity, innovation and inclusiveness.' I agree, and I hope that the path laid out in this book attracts many followers. **President Jimmy Carter**, 39th President of the United States

Expected 27 January 2022

Hardback ISBN: 978 0 7188 9570 9
Paperback ISBN: 978 0 7188 9571 6
PDF ISBN: 978 0 7188 4831 6
ePub ISBN: 978 0 7188 4832 3

21st-Century Statecraft:
Reconciling Power, Justice and
Meta-Geopolitical Interests

Nayef R.F. Al-Rodhan

From civilisational frontier risks associated with new challenges like disruptive technologies, to the shifting nature of great-power conflicts and subversion, the 21st century requires a new approach to statecraft. In *21st-Century Statecraft*, Professor Nayef Al-Rodhan proposes five innovative statecraft concepts. He makes the case for a new method of geopolitical analysis called 'meta-geopolitics', and for 'dignity-based governance'. He shows how, in an interdependent and interconnected world, traditional thinking must move beyond zero-sum games and focus on 'multi-sum and symbiotic realist' interstate relations. This requires a new paradigm of global security premised on five dimensions of security, and a new concept of power, 'just power', which highlights the centrality of justice to state interests. These concepts enable states to balance competing interests and work towards what the author calls 'reconciliation statecraft'. Throughout, Professor Al-Rodhan brings his philosophical and neuroscientific expertise to bear, providing a practical model for conducting statecraft in a sustainable way.

A unique and intellectually courageous undertaking that will help us gain deeper insights into the many dimensions of current and future security challenges. **Ambassador Rolf Ekéus**, Chairman of the Stockholm International Peace Research Institute (SIPRI), Stockholm, Sweden

Expected 31 March 2022

Hardback ISBN: 978 0 7188 9574 7
Paperback ISBN: 978 0 7188 9575 4
PDF ISBN: 978 0 7188 4835 4
ePub ISBN: 978 0 7188 4836 1

BV - #0021 - 280921 - C0 - 234/156/19 - PB - 9780718895730 - Gloss Lamination